# MICROSOFT ACCESS

## ALL-IN-ONE GUIDE

Beginner to Expert Guide to Master Microsoft Access with Ease + Secrets to Professional Database Management

# D-WYSE

Copyright © 2022 **D-WYSE**

**All Rights Reserved**

This book or parts thereof may not be reproduced in any form, stored in any retrieval system, or transmitted in any form by any means—electronic, mechanical, photocopy, recording, or otherwise—without prior written permission of the publisher, except as provided by United States of America copyright law and fair use.

**Disclaimer and Terms of Use**

The author and publisher of this book and the accompanying materials have used their best efforts in preparing this book. The author and publisher make no representation or warranties with respect to the accuracy, applicability, fitness, or completeness of the contents of this book. The information contained in this book is strictly for informational purposes. Therefore, if you wish to apply the ideas contained in this book, you are taking full responsibility for your actions.

*Printed in the United States of America*

# CONTENTS

- CONTENTS ........................................................................................................... III
- INTRODUCTION ................................................................................................... 1
- PART 1 .................................................................................................................. 3
- ACCESS BUILDING BLOCKS ................................................................................... 3
- CHAPTER 1 ............................................................................................................ 4
- AN INTRODUCTION TO DATABASE DEVELOPMENT ............................................. 4
  - THE DATABASE TERMINOLOGY OF ACCESS ..................................................... 4
    - *Databases* ................................................................................................. 4
    - *Tables* ...................................................................................................... 6
    - *Records and Fields* ................................................................................... 7
    - *Values* ...................................................................................................... 8
  - RELATIONAL DATABASES .................................................................................. 8
  - ACCESS DATABASE OBJECTS ............................................................................ 9
    - *Tables* ...................................................................................................... 9
    - *Queries* .................................................................................................... 9
    - *Data-entry and display forms* .................................................................10
    - *Reports* ...................................................................................................10
    - *Macros and VBA* .....................................................................................11
  - PLANNING FOR DATABASE OBJECTS ...............................................................12
    - *A Five-Step Design Method* ....................................................................13
    - *Step 1: The overall design from concept to reality* ................................13
    - *Step 2: Report design* .............................................................................15
    - *Step 3: Data design* ................................................................................15
    - *Step 4: Table design* ...............................................................................17
    - *Step 5: Form design* ...............................................................................21
- CHAPTER 2 ...........................................................................................................22
- GETTING STARTED WITH ACCESS ........................................................................22
  - THE ACCESS WELCOME SCREEN .....................................................................22
  - HOW TO CREATE A BLANK DATABASE ............................................................23
  - THE ACCESS 2022 INTERFACE .........................................................................27
    - *The Navigation pane* ..............................................................................28
    - *Custom* ..................................................................................................28
    - *Object Type* ...........................................................................................29
    - *Tables and Related Views* ......................................................................29
    - *Created Date* .........................................................................................30
    - *Modified Date* .......................................................................................30
    - *The Ribbon* ............................................................................................31

 *The Quick Access toolbar* ........................................................................................... *33*

**PART II** ............................................................................................................................**35**

**UNDERSTANDING ACCESS TABLES** ..............................................................................**35**

**CHAPTER 3** ......................................................................................................................**36**

**CREATING ACCESS TABLES** ..........................................................................................**36**

 TABLE TYPES ........................................................................................................................ 36
  *Object tables* ............................................................................................................... *36*
  *Transaction tables* ...................................................................................................... *36*
  *Join tables* ................................................................................................................... *37*
 CREATING A NEW TABLE ....................................................................................................... 37
  *Designing tables* ......................................................................................................... *38*
 USING THE DESIGN TAB ......................................................................................................... 42
  *Primary Key* ................................................................................................................. *43*
  *Insert Rows* .................................................................................................................. *43*
  *Delete Rows* ................................................................................................................ *44*
  *Property Sheet* ............................................................................................................ *44*
  *Indexes* ......................................................................................................................... *44*
 WORKING WITH FIELDS ......................................................................................................... 44
  *Naming a field* ............................................................................................................ *44*
  *Specifying a data type* ................................................................................................ *45*
  *Entering a field description* ....................................................................................... *49*
  *Specifying data validation rules* ................................................................................ *49*
 CREATING TBL CUSTOMERS .................................................................................................. 50
  *Using AutoNumber fields* ........................................................................................... *50*
  *Completing tbl customers* ......................................................................................... *50*
 CHANGING A TABLE DESIGN ................................................................................................. 51
  *Inserting a new field* ................................................................................................... *52*
  *Deleting a field* ........................................................................................................... *52*
  *Changing a field location* .......................................................................................... *53*
  *Changing a field name* .............................................................................................. *54*
  *Changing a field size* ................................................................................................. *54*
  *Handling data conversion issues* ............................................................................... *54*
 ASSIGNING FIELD PROPERTIES ............................................................................................... 55
  *Common properties* ................................................................................................... *56*
  *Format* ......................................................................................................................... *58*
  *Number and currency field format* ........................................................................... *59*
  *Custom numeric format* ............................................................................................. *59*
  *Built-in Date/Time formats* ....................................................................................... *60*
  *Custom dates and time formats* ................................................................................ *60*
  *Short Text and Long text field formats* ..................................................................... *62*
  *Input Mask* .................................................................................................................. *62*

    *Caption* ............................................................................................................................ 64
  Validation Rule and Validation Text ................................................................... 65
    *Required* ......................................................................................................... 66
    *Allow Zero Length* ......................................................................................... 67
    *Indexed* ........................................................................................................... 67
  Understanding tbl Customers Field Properties ............................................... 68
  Setting the Primary Key .......................................................................................... 69
    *Choosing a primary key* ................................................................................ 69
    *Creating the Primary key* .............................................................................. 70
    *Creating composite primary keys* ................................................................. 71
  Indexing Access Tables ............................................................................................ 72
    *The importance of indexes* ........................................................................... 73
    *Multiple-field indexes* .................................................................................... 74
    *When to index tables* ................................................................................... 76
  Printing a Table Design ........................................................................................... 77
  Saving the Completed Table .................................................................................. 77
  Manipulating Tables ................................................................................................ 79
    *Renaming tables* ........................................................................................... 79
    *Deleting tables* ............................................................................................. 79
    *Copying tables in a database* ....................................................................... 80
  Copying a table to another database ................................................................... 81
  Adding Records to a Database Table .................................................................... 82
  Understanding Attachment Fields ......................................................................... 83
  Adding an attachment field in the Datasheet view ........................................... 83
  Adding an attachment field in the Design view ................................................. 84

# CHAPTER 4 ............................................................................................................... 85

# UNDERSTANDING TABLE RELATIONSHIPS .................................................. 85

  Building Bulletproof Databases ............................................................................. 85
  Data Normalization and Denormalization ......................................................... 87
    *First normal form* .......................................................................................... 88
    *Second normal form* ..................................................................................... 88
    *Identifying entities* ........................................................................................ 89
    *Less obvious entities* ..................................................................................... 89
    *Breaking the rules* ........................................................................................ 90
    *Third normal form* ........................................................................................ 90
    *Denormalization* ........................................................................................... 91
  Table Relationships ................................................................................................. 92
    *Connecting the data* ..................................................................................... 93
    *One-to-one* .................................................................................................... 93
    *One-to-many* ................................................................................................. 94
    *Many-to-many* .............................................................................................. 95
  Integrity Rules .......................................................................................................... 96

*No primary key can contain a null value* .................................................................. *98*
*All foreign key values must be matched by a corresponding primary key* ........................ *99*
*Keys* ............................................................................................................................. *100*
*Deciding on a primary key* ........................................................................................... *101*
*Looking at the benefits of a primary key* ..................................................................... *102*
*Designating a primary key* ........................................................................................... *102*
*Single-field versus composite primary key* ................................................................... *103*
*Natural versus surrogate primary keys* ........................................................................ *103*
*Creating primary keys* .................................................................................................. *104*
CREATING RELATIONSHIPS AND ENFORCING REFERENTIAL INTEGRITY ............................................. 104
*Specifying the join type between tables* ...................................................................... *105*
*Enforcing referential integrity* ...................................................................................... *107*
VIEWING ALL RELATIONSHIPS ..................................................................................................... 108
*Deleting relationships* .................................................................................................. *110*
FOLLOWING APPLICATION-SPECIFIC INTEGRITY RULES ..................................................................... 110

# CHAPTER 5 ............................................................................................................... 111

# WORKING WITH ACCESS TABLES ............................................................................... 111

UNDERSTANDING DATASHEETS ................................................................................................. 111
LOOKING AT THE DATASHEET WINDOW ..................................................................................... 112
MOVING WITHIN A DATASHEET ................................................................................................. 113
USING THE NAVIGATION BUTTONS ............................................................................................ 114
EXAMINING THE DATASHEET RIBBON ........................................................................................ 115
*Views* ........................................................................................................................... *115*
*Clipboard* ..................................................................................................................... *115*
*Sort & Filter* ................................................................................................................. *115*
*Records* ........................................................................................................................ *115*
*Find* .............................................................................................................................. *116*
*Window* ....................................................................................................................... *116*
*Text formatting* ........................................................................................................... *116*
OPENING A DATASHEET ............................................................................................................ 117
ENTERING A NEW DATA ........................................................................................................... 117
*Saving the record* ........................................................................................................ *119*
UNDERSTANDING AUTOMATIC DATA-TYPE VALIDATION ................................................................ 120
KNOWING HOW PROPERTIES AFFECT DATA ENTRY ....................................................................... 120
*Standard text data entry* ............................................................................................. *121*
*Date/Time/data entry* ................................................................................................. *121*
*Number/Currency Data entry with data validation* .................................................... *121*
*OLE object data entry* .................................................................................................. *122*
*Long Text field data entry* ........................................................................................... *122*
NAVIGATING RECORDS IN A DATASHEET .................................................................................... 123
*Moving between records* ............................................................................................ *124*
FINDING A SPECIFIC VALUE ....................................................................................................... 124

CHANGING VALUES IN DATASHEET .................................................................................................. 126
    *Manually replacing an existing value* ........................................................................... *126*
    *Changing an existing value* ............................................................................................ *127*
USING THE UNDO FEATURE ............................................................................................................. 129
COPYING AND PASTING VALUES ..................................................................................................... 130
REPLACING VALUES ........................................................................................................................ 130
ADDING NEW RECORDS .................................................................................................................. 132
DELETING RECORDS ........................................................................................................................ 133
DISPLAYING RECORDS .................................................................................................................... 134
    *Changing the field order* ................................................................................................. *134*
    *Changing the field display width* .................................................................................... *134*
    *Changing the record display height* ............................................................................... *135*
CHANGING THE DISPLAY FONTS ..................................................................................................... 135
    *Displaying all cell gridlines and alternate row colors* .................................................... *136*
ALIGNING DATA IN COLUMNS ........................................................................................................ 137
    *Hiding and unhiding columns* ......................................................................................... *138*
    *Freezing columns* ............................................................................................................ *138*
SAVING THE CHANGED LAYOUT ..................................................................................................... 139
    *Saving a record* ............................................................................................................... *140*
SORTING AND FILTERING RECORDS IN A DATASHEET .................................................................... 140
    *Sorting records* ................................................................................................................ *140*
    *Filtering a selection* ........................................................................................................ *141*
FILTERING A FORM ......................................................................................................................... 143
AGGREGATING DATA ...................................................................................................................... 143
PRINTING RECORDS ........................................................................................................................ 144
PREVIEWING RECORDS ................................................................................................................... 145

# CHAPTER 6 .................................................................................................................. 147

# IMPORTING AND EXPORTING DATA ............................................................................. 147

HOW ACCESS WORKS WITH EXTERNAL DATA ................................................................................. 147
    *Types of external data* .................................................................................................... *147*
    *Ways of working with external data* .............................................................................. *148*
    *When to link to an external data* .................................................................................... *148*
    *When to import external data* ........................................................................................ *149*
    *When to export data* ...................................................................................................... *150*
OPTIONS FOR IMPORTING AND EXPORTING ................................................................................... 150
IMPORTING EXTERNAL DATA ......................................................................................................... 151
    *Importing from another Access database* ..................................................................... *152*
    *Importing from an Excel spreadsheet* ............................................................................ *154*
    *Importing a SharePoint list* ............................................................................................ *156*
    *Importing data from text files* ........................................................................................ *157*
    *Delimited text files* ......................................................................................................... *157*
    *Fixed-width text files* ..................................................................................................... *158*

| | |
|---|---|
| *Importing and exporting XML documents* | *160* |
| *Importing and exporting HTML documents* | *162* |
| IMPORTING ACCESS OBJECTS OTHER THAN TABLES | 163 |
| *Importing an Outlook folder* | *164* |
| EXPORTING TO EXTERNAL FORMATS | 165 |
| *Exporting objects to other Access databases* | *165* |
| *Exporting through ODBC drivers* | *166* |
| EXPORTING TO WORD | 168 |
| *Merging data into Word* | *168* |
| PUBLISHING TO PDF OR XPS | 169 |

## CHAPTER 7 ..... 172

## LINKING TO EXTERNAL DATA ..... 172

| | |
|---|---|
| LINKING EXTERNAL DATA | 172 |
| IDENTIFYING LINKED TABLES | 173 |
| *Limitations of linked data* | *173* |
| LINKING TO OTHER ACCESS DATABASE TABLES | 175 |
| LINKING TO ODBC DATA SOURCES | 177 |
| LINKING TO NON-DATABASE DATA | 178 |
| *Linking to Excel* | *178* |
| *Linking to HTML files* | *179* |
| *Linking to text files* | *180* |
| WORKING WITH LINKED TABLES | 181 |
| SETTING VIEW PROPERTIES | 181 |
| SETTING RELATIONSHIPS | 182 |
| OPTIMIZING LINKED TABLES | 182 |
| DELETING A LINKED REFERENCE | 183 |
| VIEWING OR CHANGING INFORMATION FOR LINKED TABLES | 183 |
| REFRESHING A DATA SOURCE AND ITS LINKED TABLES | 184 |
| SPLITTING A DATABASE | 185 |
| *The benefits of splitting a database* | *186* |
| KNOWING WHERE TO PUT WHICH OBJECTS | 187 |
| *Using the Database Splitter add-in* | *187* |

## PART III ..... 188

## WORKING WITH ACCESS QUERIES ..... 188

## CHAPTER 8 ..... 189

## SELECTING DATA WITH QUERIES ..... 189

| | |
|---|---|
| INTRODUCING QUERIES | 189 |
| *What Queries can do* | *189* |
| *What Queries return* | *190* |

| | |
|---|---|
| CREATING A QUERY | 191 |
| ADDING FIELDS TO YOUR QUERIES | 193 |
|    *Adding a single field* | *193* |
|    *Adding multiple fields* | *194* |
| RUNNING YOUR QUERY | 195 |
| WORKING WITH QUERY FIELDS | 195 |
|    *Selecting a field in the QBD grid* | *196* |
|    *Changing field order* | *196* |
| RESIZING COLUMNS IN THE QBD GRID | 196 |
|    *Removing a field* | *197* |
|    *Inserting a field* | *197* |
|    *Hiding a field* | *198* |
|    *Changing the sort order of a field* | *198* |
| ADDING CRITERIA TO YOUR QUERIES | 198 |
|    *Understanding selection criteria* | *199* |
|    *Entering simple string criteria* | *199* |
|    *Entering other simple criteria* | *199* |
| PRINTING A QUERY'S RECORDSET | 200 |
| SAVING A QUERY | 200 |
| CREATING MULTI-TABLE QUERIES | 201 |
|    *Viewing table names* | *202* |
|    *Adding multiple fields* | *202* |
|    *Recognizing the limitations of multi-table queries* | *202* |
|    *Overcoming query limitations* | *205* |
|    *Updating a unique index (primary key)* | *205* |
|    *Replacing existing data in a query with a one-many relationship* | *205* |
|    *Updating fields in queries* | *205* |
| WORKING WITH THE TABLE PANE | 206 |
|    *Looking at the join line* | *206* |
|    *Moving a table* | *206* |
|    *Removing a table* | *207* |
|    *Adding more tables* | *207* |
| CREATING AND WORKING WITH QUERY JOINS | 208 |
| UNDERSTANDING JOINS | 208 |
|    *Inner joins* | *208* |
|    *Outer joins* | *209* |
|    *Full outer joins* | *209* |
|    *Cross joins* | *209* |
|    *Unequal join* | *209* |
|    *Leveraging ad hoc table joins* | *209* |
|    *Specifying the type of join* | *210* |
|    *Deleting joins* | *210* |

# CHAPTER 9 ............................................................................................................ 211
# USING OPERATIONS AND EXPRESSIONS IN ACCESS ............................................. 211

## Introducing Operators ........................................................................................ 211
### Types of operators ............................................................................................ 211
### Mathematical operators .................................................................................... 211
### Comparison operators ...................................................................................... 213
### String operators ................................................................................................ 213
### Boolean(logical) operators ............................................................................... 213
### Miscellaneous operators ................................................................................... 214
### The Between……And operator ......................................................................... 214
### The In operator .................................................................................................. 214
### The Is operator ................................................................................................... 214
## Operator Precedence .......................................................................................... 215
## The mathematical precedence ........................................................................... 215
### The comparison precedence ............................................................................ 216
### The Boolean precedence .................................................................................. 216
## Using Operators and Expressions in Queries .................................................... 216
### Using query comparison operators ................................................................. 217
### Understanding complex criteria ..................................................................... 217
### Using functions in select queries .................................................................... 218
### Referencing fields in select queries ................................................................ 218
## Entering Single-Value Field Criteria ................................................................. 218
### Entering character (Text or Memo) criteria .................................................. 218
### The Like operator and wildcards .................................................................... 219
### Specifying non-matching values ..................................................................... 220
### Entering numeric criteria ................................................................................. 220
### Entering true or false criteria .......................................................................... 220
### Entering OLE object criteria ............................................................................ 221
## Using Multiple Criteria in a Query .................................................................... 221
### Understanding an OR operation ..................................................................... 221
### Specifying multiple values with the Or operator .......................................... 222
### Using the Or cell or the QBD pane ................................................................. 222
### Using a list of values with the In operator .................................................... 222
### Using And to specify a range ........................................................................... 223
### Using the Between… and And operator ........................................................ 223
### Searching for null data .................................................................................... 223
## Entering criteria in multiple fields .................................................................... 224
### Using And and Or across fields in a query .................................................... 224
### Specifying Or criteria across fields in a query ............................................. 224
### Using And and or together in different fields ............................................... 225
### A complex query on different lines ............................................................... 225

# CHAPTER 10 ......................................................................................................... 225

## GOING BEYOND SELECT QUERIES ................................................................................... 225

### Aggregate Queries ........................................................................................................ 225
#### Creating an aggregate query ................................................................................. 226
### About aggregate functions ...................................................................................... 227
#### Group By .................................................................................................................. 227
#### Sum, Avg, Count, StDev, Var ................................................................................. 227
#### Min, Max, First, Last ............................................................................................... 228
#### Expression, Where .................................................................................................. 229
### Action Queries ............................................................................................................ 230
#### Make-table queries ................................................................................................. 230
#### Delete queries .......................................................................................................... 232
#### Append queries ....................................................................................................... 233
#### Update queries ........................................................................................................ 234
#### Crosstab Queries ..................................................................................................... 235
#### Creating a crosstab querying using the Crosstab Query Wizard ..................... 235
#### Creating a crosstab query manually .................................................................... 237
#### Using the query design grid to create your crosstab query ............................. 237
#### Customizing your crosstab queries ..................................................................... 238
#### Defining criteria in a crosstab query ................................................................... 238
#### Changing the sort order of your crosstab query column headings ................ 238
### Optimizing Query Performance ............................................................................... 239
#### Normalizing your database design ...................................................................... 240
#### Using indexes on appropriate fields .................................................................... 240
#### Optimizing by improving query design .............................................................. 241
#### Compacting and repairing the database regularly ............................................ 241

## PART IV ................................................................................................................................ 244

## ANALYZING DATA IN MICROSOFT ACCESS ................................................................ 244

## CHAPTER 11 ........................................................................................................................ 245

## TRANSFORMING DATA IN ACCESS .............................................................................. 245

### Finding and Removing Duplicate Records ............................................................ 245
#### Defining duplicate records .................................................................................... 245
#### Finding duplicate records ..................................................................................... 245
#### Removing duplicate records ................................................................................. 246
### Common Transformation Tasks .............................................................................. 247
#### Filling in blank fields ............................................................................................. 247
#### Concatenating ......................................................................................................... 247
#### Concatenating fields .............................................................................................. 247
### Augmenting field values with your own text ....................................................... 247
#### Changing case ......................................................................................................... 248
#### Removing leading and trailing spaces from a string ........................................ 248

*Finding and replacing specific text* .................................................................. *248*
*Adding your own text in key positions within a string* ........................................ *249*
PARSING STRINGS USING CHARACTER MARKERS ..................................................... 250
*Query 1* ............................................................................................. *250*
*Query 2* ............................................................................................. *250*

# CHAPTER 12 ........................................................................................... 251

# WORKING WITH CALCULATIONS AND DATES ............................................. 251

## USING CALCULATIONS IN YOUR ANALYSES ................................................ 251
*Common calculation scenarios* ............................................................. *251*
*Using constants in calculations* ............................................................ *252*
*Using fields in calculations* .................................................................. *252*
*Using the results of aggregation in calculations* ....................................... *252*
*Using the results of one calculation as an expression in another* ................. *252*
*Using a calculation as an argument in a function* ..................................... *253*
*Constructing calculations with the Expression Builder* ............................... *253*

## COMMON CALCULATION ERRORS ............................................................ 254
*Understanding the order of operator precedence* ..................................... *254*
*Watching out for the null values* ........................................................... *254*
*Watching the syntax in your expressions* ................................................ *255*

## USING DATES IN YOUR ANALYSES ........................................................... 255
*Simple date calculations* ..................................................................... *255*
*Advanced analysis using functions* ........................................................ *256*
*The Date function* .............................................................................. *256*
*The Year, Month, Day, and Weekday functions* ........................................ *256*
*The Date add function* ........................................................................ *256*
*Grouping dates into quarters* ............................................................... *257*
*The DateSerial function* ...................................................................... *258*

# CHAPTER 13 ........................................................................................... 259

# PERFORMING CONDITIONAL ANALYSES ................................................... 259

## USING PARAMETER QUERIES ................................................................. 259
*How parameter queries work* ............................................................... *259*
*Ground rules of parameter query* .......................................................... *260*
*Working with parameter queries* ........................................................... *260*
*Working with multiple parameter conditions* ........................................... *261*
*Combining parameters with operators* ................................................... *261*
*Combining parameters with wildcards* ................................................... *261*
*Using parameters as calculation variables* ............................................... *261*
*Using parameters as function arguments* ................................................ *261*

## USING CONDITIONAL FUNCTIONS .......................................................... 262
*The IIf function* ................................................................................. *262*

>    *Using IIf to avoid mathematical errors* ........................................................................ 262
>    *Saving time with IIf* .................................................................................................... 262
>    *Meeting IIf functions for multiple conditions* .......................................................... 263
>    *Using IIf functions to create crosstab analysis* ....................................................... 263
>    *The switch function* ................................................................................................... 263
>   COMPARING THE IIF AND SWITCH FUNCTIONS ............................................................... 263

# CHAPTER 14 ............................................................................................................. 265

# THE FUNDAMENTALS OF USING SQL ............................................................................ 265

>   UNDERSTANDING BASIC SQL .......................................................................................... 265
>    *The SELECT statement* ............................................................................................... 265
>    *Selecting specific columns* ........................................................................................ 266
>    *Selecting all columns* ................................................................................................ 266
>    *The WHERE clause* .................................................................................................... 266
>    *Making sense of joins* ................................................................................................ 266
>    *Inner joins* .................................................................................................................. 266
>    *Outer joins* ................................................................................................................. 266
>   GETTING FANCY WITH ADVANCED SQL STATEMENTS ..................................................... 267
>    *Expanding your search with the Like operator* ....................................................... 267
>    *Selecting Unique values and rows without grouping* .............................................. 267
>    *Grouping and aggregating with the GROUP BY clause* ......................................... 268
>    *Setting the sort order with the ORDER BY Clause* ................................................. 268
>   CREATING ALIASES WITH THE AS CLAUSE ..................................................................... 269
>    *Creating a column alias* ............................................................................................ 269
>    *Creating a table alias* ............................................................................................... 269
>   SHOWING ONLY THE SELECT TOP OR SELECT TOP PERCENT ................................... 269
>    *Top values queries explained* .................................................................................... 270
>    *The SELECT TOP statement* ...................................................................................... 270
>    *The SELECT TOP PERCENT Statement* .................................................................... 270
>   PERFORMING ACTION QUERIES VIA SQL STATEMENTS .................................................. 270
>    *Make-table queries translated* .................................................................................. 270
>    *Append Queries translated* ....................................................................................... 270
>    *Update queries translated* ........................................................................................ 271
>    *Delete queries translated* .......................................................................................... 271
>    *Creating Crosstabs with the TRANSFORM statement* ............................................ 271
>   USING SQL-SPECIFIC QUERIES ....................................................................................... 271
>    *Merging data sets with the UNION operator* .......................................................... 271
>    *Creating a table with the CREATE TABLE statement* ............................................ 272
>   MANIPULATING COLUMNS WITH THE ALTER TABLE STATEMENT .................................. 272
>    *Adding a column with the ADD clause* .................................................................... 272
>    *Altering a column with the ALTER COLUMN clause* .............................................. 273
>    *Deleting a column with the DROP COLUMN clause* ............................................... 273
>    *Dynamically adding primary keys with the ADD constraints clause* ..................... 273

*Creating pass-through queries* ............................................................................................ 274

## CHAPTER 15 ........................................................................................................................ 276

## SUBQUERIES AND DOMAIN AGGREGATE FUNCTIONS ........................................................ 276

### ENHANCING YOUR ANALYSES WITH SUBQUERIES ........................................................................... 276
*Why use Subqueries?* ............................................................................................................ 277
*Subquery ground rules* ......................................................................................................... 277
*Creating Subqueries without typing SQL statements* ......................................................... 278
*Using IN and NOT IN with Subqueries* ................................................................................. 278
*Using Subqueries with comparison operators* ..................................................................... 278
*Using Subqueries as expressions* .......................................................................................... 279
*Using correlated Subqueries* ................................................................................................ 279
*Uncorrelated Subqueries* ...................................................................................................... 280
*Correlated Subqueries* .......................................................................................................... 280
*Using a correlated subquery as an expression* ................................................................... 280
*Using Subqueries with action queries* .................................................................................. 280
*A subquery in a make-table query* ...................................................................................... 280
*A subquery in an append query* ........................................................................................... 281
*A subquery in an update query* ............................................................................................ 281
*A subquery in a delete query* ............................................................................................... 281

### DOMAIN AGGREGATE FUNCTIONS ................................................................................................. 282

### UNDERSTANDING THE DIFFERENT DOMAIN AGGREGATE FUNCTION ................................................. 282
*DSum* ...................................................................................................................................... 282
*DAvg* ....................................................................................................................................... 282
*DCount* ................................................................................................................................... 282
*DLookup* ................................................................................................................................. 283
*DMin an/d Dmax* ................................................................................................................... 283
*DFirst and DLast* .................................................................................................................... 283
*DStDev, DStDevp, DvarP* ....................................................................................................... 283
*Examining the syntax of domain aggregate functions* ...................................................... 283
*Using no criteria* .................................................................................................................... 283
*Using text criteria* .................................................................................................................. 284
*Using domain aggregate function* ....................................................................................... 284
*Calculating the percent total* ............................................................................................... 284
*Creating a running count* ..................................................................................................... 284
*Using a value from the previous record* .............................................................................. 284

## CHAPTER 16 ........................................................................................................................ 285

## RUNNING DESCRIPTIVE STATISTICS IN ACCESS ................................................................. 285

### BASIC DESCRIPTIVE STATISTICS ...................................................................................................... 285
*Running descriptive statistics with aggregate queries* ...................................................... 285
*Determining rank, mode, and median* ................................................................................ 285

*Ranking the records in your data set* ............................................. 285
*Getting the mode of a data set* ..................................................... 286
*Getting the median of a data set* .................................................. 286
*Pulling a random sampling from your data set* ........................... 286
ADVANCED DESCRIPTIVE STATISTICS ......................................................... 287
*Calculating percentile making* ..................................................... 287
*Determining the quartile standing of a record* ............................ 287
*Creating a Frequency distribution* ............................................... 288

# PART V .................................................................................................. 290

# WORKING WITH ACCESS FORMS AND REPORTS ................................ 290

# CHAPTER 17 ......................................................................................... 291

# CREATING BASIC ACCESS FORMS ...................................................... 291

WORKING WITH FORM VIEWS ................................................................... 291
UNDERSTANDING DIFFERENT TYPES OF FORMS ........................................... 292
*Switchboard Form* ....................................................................... 293
*Dialog Box form* .......................................................................... 293
*Data Entry Form* ......................................................................... 293
*Record Display Form* ................................................................... 293
*Creating new forms* ..................................................................... 294
*Using the Form command* ........................................................... 294
*Using the Form Wizard* ............................................................... 294
*Looking at special types of form* .................................................. 295
*The navigation forms* .................................................................. 295
*Multiple-item forms* ..................................................................... 295
*Split forms* ................................................................................... 296
*Datasheet forms* .......................................................................... 296
*Resizing the form area* ................................................................ 297
*Saving your form* ........................................................................ 297
WORKING WITH CONTROLS ...................................................................... 298
*Categorizing controls* .................................................................. 298
*Adding a control* ......................................................................... 298
*Using the Control group* .............................................................. 299
*Using the field list* ....................................................................... 299
*Selecting and deselecting controls* ............................................... 299
*Selecting a single control* ............................................................. 300
*Selecting multiple controls* .......................................................... 300
*Deselecting controls* .................................................................... 300
*Manipulating controls* ................................................................. 300
*Resizing a control* ....................................................................... 300
*Sizing controls automatically* ...................................................... 301
*Moving a control* ........................................................................ 301

  *Aligning controls* ................................................................................................ *301*
  *Modifying the appearance of control* ................................................................. *302*
  *Grouping controls* .............................................................................................. *302*
  *Copying a control* .............................................................................................. *302*
  *Deleting a control* .............................................................................................. *303*
  *Reattaching a label to control* ........................................................................... *303*
 INTRODUCING PROPERTIES ................................................................................................ 303
  *Displaying the Property Sheet* ........................................................................... *304*
  *Getting acquainted with the Property Sheet* ..................................................... *305*
  *Changing a control's property setting* ................................................................ *305*
  *Naming control labels and their captions* ......................................................... *305*

# CHAPTER 18 ........................................................................................................................ 307

# WORKING WITH DATA ON ACCESS FORMS ......................................................................... 307

 USING FORM VIEW ............................................................................................................ 307
 LOOKING AT THE HOME TAB OF THE RIBBON ....................................................................... 308
  *The views group* ................................................................................................. *308*
  *The Clipboard group* .......................................................................................... *308*
  *The Sort & Filter group* ...................................................................................... *309*
  *The Records group* ............................................................................................. *309*
  *The find group* ................................................................................................... *309*
  *The Window group* ............................................................................................ *309*
  *The Text Formatting group* ................................................................................ *310*
  *Navigating among fields* .................................................................................... *310*
  *Moving among records in a form* ...................................................................... *311*
  *Knowing which controls you can't edit* .............................................................. *311*
  *Working with pictures and OLE objects* ............................................................. *311*
  *Entering data in the Long Text field* ................................................................... *311*
  *Entering data in the Date field* .......................................................................... *311*
  *Using option group* ............................................................................................ *312*
  *Using combo boxes and list boxes* ..................................................................... *312*
  *Switching to Datasheet view* ............................................................................. *313*
  *Saving a record* .................................................................................................. *313*
 PRINTING FORM ............................................................................................................... 313
  *Changing the title bar text with the Caption property* ...................................... *314*
  *Creating a bound form* ...................................................................................... *315*
  *Specifying how to view the form* ....................................................................... *315*
  *Removing the Record Selector* ........................................................................... *315*
 ADDING A FORM HEADER OR FOOTER ................................................................................. 316
 WORKING WITH SECTION PROPERTIES ................................................................................. 316
  *The Visible property* ........................................................................................... *316*
  *The Height property* ........................................................................................... *316*
  *The Back Color property* .................................................................................... *316*

    *The Special Effect property* ........... 316
    *The Display When property* ........... 316
    *The printing properties* ........... 317
  Changing the Layout ........... 317
    *Changing a control's properties* ........... 317
    *Setting the tab order* ........... 317
    *Modifying the format of text in a control* ........... 318
    *Using the Field List to add controls* ........... 318
  Converting a Form to a Report ........... 318

# CHAPTER 19 ........... 320

# WORKING WITH FORM CONTROLS ........... 320

  Setting Control Properties ........... 320
    *Customizing the default properties* ........... 320
    *Looking at common controls and properties* ........... 321
    *The Text Box control* ........... 321
    *The Command Button control* ........... 321
    *The Combo Box and List Box controls* ........... 321
    *The Checkbox and Toggle Button controls* ........... 322
    *The Options Group control* ........... 322
    *The Web Browser control* ........... 323
    *Creating a Calculated Control* ........... 323
  Working with Subforms ........... 324
  Form Design Tips ........... 324
  Using the Tab Stop property ........... 324
    *Tallying check boxes* ........... 325
    *Setting up combo boxes and list boxes* ........... 325
  Tackling Advanced Forms Techniques ........... 327
    *Using the Page Number and Date/Time controls* ........... 327
    *Morphing a control* ........... 327
    *Using the Format Painter* ........... 328
    *Offering more end-user help.* ........... 328
    *Adding background pictures* ........... 328
    *Limiting the records shown on a form* ........... 330
    *Using the Tab Control* ........... 330
  Using Dialog Boxes to Collect Information ........... 330
    *Designing the query* ........... 331
    *Setting up the command buttons* ........... 331
    *Adding a default button* ........... 331
    *Setting a Cancel button* ........... 331
    *Removing the control menu* ........... 331
    *Designing a Form from Scratch* ........... 332
    *Creating the basic form* ........... 332

| | |
|---|---|
| Creating a subform | 332 |
| Adding the subform | 334 |
| Changing the form's behavior | 334 |
| Setting the form's properties | 334 |
| Looking up values during data entry | 335 |
| Saving the record | 335 |
| Changing the form's appearance | 335 |

## CHAPTER 20 .................................................................................................. 336

## PRESENTING DATA WITH ACCESS REPORTS .................................................... 336

### Introducing Reports .................................................................................... 336

| | |
|---|---|
| Identifying the different types of reports | 336 |
| Tabular reports | 336 |
| Columnar reports | 336 |
| Mailing label reports | 337 |
| Distinguishing between reports and forms | 337 |

### Creating a Report from Beginning to End ................................................... 337
### Defining the report layout .......................................................................... 337

| | |
|---|---|
| Assembling the data | 338 |
| Creating a report with the Report Wizard | 338 |
| Creating a new report | 338 |
| Selecting the grouping levels | 339 |
| Defining the group data | 339 |
| Selecting the sort order | 340 |
| Selecting summary options | 340 |
| Selecting the layout | 340 |
| Opening the report design | 341 |
| Adjusting the report's layout | 341 |
| Choosing a theme | 341 |
| Creating new theme color schemes | 341 |
| Using the Print Preview window | 342 |
| Publishing in alternate formats | 342 |
| Viewing the report in Design view | 343 |
| Printing or viewing the report | 343 |
| Printing the report | 343 |
| Viewing the report | 343 |
| Saving the Report | 343 |

### Banded Report Design Concepts ................................................................. 344

| | |
|---|---|
| The Report Header section | 344 |
| The Page Header section | 344 |
| The Group Header section | 344 |
| The Detail section | 345 |
| The Group Footer section | 345 |

*The Page Footer section* ................................................................................................. *345*
*The Report Footer section* ............................................................................................. *345*
CREATING A REPORT FROM SCRATCH ................................................................................ *345*
*Creating a new report and binding it to a table* ........................................................... *345*
*Defining the report page size and Layout* ..................................................................... *346*
*Placing controls on the report* ...................................................................................... *346*
*Resizing a section* ......................................................................................................... *347*
*Modifying the appearance of a text in a control* .......................................................... *347*
*Working with Text BOX controls* ................................................................................... *348*
*Adding and using Text Box controls* ............................................................................. *348*
*Entering an expression in a Text box control* ............................................................... *348*
*Sizing a Text Box control or Label control* .................................................................... *348*
*Deleting and cutting attached labels from Text Box controls* ...................................... *348*
*Pasting labels into a report section* .............................................................................. *348*
*Moving Label and Textbox controls* ............................................................................. *349*
*Modifying the appearance of multiple controls* ........................................................... *349*
*Changing Label and Textbox control properties* .......................................................... *349*
*Growing and shrinking Text Box controls* .................................................................... *349*
SORTING AND GROUPING DATA ......................................................................................... *350*
*Creating a group header or footer* ............................................................................... *350*
*Sorting data within groups* ........................................................................................... *350*
*Removing a group* ........................................................................................................ *350*
*Hiding a section* ............................................................................................................ *351*
*Sizing a section* ............................................................................................................. *351*
*Moving controls between sections* ............................................................................... *351*
*Adding page breaks* ...................................................................................................... *351*
IMPROVING THE REPORT'S APPEARANCE ........................................................................... *351*
*Adjusting the page header* ........................................................................................... *352*
*Creating an expression in the group header* ................................................................ *352*
*Creating a report header* .............................................................................................. *352*

# CHAPTER 21 ............................................................................................................... 354

# ADVANCED ACCESS REPORT TECHNIQUES .............................................................. 354

GROUPING AND SORTING DATA ......................................................................................... *354*
*Grouping alphabetically* ............................................................................................... *354*
*Grouping on date intervals* ........................................................................................... *355*
*Hiding repeating information* ....................................................................................... *355*
*Hiding a page header* ................................................................................................... *356*
*Starting a new page number for each group* ............................................................... *356*
FORMATTING DATA ............................................................................................................ *356*
*Creating numbered lists* ............................................................................................... *357*
*Creating bulleted lists* ................................................................................................... *357*
*Adding emphasis on the run time* ................................................................................ *358*

  *Avoiding empty reports* .................................................................................................. *358*
  *Inserting vertical lines between columns* .................................................................. *358*
  *Adding a blank line* ......................................................................................................... *359*
  *Even-odd page printing* .................................................................................................. *359*
  *Using different formats in the same text box* ............................................................ *359*
  *Centering the title* ........................................................................................................... *360*
  *Aligning control labels* ................................................................................................... *360*
  *Micro-adjusting controls* ................................................................................................ *360*
 ADDING DATA ............................................................................................................................... 360
  *Adding more information to a report* ......................................................................... *360*
  *Adding the user's name to a bound report* ................................................................ *361*
 ADDING EVEN MORE FLEXIBILITY ............................................................................................... 361
  *Displaying all reports in a combo box* ........................................................................ *361*
  *Fast printing from queried data* ................................................................................... *362*
  *Using snaking columns in a report* .............................................................................. *362*
  *Exploiting two-pass report processing* ........................................................................ *363*
  *Assigning unique names to controls* ........................................................................... *363*

**PART VI** .................................................................................................................................... **364**

**MICROSOFT ACCESS PROGRAMMING FUNDAMENTALS** ............................................................ **364**

**CHAPTER 22** ............................................................................................................................... **365**

**USING ACCESS MACROS** ........................................................................................................... **365**

 AN INTRODUCTION TO MACROS .................................................................................................. 365
  *Creating a macro* ............................................................................................................. *365*
  *Assigning a macro to an event* ..................................................................................... *367*
 UNDERSTANDING MACRO SECURITY ........................................................................................... 367
  *Enabling sandbox mode* ................................................................................................. *368*
  *The Trust Center* .............................................................................................................. *368*
 MULTI-ACTION MACROS ............................................................................................................ 370
 SUBMACROS ............................................................................................................................... 370
 CONDITIONS ............................................................................................................................... 371
  *Opening reports using conditions* ................................................................................ *371*
  *Multiple actions in conditions* ...................................................................................... *371*
 TEMPORARY VARIABLES ............................................................................................................. 371
  *Enhancing a macro you've already created* ............................................................... *372*
  *Using temporary variables to simplify macros* .......................................................... *372*
  *Using temporary variables in VBA* .............................................................................. *372*
 ERROR HANDLING AND MACRO DEBUGGING ............................................................................. 373
  *The OnError action* ........................................................................................................ *373*
  *The MacroError object* ................................................................................................... *373*
  *Debugging macros* .......................................................................................................... *374*
  *Embedded Macros* ........................................................................................................... *374*

Macros versus VBA Statements .......... 374
    *Choosing between macros and VBA* .......... *375*
    *Converting existing macros to VBA* .......... *375*

## CHAPTER 23 .......... 376

## USING ACCESS DATA MACROS .......... 376

Introducing Data Macros .......... 376
Understanding Table Events .......... 376
    *"Before events* .......... *376*
    *"After" events* .......... *377*
Using the Macro Builder for Data Macros .......... 377
Understanding the Action Catalog .......... 377
    *Program flow* .......... *378*
    *Data blocks* .......... *378*
    *Data actions* .......... *378*
Creating Your First Data Macro .......... 378
Managing Macro Objects .......... 379
    *Collapsing and expanding macro items.* .......... *379*
    *Moving macro items* .......... *379*
    *Saving a macro as XML* .......... *379*
Recognizing the Limitations of Data Macros .......... 379

## CHAPTER 24 .......... 381

## GETTING STARTED WITH ACCESS VBA .......... 381

Introducing Visual Basic for Applications .......... 381
Understanding VBA Terminology .......... 381
Starting with VBA Code Basics .......... 382
Creating VBA Programs .......... 382
    *Modules* .......... *383*
    *Procedures and functions* .......... *383*
Working in the code window .......... 384
    *White space* .......... *384*
    *Line continuation* .......... *384*
Multi-statement lines .......... 384
    *IntelliSense* .......... *385*
    *Compiling procedures* .......... *385*
    *Saving a module* .......... *385*
Understanding VBA Branching Constructs .......... 386
    *Branching* .......... *386*
    *The If keyword* .......... *386*
    *The Select case...End Select statement* .......... *386*
    *.Looping* .......... *387*

  *The Do... Loop statement* ............................................. *387*
  *.The For... Next statement* ........................................... *387*
 WORKING WITH OBJECTS AND COLLECTIONS ........................................ 387
 PROPERTIES AND METHODS ........................................................ 388
  *Properties* ................................................................ *388*
  *Methods* .................................................................. *388*
  *The With statement* ...................................................... *388*
  *The For Each statement* .................................................. *389*
 EXPLORING THE VISUAL BASIC EDITOR ............................................. 389
  *The Immediate window* .................................................... *389*
  *The Project Explrer* ..................................................... *389*
 THE OBJECT BROWSER ............................................................ 390
  *VBE options* ............................................................. *390*
  *The Editor tab of the Options dialog box* ................................ *390*
  *The Project Properties dialog box* ....................................... *390*

## CHAPTER 25 ................................................................. 391

## MASTERING VBA DATA TYPES AND PROCEDURES ...................................... 391

 USING VARIABLES .............................................................. 391
  *Naming variables* ........................................................ *391*
  *Declaring variables* ..................................................... *392*
  *The Dim keyword* ......................................................... *392*
  *The Public keyword* ...................................................... *393*
  *The Private keyword* ..................................................... *393*
 WORKING WITH DATA TYPES ...................................................... 393
  *Forcing explicit declarations* ........................................... *393*
  *Using a naming convention with variables* ................................ *394*
  *Understanding variable scope and Lifetime* ............................... *394*
  *Examining scope* ......................................................... *394*
  *Determining a variable lifetime* ......................................... *395*
  *Deciding on a variable's scope* .......................................... *395*
  *Using constants* ......................................................... *395*
  *Declaring constants* ..................................................... *395*
  *Using a naming convention with constants* ................................ *396*
  *Working with arrays* ..................................................... *396*
  *Fixed arrays* ............................................................ *396*
  *Dynamic arrays* .......................................................... *396*
  *Array functions* ......................................................... *397*
 UNDERSTANDING SUBS AND FUNCTIONS ............................................. 397
  *Understanding where to create a procedure* ............................... *398*
 CALLING VBA PROCEDURES ....................................................... 398
  *Creating subs* ........................................................... *398*
  *Creating Functions* ...................................................... *399*

*Handling parameters* ............................................................................. *399*
  *Calling a function and passing parameters* ........................................ *399*
  SIMPLIFYING CODE WITH NAMED ARGUMENTS ................................................. 399

# CHAPTER 26 ............................................................................................ 400

# UNDERSTANDING THE ACCESS EVENT MODEL ............................................. 400

  PROGRAMMING EVENTS ........................................................................... 400
  UNDERSTANDING HOW EVENTS TRIGGER VBA CODE ................................... 400
    *Creating event procedures* ................................................................ *401*
  IDENTIFYING COMMON EVENTS .................................................................. 401
    *Form event procedures* ..................................................................... *403*
    *Essential form events* ....................................................................... *403*
  FORM MOUSE AND KEY-BOARD EVENTS ....................................................... 404
    *Form data events* ............................................................................. *405*
  CONTROL EVENT PROCEDURES ................................................................... 405
    *Report event procedures* .................................................................. *406*
    *Report section event procedures* ....................................................... *407*
  PAYING ATTENTION TO EVENT SEQUENCE .................................................... 407
    *Looking at common event sequences* ................................................ *408*
  WRITING SIMPLE FORM AND CONTROL EVENT PROCEDURES ........................... 409
  OPENING A FORM WITH AN EVENT PROCEDURE ............................................ 409
    *Running an event procedure when closing a form* ............................. *410*
    *Using an event procedure to confirm record deletion* ......................... *410*

# CHAPTER 27 ............................................................................................ 411

# DEBUGGING YOUR ACCESS APPLICATIONS ............................................... 411

  ORGANIZING VBA CODE ........................................................................... 411
  TESTING YOUR APPLICATIONS .................................................................... 412
    *Testing functions* .............................................................................. *413*
    *Compiling VBA code* ......................................................................... *413*
  TRADITIONAL DEBUGGING TECHNIQUES ...................................................... 414
    *Using MsgBox* .................................................................................. *414*
    *Using Debug.Print* ............................................................................ *414*
  USING THE ACCESS DEBUGGING TOOLS ....................................................... 414
    *Running code with the Immediate Window* ....................................... *414*
  SUSPENDING EXECUTION WITH BREAKPOINTS .............................................. 415
  LOOKING AT VARIABLES WITH THE LOCALS WINDOW ..................................... 416
    *Setting watches with the Watches window* ....................................... *416*
  USING CONDITIONAL WATCHES .................................................................. 417
    *Using the Call Stack window* ............................................................. *417*
  TRAPPING ERRORS IN YOUR CODE .............................................................. 417
    *Understanding error trapping* ........................................................... *418*

      *On Error Resume Next* ............................................................................................... *418*
      *On Error Goto 0* ......................................................................................................... *418*
      *On Error GoTo Label* ................................................................................................. *418*
   THE RESUME KEYWORD ........................................................................................................... 419
   THE ERR OBJECT ....................................................................................................................... 419
   INCLUDING ERROR HANDLING IN YOUR PROCEDURES ............................................................... 420

## PART VII .............................................................................................................................. 421

## ADVANCED ACCESS PROGRAMMING TECHNIQUES ........................................ 421

## CHAPTER 28 ........................................................................................................................ 422

## ACCESSING DATA WITH VBA ............................................................................................ 422

   WORKING WITH DATA ............................................................................................................. 422
   UNDERSTANDING DAO OBJECTS ............................................................................................ 423
      *The DAO DBEngine object* ....................................................................................... *424*
      *The DAO Workspace object* ..................................................................................... *424*
      *The DAO Database object* ........................................................................................ *424*
      *The DAO TableDef object* ......................................................................................... *425*
      *The DAO QueryDef object* ........................................................................................ *426*
      *The DAO Recordset object* ....................................................................................... *426*
      *Navigating recordsets* ............................................................................................... *427*
      *Deleting the record set end or beginning* ................................................................ *428*
      *Counting records* ...................................................................................................... *428*
      *The DAO Field objects (recordsets)* ......................................................................... *428*
   UNDERSTANDING ADO OBJECTS ............................................................................................ 429
      *The ADO Connection object* .................................................................................... *429*
      *The ADO Command object* ...................................................................................... *430*
      *The ADO Recordset object* ....................................................................................... *430*
   WRITING VBA CODE TO UPDATE A TABLE ............................................................................. 430
      *Updating fields in a record using ADO* .................................................................... *430*
      *Updating a calculated control* .................................................................................. *430*
      *Checking the status of a record deletion* ................................................................. *431*
      *Eliminating repetitive code* ....................................................................................... *431*
      *Adding a new record* ................................................................................................ *431*
      *Deleting a record* ..................................................................................................... *431*
      *Deleting related records in multiple tables* ............................................................. *431*

## CHAPTER 29 ........................................................................................................................ 433

## ADVANCED DATA ACCESS WITH VBA ............................................................................ 433

   ADDING AN UNBOUND COMBO BOX TO A FORM TO FIND DATA ............................................ 433
      *Using the Find a Record method* ............................................................................. *433*
      *Using a bookmark* .................................................................................................... *434*

FILTERING A FORM .................................................................................................434
   Filtering with code ..................................................................................434
   Filtering with a query .............................................................................435
   Creating a parameter query ...................................................................435
   Creating an interactive filter dialog box .................................................435
   Linking the dialog box to another form ..................................................435

**CHAPTER 30** ...............................................................................................................436

**CUSTOMIZING THE RIBBON** ................................................................................436

THE RIBBON HIERARCHY ......................................................................................436
   Controls for Access Ribbons ..................................................................436
SPLITBUTTON .........................................................................................................437
   Menu ......................................................................................................437
   Gallery ....................................................................................................437
   Button ....................................................................................................437
   ToggleButton .........................................................................................437
   ComboBox .............................................................................................437
   CheckBox ...............................................................................................438
   Special Ribbon features .........................................................................438
   SuperTips ...............................................................................................438
   Collapsing the Ribbon ............................................................................438
EDITING THE DEFAULT RIBBON ...........................................................................438
WORKING WITH THE QUICK ACCESS TOOLBAR ...................................................439
DEVELOPING CUSTOM RIBBONS .........................................................................440
   The Ribbon creation process .................................................................440
USING VBA CALLBACKS ........................................................................................440
CREATING A CUSTOM RIBBON ............................................................................441
   Step 1: Design the Ribbon and build the XML .......................................441
   Step 2: Write the callback routines .......................................................441
   Step 3: Create the USysRibbons table ...................................................442
   Step 4: Add XML to USysRibbons ..........................................................442
   Step 5: Specify the custom Ribbon property ........................................443
THE BASIC RIBBON XML ......................................................................................443
   Adding Ribbon Controls .........................................................................443
   Specifying imageMso .............................................................................443
   The Label controls .................................................................................444
   The Button control .................................................................................444
   Separators .............................................................................................444
   The CheckBox control ............................................................................444
   The Dropdown control ..........................................................................444
   The SplitButton Control .........................................................................445
ATTACHING RIBBONS TO FORMS AND REPORTS ...............................................445
REMOVING THE RIBBON COMPLETELY ...............................................................445

## CHAPTER 31 .......... 446
## PREPARING YOUR ACCESS APPLICATION FOR DISTRIBUTION .......... 446

### Defining the Current Database Options .......... 446
- Application options .......... 446
- Application Icon .......... 446
- Display Form .......... 447
- Display Status Bar .......... 447
- Document Window Options .......... 447
- Use Access Special Keys .......... 447
- Compact on Close .......... 447

### Remove Personal Information from File Properties on Save .......... 448
- Use Windows Theme Controls on Forms .......... 448
- Enable Layout View .......... 448

### Enable Design Change for Tables in Datasheet View .......... 448
- Check for Truncated Number Fields .......... 448
- Picture Property Storage Format .......... 449

### Navigation options .......... 449
- The Display Navigation Pane check box .......... 449
- The Navigation Options button .......... 449

### Ribbon and toolbar options .......... 449
- Ribbon Name .......... 449
- Shortcut Menu Bar .......... 449
- Allow Full Menus .......... 450
- Allow Default Shortcut Menus .......... 450
- Name AutoCorrect Options .......... 450

### Developing the Application .......... 450
- Building to a specification .......... 450
- Creating documentation .......... 451
- Documenting the code you write .......... 451
- Documenting the application .......... 451
- Testing the application before distribution .......... 451
- Polishing Your Application .......... 451

### Giving your application a consistent look and feel .......... 452
- Adding common professional components .......... 452
- A splash screen .......... 452

### An application switchboard .......... 452
- An About box .......... 453
- The status bar .......... 453
- A progress meter .......... 453
- Making the application easy to start .......... 453

### Bulletproofing an Application .......... 453
- Using error trapping on all Visual Basic procedures .......... 454

- *Maintaining usage logs* .................................................. *454*
- *Separating tables from the rest of the application* ................ *454*
- *Building bulletproof forms* ............................................. *454*
- *Validating user input* .................................................... *455*
- *Using the /runtime option* ............................................. *455*
- *Encrypting or encoding a database* ................................. *455*
- REMOVING A DATABASE PASSWORD .................................... 456
  - *Protecting Visual Basic code* ......................................... *457*
- SECURING THE ENVIRONMENT ............................................. 457
  - *Setting startup option in code* ....................................... *457*
  - *Disabling startup bypass* .............................................. *458*
- SETTING PROPERTY VALUES ................................................ 458
- GETTING PROPERTY VALUES ................................................ 460

# CHAPTER 32 ........................................................................ 461

# INTEGRATING ACCESS WITH SHAREPOINT ............................ 461

- INTRODUCING SHAREPOINT ................................................ 461
- UNDERSTANDING SHAREPOINT SITES ................................... 462
  - *SharePoint documents* .................................................. *462*
  - *SharePoint lists* ........................................................... *462*
- SHARING DATA BETWEEN ACCESS AND SHAREPOINT ............. 463
  - *Linking to Sharepoint lists* ............................................ *463*
- IMPORTING SHAREPOINT LISTS ........................................... 463
- EXPORTING ACCESS TABLES TO SHAREPOINT ....................... 464
- MOVING ACCESS TABLES TO SHAREPOINT ........................... 464
- USING SHAREPOINT TEMPLATES ......................................... 465
- CONCLUSION .................................................................... 465

# INDEX ................................................................................. 466

# INTRODUCTION

Microsoft Access is known all over the world as a database management system(DBMS) created by Microsoft that brings together the relational Access Database Engine(ACE) together with a graphical user interface (GUI) and other tools used in the development of software.

Access is a part of the Microsoft 365 suite of applications which is embedded in the very professional and much higher editions or sold differently. It has the ability to save its own format with the use of the Access Database Engine( used to be known as Jet Database Engine). With this application, you can also choose to link up directly with data that has been saved in some other applications and databases.

Access has tables that provide support for different field types, and referential integrity which includes deletes and cascading updates. It also has query interface forms that can be displayed and also has data inserted, and reports for the purpose of printing.

The main idea behind the creation of Access was so that end users would have the opportunity of accessing data from just about any source. Some of the other features this amazing application has includes; exporting and Importing data to various formats such as Outlook, Excel, dBase, Paradox, SQL Server, Oracle, etc. With this application you can also choose to have data linked right where the data is and make use of it for the purpose of viewing, editing, querying, and also reporting. With this, the data in existence changes, and Access will make use of the latest data.

Another premium benefit of this application from the perspective of a programmer is its compatibility with SQL (Structured Query Language)- you can have queries viewed either graphically or being edited as SQL statements and you can make use of SQL statements directly in Macros and VBA modules in other to makes changes to Access tables. Users also get to mix and make use of bix Macros and VBA for both logic and programming forms and also give possibilities that are object-oriented.

In our world today, there is so much data flying around with higher demands for extremely complex analysis of data with data analysts having a need for some very useful tools which is where this book comes into play. With the use of this book, you will be introduced to Access and you will also learn the different ways in which you can make use of Access to further improve your day-to-day management and analysis of data.

This book has been written in such a way that it will help you prove your skillset not minding the level at which you are(beginner, intermediate or progressional). If you are new to access and database management in general it's best you start at the beginning so you get familiar with the application and also get used to building other Access applications. You will also get to learn about Visual Basic for Applications (VBA) programming.

Through all, this book has mind-engaging chapters that will help you get started properly and take you all the way to the top. Enjoy, Learn and Practice as you read along.

# PART 1
# ACCESS BUILDING BLOCKS

In reference to what a building block is, this book has been designed to take you gradually from one step to another with each part containing chapters and also examples that are detailed and drive home the point.

In this part, you will be introduced to various topics that are rudimentary and necessary for you to be successful with using a database and you will also learn how to ensure data is normalized and well implemented so you can have an effective table. Ensure you spend more time in this part this way you will have all the fundamental knowledge needed but if you are already familiar with database design you can skim through pages to serve as revision and you might also learn new things as well.

# CHAPTER 1
# AN INTRODUCTION TO DATABASE DEVELOPMENT

Database development is quite unique and it is not the same way you play around with your computer. As against other applications like PowerPoint and Excel where you just have to be creative, there's a need for you to have basic foundational knowledge in database development. This chapter covers basic fundamental knowledge that you need to learn and cannot do without as it pertains to this application and the development of databases in general.

## The Database terminology of Access

With Access, you get to make use of almost all the basic terminologies that there are with databases. These terms include the database itself, records, tables, fields, and also values that show a hierarchy from the smallest to the largest and vice versa. All of the above-mentioned terms are equally used in almost all database systems with the inclusion of structured Query Language (SQL).

## Databases

Databases can be defined as an organized medium of collecting information, or data that has been stored electronically in a computer. Usually, a database is managed by a database management system ( DBMS). Both data and DBMS and the various applications that are related to them are known as a database system often simply called a database.

Though I have mentioned databases being electronic, there are also manual databases that are widely known as the filing systems or manual databases systems.

With the use of manual database systems, you basically have a particular way of filling out forms. Information is accessed manually by having to open a file cabinet, take out a file or folder and then locate the piece of paper. Users will fill out the forms via any method most comfortable to them. You can also make use of a spreadsheet in the analysis of data or have it displayed in another interesting manner.

Data that are found in the most common type of databases that are widely used in today's world are basically in rows and columns in various tables in order to make the processing and querying of data very efficient. With this, the data will be accessed, modified, controlled, organized, and modified with ease. Note that most databases make use of structured Query Language(SQL) in writing and querying data.

There are various types of databases. The one you decide to make use of is most dependent on how the organization plans to make use of the data.

**Below is a description of just a few of the databases we have;**

- **Relational database**: This database became widely known in the 1980s. Items within a relational database are well arranged as a set of tables that has rows and columns. The relational database technology offers the most flexible and efficient method of gaining access to information that has been well structured.

- **Object-oriented database**: Information found in an object-oriented database is represented in the form of objects similar to object-oriented programming.

- **Distributed databases**: This type of database has about two or more files that can be found in different locations. The database can be saved on various computers that are found right within the same location or diverged over various networks.

Access databases are just an automated method of the filing and retrieval functions of a paper filing system. Access databases help with the storing of information in a well-structured manner. Having data stored in a very precise format helps a database management system such as Access to turn data into very useful information. In Access, a database is just more than a collection of tables, it includes various types of objects including queries, forms, macros, reports, and code modules. Upon opening an Access database, the various objects will be opened up for you to work with. You can also choose to open various copies of Access at the same time and work at the same time also with more than a single database if need be.

## Tables

Tables primarily are database objects that have all of the data in a database. In tables, data is arranged in columns and rows format which is much like a spreadsheet. Each row shows a unique record and columns display a field on the record. For instance, a table that had the data of an employee for a company might have a row for each of the employees and the columns displaying employee information like the name of the employee, address, job title, and also mobile number.

**There are actually certain things to take note of with tables, they are;**

- The number of tables that are in a database is limited only by just the number of objects that are allowed in a database. Primarily, a standard user-defined table can have up to about 1,024 columns. The storage capacity of the server helps to bring a limit to the number of rows in the table.

- Properties can be assigned to various tables and to each column that exists in the table to bring control to the data that is allowed. For instance, a constraint can be created on a column such that it will disallow null values or make provision for a default value if the value is not indicated or you can also choose to assign a key Constraint on the table one that ensures the enforcement of uniqueness or help with the definition of a relationship that exists between tables.

- Data that exists within tables can be compressed by either pages or rows. The compression of data can enable rows to be saved on a page.

**The various types of tables that exist include;**

- **Partitioned Tables:** These can be described as tables that have their data divided in a horizontal manner that can be spread across more than just one filegroup in a database. Partitioning ensures that large tables or indexes are very manageable due to the fact that it allows you to gain access or manage subsets of data swiftly and efficiently while also having to keep the integrity of the collection as a whole.

- **Temporary Tables**: Here there are two types of tables which are local and global. They are quite different in terms of their names, availability, and visibility. Local temporary tables have just a single number sign(#) as the first character of their names they are much visible basically to the current connection for the user and they are also deleted when the user disconnects. With global temporary tables, there are two number signs(##) as the first characters of their names hence they are only visible to users just after they have been created and they are equally deleted when all of the users referencing the table disconnect.

In Access, a table is known to be an entity. In designing tables and also when you are working on some Access applications, you must bear in mind the way the tables and other database objects display the physical entities controlled by the database and also how the entities are related to one another. When you have built the table, you can view it in a spreadsheet-like manner which is known as a datasheet that has rows and columns.

## Records and Fields

Records and Fields are embedded in what is known as a datasheet and are divided into rows and columns with the first row having the names of the fields in the database.

The row comprises just one record that contains fields that also have a relationship with that same record. When in a manual system(filling), the rows are individual forms like sheets of paper and then the fields can be described as the blank areas that you fill in on a printed form.

A single column is a field that contains various properties that indicate the specific type of data that is embedded in the field and it also shows how the day and the field should be managed by Access. **These properties include;** the name of the field(company) and also the type of data in the field (text). A field can also contain some other properties too such as the Address field's Size property that tells Access the maximum number of characters that can be allowed for the address.

## Values

Simply put, values can be defined as an intersection of both a record and a field. For example, the English Premier League can be a field, and then Chelsea Football club can be a data entered to represent a value of the field. There are certain basic rules that control how data is infused into an Access table.

## Relational Databases

A database that has been designed properly offers you so much access to up-to-date and accurate information. Since a correct design is important if you want to achieve your goals when you are having to work with databases, there is also a need to invest quality time so that you can learn the principles of good design that make sense. In the end, there is every possibility you end up with a database that meets all of your needs and is also quite flexible.

Access data is usually stored in related tables such that the data in one table is related to the data in another table. Access keeps the relationship between tables that are related thereby enabling easy access to have a customer and all of the orders of the customer extracted without having to lose any data or retrieving records that are not for the customer.

When there is more than one table, data entry will also be quite easy as well as reporting of data by the decrease in the input of data that are said to be redundant. For example, when you define two tables, if you are using an application that deals with the information of the customer, there is no need for you to have the name and address of the customer saved each time the customer makes an order or purchases an item.

When data is differentiated into various tables within a database it enables the system to be easier to maintain since all records of a given type are right within the same table. When you take out time to properly place data into different tables, there will be a reduction in the design and the amount of time expended. This process is often known as normalization.

# Access Database Objects

Doesn't matter if you are an experienced user of databases or you are just new to them, there is a need for you to have a basic understanding of some ideas before you begin to build databases. There are about six different types of objects that have all the tools and data needed for you to make use of Access. These tools are table, query, form, report, macro, and module.

## Tables

As earlier discussed, tables are quite very important when it has to do with Access databases. Tables are interacted with via an object known as a datasheet. A datasheet though similar to that of an Excel sheet helps to show the information contained in a table in a row-and-column format. A datasheet shows information in a raw form without any form of transformation or filtering. It is also known as the custom default mode for showing all the fields of a given record.

## Queries

Using a query ensures you add, delete or make changes to data with much ease in your Access database. You can also make use of queries in locating specific data quickly by having to filter on some basic criteria, you can make use of queries in calculating or summarizing data, and lastly, you can make use of queries in the automation of data management task like having to review the most recent data on a recurring basis.

In a well-designed database, the data that should be presented through a form or a report is most times located in different tables. With the use of a query, you can extract the information needed from different tables and then bring them together to show it in the form of a report. A query can be either a request for data results from a database or for action on the specific data and at times it can also be both.

With the use of a query, you can have the answer to a very direct question, run some calculations, bring together data from various tables, and add, change or delete data from a database. Due to the fact that queries are also very versatile, there are actually various types of queries, and queries are actually created based on the type of task at hand. It's also worthy to note that in Access, almost all the forms and reports are based on queries that have a combination of filter or sort data before it is shown. Queries are often retracted from macros or VBA procedures to either change, add or delete database records.

## Data-entry and display forms

Forms in Access is a database object that can be used to design a user interface for a database application. A bound form is actually one that has a direct connection to a data source like a table or query and can also be used to insert, edit or show data from that particular data source. As an alternative, you can choose to create an unbound form that has no direct link to a data source but still has the command buttons, labels, or some other controls that you might have a need for in order to operate your application.

You can make use of data entry forms in restricting access to some fields in a table. Forms can also be used for the enhancement of data validation rules in VBA code in order to run a check on the Validity of your data before it's included in the database table. Forms are oftentimes preferred over datasheets. Most times they look like paper documents and can assist the user in performing data entry tasks with so much ease. Forms have a way of ensuring that data entry is done with ease and also easy to comprehend through the guiding of users along the field of the table that is being modified.

A type of form known as the Read-only form is basically used for the sole purpose of the inquiry. These forms show some fields that are in a table. When some fields alone are shown and not all, this actually means that a user can be limited to data that are sensitive while also allowing access to other fields that are also in the same table.

## Reports

Reports basically provide a method of viewing formats and also summarizing the information that you have in your Microsoft Access database. For instance, you can choose to create a very simple report of phone numbers for all of the contacts on your phone or a summary report of the total sales across different countries or regions in a given time or period. Reports help to show your data in PDF-style formatting. Access enables an extraordinary amount of flexibility when you have to create reports.

**A report comes in very handy especially when there is a need to present the information in your database for any of the uses below;**

- Show or spread a summary of data.
- Archive snapshots of the data.
- Offer details about individual records.
- Having labels created.

With reports, you can bring together various tables such that it represents the complex relationships that exist among various sets of data. A valid example is the printing of an invoice. The table of the customer will provide the name and address of the customer and other data that are related which also includes related records that are in the sales table in order to print the individual line item information for each of the products that have been ordered. The report will also calculate the sales totals and have them printed in a special format.

## Macros and VBA

With the creation of a new database, you will have to start creating various database objects like tables, forms, and also reports. Eventually, you will get to a stage where you might have to include some sort of programming in order to have some processes automated and also help tie your database objects together. This is where the macros and VBA come into play.

In Access, programming has to do with adding functionality to the database through the use of Access macros or Visual Basic for Applications code. For instance, let's assume you have created a form and a report and you want to include a command button to the form such that when it is clicked, the report will be opened. Programming in this sense means creating a VBA procedure or a macro and then fixing the command buttons' on-click event property In such a way that when you click on the command button, it will run the macro or procedure. If you are going through a very simple procedure like having to open a report, you can choose to make use of the Command Button Wizard to get all your work done or rather have the wizard turned off and then do the programming yourself.

The choice of using either macros or VBA depends majorly on the method you have in mind to either deploy or distribute the database. For instance, if you have the database stored on your computer and you alone use the computer, if you are quite comfortable with the use of the VBA code you might then prefer to make use of the VBA to execute almost all your programming tasks. Nevertheless, suppose you have in mind that you would like to give other people access to your database by positioning it on a file server. In that case, there might be a need for you to avoid using VBA basically for security reasons.

Your decision to use either the macros or the VBA should be based on two reasons majorly which are the functionality you want and of course security. Security is quite an issue because VBA can be used to design codes that will either compromise the security of data or harm files on your computer. When using a database created by someone else, you should have VBA code enabled if only you are sure the database is from a trustworthy source. When you design a database that will be used by other people, you ought to avoid adding programming tools that will need the user to specifically grant trusted status to the database.

On the other hand, macros provide a straightforward method to deal with a lot of programming tasks like opening and closing forms and also running reports. The database of various objects such as forms and reports that you have created due to the fact that there is little syntax for you to remember can be tied together quickly. The arguments for each of the actions are shown in the Macro Builder. Macros in addition to increased security offer ease of use.

## Planning for database objects

In creating database objects like tables, forms, and reports, there is a need to conclude with a series of design tasks. When your design seems unique, your application will be superb also. When you think through your design very well, you will be able to complete any system very fast and at a more successful rate. The main reason for the design of an object is for there to be a well-laid-out path to follow during implementation.

## A Five-Step Design Method

The five design steps alongside the database system explains a lot about Access and also offer a solid foundation for the creation of database applications which include tables, queries, forms, data pages, reports, macros, and also simple VBA modules.

The time expended on each step is totally dependent on the type of database that is being built. For instance, there are times when users provide examples of a report they want to print from their Access database and the various sources of data on the report are really obvious to the extent that you will need just a few minutes to complete the design. And at other times, especially when the requirements of the user are very complex, or probably the business processes that the application provides support for need so much research, you can actually spend lots of hours or even days on just the first step.

Ensure you take adequate time to look at the design based on inputs and outputs as you are reading through each of the steps.

### Step 1: The overall design from concept to reality

Almost all software developers encounter related problems, the first of which is the determination of just how to have the needs of the end-user met in total. It is very important to have a perfect understanding of the overall requirement before narrowing down on just the details.

**For example, you might have some users that request a database that supports the following tasks;**

- Inputting and maintaining information of customers such as name, address, and also the financial history.
- Inputting and maintaining sales information like a method of payment, date of sales, total amount, the identity of the customer, and some other related fields.
- Inputting and maintaining sales line-item information especially details of the items purchased.
- Checking the information from all of the tables such as sales, customers, payments, and sales line items.

- Asking various types of questions about the information that exists in a database.
- Designing a monthly invoice report.
- Designing a customer sales history.
- Designing mailing labels and mail-merge reports.

When taking into consideration these tasks listed above, there might be a need for you to also consider other peripheral tasks that have not been listed by the user. Before you begin to design, ensure you settle down and study how the process in use currently works. To get this accomplished, you should have a thorough needs analysis of the existing system conducted and also check out how you can have it automated.

One unique method of getting this done is to make up a number of questions that give an idea about the business of the client and how the client makes use of his data.

**For instance, when you want to automate any type of business you might need to ask the following questions;**

- How are billings being processed?
- What specific reports and forms are being used at the moment?
- How are sales, customers, and some other records stored at the moment?

While asking these questions and some other related ones, the client might as well remember other things about his business that he feels you should know about.

Studying carefully all the processes that are in use at the moment can also help with getting an idea of how the business feels. There might be a need for you to revert to make more observations about the process in use and also how the employees go about their work.

As you round off preparations to have the rest of the steps completed, ensure you keep the client abreast of all the things you will be doing and also let the users have an idea of what you are doing and also ask for input on what needs to be accomplished so as to ensure the users are really on the need of it.

## Step 2: Report design

Beginning with a report might seem rather odd, this is so because in most cases users are more interested in the printed output from a database than they are in any other part of the application. Most times, a report can have almost every part of data being managed by an application. Since reports are always comprehensive, they are said to be the best way to bring together information about the requirements of a database.

You might be puzzled about which should come first when you see the reports that will be created in this part. Will it be the report layout coming first or is there a need to determine the data items and text that make you the report first. Basically, these items are considered concurrently.

Note that it is also of great importance the method employed in laying out the fields in a report. The more time you spend doing this, the easier the construction of the report will be. Sometimes, people go as far as having gridlines placed on the report so that they can perfectly identify just where every bit of data should be.

## Step 3: Data design

The next step in the design phase is to get an inventory of all the needed information by the report. One of the best approaches to this is to have data items in each of the reports listed. When doing this, take careful note of various items that are added in more than a single report. Ensure the same name is kept for a data item that you have in more than one report since the data item is basically the same item.

| Customers Report | Invoice Report |
|---|---|
| Customer Name | Customer Name |
| Street | Street |
| City | City |

| State | State |
|---|---|
| Zipcode | Zipcode |
| Phone Numbers | Phone Numbers |
| Email Address | |
| Web Address | |
| Discount Rate | |
| Customer Since | |
| Last Sales Date | |
| Sales Tax Rate | |
| Credit Information (four fields) | |

Check the table below to have an idea of the Customer-Related Data Items that can be found in a report.

As shown above, when you compare the type of customer information that is needed for each of the reports, there are lots of common fields. Almost all the customer data fields can be found in both reports. The table above only shows some of the fields that are used in each of the reports- those that are related to customer information. Since the rows that are related including their field names are similar, with ease you can always ensure you have all the data at your disposal. Even though having to find items with ease is not important for this very small database, it will be very important when there is a need for you to deal with bigger tables that have various fields.

Upon the extraction of the data of customers, you can then proceed to the sales data. In cases such as this, there is a need for the analysis of only the Invoice report for data items that are pertinent to sales.

**Step 4: Table design**

This might look much like the most difficult aspect, here you have to decide the fields that are needed for the tables that will ultimately make up the reports. When you check the numerous fields and calculations that make up the documents you have at your disposal, you then start to see the fields that belong to the various tables in the database. As for this moment, add all of the fields you must have extracted. You should have others added much later also even though some fields won't be displayed in the table.

It's of utmost importance to know that there is no need for the addition of every bit of data into the table of the database. For instance, users might have a need to include bank holidays and other out-of-office days in the database in order to make it much easier to know the particular

| Customer Data | Invoice Data | Line Items | Payment Information |
|---|---|---|---|
| Customer Company Name | Invoice Number | Product Purchased | Payment Type |
| Street | Sales Date | Quantity Purchased | Payment Date |
| City | Invoice Date | Description of Item Purchased | Payment Amount |
| State | Discount( overall for this sale) | Price of Item | Credit Card Number |
| Zipcode | Tax Rate | Discount for Each Item | Expiration Date |
| Phone Numbers (two fields) | Taxable? | | |
| Email Address | | | |
| Web Address | | | |
| Discount | | | |

| | | | |
|---|---|---|---|
| Rate | | | |
| Customer Since | | | |
| Last Sales Date | | | |
| Sales Tax Rate | | | |
| Credit Information (four fields) | | | |

employees available for each day. Nevertheless, it can be very easy to complicate the initial design of an application by including too many ideas during the initial development phases. Since Access tables are very easy to alter later, the best approach might then be to set aside all of the items that are not so important until the completion of the initial design. In general, it is not so difficult to accept user requests after the database development project is underway.

When you must have made use of each report to show all of the data, it's high time you then began to consolidate the data by purpose and then look to make a comparison with the data that can be found across those functions also. In doing this, you need to first take a look at the customer information and then have it combined with all the varicus fields in order to design a single set of data items. Once that has been done, repeat the same for sales information and also the line-item information. The table helps with data comparison of data items from groups of information.

When goods and data are compared, it can be a very good way to begin to design individual tables but you still have a lot of tasks ahead of you.

As you continue to add more knowledge about how to make a data design, you also will learn that the customer data ought to be split into two distinct groups. Some of these items are used just once for each of the customers and the other items may be used more than just once. A clear example is the Sales column- the payment information can have various lines of information.

There is a need for you to further break all of these types of information into their own columns, hence differentiating all related types of items in their own columns, this can be said to be an example of the normalization part of the design process. For instance, a customer might have different contracts with the company or make lots of payments for just one sale. This way the data must have already been broken down into three categories which are; Customer data, invoice data, and line-item details.

Bear in mind that a customer might have various invoices and each of the invoices might have various line items on it. The invoice-data category has information about individual sales and the line-items category has information about each invoice. Take note that a relationship exists between these three columns, for instance, a customer can have various invoices and each invoice might have to contain various line items.

There can be a difference in the relationship with tables, for instance, a sales invoice has one and just one customer while each of the customers might have more than one sales. Many similar relationships can be found between the sales invoice and the line items of the invoice.

Database table relationships need a much distinct field in the tables that are involved in a relationship. A distinct identifier in each of the tables will help the database engine to have related data joined and extracted.

The sales table alone has a unique identifier which is the invoice number which means that there is a need for the inclusion of at least one field to each of the other tables so as to serve as the link to other tables. The database engines make use of the relationship that exists between customers and invoices to link customers and their invoices. The use of key fields helps with the facilitation of relationships between tables.

**Step 5: Form design**

When you must have created the data and made an establishment of the table relation, you can then begin to create your own forms. Forms are made up of fields that can either be entered or viewed in the Edit mode. Generally, Access screens ought to look a lot more like the forms that are used in a manual system.

**In the creation of forms, there is a need for you to place three different types of objects on the screen;**

- **Labels and text-box data-entry fields**:  The fields that are located on the Access forms and reports are known as controls.
- Special controls (command buttons, multiple-line text boxes, options buttons, list boxes, checkboxes, business graphs, and pictures).
- Graphical objects to enhance the forms( colors, lines, rectangles, and three-dimensional effects).

Generally, if the form is being created from a printed form that is already in existence, the Access-data entry form should also lock like the printed form itself. The fields ought to be in the same relative place on the screen as they are also in the printed counterpart.

Labels show messages, titles, or captions. Text boxes offer an area where you can input or display text or numbers that are present in your database. Checkboxes show a condition and are either unchecked or checked. Other types of controls that are available with Access have command buttons, list boxes, combo boxes, option buttons, toggle buttons, and other option groups.

# CHAPTER 2
# GETTING STARTED WITH ACCESS

This chapter will bring to your understanding all of the major components of the Microsoft Access user interface.

## The Access Welcome Screen

Upon the opening of Access 2022, you will see the default welcome screen. The welcome screen offers various options for opening an Access database that is already in existence or you might have to create a new database.

In the upper left corner of the welcome screen, the recent selection will be shown there. The files that are displayed here are databases that you have opened before with the use of Access 2022. Simply click on any of the database files to have them opened there. Note that Microsoft Access does not separate databases that exist from the database that has been deleted when the Recent section is populated. This simply means that you can see a database in the recent list that you are sure has been deleted. When you click on an already deleted database in the recent list, an error message will be activated which will state that Access cannot locate the database.

**Underneath the Recent section option, you will see a hyperlink named Open Other Files.**

- Click on **this link (hyperlink)** to search for and also open a database on your computer or your network.

At the very top of the welcome screen, you can search for Access database templates online. Basically, these templates are starter databases that have different purposes. Microsoft ensures that they are made available free of charge.

At the center of the welcome screen, various templates that have already been created will be displayed and you can simply click them to download and make use of them. Microsoft established the online templates repository as a medium to offer people the opportunity to download or completely built Access applications. The template databases cover various business requirements, like inventory control and management of sales. You can decide to take some time to check the online templates this way you know the exact one you need and then download it. Also at the center of the welcome screen, there will also be an option for Blank Database. With this option, you can design a totally new database.

## How to Create a Blank Database

When you start Access at first, or if you have a database closed without closing Access, the Microsoft Office Backstage view is shown.

The backstage view can be said to be a starting point from which you can choose to create a new database, have an already existing database opened, view content from office.com- anything you can make Access to do to a database file or outside of a database as opposed to being within a database.

When you open Access, the Backstage view shows the New tab option. **The new tab offers various ways that you can use to design a new database;**

- **A blank database**: if preferred, you can choose to start from scratch. This can be said to be a very good option if you have special design requirements or have data that are already existing that you might need to accommodate or incorporate.
- **A template that is installed with Access**: for this option, you can choose to begin a new project and you might also like a head start. Access comes with various templates that are installed by default.
- **A template from office.com**: alongside the various templates that come with Access, you can locate much more templates on office.com. This is so simple that you don't have to open a browser; the templates are made available on the New tab.

Microsoft Access comes with a number of templates that you can use as a starting point. Templates are ready-to-use databases that have all the tables, queries, forms, macros, and reports that you need to perform some very special tasks. For instance, there are certain templates that can be used to track issues, manage contacts or keep records of basic expenses. There are also some templates that have some sample records that help in the demonstration of how they can be used.

If any of these templates fits your needs, making use of them is actually the fastest way to start a database. Nevertheless, if you have data in another program that you would like to bring into Access, you might make the decision that it is better to design a database without having to make use of a template. Templates have a structure that has been defined already and it might also need a lot of work to adapt your already existing data to the structure of the template.

- If a database has already been opened, locate **the file tab** then click on the **close button**. The backstage view will then be displayed on the new tab.

- Various types of templates can be found in the new tab and some of them are already built into Access. You can choose to **download more templates** from office.com.

- Choose the **preferred template** you will like to use.

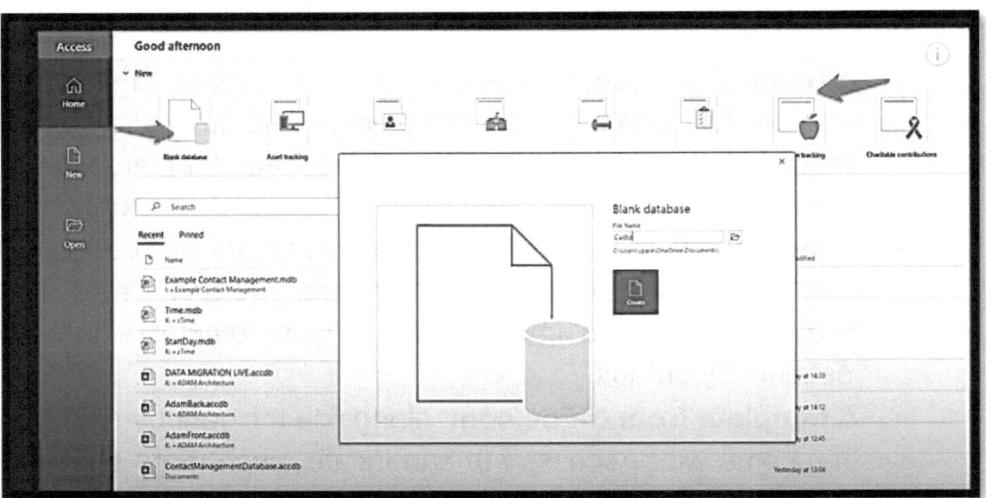

- Next, Access will suggest a file name for your database in the File Name box you can also change the file name if you choose to. To have the database in various folders saved from the one that is being shown underneath the name of the file name box, browse to the folder you would like to save it then click on the **OK option**.

Additionally, you can choose to create your own database and link it to a SharePoint site.
- Click on the **Create option**. Access creates a database from the template you have chosen and then opens the database. For almost all templates, a form will be displayed that will enable you to begin to insert data. If your template has various sample data, you can choose to delete each record by clicking on the record selector and then do any of the following;
  - On the Home tab, in the Record group option, click on the **Delete button**.
- When you want to start to design data, select the **first empty cell** on the form and start **to type**. Make use of the navigation pane to browse for other forms or reports that you might have a need to use. There are some templates that have a navigation form that enables you to navigate between the different databases that exist.

If you are not interested in making use of a template you can choose to create your own database by simply building your own tables, forms, reports, and some other database objects.

**In most cases, this might involve either one or both of the following;**

- Inserting, pasting, or bringing in data into the table when you design a new database, and then repeating the process with new tables that you must have created by making use of Table command on the Create tab.
- Importing data from some other sources and also creating new tables in the same process.

**To create a blank database;**

- Locate the **file tab**, click on the **new button** then click on **Blank Database**.

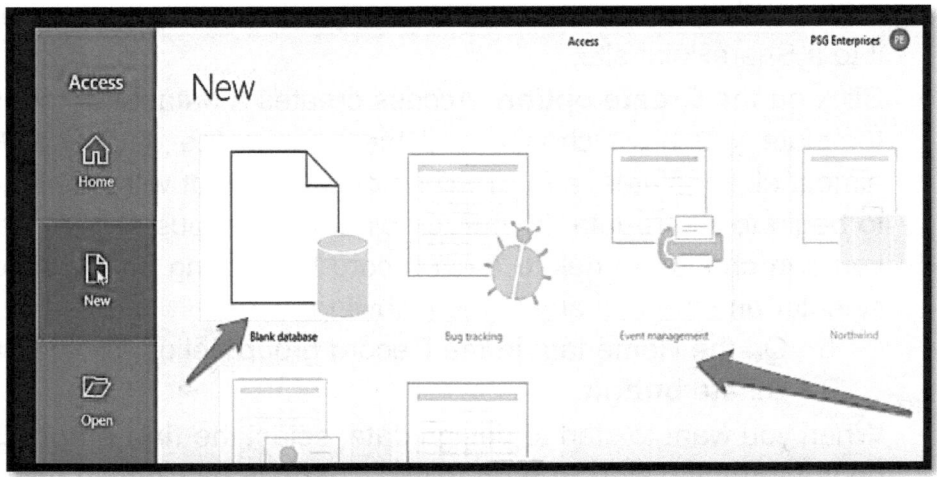

- Insert a name in the File Name box. If you would like to change the location of the file from the default, choose to **Browse** so as to get a location to put the database, browse to the location then click on the **OK button**.

- Click on the **Create option**.

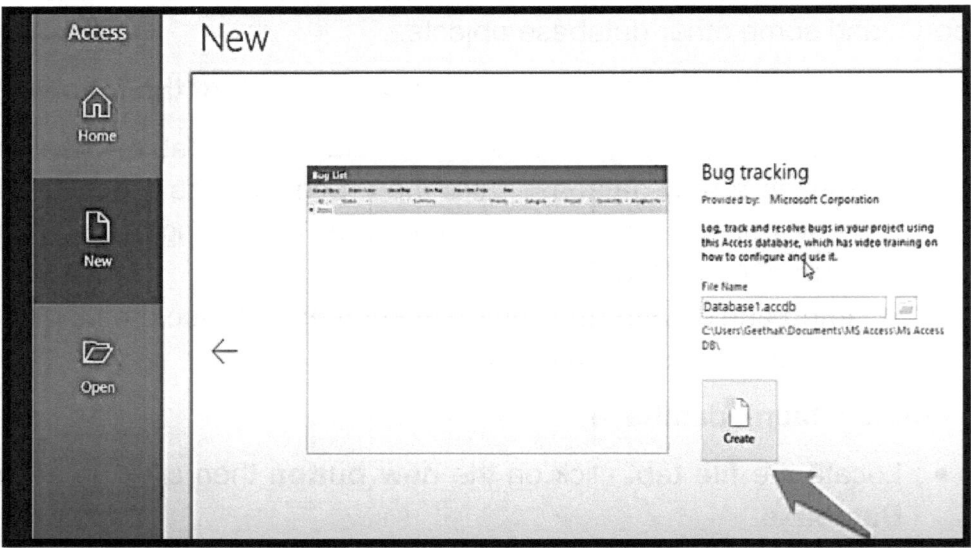

Access designs the database with an empty table which is named Table1 and then opens Table1 in the Datasheet view. The cursor is placed in the empty cell in the click to **Add column**.

- You can then begin to include data or you can choose to have the data pasted from another source.

Inserting data in a Datasheet view is created to be very close to working in an Excel worksheet. The table structure is then created while you enter data. Upon adding a new column to the datasheet, a new field is then defined in the table. Access will then automatically set each field's data type based on the data you must have inserted.

**If you don't have a need to insert data in Table1;**

- Simply click on the **close button**. If you have made changes to the table, Access will then prompt you to **save the changes**.
- Click on the **yes button** to save the changes, click on the **no button** if you want to discard them, or click on the **cancel button** to leave the table open.

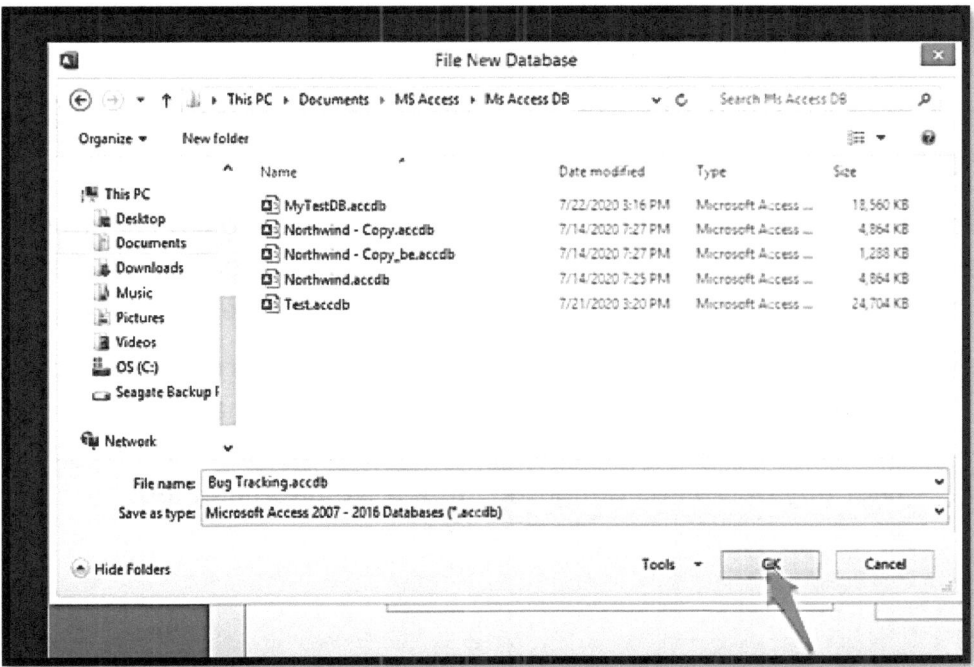

## The Access 2022 Interface

After you must have created or opened a new database, the Access screen will then be opened fully. At the top of the screen is the Access Ribbon. On the left, you will find the navigation pane. These two components are key and make up the bulk of the Access interface. Also, you can make use of the Quick Access toolbar, which you can customize with the commands you use most of the time.

## The Navigation pane

The navigation pane is the main method of viewing and accessing all your database objects and it displays on the left side of the Access window by default. The navigation pane located on the left side of the screen shows tables, queries, forms, reports, and other Access object types. You can also use it to show a combination of various types of objects.

**The navigation options are divided into two categories:**

- Navigate **To Category and Filter By Group**.
- To begin with, you have to choose **an option under Navigate To Category,** and then you can choose **an option under Filter By Group.** The Filter By Group options you are presented with are dependent on the Navigate To Category option you have selected.

## Custom

The Custom option designs a new grouping in the navigation pane. It has objects that can be moved and placed in the tab area. Items that are added to a custom group still show in their various object-type views.

- When you choose **custom**, **the Filter By Group category** is populated with all of the customer groups that have been created before. You can make use of the **Filter By Group category** to filter any of the custom groups that have been created.

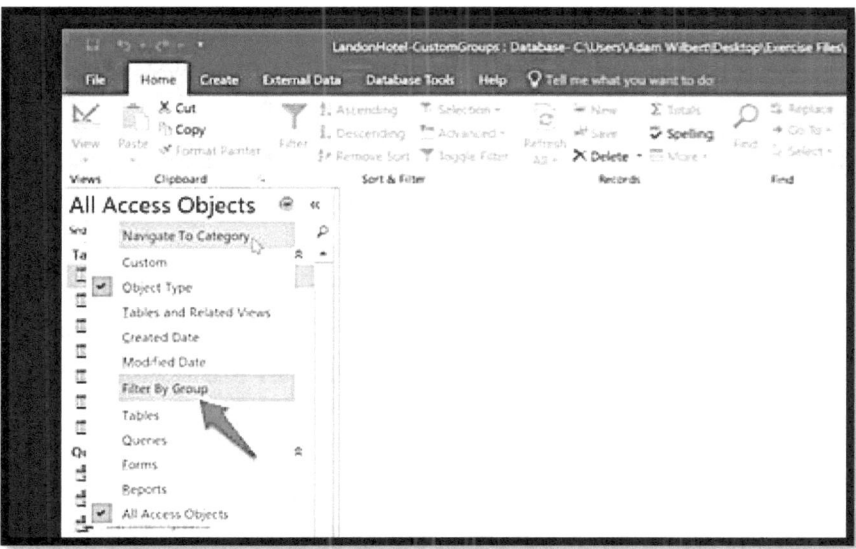

## Object Type

The Object Type option is very similar to the previous versions of Access. **When you choose the Object Type, the following options are under Filter By Group:**

- Tables
- Queries
- Forms
- Reports
- All Access Objects

By default, the navigation pane displays all of the objects in the database in use.

- Choose **All Access Objects** when you must have been working with anyone of the filtered views and wish to see all of the objects in the database.

## Tables and Related Views

A bit of explanation is needed to be done here. Access ensures it keeps the developer informed of the hidden connections that can be found between objects that can be found in the database. For instance, a specific table can be used in a number of queries or referenced from either a report or a form. Selecting Tables and Related Views enables you to know the objects that must have been affected by each of the tables.

- When you choose **Tables and Related Views**, the **Filter By Group category** will then be populated by the Tables in your database.
- Choosing each object that is in the **Filter By Group category** will also filter the list to that specific object and all of the other dependent and precedent objects that are related to it.

## Created Date

The created date option helps with the grouping of database objects by the date in which it was created. This setting is quite useful when you need to know just when an object was created.

- When you choose the **Created Date option**, some or all of the options below will be made available under the Filter By Group:
- Today
- Yesterday
- Last Week
- Two Weeks Ago
- Older

## Modified Date

This option helps in grouping objects based on the date they were modified. This is a little more like the created date option. And just like it, **when you choose this option also some or all of the options below will be made available under the Filter By Group:**

- Today
- Yesterday
- Last Week
- Two Weeks Ago
- Older

## The Ribbon

The Ribbon can be described as the main replacement for the menus and the toolbars and also offers the main command interface in Access. One of the main advantages of the ribbon is that it is said to consolidate, in a single place, all the various tasks or points of entry that formerly do require menus, toolbars, task panes, and some other UI components to display. With this, you have just one place where you can search for commands rather than you searching through different places.

When a database is opened, the ribbon will be displayed at the very top of the main Access window, where it shows the commands in the active command tab. The ribbon has a lot of command tabs that have commands embedded in them.

In Access, the main command tabs are File, Home, Create, External Data, and Database Tools. Each of these command tabs has groups of commands that are quite related and these groups show some of the newly added users' interfaces like the gallery which is simply a new type of control that displays choices visually.

- **File**: Upon clicking on **the File tab**, the **Office Backstage view** will be opened. The backstage view has a number of different options for the creation of **databases, opening databases, saving, and Configuring databases**.

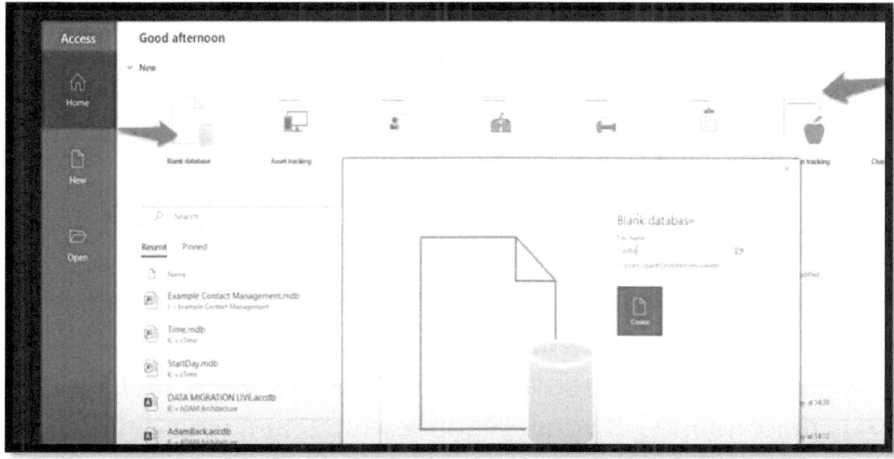

- **Home**: The theme of the Home tab is used often. This is where you get to find all unrelated commands that are used often when you are working with Access. For instance, there are certain commands for formatting, copying and pasting, sorting, and filtering.

- **Create**: This tab has commands that design the different types of objects in Access. This tab is actually where most of the work is done and you are sure to spend a lot of time there. Here you can start the creation **of tables, forms, queries, reports, and macros**.

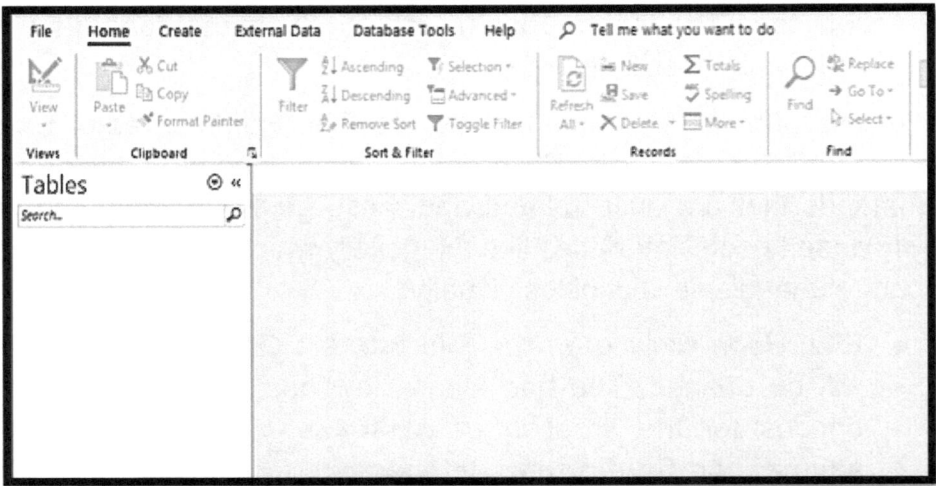

- **External Data**: This tab is specially dedicated to the integration of Access with some other sources of data. On this tab, you can locate commands that enable you to have data imported and exported and also have connections established to databases that are outside and also work with SharePoint or some other platforms.

- **Database Tools**: This tab has commands that specifically deal with the inner dealings of your database. Here you can find tools to help create some relationships between tables, analyze the performance of your database, document your database, and also compact and repair your database.

- **Help**: There is a help tab in Access 2022 that doesn't have a database functionality though it helps with the provision of various links which supports training.

## The Quick Access toolbar

The Quick Access Toolbar is a toolbar that is just adjacent to the ribbon and allows for one-click access to various commands. The default set of commands are saved, undo, and redo and you can also choose to customize the Quick Access Toolbar such that it will include some other commands that are often used. There is also an opportunity to alter the placement of the toolbar and have it changed from the default small size to a much larger size. The small toolbar will be displayed next to the command tabs on the ribbon. When there is a need to change to the larger size, the toolbar will then be displayed below the ribbon with its full width extended.

- When you click on the **drop-down arrow** close to the Quick Access toolbar, you will discover that there are more commands available. If you would like to add any of these commands to the Quick Access toolbar simply **fix a checkmark** close to it.

Note that you are not limited to the commands that are being displayed in the drop-down list. You can choose to add any kind of command you like.

**Follow the steps below to add a command to the Quick Access toolbar;**

- Choose **the drop-down arrow** that is close to the Quick Access toolbar and then choose the More Commands option. This will then display the dialog box of the Quick Access toolbar.
- In the Choose Commands From the drop-down list on the left side, choose **All Commands**.

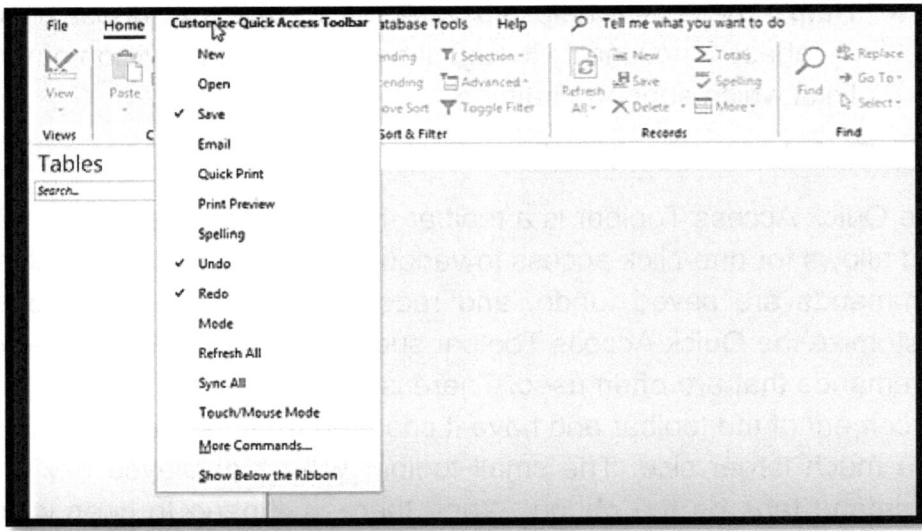

- From the alphabetical list of commands, choose **the one** you have the most interest in and then select **the Add button**.
- When you are done, select **the OK button**.

The above chapter fully describes the Access welcome screen in full, describes the navigation pane, tables, and other related views, and also the Quick Access toolbar. By now I would expect that you know how to design a database, work with the Table Design and also insert and delete rows.

# PART II
# UNDERSTANDING ACCESS TABLES

The chapters in this aspect throw more light on the various techniques that can be used to create and also manage Access database tables, the main part of any application that is being built in Access.

These chapters are way beyond merely describing how tables can be built. You will learn the basic concepts that are very important in the use of capabilities that have been documented in the other parts of this book.

# CHAPTER 3
# CREATING ACCESS TABLES

This chapter is all about the creation of tables and all that has to do with tables basically. Here you get to establish the database containers in order to get hold of tables, forms, queries, reports, and also code that you build even as you learn more about Access.

## Table Types

With Microsoft Access, a table is just the same as a table that contains data but when it comes to Access applications, various tables serve different purposes. There are about three types of tables that a database table can fit into; an object table, a transaction table, or a join table. When you know the exact type of table you create will also help you to know just how it should be created.

## Object tables

This is the most common type of table. Each record of this type of table contains information that deals with a real-world object. A customer is said to be a real-world object and also a record in a table is usually known as tblCustomers and it holds information about that particular customer. The fields that are in an object table show the characteristics of the object they also represent.

A City field talks more about one characteristic of the customer which is known as the specific city where the customer can be found. When an object is being created, it is ideal to think about the characteristics of that particular object that ensure it is unique or that is also very important.

## Transaction tables

After the object table the next very common table is the transaction table. Each record of a transaction table contains information about a particular event. When you place an order for a pen, that can be said to be an example of an event. If you would like to have the details of all of the orders, there might be a need for you to name a **table tbl PenOrders.**

Most of the time, transaction tables have a Date/Time field due to the fact that the specific time the event takes place in a very important piece of information to take note of. One other very common type of field is a field that refers to an object table like a reference to the customer in tblCustomers that placed the order. When you are about to create a transaction table, ensure you think about the information that has been created by the event and also those that were involved.

## Join tables

Join tables are pretty much easy to design and are of extreme importance to a well-designed database. Oftentimes, relating two tables is a very simple process but there are times when the relationship becomes unclear. Using a book as an example, if a customer orders a book, it can have many authors, and also an author can have more than one book too.

When this kind of relationship occurs, it is known as a many-to-many relationship, a join table will be in the middle of both tables. A join table most times has a name that shows the association like a tblAuthorBook. A join table basically has just three fields: a reference to one side of the association, a unique field to identify each record, and a reference to the other side of the association.

# Creating a New Table

Creating a new database table is so much fun and can be much science-based as it requires one or two things about art also. Before creating a database, there is a need for you to have prior knowledge of the requirements of the user, this will ensure you build a table that meets the needs of the user directly.

It's always a very good idea for you to begin with planning tables before making use of Access tools to add tables to the database. A lot of tables, most especially those that are quite small, do not actually need a whole lot of planning before you include them in the database

For instance, you don't need to plan so much if all you want to do is design a table that contains information like the names of states and countries. Nevertheless, there are actually more complex entities that will require more planning to be done. They require lots of time and a considerable amount of energy to be put into it.

Note that if you don't carefully plan before designing a table, this doesn't mean all had gone wrong as you can always make adjustments to the table you must have created much later but this will be wasting a whole lot of time which could have been avoided with adequate planning.

## Designing tables

There are lots of steps involved in designing tables.

**When you follow the steps in the order below, your table design can be created with so much ease requiring little or no effort:**

- Create **the new table**.
- Insert **the field names, data types, properties, and descriptions**.

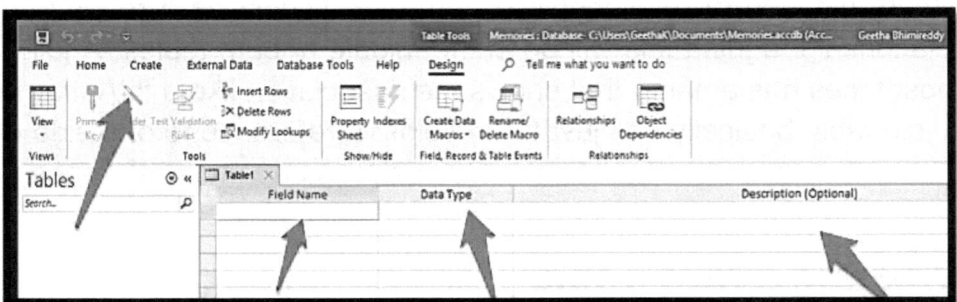

- Fix the **table's primary key**.

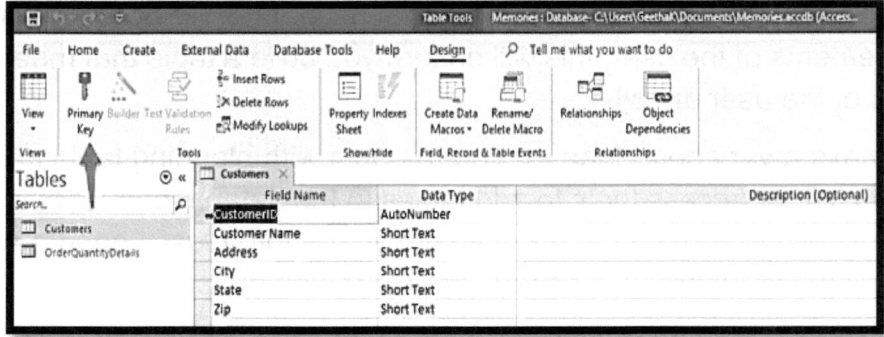

- Create **various indexes for appropriate fields**.
- Finally, ensure you **save the table's design**.

Most of the time, you can never really finish building a table as it were, this is because the scope of the business might change or the needs of the user increase hence there will be a need for the modification of the table which is usually done in the design view. Basically, most of the things done in the database on an application are done by the objects that are already existing in the database. Either object you added yourself or objects that were added by another developer at a point in time. Through it all, maintaining a database component that has already been created is almost the same as building that same component all over again.

**There are basically two different ways tables can be added to the Access database and both methods are through the Tables group on the Create tab;**

- **Clicking the Table button**: When you use this method, a new table will be added to the Datasheet view to the database that has just one Auto number field named ID.

    Here, you will notice an option named Click **to Add column**, this option is intended to allow users to quickly include fields to a table. All that is left of you to do is to just insert data in the new column. **This is done by;**

    - Right-clicking **the heading of the field.**
    - Clicking **on rename field.**
    - Insert **a name for the field.**

    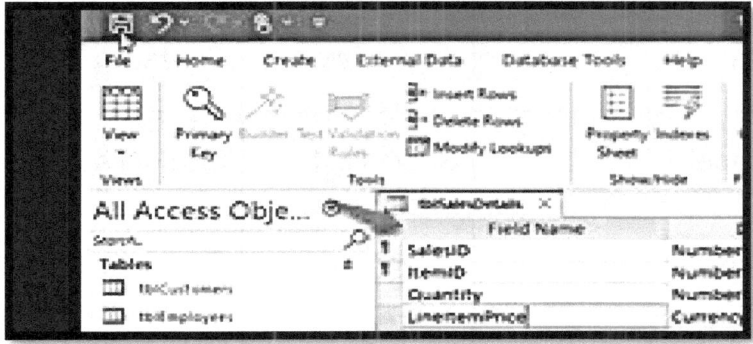

    Once you have added the new column, the tools that are on the Fields tab if the Ribbon enabled you to fix the very type of data for the field alongside its formatting, validation rules, and some other properties.

- **Clicking the Table Design button**: this method adds a table in the Design view to the database. The table designer is much easier to come to terms with and all of the columns are well labeled. To the very far left is the Field Name column where names of fields are added to the table. The data type is added to each of the fields on the table and also there is always a provision for a description field.

**Study the basic design of the table below;**

| Field Name | Data Type | Description |
|---|---|---|
| CustomerID | AutoNumber | Primary key |
| Company | Short Text | Contact's; employer or some other affiliations. |
| Address | Short Text | Contact's address |
| City | Short Text | Contact's city |
| State | Short Text | Contact's state |
| zipcode | Short Text | Contact's zip code |
| Phone | Short Text | Contact's phone |
| Fax | Short Text | Contact's fax |

| Email | Short Text | Contact's email address |
|---|---|---|
| Website | Short Text | Contact's web address |
| OrigCustomerDate | DateTime | Date the contact first bought something from SimAde Limited |
| CreditLimit | Currency | Customer's credit limit in Euro |
| CreditBalance | Currency | Customer's current balance in Euro |
| Credit Status | Short Text | General description of the customer's credit status |
| LastSalesDate | DateTime | Most recent or the last date the customer bought something from SimAde Limited |
| TaxRate | Number (Double) | Sales tax that is applicable to the customer. |
| DiscountPercent | Number | Customary discount |

|  | (Double) | provided to the customer |
|---|---|---|
| Notes | Long Text | Notes and observations as it pertains to this customer |
| Active | Yes/No | If the customer will still be buying things from SimAde Limited |

Note that the above fields containing ShortText are using the default 255 character Field Size. Though it is not very likely that a person's name will take up 255 characters, it costs nothing to make provision for names that are quite long.

**Let me quickly add that the Table Design window consists of two major areas;**

- **The field entry area**: This option is always located at the top of the window and is used to insert the name of the field and also the type of data. You can also choose to **add an optional description**.
- **The field properties area**: This is usually at the bottom of the window and it is the place where the properties of the field are specified. Some of these properties include; the size of the field, format, input mask, and default value amongst other things. The main properties that are shown in the properties area are based on the data type field.

## Using the Design tab

The design tab of Access has a lot of controls that help with the creation of a new table definition. The controls on the Design tab affect the important table design considerations.

## Primary Key

Whenever you create a Microsoft Access table, Access will automatically create a primary key to the database table, but you can also indicate the specific field you want as the primary key for your database table.

The primary key in Access is a field or perhaps a set of fields that have distinct values all through the tables. The primary key provides lots of characteristics like unique identification if each row in the database contains a value, this value never changes and the row is also never empty.

Traditionally you will always find the primary key at the top of the list of fields in the table although it can be found anywhere right within the table's design.

## Insert Rows

When you click on this option, a blank row will be inserted above the position that the mouse cursor is occupying.

- For instance, if the cursor is at the second row of the Table Designer when you **click on the Insert Rows button** an empty row will be inserted in the second position which will move the second row to the third position.

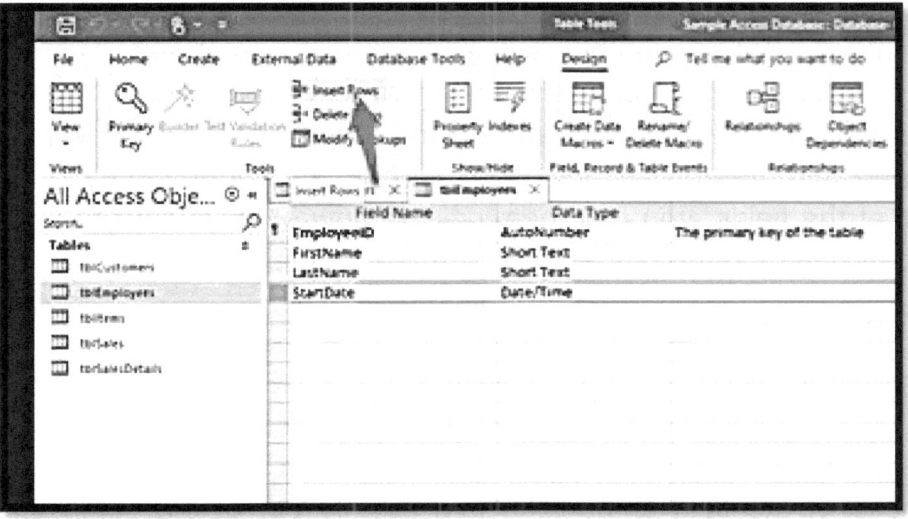

## Delete Rows

When you click on this option it takes off a row from the table's design.

- Note that **clicking on this row** activates the deletion immediately; there is no prompt to confirm the deletion before the row is removed.

## Property Sheet

This button when clicked opens up the Property Sheet for the whole table. Some of these properties allow the specification of very important table characteristics like validation rules to be applied to the whole of the table or provision of alternate sort order for the table's data.

## Indexes

Index helps Access to locate and sort records at a much faster pace. An index stores the location of records based on the field or fields as the case may be, that you have chosen to index. After Access must have obtained the location from the index, it can then have the data retrieved by simply moving it to the correct location.

# Working with fields

Fields are created simply by inserting a field name and a field data type in the upper part of the field entry area of the Table Design window. The Description property can be used as an indication of the field's purpose. The description shows up in the status bar at the lower part of the screen when data is being inserted and it can be very useful to those that are working with the application. Upon inserting the name and data type of each of the fields, you can then indicate how each of the fields will be used by inserting the properties in the field properties area.

## Naming a field

Whatever name you decide to give to a field, ensure that it is a name that describes the field well enough to the user of the system, to Access, and also to you as a developer. They should be long enough in order for the purpose of the field to be identified quickly but at the same time, it shouldn't be too long.

**If you want to insert a name for a field, place the pointer in the first row of the Table Design window beneath the Field Name column then insert a valid name ensuring that the rules below are observed;**

- Field names can include spaces. The spaces should be avoided in field names for the exact same reasons they are avoided in table names.
- You cannot make use of low-order ASCII characters, for instance, Ctrl+J or Ctrl+L.
- You cannot start with a blank space.
- Field names can be from 1 to 64 characters in length.
- Field names can include letters, numbers, and special characters with the exception of period (.), exclamation point (!), accent grave('), and brackets ([]).

Field names can be inserted in the uppercase, lowercase, or mixed case. If for any reason a mistake is made when you are typing the field name, place the cursor just where you need correction to be made and insert the change. You can also change the name of a field at any point in time, even if the table has data in it.

Note that Access is not case sensitive, as such the database itself doesn't mind if you name a table tblCustomers or TblCustomers. If you decide to choose uppercase, lowercase, or mixed case characters it is entirely up to you but not any choice you make should be aimed at making the names of the table descriptive and also easy to read.

Also, when you must have saved a table if for any reason you make changes to the field name used in queries, forms, or reports you must also change it in the objects too. One of the main causes of errors in Access applications has to do with a change of names of basic database objects like tables, and fields and not affecting those changes all through the database.

## Specifying a data type

It isn't just enough to insert a field, you must also indicate the type of data that will be found in each of the fields. In Access, you can decide to make any choice out of the several data types.

**The data types that are available are shown below;**

| Data Type | Type of Data Stored | Storage Size |
|---|---|---|
| Short Text | Alphanumeric characters | 255 characters or lesser |
| Long Text | Alphanumeric characters | 1GB of characters or lesser |
| Number | Numeric values | 1,2,4, or 8 bytes; 16 bytes for Replication ID (GUID) |
| Large Number | Numeric values | 8 bytes |
| Date/Time | Date and time data | 8 bytes |
| Currency | Monetary data | 8 bytes |
| Auto Number | Automatic number increments | 4 bytes; 16 bytes for Replication ID (GUID) |
| Yes/No | Logical values: Yes/No, True/False | 1 bit (0 or -1) |
| OLE Object | Pictures, graphs, sound, video | Up to 1GB (disk space limitation) |

| Hyperlink | link to an Internet resource | 1GB of characters or much less |
|---|---|---|
| Attachment | A special field that allows you to attach external files to an Access database. | Varies by attachment |
| Calculated | A field that saves a calculation based on all the other fields that are in the table | Determined by setting the Result Type property |
| Lookup Wizard | Shows data from another table | Generally 4 bytes |

**There are certain questions you need to have answers to before you make your choice of data type for the new fields in your tables;**

- **What is the data type?** Ensure the data type shows the data that is stored in the field. For example, choose one of the numeric data types to save numbers like quantities and prices. Ensure you don't save data such as phone numbers or social security numbers in numeric fields, however; your applications will not be able to perform numeric operations like addition or multiplication on phone numbers. Rather, it will make use of fields for common data like Social Security numbers and phone numbers.

- **What are the possible storage requirements of the data type you have chosen?** Though you can make use of the Numeric data type with a field size or a long integer in the place of an integer or byte, the storage requirements of s long integer(4 bytes) are actually two times that of the Integer itself. What this means is that two times as much memory is needed to use and also have the number manipulated, and also two times as much disk space is needed to have its value stored. Ensure you make use of the smallest data type/field size you can that will eventually still contain the largest value you will ever have in that field.

- **Will there be a need for you to sort or have the field indexed?** Since they have a binary nature, Long Text and OLE object fields cannot be sorted nor can they be indexed. Make use of Long Text sparingly. The overhead needed to save and work with Long Text fields is quite considerable.

- **What is the impact of the data type on sorting requirements?** Numeric data actually sorts in a much different manner from text data. With the use of numeric data type, a sequence of numbers will sort as expected: 1,2,3,4,5,10,100. The very same sequence saved às text data will be sorted as 1,10,100,2,3,4,5. If it is necessary to sort text data in a numeric sequence, there will be a need for you to apply a conversion function to the data first before you can begin sorting.

- **Is the data text or date?** Whenever you are working with dates, it is almost always better for you to have the data stored in a Date/Time field than as a Short Text field. Text Values sort quite differently from dates which have the ability to cause upsets to reports and other output that depend on a chronological order. Resist the urge to save dates in one Date/Time field and time in a separate Date/Time field. The Date/Time field is designed specifically to deal with both dates and times, and also it is very much easy to show just the date or time portion of a Date/Time value. A Date/Time field is also expected to save discrete date and time, and not a time interval. If it is very important for you to keep track of durations you can make use of two Date/Time fields- one to record the start time and the other to record the end or probably a Long Integer field to save the number of elapsed seconds, minutes, hours, and so on.

- **What reports will be needed?** You will be unable to sort or group Long Text OLE data on a report. If it is important to prepare a report based on Long Text or OLE data, simply include a Tag field such as a date or sequence number which can be used to offer a sorting key to the table.

## Entering a field description

Inserting a description for a field is not compulsory, it is used only to help you remember what the field is about or to let another developer know what the field is about. Most times, the description column is not used at all, or you make use of it for fields that do not have a very obvious purpose.

If you insert a field description, it will be displayed on the status bar anytime you make use of that field in Access within the datasheet or form. Field description helps to state specifically a field that has an ambiguous purpose or offer the user a more complete explanation of the appropriate values for the field when the data is being entered.

## Specifying data validation rules

Data can be vetted or validated in Access desktop databases immediately after it is being inserted with the use of validation rules. The expression builder can be used to help you format the rule rather quickly and without any form of delay. You can choose to set validation rules in either table design or table datasheet View.

**There are basically three types of validation rules in access;**

- **Field Validation Rule**: Field validation rule can be used and the specification of a criterion that all field values must meet is not compulsory for you to indicate the current field as part of the rules. you should only do that if you're using the field in a function. With the use of an input mask, it is much easier to insert restrictions on any type of character in a field. For example, you can have a date field that has a validation rule that disallows values and the past.

- **Record Validation Rule:** You can use a record validation rule to indicate a condition that all records must ensure they satisfy. You can compare values across different fields with the use of a record validation rule. For example, if you have a record with two date fields there might be a need for the value of a field to always go before the value of the other field.

- **Validation on a form:** You can make use of the Validation Rule property of a control on a form in order to indicate a particular criterion that all values need to add to that control. The validation rule control property works similarly to a field validation rule. Typically you use a validation form rule rather than a field validation rule if only the rule was indicated only to that form and not to the table no matter where it has been used.

The last major design is of major concern to data validation which of course becomes very necessary as users insert data. You will definitely need to ensure that only data that is good finds its way into your system. There is a need to deal with various types of data validation. you can test for individual items that you know, and ensure you stipulate the gender field which of course can only accept the male and female values or unknown.

## Creating tbl Customers

When working with different types of data, you should be prepared to create the final working copy of tbl customers.

### Using AutoNumber fields

Access ensures that it provides important considerations to Autonumber Fields. You will not be able to alter a field that has been defined before from another type to AutoNumber if any data has been included in the table. If you attempt to alter a field that is already in existence to an AutoNumber, there will be an error prompt saying;

> Once you enter data in a table, you can't change

There will be a need for you to include a new AutoNumber field and then you can begin working with it rather than changing a field that is already existing AutoNumber.

### Completing tbl customers

When viewing tbl customers' design view, you are then ready to finalize all that have to do with its design. All you have to do is insert the field names and data into the table. On the next page, I'll be explaining how to alter fields that are already existing which also includes organizing the field order, altering a field name, and also deleting a field.

**Below are the steps for adding a field to a table structure;**

- Place **the cursor** in the field name column in the room where you want the field to appear.
- Insert **the field name** and press **enter** or you can also choose to press the **tab button** in order to move the data type column.
- Choose **the field data** type from the list that drops down in the data type column.
- If you need to, you can add a **description** for the field in the description column.

Go through each of the steps again to design each of the data entry fields for tbl customers. You can choose to press down the arrow key in order to move between rows and you can also make use of the mouse and click on any of the desired rows. For a shorter method, you can choose to tap the F6 button so as to switch the focus from the top to the bottom of the table design window.

## Changing a Table Design

No matter how well you must have designed your table, every table will require a change from time to time. You might discover that you have a need to include another field, remove an existing one, change the name of a field or the data type, or simply have to reorganize the order of the names of the field.

Although the design of a table can be changed at any point in time you must act every time and also ensure that you give special consideration to the table that has data in them. ensure that you are very careful with the changes you make so as to avoid damaging the data in the table like making text Fields smaller or having to change the field size property of number fields.

Whenever you wish, you can always include a new field to a table without having any issues but you might experience a little bit of difficulty if you attempt to change Fields that are already existing. it is actually not advanced to change the name of the field after you must have used the table in an application however there are exceptions to this.

## Inserting a new field

At one point or the other you might have a need to insert a new field. **Follow the steps below to have a new field inserted.**

- Locate **the table design window**.
- Put **your cursor** on a field that is already existing.
- Right-click **on a field** in the table designs surface.
- Choose to **insert rows** or you can also choose to click **the insert rows button** on the Design tab on the ribbon.
- Once this has been done a new row will be added to the table after which you can then insert a new field definition.

When you insert a field, this does not in any way disturb other fields or data contained in Other fields that are already existing. If you have queries, forms, or reports that you're making use of in the table there might be a need for you to add the field to those objects as well.

## Deleting a field

You can make a mistake when you are creating a table. No one is perfect. **There are basically three ways to delete a field.**

- Choose **the field by selecting the role selector** and then press the select button.

- Right-click **on the field** you have chosen and click on **delete rows** from the shortcut menu.

- Choose **the field** and click on the **delete rows** button from the tools group on the Design tab on the ribbon.

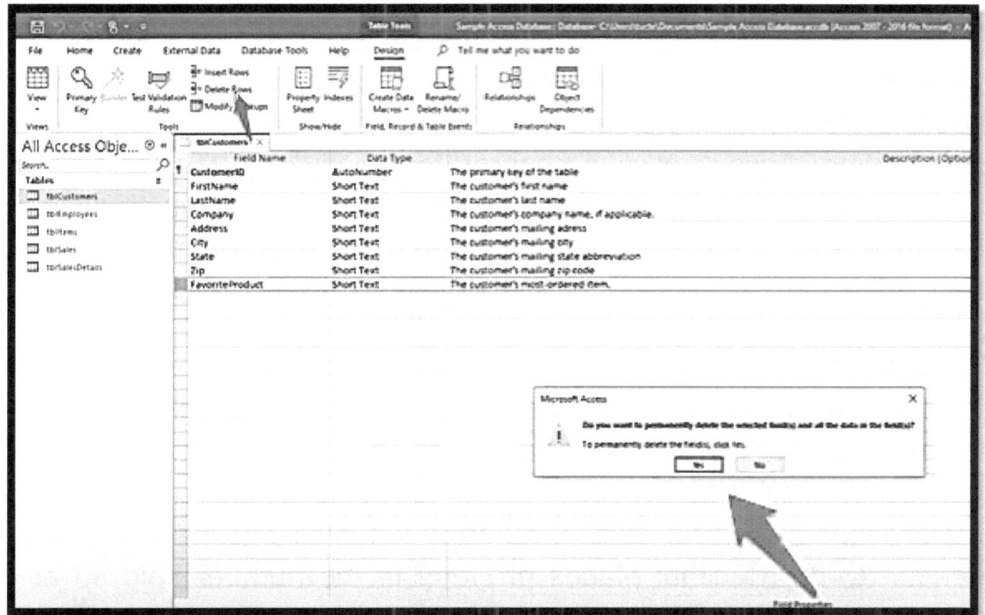

Anytime you delete a field that contains data you will always see a warning sign that you will lose data in the table for the chosen field. If the data contains tables ensure that you really want to delete the data for that field. note that you will also have to delete the same field from, queries, forms, reports, macros, and VBA code that use the name of the field.

If for any reason a field is deleted you must also fix all references to that field all through access. since you can make use of a field name in forms, queries, reports, and even table data validation hence you must examine your system very well to locate any instances in which there might be a need for you to make use of the specific field name.

## Changing a field location

A field is not expected to be static, the order of your field as you must have inserted them in the table's design determines the left to right column sequence in the tables datasheet view. if for any reason you choose that your field should be reorganized,

- Click on **the field selector** and with the use of the mouse move the field to your preferred location.

## Changing a field name

If you so wish you can also make changes to the name of the field by choosing the name of the field in the table design window and inserting a new name. Access always ensures that it updates the table design automatically. As long as you are designing a new table this process can be quite easy. but if you are changing the name of a field that is already existing this can cause slight problems as earlier discussed.

## Changing a field size

Have you made a mistake while designing the size of a flute making a few times larger is quite simple in a design table. All you need to do is increase the field size property for the text field or indicate an entirely different field size for a certain number of Fields ensure that you pay attention to the decimal places property in the number field so as to ensure that you do not choose a new size that supports fewer decimal places than you already have.

Whenever there is a need to make a field size smaller ensure that none of the data in the table is larger than the new field width. When you choose a smaller field size you might lose data in the process.

## Handling data conversion issues

After all the effort you must have put in, if it becomes necessary for you to change the data type of a field that contains data then you might have to suffer the loss of data as the data type conversion takes place.

**You should also be aware of the effects of a data type conversion on data that is existing;**

- **Any data type to AutoNumber**: cannot be done. The Auto Number field type must be created from scratch in a new field.
- **Short Text to Number, Currency, Date/Time, or Yes/No**: Most times, the conversion might take place without any damage to the data. Values inserted that happen to be inappropriate will be deleted automatically.
- **Long Text to Short Text**: A straightforward conversion that doesn't involve corruption of data. Any text that is much longer

than its field size indicated for the Short Text field will be lost and truncated.
- **Number or Large Number to Short Text**: There will be no loss of information. the number value will be converted to text with the use of the general number format.
- **Number or Large Number to Currency**: Since the currency data type makes use of a fixed decimal point some precision might be lost even as the number is truncated.
- **Date/Time to Short Text**: There will be no loss of information. The date and time will also be converted to text with the general date format.
- **Currency to Short Text**: There will also be no lots of information. as a currency value will be converted to text without the use of the currency symbol.
- **Currency to Number**: this is a simple and straightforward conversion. However, some data might be lost as the currency value is converted to feet into the new number field. For example, when you are converting currency to a Long integer the decimal portion will be cut off.
- **AutoNumber to Short Text**: Here, the conversion takes place without loss of data except in cases where the rest of the text field is not able to hold the entire Auto number value. In this case, the number will then be truncated.
- **AutoNumber to Number**: This is also simple and straightforward although some data might also be lost as the Autonumber value is changed to fit the new number field. For example, if the auto number is larger than 32,767 it will be truncated when it is changed to an integer field.
- **Yes/No to Short Text**: Simple conversion of Yes/No value to the text. No loss of data.

## Assigning field properties

All tables in access are made up of Fields. The properties of a field describe the features and behavior of data that will be added to that field. A field's data type is the most important property since it also helps with the determination of the kind of data the field can store.

The field properties that are built into the Access table are very powerful tools that can help you manage the data in your tables. Most times, the field property is informed by the database engine Which in turn means that the property is constantly being applied anywhere the value of the field is used period for example if you have set the default value property in the design table the default value will be available in the tables datasheet view but on forms and in queries.

As a matter of fact, field properties are also among the various differences that exist between access tables and Excel worksheets. Having a proper understanding of field properties is just one of the numerous skills that are needed to start using an access table to store data as opposed to using an Excel worksheet.

All of the field data types have their own set of properties. For example, Number fields have a decimal place property and Short Text fields have a Text Align property. Although many data types share a number of properties there are quite a lot of different field properties to make it easy to become confused or to use the properties incorrectly.

## Common properties

**Below is a list of all the general properties that you might need and it is based on the data type you must have chosen.**

- **Field Size**: This option when applied to Short Text fields, limits the size of the field to the indicated number of characters. Always note that the default number is 255.
- **New Values**: This option applies to the auto number field. It also allows for the specification of random type or increment.
- **Format**: this option helps to change the way the data shows after you must have inserted it in regards to the uppercase, date, and so on. There are various types of formats that can be used to access data. Lots of these differences will be explained much later.
- **Input Mask**: This option is used for the entry of data into a format that has already been predefined such as phone numbers, zip codes, social security numbers, and dates. This option is applicable to both numeric and text data types.

- **Caption**: this is an optional label that is used instead of the name of the field. Microsoft Access makes use of caption property when it has to display control in a datasheet or on a form or on a report.
- **Decimal Places**: This option also helps with the specification of the number of decimal places for the currency number and large number data types.
- **Default Value**: This is the value automatically offered for new data entry into the field. This value can be just any value as long as it is appropriate for the field data type. A default value is no more than an initial value; you can have it changed when you are inserting data. if you want to indicate a value all you have to do is include the value you desire into the default value property setting. Always note that a default value can either be an expression in a number or a text string.
- **Validation Rule**: This option helps in ensuring that the data inserted into the field conforms to some business rule like greater than zero.
- **Validation Text**: This is a message displayed when data fails validation.
- **Required**: this option helps to specify if there is any need for you to enter a value into a field.
- **Allow Zero Length**: This option helps with the determination of entering an empty string into a Short Text or Long Text field in order to have it distinguished from a null value.
- **Indexed**: this option helps to speed up data access and also reduces data to unique values. Much later in this chapter, indexing is explained better.
- **Unicode Compression**: this option is used for multi-language applications. It requires two times the data storage but it allows office documents which include Microsoft Access reports to be shown in a correct manner regardless of the language or symbol that has been used. generally, Unicode is of no value only if the application is likely to be in an alien environment.
- **IME Mode**: This is also known as the kanji conversion mode property and it is used to display if the Kanji mode is kept in use

when the control has been lost. The setting of this option is of no relevance in English or European language applications.
- **IME Sentence Mode:** This option is used in the determination of the sequence mode of various fields of a table or controls of a form that changes when the focus moves in or out of the field. The settings of this option also have no significance in English or European language applications.

## Format

The format property can be used in the customization of the way numbers, dates, times, and text are shown and printed. When it is set at the table level the format will be in effect all through the application. There are various format options for each data type.

Microsoft Access offers built-in format options for almost all field data types. The exact format that is used to show field values can be influenced by the region and language settings in Windows settings. Note that the format property affects only the way a value is shown but does not affect the value itself or how the value is saved in the database.

You can always make use of any of the predefined formats or you can choose to create a custom format with the use of formatting symbols. For control, you can choose to set this property in the controls property sheet. for a field, you can also choose to set this property in the table design view or in the design view of the query window. There is also an option for you to make use of macro or Visual Basic for Application (VBA) code.

If you decide to build a custom format you should then construct a string in the field format property box. There are various symbols that you can use for each data type.

**Microsoft Access provides a global formats specification that is to be used in any custom format.**

- **Space**: this helps to show space as characters.
- **SomeText**: this helps to show the texts that are in between quotes as literal text.
- **! exclamation point**: this helps to have the display Left-aligned.
  - **asterisk**: this helps to fill all empty space for the next character.

- **\ backslash**: this helps to display the next character as a literal text. it uses the backslash to show characters that basically have no special meaning to Microsoft Access.
- **Color**: this helps to show the outputs in the color either black blue green red magenta yellow or white and will be shown between the brackets.

It is worthy to note that the format property will always take precedence if perhaps both a format and an input mask have been defined.

**Let us consider some types of formats below;**

# Number and currency field format

There are various field formats for number and currency fields. You can make use of one of the built-in formats or you can also choose to construct a custom format for yourself.

- **General number**: this is the number that is shown in the formats in which it was inserted.
- **Currency**: this helps add a thousand commas and includes a decimal point to be two digits to the right side of the decimal, after which it will enclose negative numbers in parentheses. A currency field is displayed with the currency symbol which can either be a dollar sign or euro sign as specified by the region and language settings in Windows settings.
- **Fixed**: this always shows at least a digit to the left and two digits to the right side of the decimal point.
- **Percent**: here the number value is usually multiplied by 100 and a percent sign will then be added to the right side.
- **Scientific**: scientific notation is usually used to show the number.
- **Euro**: helps to add the Euro currency as a prefix to the number.

# Custom numeric format

**Customers are designed when there is a combination of a number of symbols to create a format. the symbols that are used with number and currency fields are listed here;**

- **. Period**: helps with specifying the exact place where the decimal point should be displayed.
- **, comma**: helps with separating values.
- **0 zero**: this is a placeholder for a digit.
- **# pound sign**: this is a placeholder for nothing or for a digit.
- **$ dollar sign**: this shows the dollar character sign.
- **% percent sign**: this helps with the multiplication of the value given by 100 and includes a percent sign to the right side.
- **E - OR e**: makes use of scientific notation to show the number. It makes use of a minus sign to show a negative exponent and displays no sign at all to show a positive exponent.
- **E+ OR+e**: makes use of scientific notation to show the number. It also uses a plus sign to show a positive exponent.

## Built-in Date/Time formats

Below are Built-in dates and times for months. always note that all the examples given are based on the English United States region and language settings in Windows settings.

- **General Date**: if for any reason the value only contains a date you are not expected to display a time value and also if the value contains a time you are not expected to display the date. Dates are displayed in the built-in short date format (m/d/yyyy), While the time data is shown in the long time format.
- **Long Date**: Friday, May 20, 2022.
- **Medium Date**: 20-MAY-15
- **Short Date**: 20/05/2022
- **Medium Time**: 8:32 pm
- **Short Time**: 20:32

**Always note that date and time formats are being influenced by the region and language settings in Windows settings.**

## Custom dates and time formats

**Custom formats are designed by the construction of a very specific string that contains the symbols below;**

- **: Colon**: this helps to separate time elements such as hours, minutes, and seconds.
- **/ Forward flash**: this is in The Separation of date elements like days, months, or years.
- **C**: this helps to instruct Microsoft Access to make use of the built-in general date format.
- **d**: this helps to show the day of the month as either one or two digits. (1-31)
- **dd**: this helps to show the date of the month with the use of two digits. (01-31)
- **ddd**: this helps to show the day of the week as a three-character abbreviation( Sun, Mon, Tue, Wed, Thu, Fri, Sat)
- **dddd**: this option makes use of the full names of the days of the week( Sunday Monday Tuesday Wednesday Thursday Friday Saturday)
- **ddddd**; makes use of the built-in Short Date format.
- **dddddd**; makes use of the built-in Long Date format.
- **w**: makes use of numbers to show the day of the week
- **ww**: this helps in showing the week of the year.
- **m**: shows the month of the year with the use of one or two digits.
- **mm**: shows the month of the year with the use of two digits adding zero as a prefix where need be.
- **mmm**: shows the month of the year as a three-character abbreviation such as Jan, Feb, Mar, Apr, May, Jun, Jul, Aug, Sep, Oct, Nov, Dec.
- **mmmm:** shows the full name of the months of the year e.g. January, February, March, etc.
- **q:** shows the date as the quarter of the year.
- **y:** shows the day of the year (1 through 366).
- **yy:** shows the year as two digits (for example, 15).
- **yyyy:** shows the year as four digits (2015).
- **h:** shows the hour using one or two digits (0–23).
- **hh:** shows the hour using two digits (00–23)
- **n:** shows the minutes using one or two digits (0–59).

- **nn:** shows the minutes using two digits (00–59).
- **s:** shows the seconds using one or two digits (0–59).
- **ss:** shows the seconds using two digits (00–59).
- **ttttt:** makes use of the built-in Long Time format.
- **AM/PM:** makes use of a 12-hour format with uppercase AM or PM.
- **am/pm:** makes use of a 12-hour format with lowercase am or pm.
- **A/P:** makes use of a 12-hour format with uppercase A or P.
- **a/p:** makes use of a 12-hour format with a lowercase a or p.

## Short Text and Long text field formats

Whenever format is applied to the Short text field it helps with the clarification of the data that is within the field. tblCustomers make use of various formats. The state text feud has a greater than sign in the former property to show the data entry in uppercase. The active field also has a yes/no format weeds lookup display control property set to Text Box.

Short text and long text Fields are usually shown as plain text by default. if a specific format is to be applied to either a short text or long text field data you are expected to make use of the symbols below in the **construction of the format;**

- **@**: A character or space is needed.
- **&**: a character is not compulsory.
- **<**: forces all the characters used to their lowercase equivalent.
- **>**: forces all characters used to their uppercase equivalents.

## Input Mask

The input mask is also a feature of access 2022. This tool helps to limit the pattern for data entry into a database. It can also help to make data entry much easier. For example, you can choose to restrict entry to only phone numbers, social security numbers, and employee IDs. With the use of this mask, there is always a requirement for input into every space and it also doesn't permit characters or spaces.

- A field input mask can be applied anywhere the Feud is shown such as query forms or reports.

- The input mask property value is a string that has about three semicolons separated sections.

The first section contains the mask itself and comprises certain symbols, the second section tells Microsoft Access if it is to store the literal characters that are included in the mosque along with other data. When you use a Zero you are telling Microsoft Access to study little characters as part of the data while 1 tells Microsoft Access to store only the data itself, the third section defines the place order character that instructs the user on the number of characters that are expected in the input area.

**Below are the characters that are used to compose the input mask string;**

- **L:** A letter from A to Z is needed.
- **?:** A letter from A to Z is not compulsory.
- **A:** A character or digit is needed.
- **a:** A character or digit is not compulsory.
- **&:** Permits any character or space (needed).
- **C:** Permits any character or space (not compulsory).
- **. (period):** Decimal placeholder.
- **, (comma):** Thousands separator.
- **: (colon):** Date and time separator.
- **; (semicolon):** Separator character.
  - **(dash):** Separator character.
- **/ (forward slash):** Separator character.
- **< (less-than sign):** changes all characters to lowercase.
  - ➤ **(greater-than sign):** changes all characters to uppercase.
- **! (exclamation point):** shows the input mask from right to left. Characters fill the mask from right to left.
- **\ (backslash):** shows the next character as a literal.
- **0:** A digit is required, and plus (+) and minus (−) signs are not permitted.
- **9:** A digit is optional, and plus (+) and minus (−) signs are not permitted.

- **#:** Optional digit or space. Spaces are taken off once the data has been saved in the table. Plus and minus signs are allowed.

Note that the same masking characters are usually used on a field property in a query or a form. An input mask is ignored when bringing in data or adding data to a table with an action query. An input mask can be overridden by the Format property assigned to a field. In this kind of scenario, the input mask is in effect only as data is imputed and reformatted based on the format when the entry has been completed.

Although input masks can be insulted manually you can create an input mask for short text or Data/Time type fields with the input mask wizard easily. The input mask wizard does not only display the name of all the predefined input masks it also is an example for each of the names. you can decide to choose from the drop-down list of predefined masks.

- Click in the **Try It text box** and then insert **a test value** to see just how the data entry will be displayed.
- When you must have chosen **an input mask,** the next wizard screen will allow you to change the mask and indicate the placeholder.
- Another wizard screen will allow you to make a decision if you want to store special characters like dashes in a social security number.
- When you must have completed the wizard Microsoft Access will automatically include the **input mask** characters in the fields property sheet.

Not that you can insert any amount of custom mask that you might need. You can also decide the international settings so that you can work with various country masks. a custom input mask that you create in one database is always available in other databases.

## Caption

Caption is the name that is shown in the title bar at the topmost part of the report. The caption property indicates what should be displayed in the default label that is attached to the control designed by dragging the field from the field list to form a report. The caption can also be displayed as the column headings in the datasheet view for tables or queries that contain the field.

You should be extremely careful while using the caption property. This is due to the fact that caption text displays as the column headings in the data view. If you are not very careful you can be misled by the column heading in a query datasheet view.

Whenever the field is displayed in a query there isn't immediate access to the field properties hence you must know that the column is basically determined by the caption property and it might not show the name of the field. It can get even more confusing if the caption assigned in the tables design view and the caption assigned in a field's property sheet in the query design view are different properties and contain different text. Note that captions can actually be as long as 2048 characters, and can be more than needed for all but the most detailed descriptions.

## Validation Rule and Validation Text

Validation rules help with the prevention of bad data from being saved in your table.Primarily they look like criteria in a query. you can create a rule for a field or for the table with the use of the properties box in table design.

When you choose a field in table design you will see its validation rule property in the lower pane.The validation rule property helps with the establishment of requirements for inputs into the field. It is usually enforced by the ACE database engine; the validation rule also makes sure that data inserted into the table conforms to the basic requirements of the application.

Validation properties are quite a good way to enforce business rules like making sure that a certain product is not sold for zero dollars or ensuring that an employee review date comes after the hire date.

The Validation Text property has a string that is shown in a message box when the input of the user does not meet the requirements of the validation rule property. The maximum length of the Validation Text property value is 255 characters. When making use of the validation rule property you are expected to indicate a Validation Text value in order to avoid unnecessary triggering of the generic message box that Microsoft

Access shows when the rule has been violated. when you make use of the Validation Text property to provide users with a helpful message it then explains acceptable values for the field.

Note that the validation rule property does not apply to check boxes option buttons or toggle buttons that are in an option group on a form. The option group itself also has a validation rule property that applies to all the controls that are in the group. Most of the time validation properties are used to make sure that some dates fall after another and also that numbers that are not negative are inserted for values like inventory quantities and also that entries are restricted to different ranges of numbers or text.

When you move a field to a form the validation rule property of the new control is not sent immediately to the validation rule of the field. To get this done you need to insert a new validation rule value in the controls property sheet then Microsoft Access will enforce the rule that has been set at the table level.

Field and control validation rule properties are also enforced when the focus must have left the table field or form control. Validation rule property that has been applied to both a field and the control that is bound to the field will be enforced for both entities. The table-level rule will then be applied as data and edited on the bound control as the focus leaves the control.

## Required

The required property always instructs Microsoft Access to require input into the field. When this option is set to yes input is needed in the field either within a table or in a control on a form that is bound to the field. Note that the value of a required field can never be NULL.

Microsoft Access database engine usually enforces the required property. An error message is usually generated any time the user tries to leave a textbox control bound to a field with the required property set to yes. The required property can be used alongside the AllowZeroLength property In determining if the value of a feud is unknown or is not in existence.

## Allow Zero Length

The Allow Zero Length Property indicates if you want a zero-length string to be a valid entry for either a short text or a long text field. **AllowZeroLength takes up the following values;**

- **Yes:** this option is used when a zero-length string is a valid entry.
- **No:** with this, the table does not accept the zero-length strings but rather brings in a null value into the field when no valid text data has been supplied.

When you combine the AllowZeroLength and required properties it allows you to know the difference that exists between data that doesn't exist and data that is totally unknown. At certain points in time, you might have a need to store the proper value in the short text or long text field.

An example of data that is not in existence can be the case of a customer who doesn't have a phone number. the field for the phone number should be set to an empty which means that you can tell the user that does not have a phone number. Another customer who is totally new to the company is expected to have a null value in the field of the phone number. This states that you don't know for sure if the customer has a phone number.

With the use of an input mask, you can help the uses of your application to differentiate when a field has a null value. The required property state determines if a null value is accepted by the field, while the AllowZeroLength property allows zero-length strings in the field. Both of these properties offer various means to know if a value is unknown or the value is absent for the field.

## Indexed

The indexed property instructs Microsoft Access that you want to make use of a field as an index in the table. indexed Fields are organized internally to speed up queries sorting and arranging of operations. If you intend to frequently add a certain field such as social security number in queries or if the field is sorted or group or reports rather frequently you should then set its index property to yes.

**The valid settings for the indexed property are as follows;**

- **No**: This means the field is not indexed period this is usually set by default
- **Yes(Duplicates OK)**: this means the field is indexed and Microsoft Access also offers duplicate values in a column. This is said to be the appropriate setting for values like names where it is likely that names like John will appear more than once in the table.
- **Yes( No Duplicates)**: This field is indexed but duplicates are not allowed in the column. You can use this setting for data that should stand out within the table like social security numbers and customers.

Note that the indexed property is set in the field properties sheet or on the tables property sheet. it is expected for you to use the tables property sheet to set multi-field indexes.

## Understanding tbl Customers Field Properties

When you must have inserted the names of the field, the data types, and the field Descriptions there may be a need for you to go back and make some adjustments to some of the fields.All fields have properties and all of these properties are different for each of the data types. In tblCustomers, there is a need for you to insert properties for the various data types.

- When you press **the F6 button** you switch between the field entry grid and the field properties pane you can also choose **to move** between different panes by choosing the pane of your choice. Some properties show a list of values that are possible together with an arrow pointing downwards when you drag the pointer into the field. when you choose the arrow the values will be displayed in a drop-down list.

The field properties pane of the table design window has a second tab which is known as the lookup tab. When you click this tab you might see a single property which is the display control property. This property can be used for Short Text, number, and Yes/No fields.

# Setting the Primary Key

Primary keys of Field forms are values that are unique all through a table when creating a Microsoft Access database. primary keys can be used to refer to an entire record with each record having a different value for the key. a table can only have a single primary key. Microsoft Access can choose to automatically design a primary key field for you when you design a table or you can choose to indicate what you want to use as the primary key.

The major function of the primary key when designing databases in Microsoft Access is to help with the implementation of relationships between tables in a relational database. You cannot declare a foreign key in table Q to relate with table R until you have defined the primary key in table Q. It is necessary because it helps you link your table to order tables with the use of the primary keys as links.

The primary key also offers a means to specifically and uniquely specify the role of data in a table when creating a Microsoft Access database. For example, in an employee table, the primary key would be the employee number which is a unique employee.

When adding primary keys to your database there are some steps you need to follow in building an Access database. Make sure you note that for a primary key to function the field most uniquely identifies each row. In tblCustomers, the CustomID field is the primary key. Every customer has a unique CustomerID value so that the database engine can distinguish one record from the other. CustomerID15 refers to just one customer in the contacts table.

## Choosing a primary key

Without the CustomerID field, there will be a need for you to depend on another field or a combination of fields for it to be unique.You will be unable to make use of the company field since more than one customer can have the same company name. Furthermore, you can't equally use the company and City field together since more than one customer can also have the same company name and the same City name.Hence, there is a need for you to develop a field or a combination of fields that ensures the uniqueness of every record.

You can solve this problem with ease when you add an AutoNumber field to play the role of the table's primary key. The primary key in tblCustomers is CustomerID, an AutoNumber field.

If you don't decide on a field as a primary key, Microsoft Access can automatically add an Auto number field and use it as the table's primary key. Note that Auto number fields are usually very good primary keys because Microsoft Access does the value creation for you. The number will never be repeated in the table and you will be unable to change the value of an auto number field.

**Below are the properties of a good primary key;**

- A good primary key identifies each record uniquely.
- A good primary key can never be null.
- A good primary key must be in existence when the record is created.
- A good primary key must be stable; it should never be changed once it has been established.
- A good primary key should be simple and straightforward and it should also have as few attributes as possible.

In conclusion, an ideal primary key is one that is a single field that is immutable and is guaranteed to be distinct within the table.

## Creating the Primary key

**You can create a primary key with any of the three methods below. you have to start with opening a table in a design view then;**

- Choose **the fields** that should be used as the primary key and click on the **primary key** button in the **Tools group** on the **Design tab of the ribbon.**

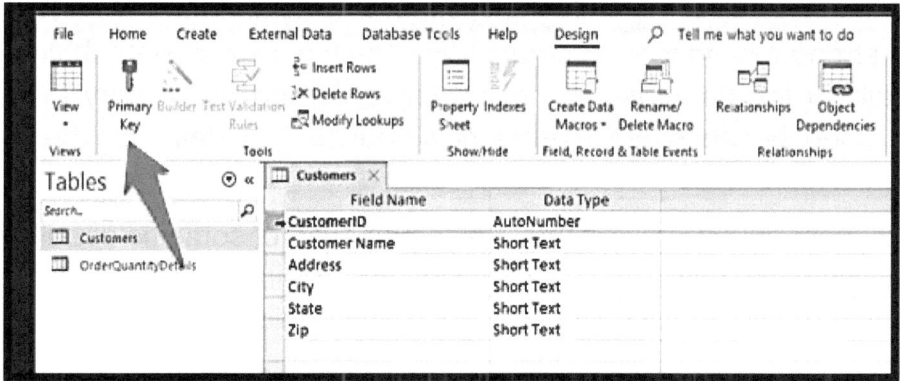

- Right-click the **field** and choose the **primary key** from the shortcut menu.
- Save the table without having to create a primary key and Microsoft Access will automatically create an Auto number field.

After you must have designated the primary key a key icon will be displayed in the gray selector area on the left of the name of the field to show that you have created a primary key.

## Creating composite primary keys

Composite keys are regarded as stable properties that make use of two different columns as the primary key. Note that a primary key must be a unique value in the table. If there is no available column that is distinct in the table you can choose to design a composite key of your choice.

A composite key makes use of combined values in the creation of a unique value in your table. primary keys are parts of good table design and they assist with query performance. composite keys are accomplished in the design view for Microsoft Access.

**To create the composite key simply;**

- Choose **the fields** you would want to add the **composite primary key**.
- Click on **the primary key button** on the tools tab of the ribbon. If you want to create a primary key from fields that are close to each other make sure you press the ctrl button when choosing the fields.

Most times composite primary keys are basically used when a developer has a strong feeling that a primary key should consist of data that occurs naturally in the database. In recent times composite primary keys are really used because developers now realize that data can be highly unpredictable.

If your users ever promised that the combination of some fields will never be duplicated in the table you will discover that things have different ways of turning out as against what has been earlier planned.

Furthermore, when making use of composite keys it is essential to maintain relationships between tables as it can become more complicated due to the fact that the fields that contain the primary keys must be duplicated in all the tables that have data that are related. When you use composite keys you are simply adding to the complexity of the database without adding stability or integrity and all the features that are desirable.

## Indexing Access Tables

Data is entered into tables in a random manner. However, the record in the orders table is always in a chronological order which is often not helpful when compiling reports that have to do with customer orders. In cases like this, you would prefer to have data entered in the customerID order.

Records are added to the Microsoft Access table in a similar manner as a fixed card. New records Are usually added against the middle of the table where logically they should belong to. in an order entry system, however, there might be a need to have new records inserted close to other records on the same customer. Unfortunately Microsoft Access tables don't work this way. The natural order of a table is usually the order in which records were added to the table which is sometimes referred to as entry order or physical order in order to emphasize that the records in the table are shown in the order in which they have been added to the table.

It is not outrightly bad to use natural order. In fact, natural order makes more sense if the table is not searched frequently or if it is a small table. There are also situations where the data being added to the table is well-ordered, to begin with. Access makes use of the index in a table just as we use the index in a book; if you want to find data Microsoft Access will look up the details location in the index. Oftentimes your table will have one or more simple indexes. A simple index is an index that has a single field in the table. a simple index can arrange the record of the table in either ascending or descending order.

If you have situations where natural order doesn't come up Microsoft Access offers indexing that can help you locate and organize records faster. you can choose to specify a logical order for the records in a table by designing and indexing on that particular table. Microsoft Access makes use of the index to keep one or more internal sort orders for the data that are in the table.

By default access fields are not indexed but it's extremely hard to think of a table that does not need any form of indexing in the next section below I'll be discussing the reasons why indexing is very important in Microsoft Access table

## The importance of indexes

Data from Microsoft shows that more than about half of all the tables that are in Microsoft Access databases have no indexes. These numbers stated do not include the tables that are not properly indexed, it only includes the tables that have no indexes at all. This shows that a lot of people do not appreciate the importance of indexing the tables in a Microsoft Access database.

Since an index means that Microsoft Access keeps an internal sort of data on the data that are in the indexed field as you can see why query performance is usually enhanced by an index. therefore you should index almost all the food that is often involved in queries or is often sorted on reports or forms.

Without the use of an index, Microsoft Access must look for each and every record in the database as a means of looking for matches. This process is popularly called table scan. you should ensure to search everything thoroughly until you get to the end of the deck before you can be sure you have found all the relevant cards in the file.

# Multiple-field indexes

**Multiple indexes also known as composite indexes are very easy to create.**

- Locate **the design view** option
- Choose **the index indexes button** on the **Design tab of Ribbon**.

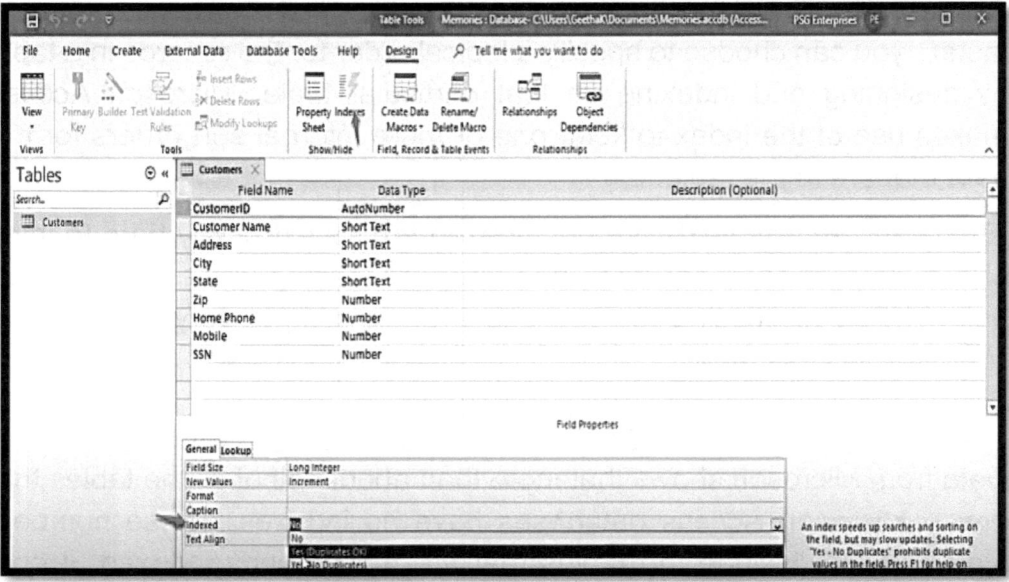

- The indexes dialogue box will then be displayed which will allow you to indicate the fields that you should include in the index.

Insert a name for the index with the use of the field name column. Make use of the drop-down list to choose the fields that you would include in the index. if any row appears immediately below the row you have just created and does not contain an index name then it is not a part of the composite index. Microsoft Access considers these two Fields when creating the sort order on this table ensuring that it speeds up queries and sorting operations in both fields.

Note that you can have up to about 10 fields added to a composite index. All that matters is that the composite index is not used as the primary key of the table, any of the fields in the composite index can remain empty.

The index properties are very easy to comprehend.

**These properties are often applied to sing-field and composite indexes also:**

- **Primary**: When this option is fixed as yes, Microsoft Access will make use of the index as the primary key of the table. You can choose to designate more than one field as the primary key, but ensure that the rules that control the primary keys are kept in mind, especially the rules that need each of the primary keys' values to be distinct and that there should be no field in the composite primary key that should be left empty. Hence, the default for the Primary property is NO.

- **Unique**: When the unique option is set to yes, this means that the index must also be unique within the table. A social security number field can be a very good candidate for a unique index since the business rule of the application might need just one and yes only one instance of a Social Security number in the table. In contrast, ensure that you do not index the last name field due to the fact names such as John and Alan are quite common and if a unique is indexed on last names like that it can only cause more problems. Anytime it is added to composite keys the combination of field values must also be unique with each of the fields within the composite key duplicating fields that can be found within the table.

- **Ignore Nulls**: If a record index field contains a null value the records index might not add anything to the overall indexing. This simply means that if a record index contains some kind of value Microsoft Access will not know where to insert the record in the table's internal index sort list. Hence, there might be a need for you to instruct Microsoft Access to ignore a record if the index value is null. By default, the Ignore Nulls property is always set to No, this actually means that Microsoft Access inserts records with a Null index value into the indexing scheme alongside any other records that have the Null index values. Ensure you test the impact of the index properties on your Microsoft Access tables and make use of the properties that perfectly suit the data that is being handled by your database.

## When to index tables

Based on the number of records that you might have in the table, the extra overhead of having to maintain an index might not make a justification for the creation of an index that goes beyond the primary key of the table. Though it might be much faster to retrieve data that does not have an index, Microsoft Access must ensure they update the information anytime records are inserted or changed in a table. In contrast, changes made to fields that are non-indexed do not need an extra file activity. Data can be gotten from fields that do not have an index at the same pace as it is gotten from fields that do have an index.

Generally, it is considered a best practice to include secondary indexes when you have a very large table and also when indexing Fields that are not primary keys helps to speed up searches. Even if you have Larger tables indexing can slow down the performance. Even records in a table will be changed frequently or new records will be added almost every time. anytime you add a record or change a record in the table Microsoft Access must also update all the indexes in the table.

**You might be thinking that since indexing is important why not just index everything contained in a table;**

First you need to know that indexes increase the size of the Microsoft Access database. If you index a table that you shouldn't this doesn't really need an index eating up a space for each record in the table. More importantly, indexes bring out a performance hit for every index on the table each time a record is added to the table.

Since Microsoft Access updates the index automatically any time a record is either added or removed from the table the internal indexing must also be adjusted for each new record. Microsoft Access makes about ten adjustments to the indexes every time a new record is included or an existing record is deleted and this can cause a noticeable delay on large tables especially if you are using a quite slow computer.

As you begin to work with Microsoft Access tables, you will likely begin with the easiest one-field indexes and move to more complex ones and then you become more familiar with the process. Ensure you keep in mind the trade-offs that exist between greater search efficiency and the overhead incurred by the maintenance of a large number of indexes on your table.

## Printing a Table Design

**To print a table design simply;**

- Click on the **Database Documenter button** that can be found in the Analyze group on the Database Tools tab of the Ribbon.

The analyze group has some tools that ensure that documenting your database objects is done with ease. Anytime you click on the Database Documenter button, the Documenter dialog box will then be displayed which allows you to choose objects that should be printed.

There is also an option for you to fix different options for printing.

**Simply:**

- Click on the **Options buttons**, and the Print Table Definition dialog box will be displayed which will allow you to choose the information needed from the Table Design to print. You can choose to print the different field names, all of the r properties, the indexes, and also their network permissions.

When you must have chosen the options that you want, Access will then generate a report. This report can be viewed in a Print Preview window or you can choose to send the report to the printer. You might also choose to save the report right within the database as part of the application's documentation.

## Saving the Completed Table

Run through the properly to ensure that it is void of any form of mistakes. Once you have done this, you can then choose to save the table design by

- Clicking on the **file** then choosing the **save option** or you click on the **save button option** on the Quick Access toolbar in the upper left part of the Microsoft Access environment.

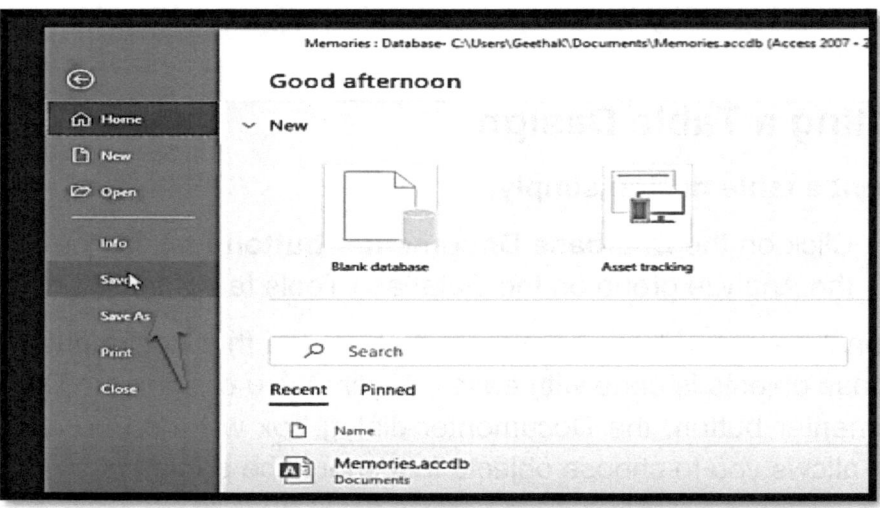

If this is the first time you're saving the table Microsoft Access requires that you give the table and name. names for tables can be up to 64 characters long and they should always follow the standard Microsoft Access object naming conventions which means they can include letters and numbers but cannot begin with a number and cannot include punctuations. if you are tempted to close a table you have not saved Microsoft Access will prompt you to save the table this way you are sure there will be no loss of data.

**If the table has been previously saved and you only want to change the name it has been saved with;**

- Click **on file** then **save as then save Object as**. Then click on the **Save As button** and insert a **different table name**.

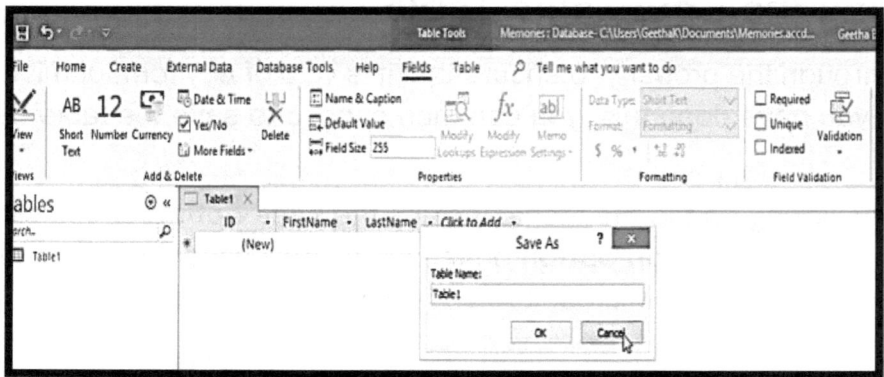

With this action, a new table will be created and the original table will be left with its original name remaining the same. If there is a need for you to delete the old table, all you have to do is to locate it in the Navigation pane and then press the delete button.

## Manipulating Tables

There might be a need for you to make copies of the tables you have added to the database as backups. In most cases, there might be a need for you to copy only the design of the table and not necessarily have to insert all the data in the table.

**Below are the table operations you can perform in the Navigation pane;**

- Changing **the names of tables**.
- Deleting **tables**.
- Copying **tables in a database**.
- Copying a **table to another database**.

## Renaming tables

**From time to time there might be a need for you to change the name of a table all you have to do is**

- Right-click on **the name of the table** in the navigation pane and choose **the name** from the drop-down list or you can choose **the table** in the navigation pane and press the **F2 button**. When you must have changed the name of the table it's being shown in the table list and it will reorganize the tables that are in the list in alphabetical order.

## Deleting tables

You created and should also be able to delete. Tables can be deleted once they have served their purpose and you are sure you will have no need for them again moving forward. **To delete a table**,

- Right-click on **the name of the table** in the navigation pane and choose **delete** from the shortcut menu or you can choose **the table** in the navigation pane and then press the **delete button**. Just like almost all conventional applications, when you press the

**delete button**, there will be a prompt that will ask you to confirm **the delete**, click on the **Yes button** to confirm and the table will be deleted.

You must note that when you press down the shift button while also pressing the delete key this action will delete the tables without requesting confirmation. If you are sure you want to delete a table you can use the combination of these two keys but if you're not quite sure it's better you use the method explained above.

## Copying tables in a database

Instead of having to create another similar table elsewhere in the database, you can choose to copy the table you want to replicate and then have it pasted just where you want the table to be.

- When you copy the table and then click on the **paste option**, the Paste Table As dialog box will then be displayed, which will also **ask you to choose from the three options below;**

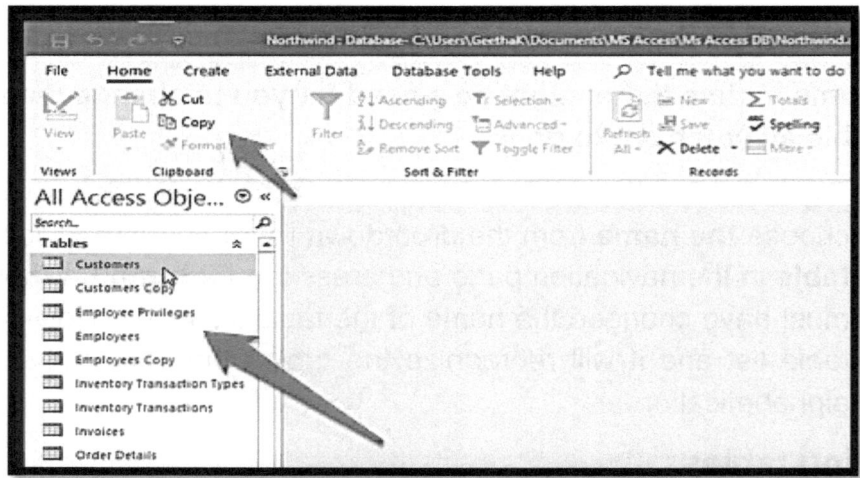

- **Structure only**: When you choose the structure only option, an empty table with the exact same design as the one you must have copied will be displayed. If you want to have a ready-made structure to which you can copy tables, this option is best to be used.
- **Structure and Data**: When you click on this option, a complete table with the data in it will be displayed.

- **Append Data to Existing Table:** This option helps to add the data of the table you must have copied to the lower part of another table. This option is quite useful if you have a need to combine tables like when there is a need for you to include data from a monthly transaction to a yearly history table.

**To have a table copied, follow the steps below;**

- Right-click on **the name** of the table in the navigation pane and choose the copy option from the shortcut menu or you can choose to click the **copy button** in the clipboard group on the home tab.
- Right-click **anywhere** in the navigation pane and choose the **paste option** from the shortcut menu or you can choose to click the **paste button** and the clipboard group on the home tab
- Once you have done that, insert the **name** of the new table.
- Choose either of the **paste options** as described above that use structure only, structure and data, or append data to an existing table.
- Finally, click on the **ok button** to complete the operation.

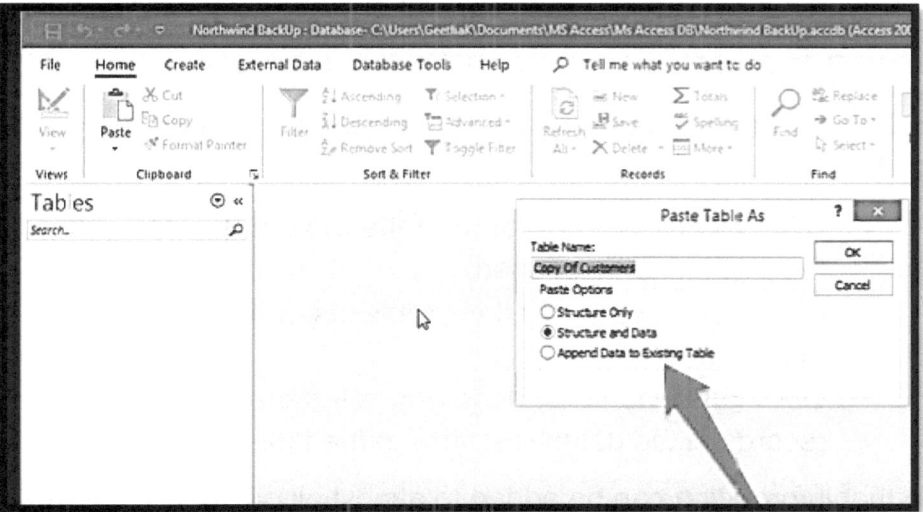

## Copying a table to another database

Just as tables can be copied within a database, you can also choose to copy tables from one database to another. You might have a need to share a common table among various systems or there might be a need for you to have a backup created on another database.

Note that when you copy tables to another database, the relationship that exists between these tables will not be copied. Microsoft Access will only copy the table design and the data to the other database. Copying a table to another database is almost the same as copying a table within the same database.

- Right-click **on the name** of the table in the Navigation pane and choose **Copy** from the shortcut menu or you can just click the copy button in the clipboard group on the home tab.
- Open the other **Microsoft Access database** and right-click **anywhere** in the navigation pane. Click on the **paste option** from the shortcut menu or you can choose the **paste button** in the clipboard group on the home tab.
- Insert the **name** of the new table.
- Choose one of the following **paste options; structure only, structure and data, or append data** to an existing table.
- Finally click on the **ok button** to have this operation completed.

## Adding Records to a Database Table

**To add records to a database table is quite very simple. All you have to do is**

- Double-click on **the name** of the table in the navigation pane to have the table opened.
- Once you have opened the table insert the **values** for each of the fields.
- Once that has been done you will then proceed with adding records in the datasheet view to the table.

Note that information can be added to almost all of the fields in the table except the Customer ID. AutoNumber fields will provide a number for you automatically.

Although records can be added directly to the table through the datasheet view as earlier stated, this method is not always recommended. Making use of forms to add records is quite better since the code that is behind a form can dynamically offer default values and also communicate with users when data is being entered.

## Understanding Attachment Fields

The attachment field in Access is used to add one or more files like documents, presentations, images, and so on to the records that are in your database.

Attachment can be used to store files in a single field and you can also use it to store different types of files in that same field. Attachments also help with the storage of data in a more efficient manner. Former versions of Access use a technology known as Object Linking and Embedding (OLE) in the storage of images or documents.

Those bitmap files can be much larger, even as much as 10 times the original file. When an image has been viewed from your database, OLE shows the bitmap image, not the original file. When you make use of attachments, you can open documents and other non-image files in their parent program, hence, right from within Access, you can locate and edit those files.

To use attachments in Microsoft Access, you must acd an attachment field to at least one of the tables in your database. Microsoft Access offers three methods in which an attachment field can be added to a table.

## Adding an attachment field in the Datasheet view

- Ensure that the table is opened in the datasheet view, click on the **first blank column** that is available. To locate a blank column, search for a new field in the column header.
- when you are on the data sheet tab, in the data type and formatting group, click on the **down arrow** close to the data type and then choose **the attachment option**. Once this has been done access will set the data type for the field to attachment and it will place an icon in the header row of the field.

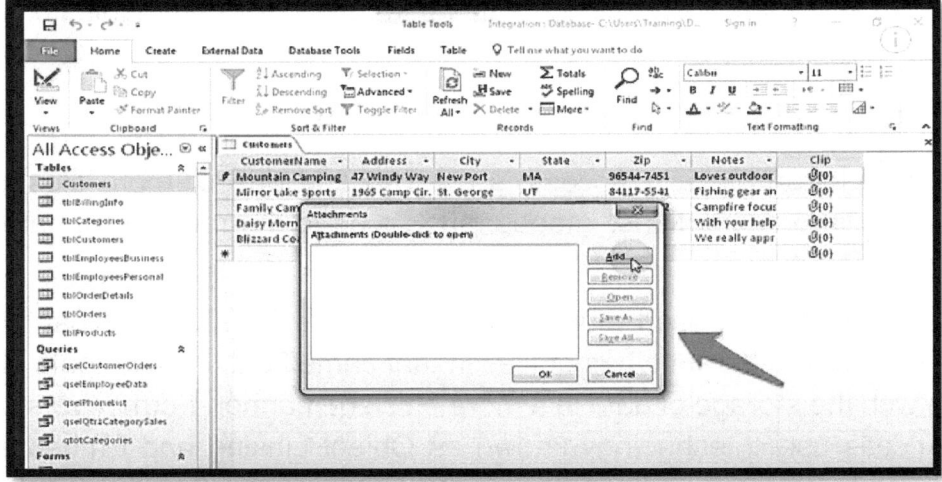

- Finally save your changes. Remember that you cannot change the new field to another data type but you can always delete the field if you think you might have made an error.

## Adding an attachment field in the Design view

- Locate the **navigation pane**, right-click **the table** that you want to change, and choose the design view option on the shortcut menu.
- When in the field name column choose a blank row and insert **a name** for your attachment field.
- In the same row under data type choose **attachment.**
- Save your changes. Just like the option above, you should always remember that you cannot convert the new field to another data type but you can choose to **delete** the field if you think you must have made an error.
- On the design tab in the Views group, choose **the arrow** that is under the fuel button and then select the **datasheet view** so as to have the table opened for use.

# CHAPTER 4
# UNDERSTANDING TABLE RELATIONSHIPS

One of the things a good database design seeks to accomplish is to take away any form of data redundancy i.e. duplicate data. If you would like to achieve this goal, you should have your data divided into various subject-based tables. This way each of the facts in the table will only be presented once.

Once this has been done, you can then offer Microsoft Access a method of bringing the dividend information back to themselves. This can be done by having common fields in tables that are quite related placed together. If you want to have this step done in a correct manner, you should then indicate these relationships within your database.

Although databases are supposed to be a model for ideal situations in the world or at the least have data managed in ideal situations, even the very complex situation is reduced to a number of relationships that exist between pairs of tables. The more complex the data managed by a table is, the more there might be a need for you to add more tables to the design.

When you are dealing with real data, however, you should always concentrate on the relationship that exists between two tables at a single point in time.

## Building Bulletproof Databases

The most common type of relationship that is used in almost all Access databases is the one-to-many relationship. In this type of relationship, each of the records in a particular table is directly related to one or more records in another table.

Imagine having a combination of these types of records, having them in just a single table instead of two or more tables. This means when there is a need to adjust the records, all you would have to create will just be new rows to accommodate the new records.

The above-described scenario is what is obtained with Excel if it is used for the purpose of a database. Since Excel is all about spreadsheets, there is no provision to have data broken into different tables, it just encourages users to have all their records kept in one large spreadsheet. **Arrangements like this can develop quite a number of problems;**

- **The table becomes too large to be properly managed**: When you have all of the records in just a single table, let's assume the table has to do with customers and placing of various items. In no time, such a table will become way too large for you to be able to manage with ease because almost all the customers will keep placing orders and with each new order placed is a record that should be updated in the table, not including all of the records like the name of the customer, phone number and address that must have already been added to the table as at when it was been created.

- **Data becomes extremely difficult to update and maintain**: When you attempt to make certain changes to a table that contains very large data, you are prone to committing so many errors, especially with tables that need to be updated frequently. The fewer records you have to change in a table the better it is for the user.

- **A monolithic table design is wasteful of disk space and other resources**: If you have a combined table, it will take up more space than necessary. When this happens, it can ultimately lead to having a slow computer if the memory of the computer is not large and it can also lead to other resources on the system being badly utilized.

With the use of a much better design like the relational design you can move the repeated data into a different table, and this will leave a field and the first table serving as reference points to the data in the second table.

The additional field needed by the relational model is just what has to be done for the efficiency that must have been gained by taking out redundant data from the table. Another advantage of having data normalized and including strict database rules for Microsoft Access applications is the fact that data will become virtually bulletproofed.

When a database is well-designed and properly managed the users know that the information will be displayed on forms and reports and it will truly show the data that has been stored in underlying tables. When a database is poorly designed it is at the risk of having its data corrupted; this means that some records might be lost sometimes and they may never get to be displayed on forms and reports even though the user must have added the data to the application.

Oftentimes, users get to trust what they can see on the screen and what is printed on the paper. Note that nothing good can come from a database that was weakly designed when you follow proper data normalization rules you can achieve a well-structured and carefully designed database

## Data Normalization and Denormalization

Normalization can be described as a process of arranging data within a database. This can include creating tables and also establishing basic relationships between the tables that have been created according to rules created to protect the data and to also make the database quite flexible by removing any form of redundancy and dependency that appears to be inconsistent.

Redundant data wastes disk space and also brings about problems with maintenance. If data that exists in more than one single place has to be changed, the data must be changed in the same method in every other place. It is quite easy to make any changes as regards a customer if only the data has been stored in the table of the customer and it isn't in any other place in the table.

There are just about a few rules for database normalization with each rule known as a normal form.

If the first rule is followed, the database can be said to be in its first normal form, and if the first three rules are kept, then the database can be said to be in its third normal form. Though there is a possibility of other forms of normalization, the third normal form is widely regarded as the highest level that is needed for almost all applications to function optimally.

As it can be with formal rules and its specification, the real-world scenarios do not allow for perfect compliance. In general, normalization needs the addition of more tables and some customers might have this quite tasking. If you have decided to violate any of the first three rules of normalization, ensure that your application expects any problem that might arise like inconsistency in dependency and redundant data.

## First normal form

**The first stage of the normalization is known as the first normal form and it needs the table to follow the following rule;**

"Each field that is in a table must have only one value, and the table must not have repeating groups of data".

A table is supposed to be a two-dimensional storage object and having to store more than one value in a field or allowing repeating groups in a table will mean a third dimension to the data in the table. What then happens when you include a third dimension in the table? Including a field is not the answer, all you need is a program and some table modifications and this does not naturally allow a dynamic number of fields.

## Second normal form

- Create **different tables** for sets of values that can be applied to more than one record.
- Relate **the table** that must have been created with a foreign key.

All the second normal form is stating is that the record should not depend on anything other than the primary key of a table. For example, take into consideration a customer's address in an accounting system. The address is required by the customer's table but also by the orders, shipping, invoices, Accounts receivable, and also collections tables. Rather than having to save the address of the customer as a different entity in each of these tables, save it in a single place either save it in a separate address table or in the customer's table.

## Identifying entities

There are times when it seems very hard to be able to distinguish certain entities as you might think that some entities are not integral to the other hence making the mistake of taking them off the table. For example, if you have a table that shows the names of customers as well as the order the customer places per time, if you have a need to alter the name of the customer this would in no way affect the order. To solve this problem, it is best you create different tables of the customers and also another of what the customer orders.

**Follow the steps below to get this done;**

- Click on the **Table design** that can be found on the **Create tab** of the ribbon.
- Insert an **AutoNumber field** and give it your **preferred name**.
- Choose the **Primary key** option on the **Table Tools Design tab** of the ribbon.
- Include a **Short Text field** and **name it**.
- Make sure you set the field size of the above name to 50.
- Finally, **save the table.**

With this, you can then choose to add some more information about the customer such as their mailing address and phone numbers. This will have the data moved into 2NF since you will be moving data that is not integral to its own table.

## Less obvious entities

Customers and what they order about physical objects can be identified as separate entities easily. Now I will be looking at having to separate the order and the details of the other. Getting the details of the order into the second normal form can be done by simply putting the information Integral to the order as a whole in a different table from the information for each line on the order. Have a new table created and move all the order details into it, this will effectively separate the order from the order details.

The breaking of a table into individual tables with each of the tables describing some aspect of the data is known as decomposition. Note that decomposition is an important part of the process of normalization. Though the tables that have been newly created might appear to be smaller than the original table, the data contained in the tables are still the same as in the previous table.

## Breaking the rules

You might not be able to follow the rules at all times, there are times when you might find it necessary to break the rules, but this is somewhat normal. For example, let us assume that bookstores are entitled to certain discounts which are dependent on the volume of purchases over the last year.

When following the rules strictly, the discount percentage is expected to be included in the general table of the bookstore since the discount is based on the customer and not on the order. But probably, the discount is applied to each of the orders which might seem arbitrary but can happen if the wholesaler allowed the sales personnel to give out special deals for some customers.

With this, there might be a need for you to include a discount column in the table which contains book order information, even if this means that you will have to duplicate records. If this happens to occur, you would have only broken the second normal form. The default discount is placed directly on the customer while the actual discount is based directly on the order.

## Third normal form

- Eliminate **fields** that do not in any way depend on any key.

Values in a record that are not really a part of that record key do not belong in the table in any way. Generally speaking, anytime the contents of a group of fields are to be applied to more than one record in the table, there might be a need for you to consider placing those fields in a different table.

For instance, in an employee recruitment table, the name and the address of the university of a candidate might not be added. But there is a need for a complete list of the universities in case there is a need for group mailings. If the information that deals with the university is saved in the table of the candidate, there will be no way to have a list of the universities with no current candidates. To solve this problem, all you have to do is to create a different table for universities and then have it linked to the Candidate's table with a university code key.

Following the third normal form strictly though can be desired theory wise is not always possible practically. If you have a customer table and there is a need for you to remove all of the possible inter-field dependencies, you must create different tables for cities, Zip Codes, sales representatives, customer classes, and some other factors that might happen to be duplicated in various records. In theory, it is worth going after normalization. However, lots of smaller tables degrade performance or go beyond open file and memory capacities.

It can actually be more feasible for you to apply the third normal form to data that changes often alone. If some fields that are dependent remain, design your application so it needs the user alone to make some verifications for all the related fields when anyone has been altered.

Based on the applications you decide to create, you might deem it fit to save calculated data in tables, especially if having to perform the calculation can be quite lengthy, or if the saved value is needed as an audit check on the calculated value printed on reports. It might be much more efficient to perform the calculations when inserting data rather than when printing reports.

Though you can always have higher levels of normalization, which can be found in most database applications, the third normal form is way more adequate. If you cannot attain the third normal form at the very least you should strive to get the first normal form in your tables by taking off redundant or data that might be repeated to another table.

## Denormalization

Denormalization can be said to be a process of including precomputed redundant data to an otherwise normalized relational database in a bid to help improve the read performance of the database. Note that there are times when you might generally decide to have to denormalize databases by yourself.

Basically, data is normalized so as to help with the improvement of the performance of your database. For example, no matter how much time and effort you spend in carefully creating a table, it might still be quite stressful having to look for something even when you must have indexed properly and also done the proper normalization. Likewise, some values that have been calculated might take a considerable amount of time to calculate. It might be much easier to save a value that has already been calculated than to calculate such values on the go, especially when the computer you are working with doesn't have a large memory or it is relatively slow.

Another reason why denormalization of data is usually done is for the provision of the ability to bring back a document as it had been produced before. Note that almost all the steps that have to be taken to have data denormalized have to result in more programming time which is needed to have both the data and user protected from the various problems that might arise from an unnormalized design.

Ensure you have all you have done to denormalize a design documented. It is basically possible that either you or some other person will be called to provide maintenance services or to include another feature to the application. In a bid to have the design optimized, whatever you might have done and spent a lot of time and energy on might be undone if you have left design elements that look like they will be violating the rules of normalization.

Always bear in mind that the main purpose of denormalization is for the sake of reporting or for performance-related purposes such as just maintaining the table.

## Table Relationships

Most of the time, people begin with the use of spreadsheet applications such as Excel in the building of a database. This can be said to be quite unfortunate as it doesn't introduce them to the complexity of a database structure since spreadsheets only store data as a two-dimensional worksheet( rows and columns) without any provision of an easy way to aid the connection of individual worksheets together. Each cell of a worksheet has to be connected manually to the cells in the other worksheet it corresponds to, this process can be quite exhausting.

Storage objects with just two dimensions like worksheets are known as a flat-file databases because they don't have the three-dimensional quality of relational databases. Although, with the use of clever programming in the Excel VBA language, it can be quite possible and also easy to have the data in a worksheet linked to the data in another worksheet. It can also be possible to change the data in individual rows though such an effort is not ideally needed when you make use of a relational database like Microsoft Access.

## Connecting the data

The Primary key of a table helps to uniquely identify the records that are in that table. This can also basically help with connecting data that are in a particular table with the data in another table. For example, if you have a table of employee data the security number of the employee might be a combination of first and last names or an employee ID might also be used as the primary key. Now let's assume The employee ID is used in choosing the primary key for the employee's table whenever the relationship to the payroll table is created the employee ID field will then be used to link or connect the tables together. In books such as this and almost every other book that is about relational databases like Microsoft Access they're basically three types of relationships that can be found **between tables they are;**

- One-to-one
- One-to-many
- Many-to-many

## One-to-one

In a one-to-one relationship each record in the first table ought to have only one matching record in the second table, and each record in the second table should also have only one matching record in the first table.

This relationship is not common because oftentimes the information related in this manner is saved in just a single table. You might make use of a one-to-one relationship in the dividing of a table with various fields or isolate parts of a table for security reasons or rather store information that applies to only a subset of the main table. Whenever you notice such a relationship, ensure that both tables share a common field.

Another instance of a one-to-one relationship can be described as a situation known as subtyping. For instance, your database might contain a customer's table and also a vendor's table. if both your customers and vendors are businesses a lot of the information for both entities might end up being similar. in such a case you might want to have a company's table that has all the data that is similar like the name of the company, the address, and the tax identification number after which your customers and when does table would include a reference to the companies table and also include some additional fields that are specific to customers and vendors respectively. the customer and vendor entities will be regarded as subtypes of the companies and related one to one.

## One-to-many

Let us consider an order tracking database that contains a customer's table and an Orders table as an example. A customer can choose to place any amount of orders. It follows that for any customer that is represented on the customer's table there might be numerous orders for that same customer represented in the orders table. The relationship between the Customers table and the Orders table is a one-to-many relationship.

To represent a one-to-many relationship in your database design, take the primary key on the one side of the relationship and include it as an additional field or fields to the table on the many sides of the relationship. In this case, for instance, you add a new field which is the ID field from the Customers table to the Orders table, and then name its customer ID. Microsoft Access can then make use of the customer number in the Orders table to find the right customer for each of the orders on the Orders table.

beyond a reasonable doubt, one-to-many relationships are the most common type of relationship encountered in relational database systems. **Below are examples of one-to-many situations;**

- **Customers and orders**: In this kind of example, the customer which is the one side has placed several orders which is the main side but all of the orders placed will still be sent to just one customer.
- **Teacher and student**: Each teacher has a lot of students but each student has just one teacher. This is in the concept of a particular class or a particular course of study or subject.
- **Employees and paychecks**: each employee has received several paychecks but each paycheck is given to just an employee.
- **Patients and appointments**: which patient houses none or multiple doctor appointments but which appointment is for just one patient.

## Many-to-many

In this relationship let's take a look at the relationship between a product's table and an Orders table. a single order can contain more than one product. On the other hand, a single product can be displayed on many orders. Therefore for each of the records that are in the order table, there can be many records in the product table.

Furthermore, for each record in the product table, there can also be many records in the Orders table. This kind of relationship is known as a many-to-many relationship. You should note that in order to know an existing many-many relationship between tables, it is very important that both sides of the relationship be considered.

To show a many-many Relationship it is necessary to create a third table which is often called a junction table that breaks down the many-to-many relationship into two one-to-many relationships. you can insert the primary key from each of the two tables into the third table. As a result of this, the third table will record each occurrence or instance of the relationship. For example, the orders table and the product table have a many-to-many relationship that is defined by the creation of two one-to-many relationships to the orders details table. One order can have many products and each of these products can be displayed on many orders.

Due to the additional complications of the junction table, many-to-many relationships are mostly considered difficult to create and maintain. Fortunately, Microsoft Access ensures that such a relationship is easy to create if only a few rules are followed. These rules are explained in certain places in this book. For example, if you want to update either side of a many-to-many relationship the junction table must contain the primary keys of both tables that are joined by the relationship.

**Below are examples of many many relationships that are commonly used in the business environment;**

- **Lawyers to clients**: each lawyer might be involved in several cases and each client might be represented by more than one lawyer in each case.
- **Patients and insurance coverage**: most people are covered by just one insurance policy. For example, if both you and your spouse are provided medical insurance by your employers you have multiple coverages.
- **Video rentals and customers**: over a period of time for example a year, each video is rented by various people while every customer would have definitely rented more than one video over the course of a year.
- **Magazine subscriptions**: most magazines have a circulation that is measured in thousands or millions. Most people who do subscribe to magazines subscribe to more than one at a time.

## Integrity Rules

Referential integrity can be described as a system of Rules that Microsoft Access makes use of in order to ensure that relationships that exist between records in tables that are related are valid and that you also do not mistakenly delete or alter data that are said to be related to one another.

Referential integrity works strictly on the bases of the key fields of the table. Referential integrity means that the database engine checks each time a key field, be it primary or foreign is either added, changed, or deleted. If a change to a value in a key field causes an invalidation of the relationship such change is said to violate referential integrity. you can set tables up in order to automatically enforce referential integrity.

Since the rules of referential integrity are enforced by the Microsoft Access database engine, data integrity is ensured anywhere the data is displayed in the database, either in tables, queries, or forms. Once the integrity requirements of your application have been established you don't have to be afraid that the data in related tables will be lost or scattered. The need for referential integrity in database applications can never be overemphasized. Lots of developers think that they can use VBA code or user interface design to prevent Orphaned records( which are always very bad in database applications).

The truth is that in almost every database the data saved in a particular table might be used in various places within the application or even in some other application that also makes use of the same data. Given the fact that many database projects elongate for so many years and among any number of developers, it is not always easy to remember the way data should be protected. Over time the best approach to ensuring the integrity of data that is stored in any database system is to make use of the power of the database engine in the enforcement of referential integrity.

**You can set referential integrity when the conditions below are true;**

- The matching field from the primary table is the primary key or has a unique index.
- Related Fields have almost the same data though there are two exceptions to this; an auto field can be related to a number field that has a field size property setting of long integer and an auto number field that has a field size property setting of replication ID can be related to a number field that has a field size property setting of replication ID.
- Both tables belong to the same Microsoft Access database. If the tables are linked tables they must also be tables in Microsoft Access format and the database in which they are

stored to set referential integrity must be opened. referential integrity cannot be enforced for linked tables from databases that are in other formats.

**The following rules apply whenever you make use of referential integrity;**

- You cannot insert a single value in the foreign key field of the table that is related but does not exist in the primary key of the primary table. Nevertheless, you can insert a Null value in the foreign key. This does specify that the records are not related. For example, you cannot have an order that is assigned to a customer that does not exist. However, it is possible to have an order that is not assigned to anyone by inserting a Null value in the Customer ID field.
- A record cannot be deleted from a primary table if matching records can be found in related tables. For instance, you cannot delete an employee record from the table of the employee if there are certain orders that are assigned to the employee in the orders table.
- The primary key cannot be changed in the primary table if that very record has other records that are related to it. For instance, an employee's ID cannot be changed if there are orders that are assigned to that employee in the Orders table.

## No primary key can contain a null value

A primary key can be described as a field in your table that offers Microsoft Access with a unique identifier for all the rows that are within a table. In a relational database like the Access database, information can be divided into different subject-based tables. You can then make use of the table relationships and primary keys will then tell Microsoft Access how information can be brought back together. Access makes use of primary key fields to swiftly associate data from various tables and bring the data together in a very meaningful way. Most times a primary key can be an ID number or a serial code. An example of a bad choice for a primary key can be a name or an address since both information can change with time.

A Null value is known as a value that can be inserted into a field or can be used in expressions or queries to specify data that is missing or data that is unknown. In Microsoft Visual Basic, the Null keyword shows a Null value. Certain fields like the primary key fields cannot contain Null.

The first referential integrity rule states that no primary key should contain a null value. The value of a field that has never been assigned a value is regarded as null. No row that exists in the database table can have a null in its primary key since the very main purpose of the primary key is to ensure that there is a guarantee of uniqueness of the row. Null values cannot be unique and the relational model will also not work if primary keys can be null. Microsoft Access will not permit you to create a field that already has null values as the primary key.

In addition, it is impossible for Microsoft Access to evaluate a null value. Since there is no existence of a null value, it cannot be compared with any other value. It is not bigger or smaller when compared with any other value; it just doesn't exist. Hence a null value can be used to search for a record in a table or rather to create a relationship between two tables.

Anytime a composite primary key that is made up of various fields is being used, all the fields in the composite key must have values. It is not permitted for any of the fields to be empty. The combination of the values in the composite primary key must be unique.

## All foreign key values must be matched by a corresponding primary key

A primary key-foreign key relationship describes a one-to-many relationship between two tables in a relational database. A foreign key can be described as a column or a set of columns that are in one table and reference the primary key columns in a different table. The primary key is known as a column and can be a set of columns also where each value is simply unique and also identifies a single row of the table.

The second referential integrity rule says that all of the foreign key values must be matched by primary keys that are corresponding. This also can mean that all the records that exist on the many sides of the table of a one-to-many relationship ought to have a record in the table that corresponds to the one side of the relationship. If there happens to be a record on the many sides of the relationship without a corresponding record on the one side of the relationship such is said to be orphaned and will be taken off the database schema. Having to identify orphaned records in a database can be very difficult. It is much better to then avoid the situation in the first place.

**The second rule simply means the following;**

- You cannot have rows added to a many side table if there is no corresponding record on the one side of the other table.
- The primary key value in a one-side table cannot be changed if the change will bring about the creation of an orphaned record.
- Deleting a row on the one side must not create an orphaned record on the corresponding many sides.

An absolutely curious Result of the rules of differential integrity is that it is very possible to have a parent record that is not matched by any corresponding child record. This means a company may have employees that have not been issued a paycheck yet. Eventually, most current records will be matched by one or more corresponding child records but this condition is not a requirement of a relational database.

## Keys

After the creation of any database table it is essential you assign each table to a primary key. With this key being assigned you can be sure that the table records will have only one unique value.

All a primary key does is to uniquely identify each record in a table. Always ensure that two records should not have the same number.

**Below are reasons why this should be totally avoided;**

- It can make updating the record of the customer almost impossible.
- You want to be sure and certain that all of the records that are in a table are accurate in order to be sure the information that is gotten from the table is accurate.
- You don't want to make the table any larger than it already is. When you add redundancies or have fields or records

duplicated, it will just complicate the database and add no value.

When you add a single unique value to each record in a table it makes the table reliable and clean; this can also be referred to as entity integrity. When you have a different primary key value in each record you can tell two records apart even if all other fields in the records are the same.

This is extremely important since you can easily have two individual customers with a common name on your table. If you indicate a primary key when you're creating a Microsoft Access table Microsoft Access will ask if you want one. If you reply by saying yes Microsoft Access will use the auto-number data type to create the primary key for the table. An Auto number field is always inserted automatically every time a record is added to the table and once the value has been established it can be changed. Additionally once any other number value has been displayed in a table the value will never be reused even if the record that has the value has been deleted and the value is no longer being displayed in the table.

## Deciding on a primary key

As earlier mentioned, the primary key is the entity that makes a record in a table unique. It is an identifier that is often a text, numeric or AutoNumber data type. To decide, you can choose to specify a method for the creation of a unique value or you can choose to allow Microsoft Access to create the primary key automatically for you with the use of the AutoNumber value.

Nevertheless, there is absolutely no major reason why the primary key value has to have a meaning to the application since its major function is simply to Make sure that each row is unique and to also provide an anchor for table relationships. Most Microsoft Access developers make use of auto-number fields as primary keys basically because they meet all the requirements of a primary key without adding to the complexity of an application.

Even though it can be extremely difficult to make use of logic in the generation of unique values for a primary key field, the simplest approach is to make use of auto-number fields for the primary keys in your table. The unique characteristic of the author number field is the fact that it cannot be changed and so it makes it ideal to be used as a primary key.

Note that AutoNumber fields are always guaranteed to be very unique but they are not guaranteed to be sequential. There are certain reasons why the gaps in AutoNumbers can be introduced like deleting records and never should you totally rely on AutoNumbers being sequential.

you might feel that sequence numbers can make it extremely difficult to search for information all you need to remember is that most times you don't use an ID field to search for the information you generally search for information based on the purpose of the table

## Looking at the benefits of a primary key

Primary key is of utmost importance in any database as it does the job of linking records together working hand in hand with the foreign key. Aside from the primary key serving as a link between tables in a database, the **primary key field in Microsoft Access has the following benefits;**

- Fields are usually indexed which helps to swiftly speed up queries searches, and sort that might have to do with the primary key field.
- Microsoft Access makes sure you include a value every time you add a record To the table with this you are guaranteed that your database tables follow strictly the rules of referential integrity
- With the addition of new records to a table, Microsoft Access checks for duplicate primary key values and also helps with the prevention of duplicate entries and ensuring that data integrity is maintained.
- by default Microsoft Access will show your data in primary key order.

## Designating a primary key

As discussed above, by now you must know that choosing a primary key is extremely important for the bulletproofing of a database design. With proper implementation, the primary key can help with the stabilization and protection of the data that must have been saved in Microsoft Access databases. Ensure you bear in mind that the main rule that governs the values that will be added to the primary key field in a table must be very unique. Additionally, you must also note that the ideal primary key must be stable.

## Single-field versus composite primary key

there are times when the ideal primary key cannot be found within a table as one value you might be able to bring Fields together to create a composite primary key. For example, you might not be able to create a primary key with the use of the first name alone but when you combine the last name and probably date of birth you might be able to come up with a unique combination of values that can be used as the primary key. This section shows that Microsoft Access has made it very easy to combine Fields as composite primary keys.

**below are things you should consider when using composite keys;**

- None of the fields in a composite key should be null
- There are times when building a composite key from naturally occurring data within the table proves to be extremely difficult.
- each of the fields can be duplicated within the table but it is impossible to duplicate the combination of composite key fields.

## Natural versus surrogate primary keys

a natural primary key can be gotten from data that is already in existence in the table like a social security number or an employee number. If there is no single field that can uniquely identify the records that are in a table it is best to combine fields to form a composite primary key.

Note that one of the greatest issues has to be that adding a record to a table is not possible if the primary key value is not known as when the record is committed to the database. Even if the temporary values are entered until the permanent value is known, the amount of fixing that will be done in related tables can also be considered.

## Creating primary keys

**To create a primary key,**

- Open **a table** in the **Design View**.
- Choose **the fields** that you will prefer to use as a primary then click on **the primary key button** on the **Table Tools Design tab of Ribbon**. If you have a need to indicate more than just a single field in the creation of a composite key, **press down the ctrl key** then choose the fields before you go ahead to click on **the primary button**.

# Creating relationships and enforcing referential integrity

With the use of the Relationship window, you can create relationships and also referential integrity rules that should be applied to the tables that are within a relationship. Whenever you want to design a permanent, managed relationship that makes sure referential integrity between Microsoft Access is easy, **follow the steps below;**

- Choose the **Database Tools Relationships**, This will then display the relationship window.
- Select the **Show Table button** option on the Ribbon or you can choose to Right-click the **Relationships window** and choose the **select Show Table option** from the shortcut menu. The Show Table dialog box will then be displayed.
- Add your **preferred table name** to the relationship window by double-clicking on **each table** in the show table dialog box, or you can choose **each table** and select the **Add button option**.
- Build a relationship by moving the **primary key field** in one table and then dropping it on the **foreign key** in the Many tables. As an alternative, you can choose to move the **foreign key field** and then drop it on **the primary key field**. Once this has been done, Access will immediately open the **Edit Relationships dialog box** in order for you to **indicate the details** about the relationship that you are about to create between the tables.

- Check the **Enforce Referential Integrity check box**. If this checkbox happens to be left unchecked, Microsoft Access will not allow you to have records deleted in the table you have chosen. In view of this box that has been checked, the deletions across the relationship will be cascaded automatically. Deletes that involve cascading can be a very delicate operation since the deletions in the Many tables happen without confirmation.
- Finally, click on the **create button**. Microsoft Access will then draw the line between tables shown in the relationships window showing the type of relationship that exists.

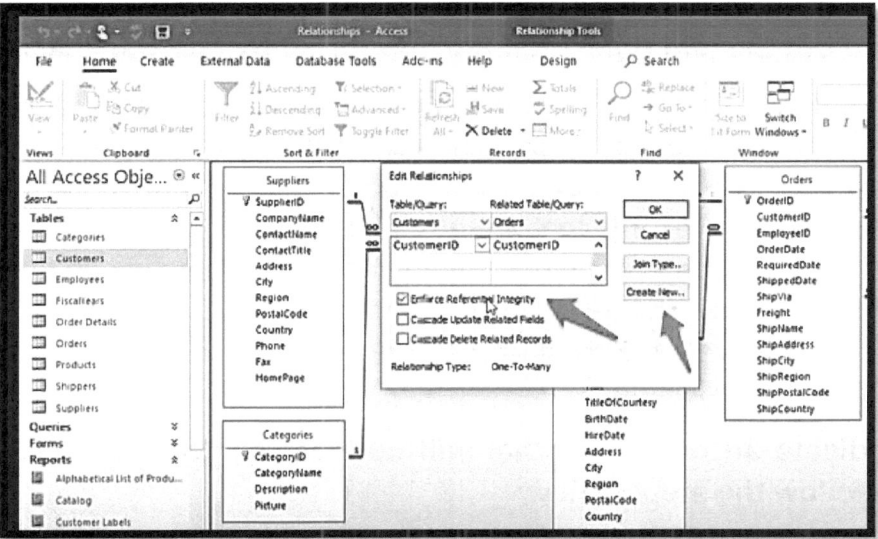

## Specifying the join type between tables

There are about four buttons on the right-hand side of the Edit Relationships dialog box.

**They are;**

- **Create**: This button takes you back to the Relationships window with the changes outrightly indicated.
- **Cancel**: This button takes off the current changes and also takes you back to the Relationships window.

- **Join Type**: The join type button when clicked, opens up the Join Properties dialog box.
- **Create New**: The create new option enables you to indicate an entirely new relationship between the two tables and fields.

By default, when a query on related tables is being processed, Microsoft Access returns only records that are displayed in both tables. When this happens such a relationship is sometimes known as the inner join since the only records that are displayed are those that can be found on both sides of the relationship.

Nevertheless, the inner join is not the only join that is supported by Microsoft Access.

**To find out the join types that are supported by Microsoft Access;**

- Choose the **Join Type button** in order to have opened the Join Properties dialog box, The alternative settings in the Join Properties dialog box enables you to indicate that you would like to see the records that are available either from the child table or from the parent table not minding if they are matched on the other side or not. This kind of join is known as the Outer join and it can come in very handy since it perfectly shows the state of the data in the application.

**To indicate an outer join that will connect customers to another table follow the steps below;**

- From the relationships window, add the two tables.
- Move the **Customer ID** from one table and drop it on the other table. The Edit Relationships dialog box will then be displayed.
- Click on the **Join Type button**. The Join Properties dialog box will then be displayed.
- Choose the **Include All Records** from one table and Only Those Records from the other table Where the Joined Fields Are Equal option button.
- Click on **the Ok button**. You will then be taken back to the Edit Relationships dialog box.
- Click on the **Create button**. This will also take you back to the Relationships window. The Relationships windows by now should

be displaying an arrow going from one table to the other table. When you get to this point, you can then set the referential integrity between the two tables on an outer join relationship.

Note that it is not compulsory for you to create a joint type for all the relationships in your database. Most developers make use of the default inner join for all the relationships that exist in the database and also to make adjustments to the joint properties data on each query in order to bring forth the desired result.

## Enforcing referential integrity

When you must have used the Edit Relationships dialog box to indicate the relationship, to have the table and related Fields verified, and also to indicate the type of join that exists between the tables you then should indicate referential integrity between the tables.

- Choose the **Enforce Referential Integrity checkbox** that can be found in the lower portion of the Edit relationship dialogue box in order to specify that you want Microsoft Access to enforce the referential integrity rules on the relationships that exist between the tables

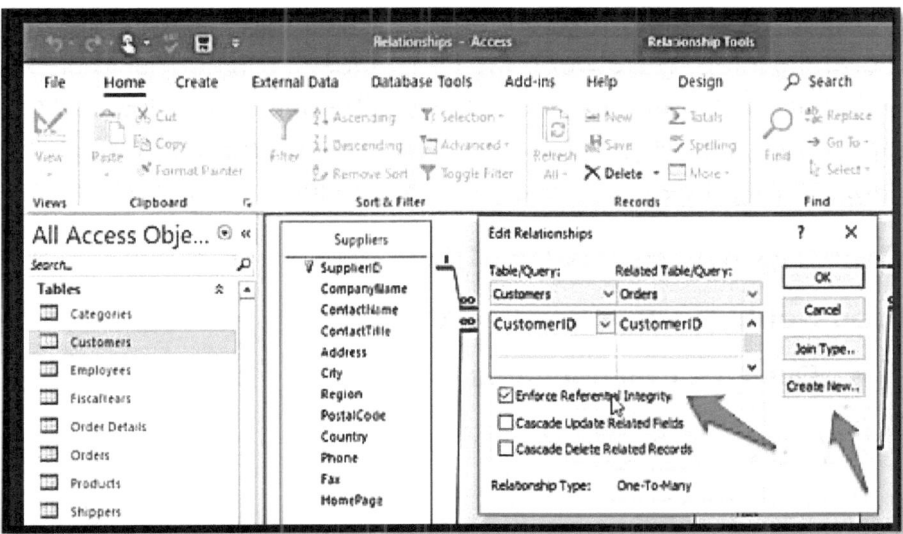

If you decide not to enforce referential integrity, you can choose to include a new record, change key Fields, or have related records deleted without warnings about referential integrity violation. With this, it is possible to change critical fields and damage the application's data. When there is no active integrity you can build tables that have orphans. With normal operations like data entry or changing of information, there should be enforcement of referential integrity rules.

There are two other options that referential integrity also enables and can be of extreme importance to you they are; cascading updates and cascading deletes. These two options can be found close to the bottom of the Edit relationships dialog box.

Note that there are times when you might find When you choose to Enforce Referential Integrity and select the create button (if you have reopened the Edit relationship dialogue box to edit a relationship), that Microsoft Access will not allow you to create a relationship and enforce referential integrity. The most likely reason for this is that you are requesting Microsoft Access to create a relationship that violates referential integrity rules like a child table with orphans in it.

When this happens Microsoft Access we warned you by displaying a message. This means that Microsoft Access cannot enforce referential integrity between the tables because the data within the tables already violates the rule. Either way, you can solve this by removing the offending records then returning to the relationship window and setting referential integrity Between the two tables. If it is normal to clean up data by deleting records depends solely on the business rules that govern the application. Deleting orders just because referential integrity cannot be enforced might be considered a very bad idea in most environments

## Viewing all relationships

**If you would like to view all relationships;**

- Open the **Relationships window**.

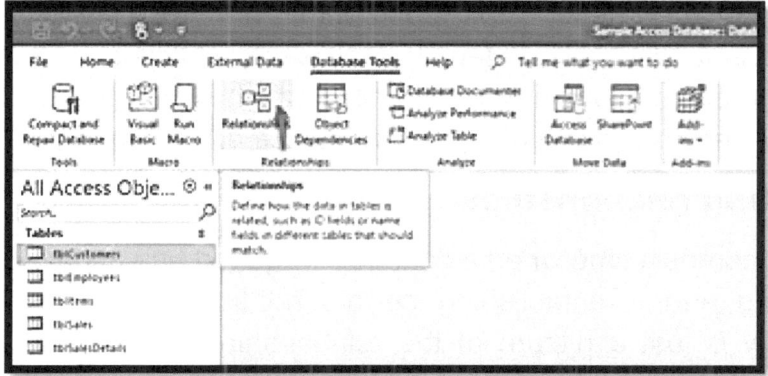

- Click on the **All Relationships** option on the Relationships Tools Design tab of the Ribbon to view all of the relationships in the database.

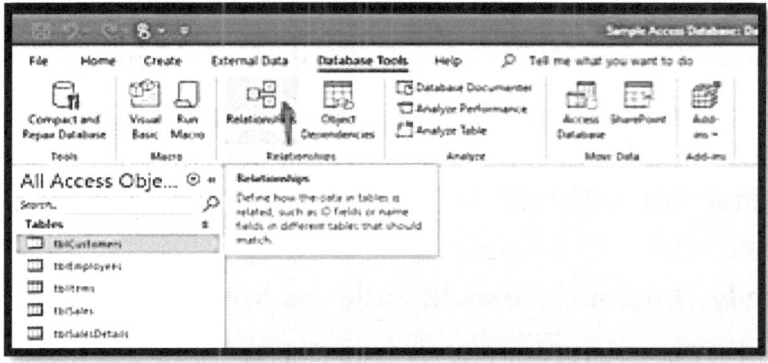

If there is a need for you to simplify the view that you can see in the Relationships window, you can then hide a relationsh p by deleting the tables that you can see in the Relationships window.

- Click on **a table** and then press the **delete key** and Access will take off the table from the Relationships window.

When a table is taken off the relationship window, this doesn't delete any relationship that can be found between the table and other tables that are in the database.

Anytime you are creating database tables, always ensure that the Required Property of the foreign key field is set to Yes. With this action, the user will be forced to insert a value in the foreign key field, while providing the relationship path between the tables.

Note that the relationships found within the Relationships window are permanent and are often managed by Microsoft Access. When permanent relationships are performed, they will be displayed in the Query Design window by default as tables are being added.

## Deleting relationships

There comes a time when a change is required and might have to do with deleting and re-establishing certain relationships. The Relationships window is just a picture of the relationships that can be found within tables. If all you do is open the relationship window and click on the delete button, the picture will be deleted but the relationship itself will still exist. There is a need for you to click on the line that connects the tables together then press the Delete button to delete the relationship and then delete all of the table pictures so as to take away the relationship totally.

# Following application-specific integrity rules

Adding to the Referential integrity rules that the ACE database engine enforces, there is also an option for you to create a number of business rules that are enforced by the applications you create in Microsoft Access.

**Basically, business rules include the following items;**
- The order-entry clerk must insert his ID number on the entry form.
- Quantities can never be less than zero.
- The unit selling price can also never be less than the unit cost price.
- The order ship data must always come after the order date.

Most times rules are included in a table at the time of design. When you enforce such a rule you go a long way to preserving the value of the data managed by the database. you can also choose to create a table-wide validation rule with the use of the validation rule property on the tables property sheet that ensures the provision of some protection for the data in the table. With this only one rule can be created for the whole table which makes it extremely difficult to offer certain validation text for all possible violations.

There are some limitations with the valuation of rule property. For example, user-defined functions in a rule cannot be used. Furthermore, you also cannot reference other fields, data in other records, or tables in your rules. validation rules help to prevent the user entry by providing warnings that the user can bypass. If there is a need for you to provide a warning but still enable the user to continue you shouldn't make use of the validation rules.

# CHAPTER 5
# WORKING WITH ACCESS TABLES

In this chapter, you will be introduced to working with a datasheet and how it can be used to insert data into a Microsoft Access table and then show the data in many different ways. With the use of the Datasheet, you can view lots of records at once in the familiar spreadsheet-style format. In this chapter you will also learn how to add records to a table, alter records and also delete records.

## Understanding Datasheets

When a table is opened or the results of a query are viewed, Microsoft Access will show the table or the query results in the Datasheet view. Table data or query results that are displayed in the Datasheet view are most commonly referred to as a datasheet. The appearance of a datasheet can be customized to show very specific data for use as a simple report.

A datasheet can be described as a visual representation of the data that is in a table, or of the results returned by a query. It shows the fields for each of the records from a table, form, or query result in a tabular format. By default, the tables and queries are always opened in the Datasheet view.

- In the Navigation Pane, right-click **on a table or query** > click on the **Open button** on the shortcut menu in order to open the table or the query as a datasheet.

When certain specific formats are applied to rows and columns or added to a Total row, a datasheet can also be used as a simple report. Scrolling upwards or downwards, you will see

the rows (records) that do not fit on the screen and when you scroll left or right you will also see the columns (fields) that do not fit.

Note that most of the behaviors that will be described in this chapter apply majorly to access forms alone. Most of the Access forms show data from just one record at a time and also any type of interaction with the data on a form like that is the same as working with data in a single row of the datasheet.

Datasheets can be customized in such a way that allows you to view data in various ways. For instance, you can have the height of the font size changed, change the column width, and also change the row heights in order to make more or less of the data fit on the screen at once. You can also choose to change the arrangement of the order of the rows and/or the columns in order to have them organized logically. It is also very much possible to have columns locked this way; they will remain in the same position even while you are scrolling to other parts of the datasheet or you can choose to hide them to make them disappear. To have records hidden, all you have to do is filter the data that does not match the specified criteria.

A datasheet is an ideal way to look at various records in a table at the same time. A single record will appear as a row in the datasheet with each of the rows having special information for that particular record. The fields will be displayed as columns in the datasheet with each column having an individual fields content. With this row and column format, you will be able to see all of the data at once.

## Looking at the Datasheet Window

Datasheet helps to organize records basically with the use of the primary key and also organizes fields by the order in the table design. Looking at the top of the Access window is located the title bar which shows the filename of the database, you can also find the Quick Access toolbar and the Ribbon. At the lower part of the Access window, you will find the status bar which shows information about the datasheet. For instance, this can contain the field description information, warning, or a progress bar.

Most of the time, error messages and warnings are always shown in dialog boxes at the center of the screen as against the status bar. If you move the arrow on the screen on some of the items in the status bar, a short message stating what the item is and sometimes what it does will be displayed.

On the right side of the Datasheet, the window is located a scroll bar that is used for showing a different subset of records. As you are moving upwards, a scroll tip will always let you know the record that will be visible first. The size of the scroll box will give you an idea of the total number of records that are shown. At the bottom of the Datasheet window also, you will find a scroll bar that shows different fields. The navigation button that is used to move among records will also be displayed in the bottom-left corner of the Datasheet window.

## Moving within a datasheet

In moving within the datasheet, all that is needed is the use of the mouse in order to show where there should be a change or where you might need to have data included. Furthermore, with the use of the ribbon tabs, the scroll bars, and the navigation button, it can be quite easy to move among fields and records.

Make this quite easy for yourself, think of the datasheet as a spreadsheet without the row numbers and the column letters. Rather, columns have field names and rows are very unique records that have values that can be easily identified in each of the cells.

**Below are the keys that are used for navigation within the datasheet;**

| Navigational Direction | Keystrokes |
| --- | --- |
| Next field | Tab |
| Previous field | Shift + Tab |

| | |
|---|---|
| The first field of current record | Home |
| Last field of current record | End |
| Next record | Downward pointing arrow |
| Previous record | Upward pointing arrow |
| First field of the first record | Ctrl+Home |
| Last field of the last record | Ctrl + End |
| Scroll down one page | PgDn |
| Scroll up one page | PgUp |
| Scroll right one page | Ctrl + PgDn |
| Scroll left one page | Ctrl + PgUp |

## Using the Navigation buttons

The navigation buttons are the six controls that can be found at the lower part of the Datasheet window which can be used to move to another record in the datasheet. The two controls to the farthest left help to move you to the first or the previous record in the datasheet, respectively. The three rightmost controls help to move you to the rightmost controls on the next record, the last record, or the most recent record in the datasheet.

- Make use of the record-number box if you know the record number or the row number by clicking on the **record-number box** and then inserting a **record number** and then pressing the **Enter button**.

# Examining the Datasheet Ribbon

The Datasheet Ribbon offers a way to get the best out of the datasheet. The Home tab has some objects that you normally should be used to and also has some new ones too.

## Views

With the Views group, you can change between the Datasheet view and the Design view.

**Both choices can be seen when you;**

- Click on the **downward pointing arrow** of the view command.

When you click the **Design View**, you will be allowed to make certain changes to the design of the object which includes table, query, and so on. When you click on the **Datasheet View**, it will take you back to the datasheet.

## Clipboard

The clipboard has options for copying and pasting objects. It also offers access to the undo drawing feature. These options work in a similar manner as in Microsoft Word or Microsoft Excel. There are three different options with the paste command and they are Paste, Paste Special, and Paste Append. With the Paste Special option, you have the option of pasting the contents that are in the clipboard in different formats such as the text and CSV. The paste appends the contents of the clipboard as a new record. All that is needed is a row that has a similar structure in the clipboard.

## Sort & Filter

This allows you to make changes to the order of the rows and also limit the rows being shown depending on the criteria you prefer.

## Records

With the record group, you can save, delete or have a new record added to the datasheet. This group also has some commands that display the totals, check spelling errors and also hide columns and change the row height and field width.

## Find

This group allows you to find and replace data and also locate specific records in the datasheet. You can make use of the Select command to choose a particular record or all of the records.

## Window

**There are two buttons in the windows group with which you can control the items like reports, tables forms and so on that are opened in the main Access window;**

- **Size to fit form**: This button when clicked helps to change the size of the form in order to fit the size set when the form was designed initially. Access forms have a border that is sizable; this means that all the user will have to do is move the form to another size.

- **Switch windows**: With the switch window button, you can choose the different open windows that you would like to work with. A form of a report that a user needs might be under another form or report and then the switch windows button also offers a very quick way to choose the objects that are at the top of the other object in the Access main window.

## Text formatting

You can make use of the text formatting group to change the look of the text fields in the datasheet. With the use of these commands, you can change the font, size, bold, italic, color, and so on. When you choose a particular font, for example, this choice will be applied to all the fields in the datasheet. Make use of the Align Right, Align Left, and center commands in the aligning of data with the chosen column.

- Click on the **gridlines command** in order to toggle the gridlines either on or off. Make use of the alternate Row color command to alter the colors of alternating rows in order to ensure that they are all the same.

Note that if the chosen field in the datasheet happens to be a long text field, the Text Formatting group will behave in a quite different manner. When you choose a Long Text field, the font attributes of the individual characters and also the words in the fields can be changed to bold, underline, italics, etc but this is only if the Text Format property is set to Rich Text.

## Opening a Datasheet

**Below are the steps to follow if you want to open a datasheet from the window of a Database;**

- Locate **tables** in the navigation pane.
- Click **twice** on the name of the table you want to open.

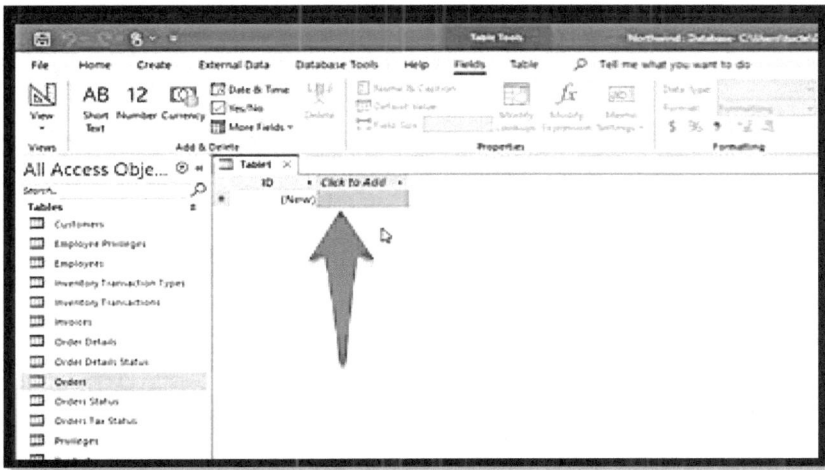

**If probably you are in any of the design windows;**

- Choose the **Datasheet View command** in the View group of the Ribbon in order to view your data in a datasheet.

## Entering a New Data

All the records that are in your table can be seen once you have the Datasheet view opened. If the table has just been created, the new datasheet will be empty. When this is the case, the first row will contain an asterisk sign in the record selector which is to let you know that it is a new record.

The Table Tools tab group that can be found in the Ribbon has almost all you will need to build a complete table. You can choose to indicate the data type, default formatting, indexing, field and table validation, and other table construction tasks from the controls in the Table Tools tab group.

**The new row will be displayed at the bottom of the datasheet when the datasheet already has the records.**

- Click on the **New command button** in the Records group of the ribbon or click on the **New Record button** below the datasheet in order to have the cursor move to the New row or better still you can choose to click on the **last row** where you can find the asterisk button.

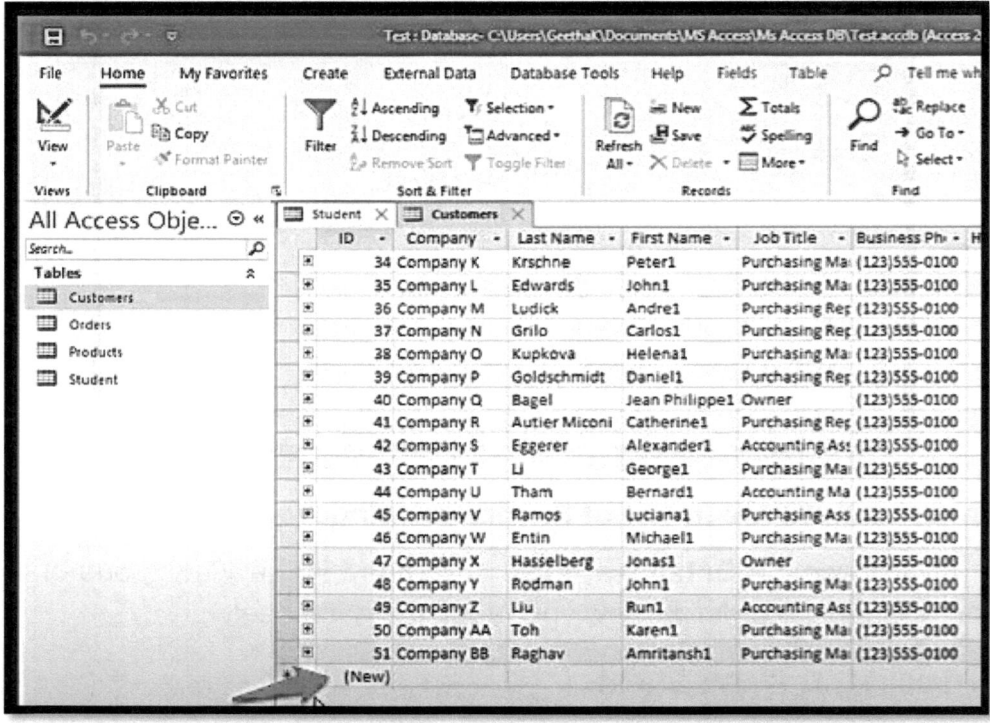

When you are about to start typing the data, the asterisk sign will turn into a pencil which is an indication that the record is being edited or a new record is being added to the datasheet.

**Follow the steps below if you would like to add a new record to the opened datasheet view;**

- Choose the **New button option** in the records group of the Home tab of the Ribbon.
- Enter the **values** for all of the fields of the table, press the **Enter button** to move between fields or you can also choose to press the Tab key.

**There are three options that are often displayed whenever you are adding or editing records in the datasheet.**

- **Record being edited**: this option displays a pencil icon.
- **Record is locked**: this option displays a padlock icon.
- **New record**: this option displays an asterisk icon.

## Saving the record

When you move to another record, the record that has been edited will be saved automatically. When you tab through all the various fields, click on the navigation buttons, and

- click on the **Save button** in the records group of the ribbon, all of these will write the edited record to the database. When the pencil icon leaves the record selector, it is a sign that the record has been saved.

**To get a record saved, all you have to do is**

- Insert the **valid values** into each of the fields. The fields are validated for data type, uniqueness, and any validation rules that might have been inserted into the validation rule property. If your table has a primary key that is not an Autonumber field, then you ought to insert **a unique value** in the primary key field to avoid the display of the error message, the best way to avoid this error message from being displayed is to make use of an AutoNumber field while the data is being inserted as the primary key of the table.

Note that if you made any mistake when inserting a record and you have already saved such a record, the undo button in the Quick Access toolbar can help to change the current record that has been edited to the last record that has not been edited then you can correct your wrong and then save the record again. When saving the record to the disk, you can also choose to make use of the shift+enter button which will help you save the record to the disk without you having to leave the record.

## Understanding automatic data-type validation

There are certain types of data that Microsoft Access automatically validates hence there is no need for you to enter any form of data validation rules for these data when the properties of the table have been indicated. These types of data are; Number/Currency, Date/Time, and Yes/No.

When you enter a letter into a Number or Currency field you won't see a warning immediately that the characters you have entered are not valid but when you leave the field or you click on another field, you will get a warning sign immediately. With this warning sign, you can choose to either enter another value or you will change the column's data type to Text so it can suit what you have inserted.

Validation of Date/Time fields is also done by accessing for date or time values that are valid. A warning message as earlier explained will also be displayed when you try to insert a date like 12/27/02 or a time like 45:16:87.

**For the Yes/No fields it is necessary that you insert any of the defined values below;**

- **Yes:** Yes, True, On,-1, or a number other than 0.
- **No**: No, false, off, or 0.

You also have the freedom to define your own values in the Format property for the field and these values will generally become the acceptable values.

## Knowing how properties affect data entry

Different data-entry technique types have to be used because field types are not all the same. Below are the various type of data entry formats that we have;

## Standard text data entry

In this data entry, assume the first field is Contact ID and it is an AutoNumber and the other fields that are in the table are Short Text fields. Simply skip the contact ID and when this has been done, enter a value in the rest of the fields and move on. The zip code will then use an input mask(0000\ -9999;0;_ ) for the data entry. Note that 9 in an input mask means an optional numeric entry. The zip code input mask needs the first 5 digits but the other 4 digits are basically optional. Unless characters are restricted with an input mask, the Short Text field allows any character.

## Date/Time/data entry

For this option it is best to have the date entry with a short date specified format like 3/17/2022, medium date 17-Mar-2022, or the long date format Thursday, 17th March 2022. Hence if you enter the date as 3/17/22 or 17 Mar 22, Microsoft Access will show the value in the specified format immediately after you exit the field. Oftentimes, dates are stored in the Database without a need for any form of formatting. This way the format you choose for a field will not affect the manner in which the data is stored.

It is worthy to note that formats also affect the display of the data, they in no way change the storage of data in the table. Generally, it is not such a good idea to add an input mask on Date/Time data. Access ensures it takes up the task of validating date and time values. Without any doubt, you are more prone to encountering problems with data entry with an input mask on a date that contains control than you are to avoid trouble by making use of an input mask.

## Number/Currency Data entry with data validation

This option allows you to insert a credit limit as you des re with the use of the validation rule. Whenever the rule is violated, a dialog box will be displayed with the validation text inserted for the field. If you want to make changes to the credit limit that you have already set, you have to do that by changing the validation rule in the table design.

The currency character that will be used by Microsoft Access is dependent on the regional settings options that have been set in the Region and Language settings in the Windows settings.

## OLE object data entry

This option is basically used to insert the Object Linking and Embedding (OLE) object into the database. Note that even if you do not see the object you can still go ahead with this option. The various objects an OLE field can hold include; Bitmap pictures, Sound files, Business graphs, and Word or Excel files.

Objects supported by an OLE server are usually saved in the Access OLE object field. These objects are inserted into a form hence you will be able to see, hear, or even make use of the value. When OLE objects show in the datasheets, you can see a text that tells what the object is all about. **OLE objects can be inserted in two different ways, they are;**

- Pasting from **the clipboard**
- Right-clicking on the **OLE Object field**, and then choosing the insert Object option from the shortcut menu.

## Long Text field data entry

This option helps with the storage of large amounts of alphanumeric data sentences and paragraphs of up to about 1GB of text for each of the fields. When you insert a long text field, you will only be able to see a few characters per time; the rest of the string will then scroll out of sight. When you press the Shift+F2 button it will show a zoom window with a scroll bar with which you will be able to see more characters per time.

The first time a text is displayed in the Zoom window, all the text will be chosen. You can choose to deselect the text by clicking anywhere in the window.

**If by mistake you happen to delete all the text or you change a particular thing you never wanted to change all you have to do is;**

- Click on the **cancel button** to go back to the datasheet with the original data of the field.

# Navigating Records in a Datasheet

At any point in time you might have a need to make changes to the records that you have already inserted into the table. This might be due to a mistake you might have made when you were entering the record initially or as a result of new information, you might want to include.

**When you want to make changes to the record in a table, begin by**

- Opening **the table** if it is not opened already.
- Click **twice** on the table you want to make changes to and this will open the table in the datasheet view.

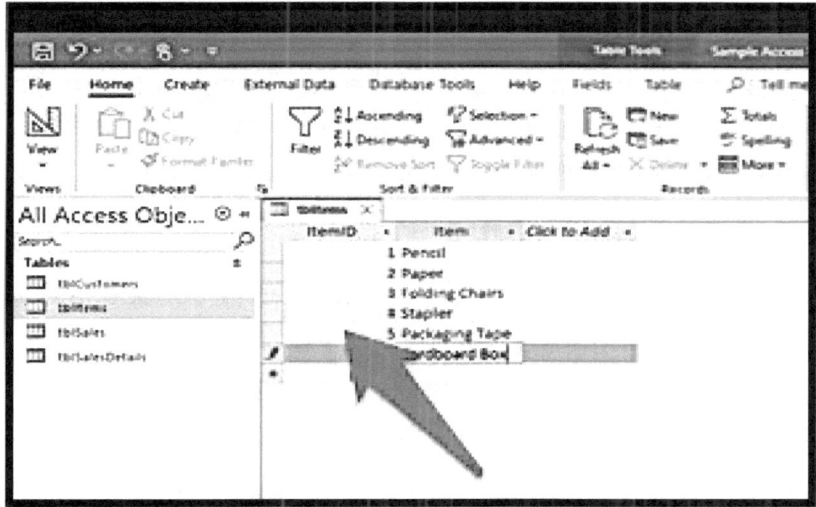

If on the other hand, you are in the design view, click on the **datasheet View button** in order to change views.

When a datasheet that has tables that are related is opened in Microsoft Access, a column with the plus sign will be included, this will help with the indication of records that are related or sub datasheets that are related.

- Click on a **plus sign** of a row in order to open the sub datasheet for the row.

## Moving between records

Moving through the records is quite easy, all you have to do is scroll through the records with the mouse and point the arrow at the record you desire. If you have a very large table, it might be quite difficult to move through all the records by merely scrolling through, you might have to make use of other methods in order to get to the desired record faster.

You can make use of the five Navigation buttons to move quickly between records. All you have to do is click on these buttons to move to your preferred records. If you know the particular number of the record you can then make use of the record number box,

- Insert the record number and then press the **Enter button**.

You can also choose to make use of the Go-To command button in the Find group of the Ribbon in order to move to the First, Previous, Next, Last, and of course the New records.

## Finding a specific value

Finding a particular value in a table can be a very serious task if you do not know the number of the record.

If you do have the number all you have to do is insert the number into the record number box and then press the **Enter button**.

**Alternatively, you can also choose to make use of any of the methods below for finding a value in a field;**

- Choose the **Find command** option from the Find group of the Ribbon.
- Click on the **Ctrl+F buttons**.

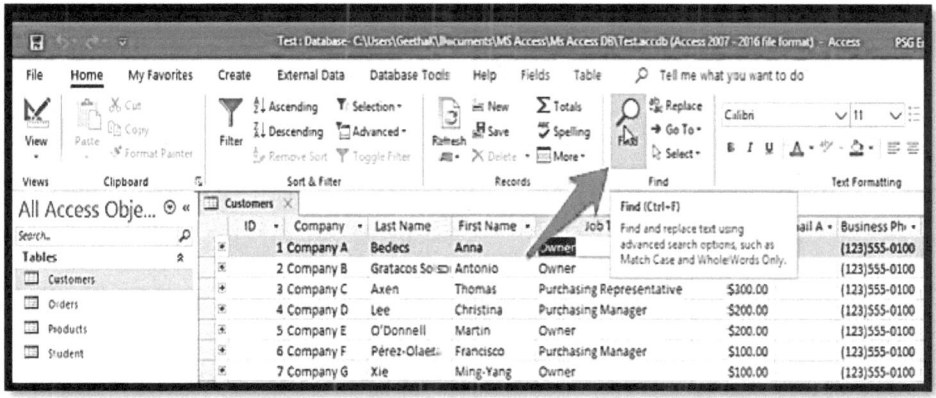

- Make use of the Search box located at the lower part of the Datasheet window.

When you make use of the first two methods listed above, it will display the Find and Replace dialog box. To have the search limited to a particular field, place the cursor in the field you want to search before opening the dialog box. Then alter the settings in the dialog box to find all searches.

With the Find and Replace box, you can gain total control over all the aspects of searches. All you have to do is insert the value you would like to search for in the Find What combo box which has a list of recent;y used searches. You can also choose to insert a particular value or make the option of using a wildcard character.

**Below is a table that contains wildcard characters;**

| Character | Description |
|---|---|
| * Asterisk | This matches any number of characters. |
| ? Question mark | This matches any single character |

| [] brackets | This matches at least one of a list of characters. |
|---|---|
| ! exclamation point | When this has brackets with it, it excludes a list of characters. |
| -hyphen | When it has brackets with it matches a range of characters |
| #hash | This matches only one number |

# Changing Values in Datasheet

If there are no values in the field that you are, you can choose to insert new values into the field. When you insert new values into a field, all you have to do is make use of the same rules as for a new record entry.

## Manually replacing an existing value

Basically, you insert a field that doesn't have characters chosen or the whole value has not been chosen. If you are making use of the keyboard, to insert a field, it's best you choose the whole value. When you then start to type, the new contents you are typing will then replace the value you have already chosen automatically and with ease.

When you choose a field, the value is not chosen yet.

**If you want to choose the whole value with the use of the mouse, make use of any of the methods below;**

- Click **inside the field** and then press **the F2 button**.
- Select **the left of the value** then press down **the left button** of the mouse and then move **the mouse** to choose the whole value.
- Choose only the left of the value when the cursor is being displayed as a large plus sign.

There might be a need for you to change a value that is already existing with the default value of the field.

**All you have to do is to**
- Choose **the specific value** then press the **Ctrl+Alt+Spacebar**. If you would like to change the value already existing with the one from the same field for the record that precedes it, Press the **Ctrl + ; (semi-colon)** to add the current date in the field.

## Changing an existing value

If you would like to change a value that is existing rather than having to **replace the whole value, make use of the mouse and;**
- Click at **the front** of any character in the field in order to activate the insert mode; the value that exists will then move to the right even as you are typing the new value.

If you press **the insert key**, your entry will then change to the Overtype mode; you will then replace a character at a time as you are typing. Make use of the arrow keys to move between characters without having to disturb them.

**You can also choose to erase the characters by simply**
- Pressing the **backspace key** this will erase to the left-hand side or you can choose to press the **delete button** and this will erase to the right-hand side.

**Below is a table that displays some of the various editing techniques;**

| Editing Operations | Keystrokes |
|---|---|
| Insert a value within the field | Choose the point of insertion with your mouse then type the new data. |

| | |
|---|---|
| Toggle the whole field and the insertion point | Press the F2 button. |
| Move the insertion point to the end of the field | Press the end button. |
| Choose the next character | Press the Shift + right arrow key |
| Choose from the point of insertion to the place where the word begins | Press the Ctrl+ Shift + left arrow key |
| Choose from the insertion point to the beginning of the field. | Press the Ctrl+Shift+Home buttons |
| Choose from the insertion point to the end of the field | Press the Ctrl + Shift +End buttons |
| Replace a value that already exists with a new value | Choose the whole value and then insert a new value. |
| Replace a value with the value of the former field | Press Ctrl + the apostrophe sign |
| Replace the current value with the default value. | Press Ctrl + Alt + Spacebar |
| Insert a line break in a Short Text or Long Text field. | Press the Ctrl + Enter buttons. |

| | |
|---|---|
| Insert the current date. | Press the Ctrl +; semi-colon |
| Insert the current time. | Press the Ctrl +: colon |
| Add a new record | Press the Ctrl + plus sign |
| Undo a change to the current field | Press the Esc button or choose the Undo button. |

Note that not all fields can be edited; the following are fields that cannot be edited: Auto number fields, Calculated Fields, and Fields in multi-user locked records.

## Using the Undo Feature

The undo button that is located on the Quick Access toolbar is most times not brightened as there is absolutely nothing to undo. Immediately you begin to edit a record, you can however make use of the button to undo the typing in the field that you are.

**You can also undo a change with the use of the Esc key;**

- When you press the **ESC key** it will cancel any changes made to the field that you are editing currently and it also can cancel the changes that have been made to the last field that you edited if you are not editing any field at the moment.
- When you press the **Esc key** two times you will undo any changes you must have made to the whole current record.

**When you must have typed a value into a field,**

Choose the **Undo button** to undo changes to that particular value. When you must have moved to another field, you can choose to undo the change to the field that prececes the value by simply **clicking** on the undo button.

**You can also undo all the changes that have been made to the current record that has not been saved all you have to do is to**

- Click on the **undo button** after you undo the field.

**After you must have saved a record you can still choose to undo the changes by**

- clicking on the **undo button**.

Nevertheless, after the next record must have been edited, changes that have been made to the record will then become permanent.

## Copying and Pasting Values

The Microsoft office or Microsoft does the job of copying or cutting data to the clipboard based on the type of data that is being copied. This isn't basically a function of Access, note that almost all the Microsoft office suite apps do this.

After copying or cutting data you can paste it into another field with the use of the paste command in the clipboard group of the Ribbon.

You can choose to cut, copy or paste data from any Windows application or from one task to another in Microsoft Access. When you make use of this technique, you can copy the whole records that exist between tables or databases and you can also choose to copy datasheet values to and from any of the Microsoft Office suites.

There are three different options with the paste command and they are; paste, paste special which provides the option of pasting in different formats, and the paste append which pastes the contents of the clipboard as a new record and also provides a row that has almost the same type of structure.

## Replacing Values

If you want to replace a value that is already existing you can find such value with ease when you make use of the Find Replace dialog box.

**Show the Find and Replace dialog box with the use of any of the following methods;**

- Press the **Ctrl +H buttons**.
- Choose the **Replace command** from the Find group of the Ribbon.

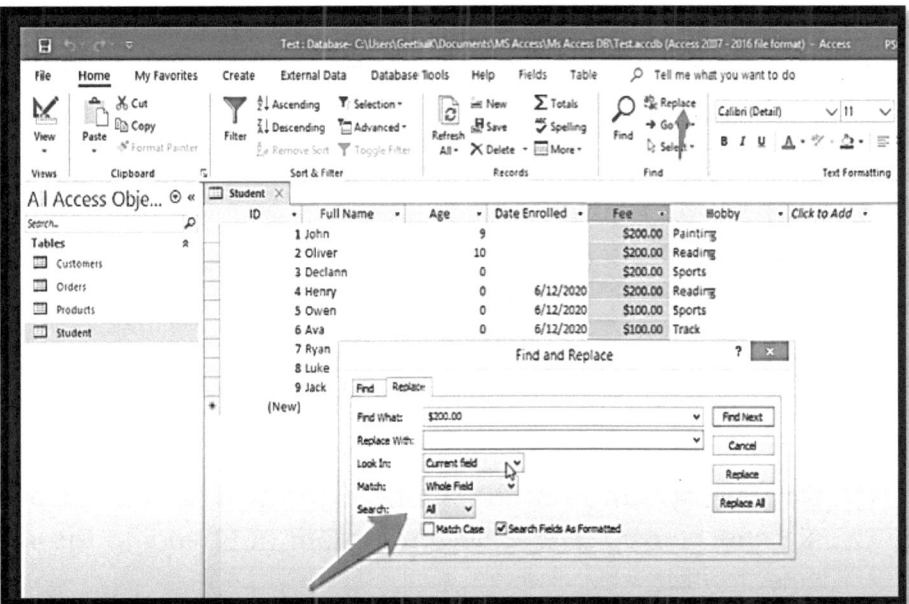

With the Find and Replace dialog box, you can replace a value that exists in the current field or in the whole table. You can also make use of it in locating a particular value and then replace it with another value everywhere that value appears on the field or table.

Once the Find and Replace dialog box is already active, you can choose the Replace tab and insert the value you are looking for in the Find What box then

- Click on the **Find Next button** in order to locate the next occurrence of the inserted value.

**You can choose your search options on the Find tab and then**

- Choose the **Replace tab** option to ensure continuity of the process.

Nevertheless, it is very much easier to do the whole process by making use of the Replace tab. Insert the value that you want to locate and the value that you will like to replace it with.

Once you have finished with the dialog box ensure you have entered the correct information then choose any of the commands that follow; find next which tries to locate the next field that has the same value that has been inserted, cancel which closes the form, and does not complete the find and replace operating, replace which replaces the value in the current field alone and finally replace all which finds all the fields with the value that has been inserted with the Replace With Value. This option is best used if you are sure you want to change all of the values in the box.

## Adding New Records

**There are different ways in which you can add a record to a datasheet and they are;**

- Choose the **last line** of the datasheet where the record pointer is an asterisk.
- Right-click on any **record selector** then click on the **New Record option** from the shortcut menu. The new record will still then be appended to the bottom not minding the record selector that was chosen.
- Press the **Ctrl + the + sign**.

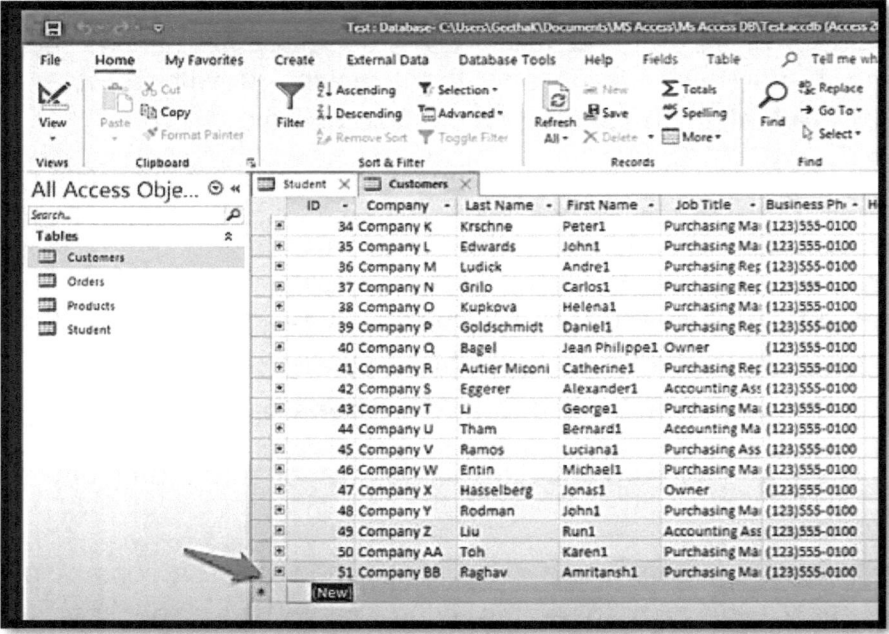

- Move to the **last record** and then click on the **downward pointing arrow key**.

Once you get to another record, insert data into the preferred fields then finally save the record.

# Deleting Records

**If you would like to delete any record in the table, follow the steps below;**

- Choose **one or more records** with the use of the record selectors.
- Click on the **Delete key** then choose the **Delete commands** on the Record group of the Ribbon or you can choose to **right-click a records selector**.

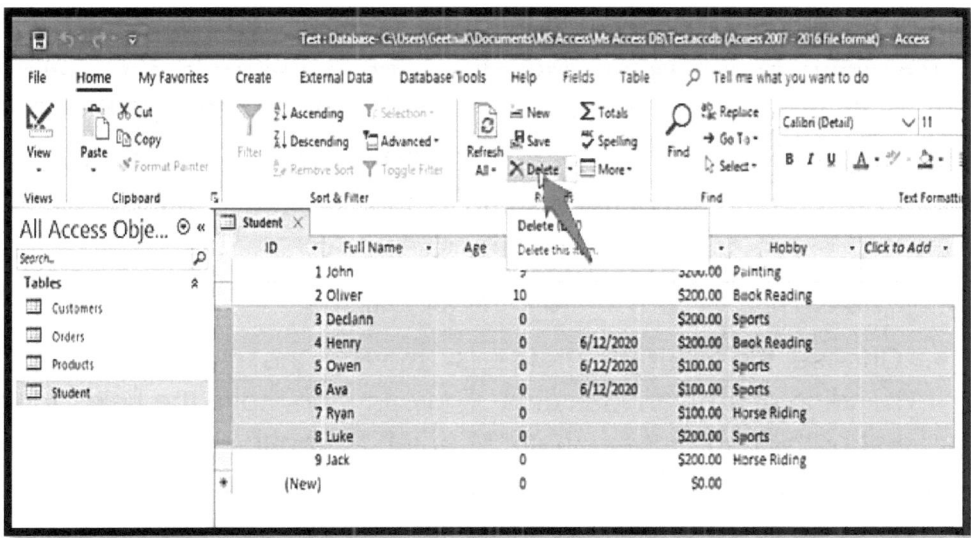

The Delete commands drop-down list has the Delete Record command which helps with the deletion of the current record even if it is not chosen. When you delete a record, a dialog box will be displayed asking to confirm the deletion.

- If you choose **the yes button**, the records will be deleted and if you choose **the No or press the Esc button**, no changes will be made.

**If you want to choose various consecutive records with the use of the keyboard,**

- Press the **Shift + Spacebar** to choose the current record and then press the Shift + downward arrow key or the shift + upward arrow key in order to extend the selection to nearby records.

# Displaying Records

There are some techniques that can help with the increment in productivity when records are either changed or added. To make the entering of data much easier, you can decide to change the field order, hide and freeze columns, change row height or column width, change the display fonts or remove gridlines.

## Changing the field order

By default, Access shows the fields that are in a datasheet in the same manner as they are displayed in the table design. There are times when it is necessary for you to see some fields that are close to each other in order to better analyze the data. If you would like to rearrange the fields,

- Choose **the column** by simply clicking on **the heading of the column** then move the column to your desired location.

With the use of this method, you can choose to move a single field or multiple fields. If you want to move multiple fields,

- Choose the **multiple fields** by moving the mouse across the heading of the various fields. You can then move the fields to the left or the right or past the right or left boundary of the window.

## Changing the field display width

The width of the field display can be changed indicating the specific width to be changed in the dialog box or moving the column border. When you move the mouse over a column border, the cursor will then change to the symbol of s double arrow.

**If you would like to make certain adjustments to the width of a field simply follow the steps below;**

- Place the **mouse arrow** between two column names on the field separator line.
- Move **the column border** to the left side to make the column smaller or the right side to make the column bigger.

Note that when you make changes to the columns that change will not affect the number of characters that are allowed in the field size of the table. All you are doing is changing the value of the amount of viewing space for the data that is in the column.

**You can also choose to resize a column by**

- Right-clicking on **the header** of the column and then choosing **Field Width** from the shortcut menu in order to show the Column Width dialog box.

**Ensure you set the number of characters you would like to fit into the column or you can choose to;**

- Click on the **Standard Width check box** in order to configure the column to its default size.
- Click on **Best Fit to Size** the column to the Widest visible value.

## Changing the record display height

There might be a need for you to make an increment to the row height in order to accept larger fonts or text that makes use of various lines. Make changes to the record(row) height of all rows by moving a row's border in order to make the height of the row larger or smaller.

**If you would like to either increase or decrease the height of a row, follow the steps below;**

- Place **the mouse arrow** between the record selectors of the two rows.
- Move the row border upwards in order to reduce the row heights or move it downwards in order to increase all of the row heights.
- You can also choose to **resize the rows** by clicking on **more > Row height** in the Records group of the Ribbon. The Row Height dialog box will be displayed when you insert the row height in point size. Ensure you check the Standard Height check box in order to return the rows back to their default size.

## Changing the display fonts

By default, Microsoft Access will show all of the data in the datasheet in the Calibri 11-point font. You can make use of the commands and the drop-down list in the Text formatting group in the Ribbon in order to make changes to the datasheet text appearance.

When you configure the font display it will affect the whole of the datasheet. If there is a need for you to see more data on the screen, you can make use of a font that is quite small. If there is a need for you to see a much bigger character, you can choose to increase the size of the font or click on the Bold button.

## Displaying all cell gridlines and alternate row colors

By default, gridlines are displayed between fields and also between records. You can choose to configure the manner in which you would like the gridlines to be displayed by making use of the Gridlines command in the Text Formatting group of the Ribbon.

**Make your choice from the options below in the Gridlines drop-down list:**

- **Gridlines**: Horizontal
- **Gridlines**: Both
- **Gridlines**: None
- **Gridlines**: Vertical

You can also change the color of the background of the datasheet and also make use of the background color and the alternate color in the Text formatting group. The color of all the rows in the datasheet will be changed by the background color palette and the alternate row color palette will change the color of the even-numbered rows.

When you must have changed the Gridlines settings or the alternate row colors, Microsoft Access will then ask if you would like to save the changes that have been made to the Datasheet layout.

- If you want the changes made to be permanent then click on the **Yes button**.

With the Datasheet formatting dialog box, you will have total control over the way the datasheet looks.

**You can open this dialog box by;**

- Clicking on the **Datasheet Formatting** launcher in the bottom right corner of the Text formatting group of the ribbon. Make use of the flat, sunken, And Raised option button beneath the Cell Effect to have the grid changed to a 3-D look.

With the use of the border and lines style drop-down list, you can make changes to the way the grid lines look. You can make changes to the styles of the Datasheet Border and also the Column Header Underline. Make a choice of a different line style for each of the selections in the first drop-down list.

**The different line styles that you can choose from are;**

- Transparent Border
- Solid
- Dots
- Double Solid
- Dash Dot
- Sparse Dots
- Dash-Dots-Dots

## Aligning data in columns

You can have data aligned to either the left, right, or the center with the use of the alignment button. Choose alignments different from the default alignments Access chooses to depend on the data type of the field. **Follow the steps below to make changes to the alignment of the data in a column;**

- Place the **cursor anywhere** within the column whose alignment you want to change.

- Choose the **Align left, center, or Align Right commands** in the Text formatting group of the ribbon.

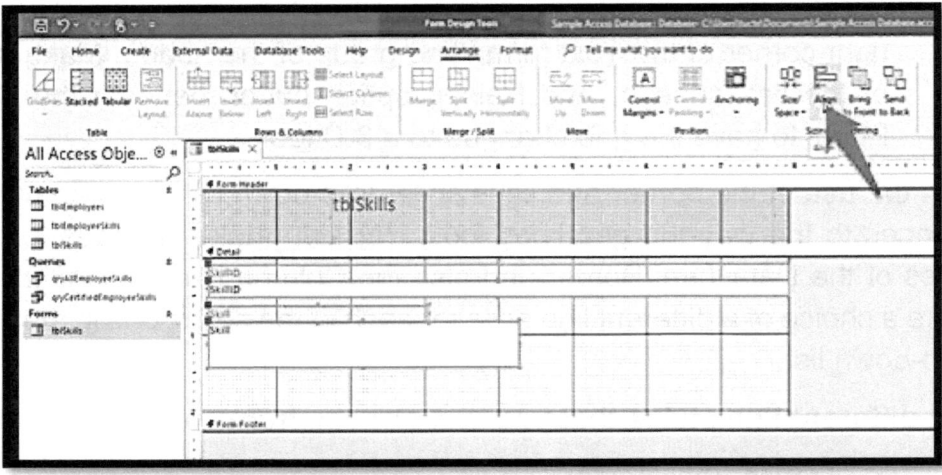

## Hiding and unhiding columns

**You can choose to hide columns by configuring the column width to 0 or by moving the column gridlines to the preceding fields:**

- Place **the cursor anywhere** within the column you want to hide.
- Click **on more,** then hide fields in the records group of the ribbon.

**When you must have hidden a column, you can choose to display the column again by simply choosing;**

- **More > Unhide Fields** in the Record groups of the Ribbon. A dialog box will be displayed enabling you to select columns that are unhidden next to each of the fields. You can also use this dialog box to hide more than one column by **unchecking** the checkbox that is close to the field you would like to hide.

## Freezing columns

Columns can scroll out of the view when you are scrolling either left or right. **To stop this from happening you can simply;**

- Choose the **More option** then choose **Freeze Fields** in the Records group of the Ribbon.

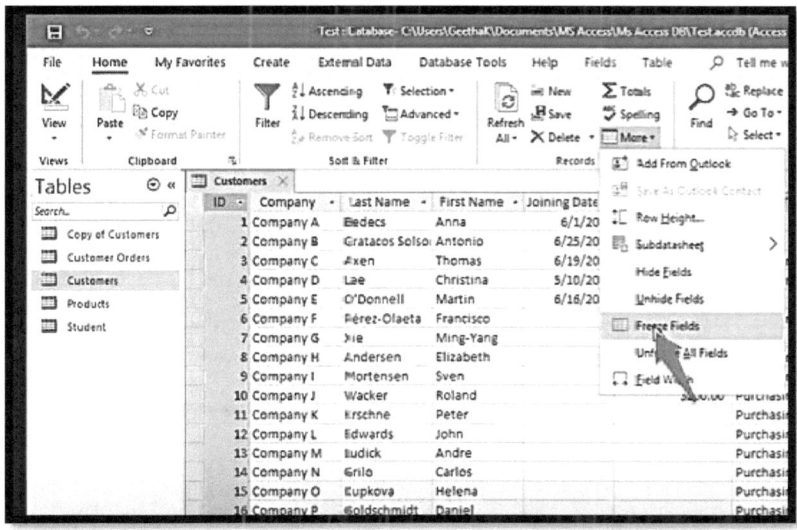

The already frozen columns will still be visible to the far left of the datasheet while the other fields will scroll out of sight in a horizontal manner. If you would like to freeze more than one field at one time, ensure you arrange the field in such a way that they are close to each other. **When you are done scrolling and you want to unfreeze the fields all you have to do is;**

- Choose the **More option** then click on **Unfreeze All Fields option**.

## Saving the changed layout

Saving the data changes is quite easy as when you leave the datasheet all the changes made to the data will be saved but there is every possibility yu lose your layout changes.

When making changes to the datasheet, you will definitely want tHe changes to be made once and for all. If you make any changes to the layout, Microsoft Access will automatically prompt you to save the changes to the layout when you close the datasheet.

- Click on the **Yes option** in order to have the changes saved. The layout can also be saved manually by clicking on the Save button in the Quick Access toolbar.

## Saving a record

Saving a record with Access is done automatically when you leave the record.

**If you are still in the record and you want to save it immediately simply;**

- Press the **Shift + Enter button** or choose the **Save option** from the Records group of the ribbon. When you close the data sheet as a whole, that also helps to save the records.

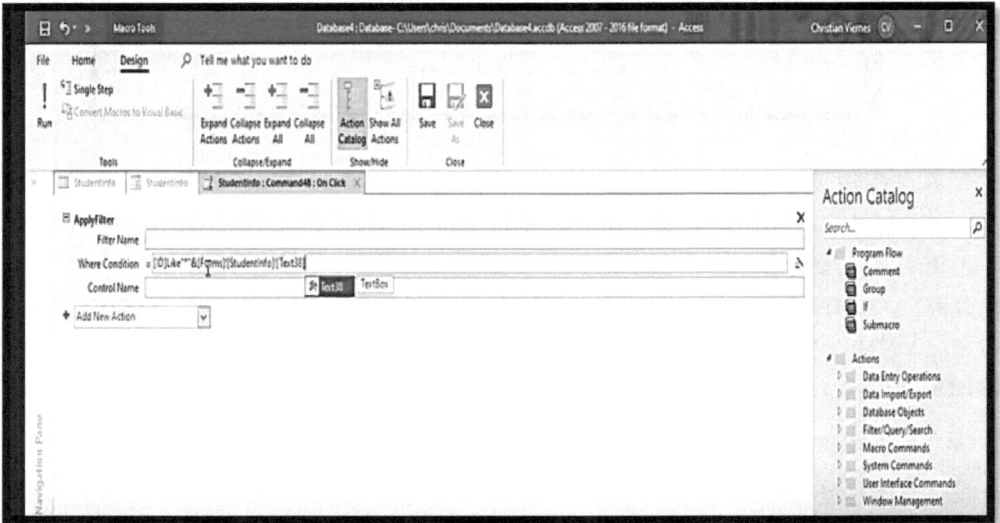

## Sorting and Filtering Records in a Datasheet

There is a group on the Ribbon known as the Sort and Filter group which helps you to reorganize the number of rows and can also help with the reduction of the number of rows. When you make use of the command in this group, the records will be displayed just in the way you would love to see them. Sorting and filtering are tools that help you customize your data and also make the data more convenient to work with.

### Sorting records

When you sort records, this means putting the records together in a logical order with like data being grouped together. As a result of this, data that has been sorted is often easier to read and understand than data that has not been sorted. By default, Microsoft Access sorts records by their ID numbers. Nevertheless, there are various other ways you can sort records.

**Let's take the data belonging to a bakery as an example and see how we can sort such data;**

- Orders can be sorted by order date or by the last name of the customer who must have placed the order.
- Customers can be sorted by their names, by the city, or the zip code where they live.
- Products the bakery offers can also be sorted by name, price, or category.

You can have text and numbers sorted in two different ways; either in ascending order or descending order. Ascending order means the arrangement will be done from the smallest to the largest and descending takes the data from the largest to the smallest.

**Follow the steps below to have records sorted;**

- Choose **the field** you want to sort by.
- Click on **the Home tab** on the Ribbon and find the Sort and Filter group.
- Sort **the field** in either ascending or descending order.
- The table will then be **sorted** by the field.
- If you would like to save the new sort, click on the **Save command option** on the Quick Access Toolbar.

# Filtering a selection

When you filter by the selection, you will be able to choose your records based on the current field value.

**There are basically four choices provided by Microsoft Access when you choose the Selection command; they are**

- Equal "Trucks"
- Does Not Equal "Trucks"
- Contains "Trucks"
- Does Not Contain "Trucks"

An area to the right side of the Navigation buttons at the lower part of the Datasheet window will let you know if the datasheet is currently filtered or not; furthermore, when the Toggle Filter command on the Ribbon is highlighted, this is an indication that the filter is in use. To filter by selection is just to keep adding values. You can always continue to choose values anytime you click on the **Selection command**.

**When you are making use of the Selection command on numeric or date fields,**

- Choose between **the commands** that are made available in order to insert a range of values. Insert the smallest and largest numbers of the oldest and newest dates in order to place a limit on the records to values that fall in the desired range.

When a datasheet has been filtered, each column will have an indicator in the heading of the column which simply lets you know that a filter has been applied to that column. when you move the mouse over the indicator you will see a screen tip that displays the filter.

- Click on **the indicator** and it will indicate additional criteria for you to make use of the shortcut menu. You can also click on the **column heading downward arrow** to have an unfiltered column displaying a similar menu.

The menu has commands that help to sort the column in either an ascending or a descending manner, have the filter cleared from the field, choose a particular filter of your choice, and then check the values you would like to see in the datasheet. The available commands will also change depending on the data type of the column. Whenever there is a case such as this, the Text Filter will allow you to insert criteria that will filter the data based on the type of data that is in it.

The checkboxes that are in this menu also have data that is displayed in the column. In this case, the choices are; Select All, Blanks, and an entry for each of these choices Mark in the table. If you want to filter data but you cannot find the value that you want to make use of and you know what the value is,

- Click on the **text filters** which can be either number filters, date filters, etc.

- Choose **one of the available commands** which will then display a dialog box wherein you can insert the desired value.

# Filtering a form

When you filter by form you will be able to insert criteria that will allow you to enter a single row on the data sheet. When you click on the Filter by Form button, it will transform the data sheet into a single row that has a drop-down list in all of the columns. The drop-down list also has all the unique values for the column. An Or tab at the lower part of the window also enables you to specify OR conditions for each of the groups.

**To filter by form simply go through the following steps below;**

- Click on the **Advanced option** then select **Filter By Form** in the Sort and Filter group of the Ribbon in order to get into the Filter by Form mode.

You can enter as many conditions as you want with the use of the Or tab. **In case you even need a more advanced tweak of your selections simply follow the steps below;**

- Click on **Advanced** then **Advanced Filter/Sort** from the **Sort & Filter group** of the Ribbon in order to get an actual Query by Example (QBE) screen that you can make use of in entering more complex criteria.

# Aggregating Data

Microsoft access data sheets offer support to a total row at the bottom of the sheets. The total row can be opened when you click the Totals button in the Record groups on the Home tab of the Ribbon. The columns in the total row can be configured to various aggregation calculations such as Sum, Average, Minimum, Maximum, Count, Standard Deviation, or Variance.

**If you would like to make use of the Total row simply follow the steps below;**

- Open **a table or form** in the Datasheet view then click on the **Totals button** in the Records group on the Home tab of the

Ribbon. Microsoft Access will then add a Total row at the lower part of the datasheet that can be found just beneath the New row.

When you click on a column in the Total row, it will change the datasheet cell to a drop-down list. The items that are in the drop-down list are specific to the data type of the column.

The Totals calculation chosen should be dynamic. When you change data in the datasheet or in an underlying table, the calculation result that is shown in the Total row will be updated automatically after a rather short delay.

When you recalculate lots of totals you will get a small performance penalty hence you might want to have the Total row hidden when you are not making use of it. The Totals option chosen for the columns in the datasheet will still be the same. If you close the datasheet for any reason and open it again, the Total row will still be there intact!

**But if for reasons best known to you, you have a need to remove the Total row,**

- Open the **datasheet** then choose the **click Totals button** in the Records group on the Ribbon.

## Printing Records

All the records in your datasheet can be printed in a simple row and column layout.

**The simplest and easiest way to print a record is to;**

- Click **on File**
- Print and **choose one of the print options.**

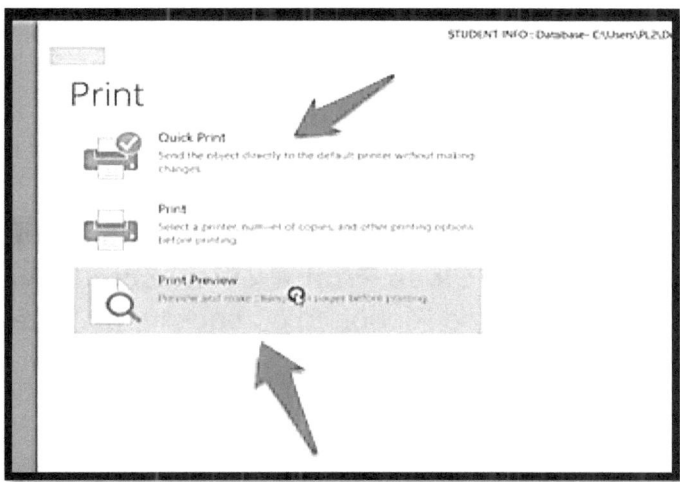

If you go straight to choosing the print option and not Quick print or print preview, Microsoft Access will show the print dialog box.

**From this box you can choose to customize your printout by choosing from various options;**

- **Copies**: this option helps to determine the number of copies that should be printed.
- **Collate**: this helps to determine the various copies that are collated.
- **Print Range**: this helps to print the whole datasheet or just the chosen pages or records.

The printout will show all the layout options that are in use when the datasheet is being printed. Columns that are hidden as of this time will not be printed. Gridlines only print when the properties of the cell gridlines are on. The printout will also show the specified row height and column width.

## Previewing Records

Even when you have all the needed information in the datasheet and you are ready to print, it is best to check all the height and width of the columns and rows to ensure they are well adjusted or if there is a need to make adjustments to your font size before printing.

**To preview your print simply**

- Click on the **print preview command** below the Print menu in order to show the Print Preview window. The default view is the first page I'm single page preview. Make use of the Ribbon commands to choose various views and you can also choose to zoom in and out.
- Click on the **print button** to print the datasheet on the printer.
- Click on the **Close Print Preview command** located on the right side of the Ribbon to go back to the Datasheet view.

# CHAPTER 6
# IMPORTING AND EXPORTING DATA

**In this chapter,** I will introduce you to importing data from a source outside the Database and also exporting data away from the Access database. I will also show you how you can create external files from the data via exporting. Importing data means you increase the data that you already have in the database like an XML file. And exporting from Access also means that you create other data away from Access databases like XML or EXCEL files which have data that is stored in Access.

## How Access Works with External Data

In the world of today exchanging data between databases is actually very possible. Information is usually always saved in a wide variety of application programs and data formats. Access databases as with some other databases have their own file format which is created specifically to offer support for rich data types like OLE objects. Most of the time, however, you need more than the Access database alone to get the job done. More times than often, there is a need to move data from one Access database file to another or make use of data from another program that has a different but unique format.

## Types of external data

External Data are those data stored outside the current database. This might be data saved in another Microsoft Access database or it might be one saved in various other file formats like ISAM(Indexed Sequential Access Method), spreadsheet, ASCII, SQL, Server Oracle, or even a text.

Microsoft Access can move data among various categories of applications which includes Windows applications, Macintosh applications, database management systems, text files, and even mainframe files.

## Ways of working with external data

Most times as earlier established there is a need for you to move data from another application to the Access database and vice versa. There might be a need to get some data that you already have in an Excel sheet. You can easily have all of that data imported automatically into the database. Microsoft Access has certain tools that can be used in the movement of data with other databases or even with a spreadsheet file.
**The various ways Access does this includes;**

- **Linking**: Linking to data designs a connection to a table that is in another Access database or rather links to the data from another format. When linking, the data in the source file format like Excel or XML is used. The linked data will still remain the main file. Note that the file that had the linked data should not be moved, changed, or deleted because if this is done Access will be unable to locate the data when next it is in need of it.
- **Importing**: When you import data from a data source like another Access database or another application database in general, the data that is imported will be converted to the appropriate Access data type, stored in a table, and also managed by Access from that point onwards.
- **Exporting**: Exporting takes data away from your Access database to another Access database or another file of an application. Unlike importing if the location of the source data is changed, this doesn't affect the exported data.

## When to link to an external data

Linking to external data is basically quite different from importing data. Linked data will still be in its native format. When you establish a link to external data, you can then build queries, forms, and reports that present such data.

After you must have designed a link to external data, the link will remain established permanently unless you remove the link by yourself.

The linked table will be displayed in the Navigation pane just like any other Access table the only difference that will be noticed will be its icon.

Furthermore, if the data allows for more than one user, the users of an application can choose to make changes to the data as can the users of the applications written in the data sources' native database formats like FoxPro, dBase, or paradox. The main difference between a linked table and a native table is simply that you cannot alter the structure of a linked table from within the Access database.

The major disadvantage of working with tables that are linked is the fact that you will not be able to enforce referential integrity between the linked tables except if the linked tables are all in the same external Access database or they are in another database that offers support for referential integrity.

When tables are linked they sometimes have very poor performance as to local tables. Based on the source and also the location of the source data, users might experience quite a little delay when a form or report that is based on linked data is opened.

## When to import external data

When you import data into an Access table, Access will make a copy of that data and then place it in the Access table. After Access must have imported the data, it will treat the data just like any other Access table. Furthermore, not you nor Access can know where the data must have come from. Hence, data that is imported provides the same performance and flexibility just like any other Access table data.

Since importing makes another copy of the data, you might feel the need to delete the old file after you must have imported the copy into Microsoft Access. However, there are times when you might want to keep the old records also.

One of the main reasons why you might import data s to tweak the data in such a way that it meets all of your needs. Once you have imported a table into an Access database, you can then work with the new table although it has been built in the current database.

With the use of linked tables though, there is a limit to the number of changes you can make. In addition, since linked tab es point to external files, which Access expects to locate in a specified location, it can make the distribution of your applications a little more difficult.

Note that if you will be exporting data often from the same source, you can choose to automate the process with the use of s macro or a VBA procedure. This can be of immense benefit for the times when you have a need to import data from an external source on a regular schedule or when you have transformations that are quite complex that must be added to the imported data.

## When to export data

There are various reasons why you might have a need to export data from a database. You might want to analyze the data and use it for another purpose, exchange data with someone else, migrate to a new software application, etc. Anytime data is exported, Microsoft Access will convert the data to an external format and then copy the data to a file that can be read with ease by another application.

Though formats that are unsupported are quite rare, there might be a need for you to work with data from a program that is not stored in an external database or file format that is supported. When such a case arises, the programs can oftentimes export or have their data converted to formats that can be recognized by Access. If you would like to use the data in these programs, have the data exported to a format that can be recognized by Access then import it into Access.

# Options for Importing and Exporting

In this section, we will be looking at the options used in importing and exporting data. Most developers like to use Access because it has the capability to use and also has databases changed among a number of applications. For example, there might be a need for you to collect data from SQL or Oracle, or even an XML document. This can be done with ease using Microsoft Access as it can move data among various categories of applications, database engines, and platforms such as mainframes and Macintosh computers.

The import and link group has the following options; New Data Source, Saved Imports, and Linked Table Manager.

**The drop-down menu of the New Data Source Option has about four categories which have various data formats like;**

- From File
    - Excel
    - HTML Document
    - XML File
    - Text File
- From Database
    - Access
    - From SQL Server
    - From Azure Database
    - dBase File
- From Online Service
    - SharePoint List
    - From Dynamics 365(Online)
    - From Salesforce
    - Data Services
- From Other Services
    - ODBC Database
    - Outlook Folder

## Importing External Data

Import had to do with bringing in an Access database. The external data will remain in its normal position but when it has been imported a copy of it will be in the Access database. When you bring in a file, Access will convert a copy of the data from an external source like SQL into records in an Access table. The external data source is not changed when importing the data. Also, note that there will be no connection to the external source upon the completion of the import process.

You can import data to new tables or tables that are a ready in existence. There is no type of data that cannot be imported to a new table. Nevertheless, there are some types of imports like spreadsheets and text files that do not have a table structure that can be used with Access. Anytime there is a case like this, Access will design a table structure for you. If you will love to have control over the table, ensure you design the table before you import it.

## Importing from another Access database

You can import data from another database into the database you are currently working on. Objects like tables, queries, forms, reports, macros, or modules can be imported.

**To complete this process simply follow the steps below;**

- Open the **destination database** you would like to import.
- Choose the **External Data tab**.
- Select **Import & Link** then choose **New Data Source> From Database> Access** then click on the **Browse button** to choose the **filename** of the source database.

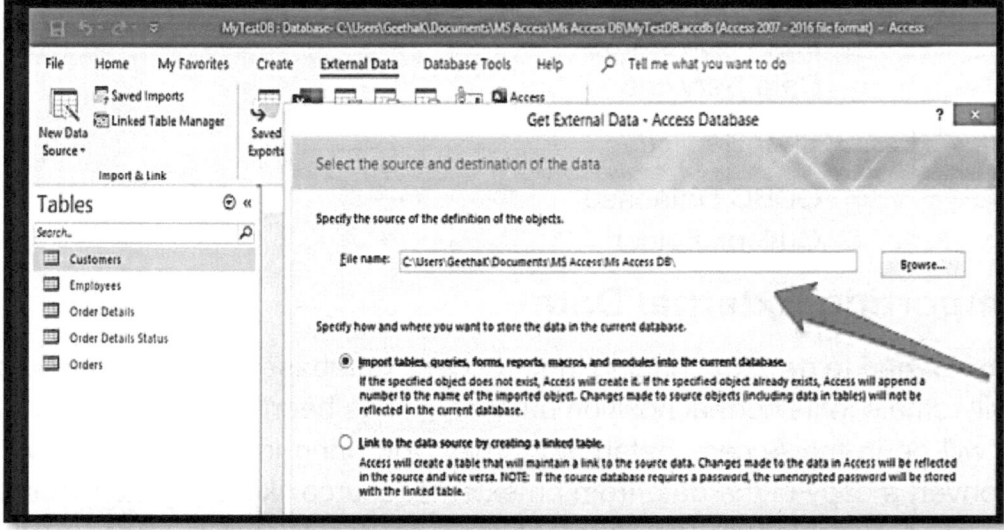

- Choose the **Import tables, Queries, Forms, Reports, Macros, and Modules** into the Current Database option button and then click on the **Ok button**.

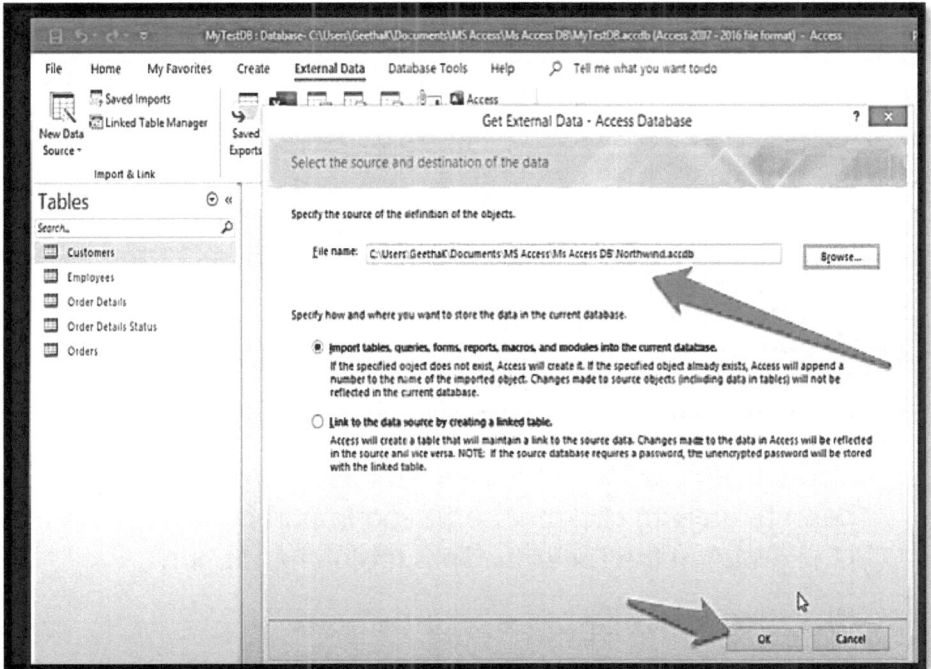

- Choose **a table** and then click on **the OK button**. If you already have an object in the destination database, a sequential number will then be added to the name of the object you just imported. For example, if the name of the object that is already there is tblprodcts then the name of the object being imported will be tblproducts1.
- Check the **Save import** steps checkbox.
- Give a name for the import process so as to make it quite easy to bring back the purpose of the saved import then click on the **Save import option**.

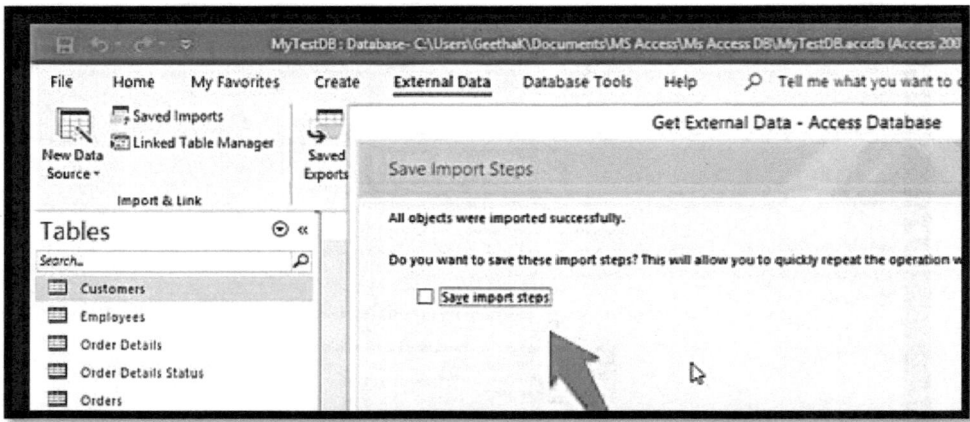

You can choose to run the saved import option much later all you need to do is to click on the Saved Imports button in the Import & Link group of the External Data tab of the Ribbon.

## Importing from an Excel spreadsheet

You can choose to import data from an Excel spreadsheet just ensure you follow the basic rule which states that each cell in a column must have the same type of data. Anytime you are about to import data into a new table, Access will make a guess at the type of data that is in the table this way it will be able to assign the data appropriately to the field it should belong.

You can import the whole data from an Excel spreadsheet or you can choose to import just the data from the named range of cells. When the range of cells is named, it can make importing pretty much easier with Microsoft Access.

**Follow the steps below to import from an Excel sheet;**

- Start by **opening the database**.
- Click on the **Import & Link option>New>Data Source> From File> Excel on the External Data tab**.

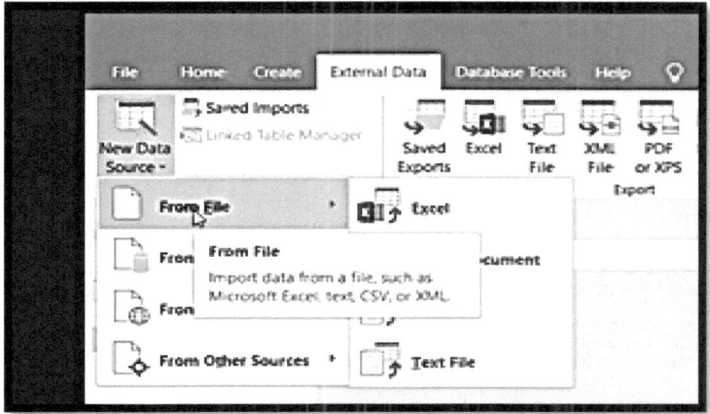

- Browse through till you get to the Excel file
- Choose **Import Source Data** into a New Table in the Current Database then Click on the **OK button.**
- Choose a **worksheet** or named range then click on the **Next button**.

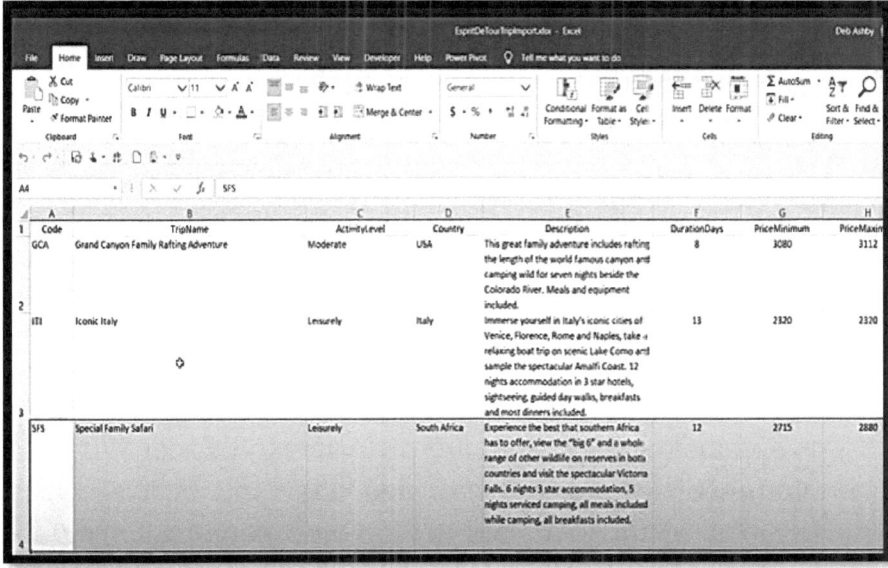

- On the next screen, choose the **First Row** that Contains Column Headings check box and then click **Next**.
- On the screen that follows, you can override the default field name and data type, remove the fields from the import and then design

an index on a field. When you are through, click on the **Next button**.
- On the next screen, configure **a primary key** for the new table and then click **Next**.
- Indicate **the name** of the new table and then click on the **finish button**.

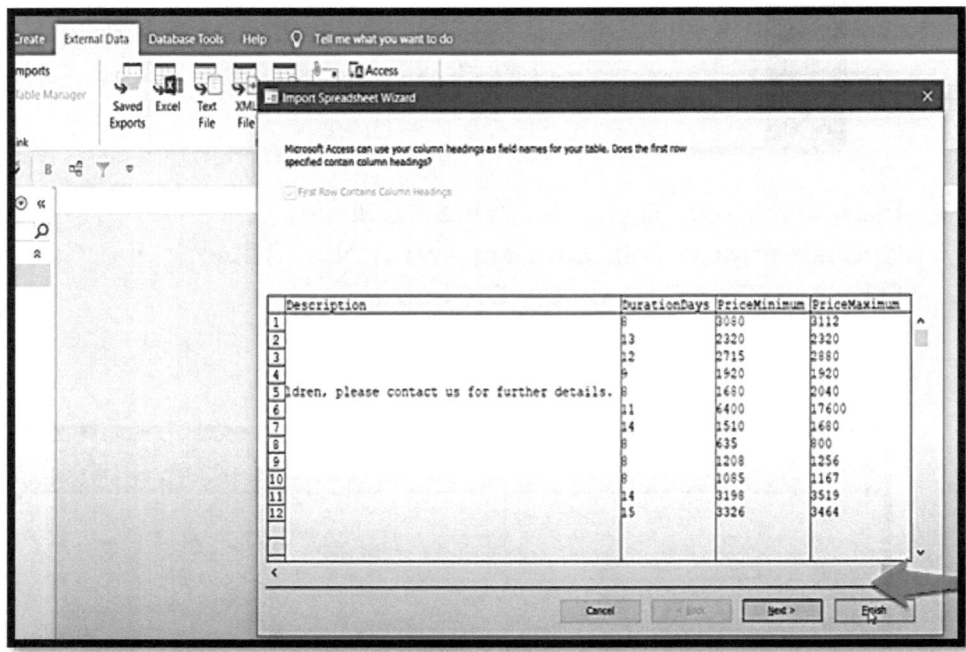

- If you would like to, save the import process for later execution.

## Importing a SharePoint list

Basically, a SharePoint list is a collection of content that has rows and columns and looks much like a table in Microsoft Excel. It can be used to store information where you can add attachments like documents or images. Since SharePoint lists are on web servers, their data can be accessed across any network that is qualified for users. With this, Access can share data virtually in any part of the world.

Microsoft Access might just continue as a component in enterprise environments since SharePoint is deployed on various corporate intranets.

## Importing data from text files

Data can be brought from a text file into Access in two different ways. If you would like to have a copy of the data then you can choose to edit the data within Access and have the file imported into a new or existing table by making use of the Import Text Wizard. If all you want to do is view the latest source data that is within Access for richer querying and reporting then you can simply create a link to the text file in your database with the use of the Link Text Wizard.

A text file has unformatted readable characters like letters and numbers and also special characters like tabs, line feeds and carriage returns. Microsoft Access offers support for the following file name extensions- .txt, .csv, .asc, and .tab.

If you would like to make use of a text file as a course file for the purpose of importing and linking, the contents of such a file must be well organized such that the linking and importing wizards will be able to divide the contents into a set of records(rows) and each record into collection fields (columns). Text files that are well organized will fall into either Delimited files or Fixed width files.

## Delimited text files

In a delimited file, each of the records will be displayed on a separate line and the fields will also be separated by a single character known as the delimiter. The delimiter can be any character that does not show in the field values like a tab, semicolon, comma, space, and so on.

**Below is an example of comma-delimited text;**
- , Company A, Anna, Bedecs, Owner
- , Company C,    Thomas, Axen, Purchasing Rep
- , Company D, Christina, Lee, Purchasing Mgr.

**If you would like to import a delimited text file, take the following steps below;**
- Start with **opening the database**.
- Choose the **External Data tab**.
- Select **Import & Link > New Data Source>From File>Text File**.

- Browse to the file, choose the **import option button** then select the **ok button**.
- On the next screen, choose **the Delimited button** and click on the **Next button**. This will then display the Text Wizard. This screen allows you to indicate the separator used in the delimited file. ( Separator is the character that I placed between fields in a delimited text file which is often a comma or semicolon although another character can also be used.
- Choose the **delimiter** that separates your fields; if the delimiter used is not a common one, click on **Other** and insert the **delimiter in the other box.**
- If the first row has field names for the table that has been imported, all you have to do is choose the **First Row Contains Field Names** checkbox after which you can then click on the **Next option**. The screen where you will see the next steps similar to the ones you will take when importing Excel worksheets. You can also make some changes like the field names, indicating a primary key and you can also save the import option for future use.

Note that the separator that should be used must not have been used in any of the fields in the text file that has the separator character as data. For example, if you have chosen to use a comma as a separator ensure that you do not use a comma in any of the fields else Access will have a problem importing the file. There is a solution to this problem however which is Making use of double-quotes. With this, the comma used in the fields will not be mistaken to be a separator. Oftentimes single or double quote marks are used for this purpose and bring a solution to the issues of special characters contained within data fields.

## Fixed-width text files

In a fixed-width file, each of the records are displayed on a separate line and the width of each of the fields will be consistent across records. For instance, the first field of every record will always be seven characters long, the second field will be twelve characters long, etc. If the actual length of a field's value is not consistent from one record to the other, the values that are not up to the required width must be padded with space characters. Below is an example of fixed-width text.

- Company      A      Anna       Bedecs      Owner
- Company      C      Thomas     Axen        Purchasing Rep.
- Company      D      Christina  Lee         Purchasing Mgr.

**Below are the steps to follow if you want to import a fixed-width text file;**

- Open the **database**.
- Choose the **External Data tab**.
- Click on **Import & Link** then select **New Data Source>From File>Text File**.
- Browse to the text file you want to import then click on the **Import button** then click **OK**. This will then show the first screen of the Import Text Wizard and it will show the data that is in the text file and allow you to make your choice between delimited or fixed-width
- Choose **Fixed Width** and select the **Next option**.
- Adjust the field widths as needed. Note that Access will always take a guess at the best breaks you should use for the fields and its guesses are based on the most consistent spacing that is across rows. With this, you can trust that the field breaks will be very consistent.
- Click on the **Advanced button** at the lower part of the wizard. This will show the Import Specification dialog box which will allow you to change the default formats for dates, times, indexing, and data types. It will also offer an option for you to skip fields that you do not wish to import.
- Make sure that the DATE Order is fixed at MDY and the Four-Digit Years check box is also chosen.
- Choose the **Leading Zeros** in the Dates check box.
- Click on the **OK button** to dismiss the Import dialog Specification dialog box.
- You can proceed with the renaming of Import Text Wizard Screens.

When text files with Data-type are imported, always ensure that you have a separator between the months, days, and year. Microsoft Access will report an error if any field is being specified as Date/Time type and no delimiter is used. Anytime you are exporting the day fields, the separator is usually not needed.

With the use of the Time Delimiter option, you can choose to indicate another separator that will be between the parts of times values that are in a text file. If you would like to change the separator all you have to do is insert another separator in the Time Delimiter box.

- Choose the **Four-Digit Years checkbox** to indicate that the year portion of a date field is formatted with about four digits. When you check this box, dates that include a century like 1981 or 2002 can be imported. Note that the default setting here is four-digit years.

## Importing and exporting XML documents

This process is quite an easy one in Microsoft Access. Basically, XML is used in the transfer of information between platforms such as applications, Operating systems, or companies. XML is used for raw data, metadata, and also the processing of data. You can say that almost all Access developers will always at a point have to either import or export data in XML format.

**Below are the steps to follow when you want to export data from Access to an XML file:**

- Open the **database.**
- Open **the field** you would like to export in the Datasheet view.
- Click on the **External Data tab** and choose **XML File** in the Export section.

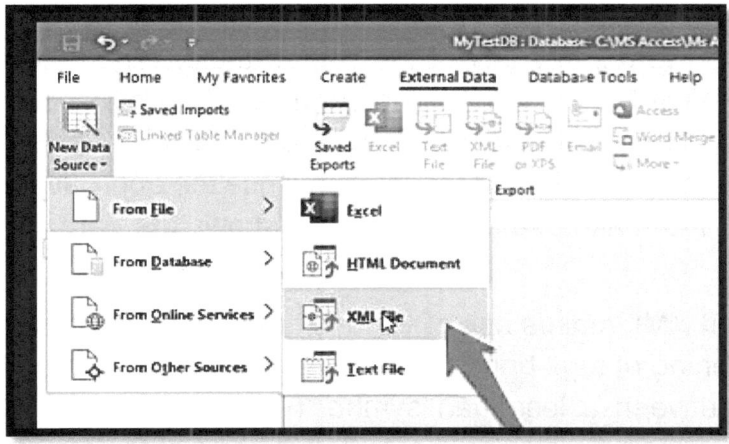

- Give the file a name that usually ends with. XML and then click on **the OK button**. This process will bring up the export dialog box which has various options which can be used to specify advanced options for the XML export process. When you click on the **More options button** another dialog box will be opened containing various important XML settings. Oftentimes, there is always a need for schema files which is needed for the perfect understanding of complex XML by some other applications. The schema file is preferred to be used because Access opens it automatically for data exported in XML format.
- Click on the **OK button** to have the process exported.

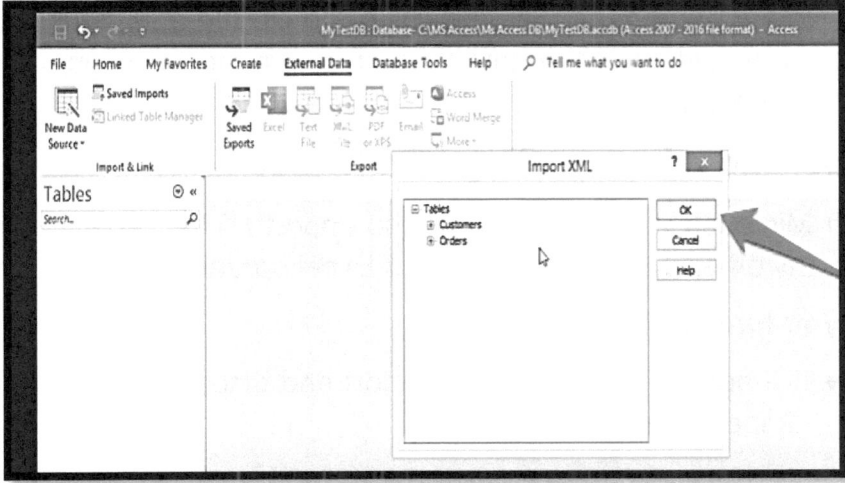

XML schema files have information like data types of each of the fields and also the primary key of the source table. When the XML export is further refined, it will indicate just how the XML data should be displayed in an application with the use of exported data. Most times there is always no need for the XML file presentation since the application that has been designed to make use of the XML file shows the data as needed by its users.

Note that XML makes use of various tags to provide context to the data. The opening of tags brings about the start of structure and also has text found between a less-than symbol (<) and a greater-than symbol(>). When the tags are closed, it signifies the end of the structure.

**Follow the steps below to have Access import XML files;**

- Click on the **Import & Link > New Data Source>From File>XML File** on the External Data tab.
- Locate the **XML file** which usually ends with.xml then click on the **Open option** then click on the **OK button**. This will also display the Import XML dialog which tells how Access will interpret the XML data.
- Click on the **OK button**.
- Click on the **Close button**.

With the completion of the above steps, Access would have perfectly imported the XML file as a table and you can then choose to rename the file. Note that the tags that are within the file tag and its closing tag will define the fields and the data that can be found between the field tags will also become the new table.

## Importing and exporting HTML documents

With Microsoft Access you can also import HTML tables with ease as with any other database, text file, or Excel spreadsheet.

**All you have to do is;**

- Choose an **HTML file** to import and also make use of the HTML import Wizard.

To begin this process you have to start by exporting a table in order to develop an HTML file then you can have the file imported back into **Microsoft Access in order to have a new table created;**

- Open the **database** and choose the **specific table** you would like to export from the Navigation pane.
- Choose the **External Data** tab then click on the **More drop-down button** that is located in the Export drop-down button then choose HTML Document.
- Ensure you **indicate an HTML file** as the export destination in the Export -HTML Document dialog box.
- Choose your **preferred HTML** output options and click on the OK button. Immediately after you click on the **OK button** the HTML export will be completed already.

Exporting Data with Formatting and Layout which is another option in the Export-HTML Document dialog box shows more export options. The most important of these options is the fact that it allows you to indicate an HTML template for your export

Importing the HTML is like importing a text file, the Import HTML Wizard also has almost the same screen options as the Import Text Wizard-like defining data types for fields and also having to identify the primary key.

## Importing Access objects other than tables

With Access you can import other objects like queries and forms into Access. You can copy the object and then have it pasted which is also the easiest way but with the import option you have more options.

**Objects are imported basically when there is a need for you to do one of the following;**

- Copy the **design and layout of a form**, a report, or some other object.
- Copy the **latest version of a form**, report, or other objects. To do this you can choose to **create an import specification** the very first time you import the object then make use of the specification to later repeat the operation.

Note that when you import an object into an Access database, there is only a little difference between opening another database and then exporting the object from the first database created.

**The two main difference that exists between importing and exporting objects are;**

- You can have more than one object imported with just one operation but you cannot export more than one object with a single operation. If there is a need for you to export more than one object it is best you open the destination the object should be and then perform an import operation from there.
- In addition to database objects, you can also choose to import relationships that exist between tables and any other import or export specification which also includes menu bars and toolbars. You can also choose to import the query as a table. Take note that these options listed are not offered with exporting.

**Follow the steps below to complete this import process;**

- Open **the database**.
- Click on the **Import & Link >New Data Source> From Database>Access** then you can choose the **option** to import from another Access database. A screen will be displayed which will let you know that you can indicate if you would like to import database objects or link to tables in an external Access database.
- Locate the **file** and then click on the **Open button** then click on the **OK button**.

Anytime you are adding tables, forms, queries, modules, or macros all in the same import, you can choose objects from each of the tables and then have all of the objects imported at once.

## Importing an Outlook folder

**Microsoft automatically saves messages, contacts, appointments, tasks, notes, and journal entries in one of the following locations;**

- In a personal storage folder which is also known as a .pst file on your computer.

- In a mailbox that can be found on the server. Your mailbox is usually found on the server if you make use of the Microsoft Exchange Server.

You can make a backup of your .pst file to bring back or move your outlook data if you happen to experience a hardware failure, lose data suddenly, or have a need to transfer data from one computer to another computer or you have to transfer data from one hard disk drive to another disk drive.

You can have outlook data imported into a new table or an already existing one, include a primary key, indicate data type, and then save the import process for much later execution.

# Exporting to External Formats

An export helps with the copying of data from an Access table to another application or data source like an XML document. The expected result makes use of the format of the destination data source and not the format of an Access database. You can choose to copy data from an Access table or query into a separate external file. You can also export tables to various other sources.

## Exporting objects to other Access databases

When you want to export an object to an Access database, you can choose to export any type of Access object (tables, queries, forms, reports, etc). As against importing which most times enables you to import lots of objects at the same time, you can only export one object per time with exporting.

**If you would like to export other objects simply follow the steps below;**

- Open the **source database** and choose **an object** that you would like to export.
- Select the **Access button** in the Export group of the External Data tab. This will then display the **Export -Access Database dialog box**.
- Make use of the **Browse button** to find the destination Access database. Make sure that the database is not opened at the time

you want to export it. If it happens to be open, there might be a conflict.
- Click on the **Save button** then click on the **OK button**. If the object you are exporting is already in the database you want to export to, you will be asked to replace the object in the target database. If you do not, you won't be able to create another object in the database you want the object to be.
- Select **Definition and Data** and then click on the **OK button**.
- The last step of the wizard will allow you to save the export configuration for later use. If you will probably be performing an export frequently, this option can come in very handy.

## Exporting through ODBC drivers

WItH Microsoft you can also export files or objects through ODBC( Open Database Connectivity). ODBC-compliant databases come with an ODBC driver that works as the connector between Access and the database. Most of the very common databases which include Access are compliant with ODBC.

**Follow the steps below to export files or objects through ODBC;**
- Open **Access** and choose **the object** you would like to export.

- Click on the **More button** then click on **ODBC Database** in the Export group of the External Data tab. This will display the Export dialog box.

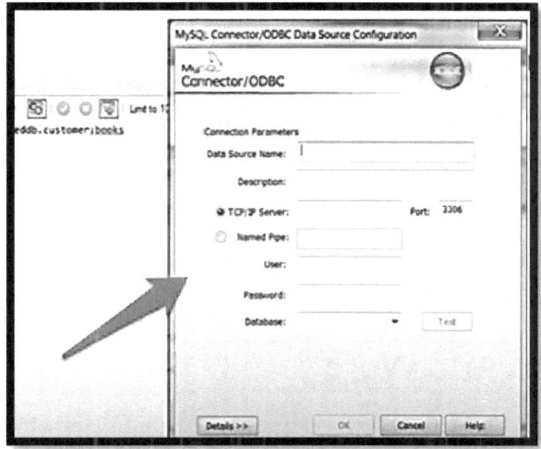

- Enter **a name** for the table or you can also choose to simply **click on the OK button** in order to make use of the default name.
- Choose the appropriate driver for your database from the **Select Data Source dialog box**.
- Lastly, save the **export steps** if need be(do so if you are exporting very often).

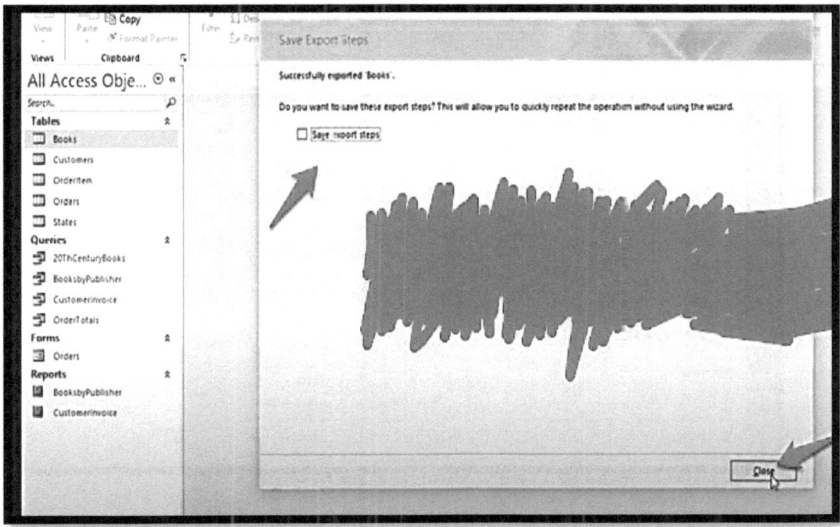

Note that some ODBC drivers will display a prompt for more information like the name of the database or the name of the table. When the export must have been completed you can make use of the table in the other database.

# Exporting to Word

With Access, there are two major ways in which you can transfer data to word; you can choose to either export to Rich Text Format (RTF) or merge Word, the Rich Text Format is a plain text file that has a very special characters which help with defining the formatting.

When you choose the option of exporting to an RTF a document with an RTF extension will be created and not a normal Word document.

## Merging data into Word

This is by far the best method of exporting Word. With Word Merge, you can gain control of where you would like your data to be used finally in a Word document. This can be of great use if you happen to be dealing with tasks like producing reports, creating file folder labels, and addressing envelopes.

**If you would like to create a file folder labels for departments in a table, go through the following steps;**

- Open the **desired table in the Datasheet view**.
- Select the **Word Merge button** in the Export group located on the **External Data tab**.

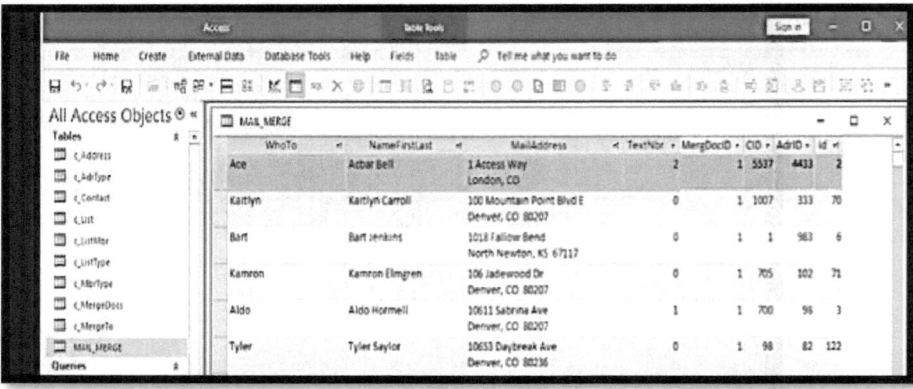

- When you are on the first screen of the Microsoft Word Mail Merge wizard, choose to **Create a New Document** and then have the data linked to it and click on the **OK button**.

- Take the steps that can be found in **Words Mail Merge Wizard**. Choose **the labels** as the document type and then choose **the style** of label you have.

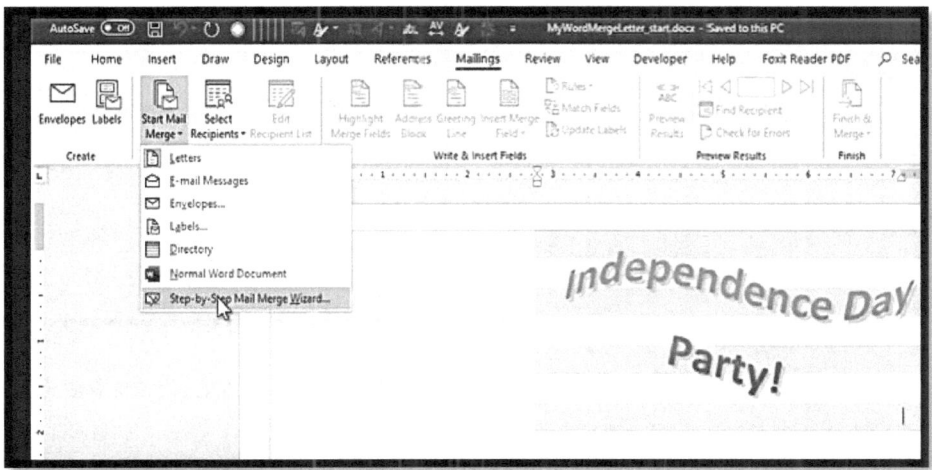

- Arrange **the names and characters** on the label and template then complete the merge process.

You can always import from Microsoft Word into Access by simply converting the Word document into a text file first, you can also choose to combine Word and Excel together in order to produce a delimited text file.

## Publishing to PDF or XPS

The main use of the PDF or XPS format is to have data displayed as it would be on a page that is printed. The dates that are shown in this format cannot be edited. You have a very small file when you are publishing to either PDF or XPS formats but this process can be of great use when you don't want the person you are sending the file to be able to alter it.

**Follow the steps below to complete this process;**

- Choose **the table** you want to publish in the navigation pane.

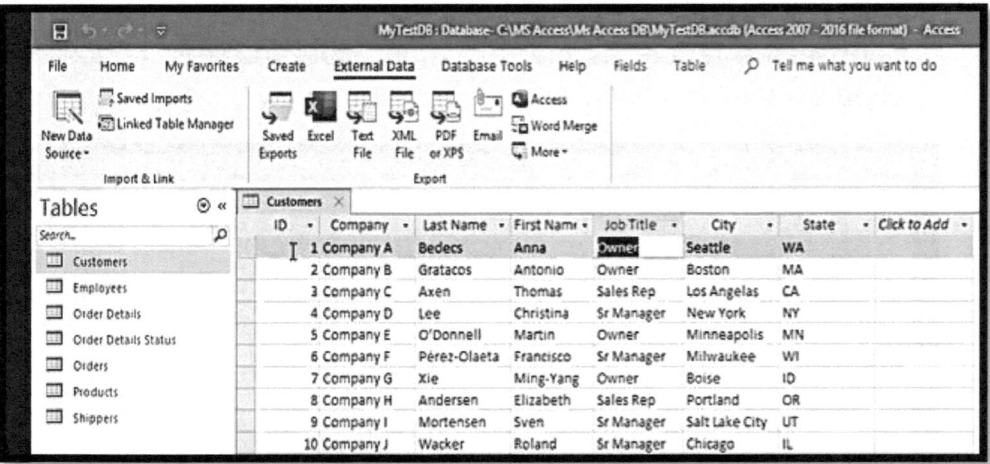

- Choose either **PDF or XPS** from the Export group on the External Data tab of the Ribbon. They will then display the Publish as PDF or XPS dialog box is displayed.

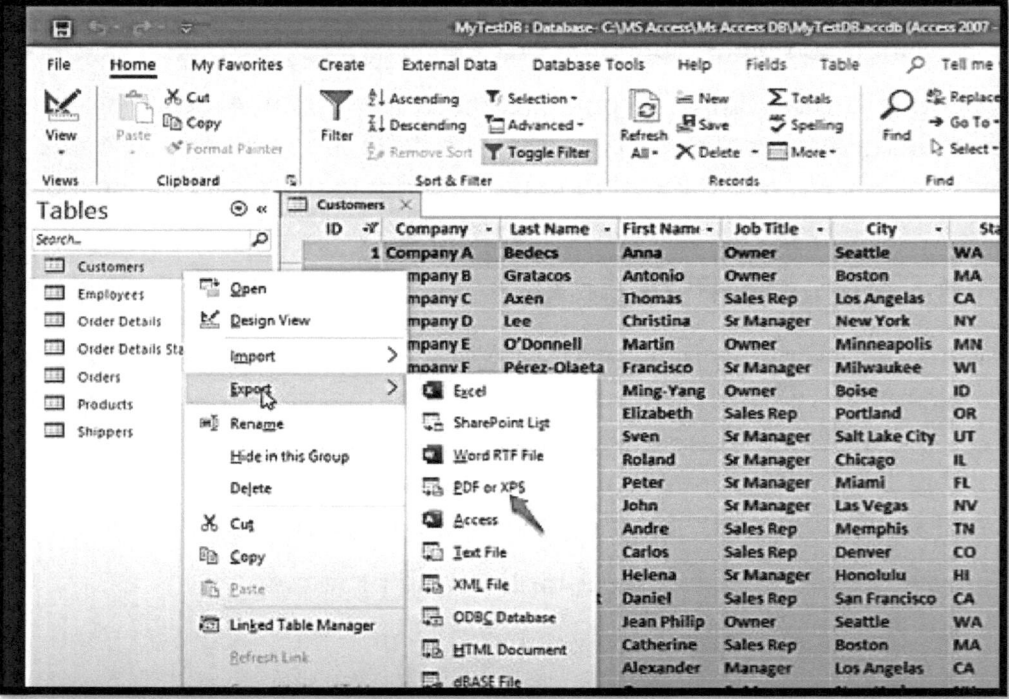

- Choose the **PDF** from the **Save As Type drop-down list**.
- Select the **Publish button**.

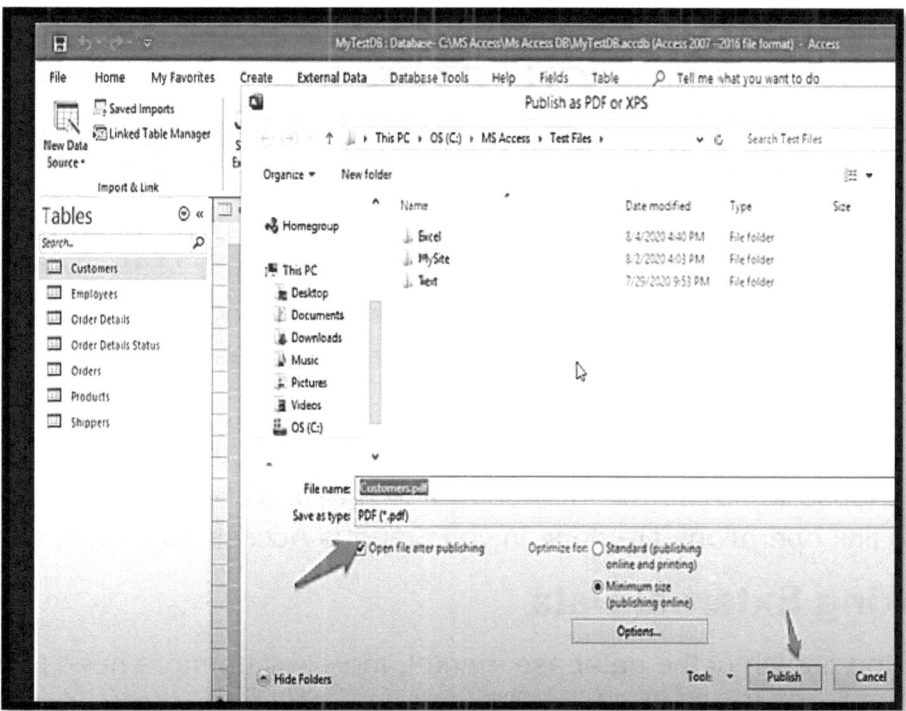

Once all of the above has been completed, you will then have a PDF file that can be opened by various PDF reader programs.

# CHAPTER 7
# LINKING TO EXTERNAL DATA

This chapter is explicitly about the use of External Data and how to go about linking data to Access. You will also learn that Access needs to make use of a particular part with each file as it cannot work with relative paths. This means that when you copy certain files, it might not work unless you link the different external files.

This chapter also points out many of the problems that can arise when you choose to link to external data; it is meant to serve as a guide as these link operations are done in your various Access applications.

## Linking External Data

With the growth of the database market, there will be more need to work with various information from different sources. You won't want to go through the hurdle of reentering information you have in either an Excel spreadsheet or an SQL server into Microsoft Access. Furthermore, with all the policies involved with external files, you won't want to take the risk so as to avoid the duplication of data.

You would like to open the Access table that has the information you need without the need of you to copy it or write a translation program in order to gain access to it.

The use of code in copying or translating data from one application to another can be very time-consuming and also quite costly. Hence there might be a need for an intermediary between the different sources of data that you have in your environment.

With Microsoft Access, you can choose to link to various tables that are in the same database systems at the same time. Upon the linkage of an external file, Access saves the link specification and makes use of the external data as though it was contained in a local table.

# Identifying linked tables

When it has to do with working with external data, there are certain database tables and some other types of files that Access links to. Access will display the names of the tables that have been linked in the object list and also make use of a special icon to specify that the table has been linked, not local. An arrow that points to an icon shows that the table name shows a linked data source.

When you must have linked an external data table to your Access database, you will then make use of it as you would in any other table. When linked data is used in Microsoft Access; the users really do not know nor care about where the data will be. All they want is the data in their preferred format. The developer will be the one that understands all the hurdles that are involved in bringing the data to the User Interface. Apart from the limitations, users might not be able to state the difference between native data and linked data.

## Limitations of linked data

Anytime you are working with linked data in Microsoft Access you ought to be aware of its critical reputation.

When you are making use of Microsoft Access in your company, there might be a need for you to also link external data with Microsoft Access since the operations in various applications cannot be thoroughly performed without the use of data that I already have in Microsoft Access. When you make use of external data with Microsoft Access there will be a need for you to link the external data with the application, with this you will be able to make use of the information in its original format.

This simply means that you will be able to make use of data from a different application in Microsoft Access. However, whenever you make a choice of linking data from external sources to Microsoft Access, there might be certain limitations.

Although Microsoft Access has given users the scope of making use of data from another application within Access, it does not grant them the access to alter the original data that makes use of Access.

**Below are some other limitations;**

- **Excel Data**: whenever you are making use of a Microsoft Excel worksheet in the Microsoft Access database, changes cannot be made to worksheets that already exist. Furthermore, adding and deleting more rows will not be possible in cases where data is linked. When data is linked, Excel Data can be used in Microsoft Access basically in a read mode.
- **Text Files**: when making use of text files in Access as linked data, the access you have to them will be a little more than just the read mode but not so much access will be granted still. Although in this option you are allowed to add rows to the already existing data, you still cannot make changes to any of the rows that are already existing nor delete any of the rows that are already existing nor can you update the ones that are already existing. This is done mainly for you to avoid any kind of breaks in the operations that are already being done with the use of the given text files.
- **HTML**: The access that is granted in this option is read-only, almost the same as the access granted when making use of Excel Data as linked data. HTML cannot be changed by any known means. You cannot also update, delete or include any more information to what has been created already in the HTML table.
- **dBase**: since this file format is readily accessible in Microsoft Access, you can make changes as much as you can with normal Access databases. Nevertheless, there is a need for you to have access to the primary key of each of the database tables. If you don't have the key, your actions might become restricted again.
- **ODBC**: This can be said to be a data access technology that makes use of the driver that is between Access files and the files from the linked data/application. This also includes applications such as SQL Server or Oracle which are also database applications. Due to the fact that the source of linked data is also a database table, you can perform operations freely be it editing, deleting, or adding data. Note that before this can be possible, the linked database must have a uniquely defined index. Hence, if you would like to make use of linked data from another database application as freely as though it were a native Access database there will be a need for you to have a unique index for all the linked

databases. It is always prudent to have a professional tool at hand so as to be able to recover files that become corrupted before the initiation of a drastic change.

## Linking to other Access database tables

You can bring in data from one Access database into another in different ways. Copying and pasting is a very simple way but the use of importing and linking provides you with a much better opportunity and also gives you better control over the data that you bring, and also over how you bring the data into the destination base.

If your organization makes use of several databases, you might want to consider the option of linking data but note that some data in tables like Employees need to be shared between various databases. Another workgroup or department should be able to make use of the data that is in your database but you should still own the structure of tables.

**Below are steps you should follow in order to link to a particular table in the database.**

- Open **the table** you want to link.
- Click on the **External Data tab** of the Ribbon, and then click on **Import & Link > New Data> From Database>Access**. This will then display the Get External Data -Access Database dialog box.

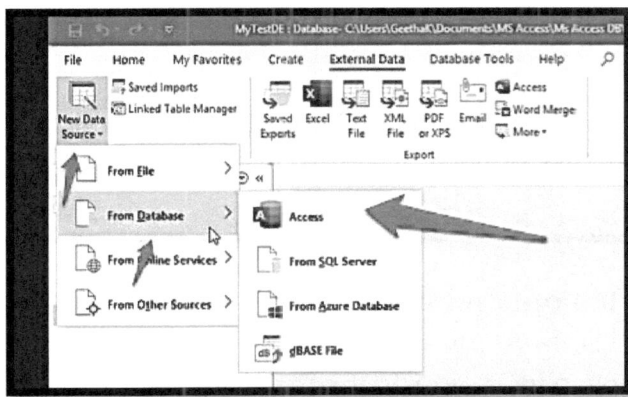

- Click on the **Browse option**.

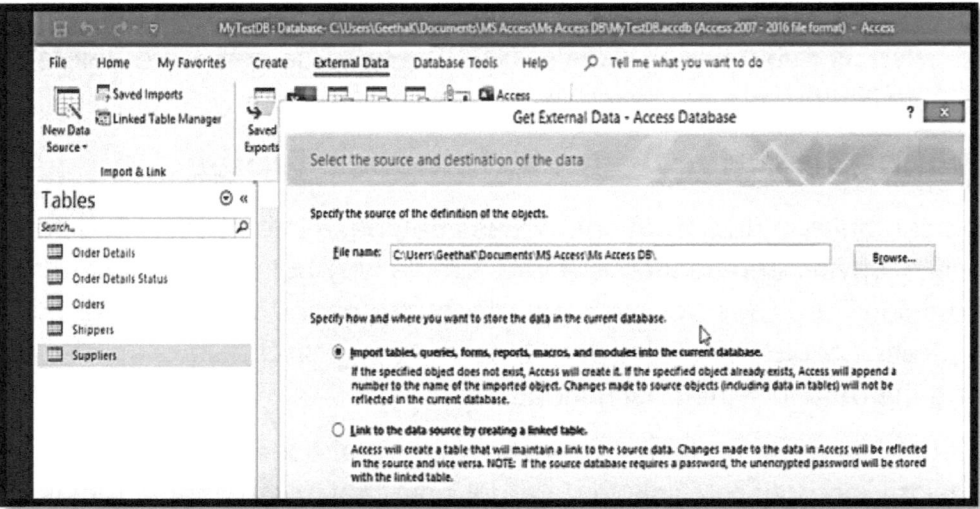

- Find the data you want to link then click on **open**.

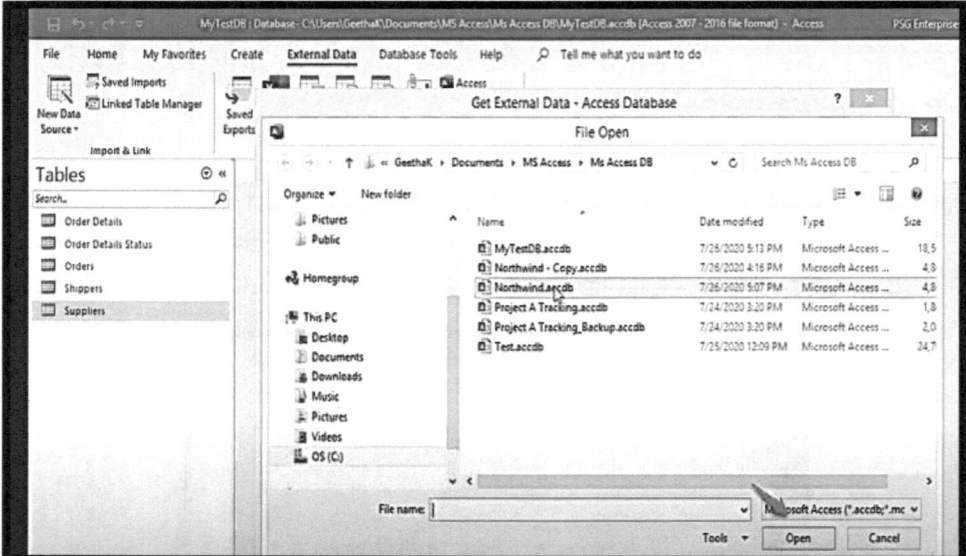

- Choose the **option button** for linking and click on **OK** in the Get External Data-Access Database dialog box. The Link Tables dialog box allows you to choose one or more tables from the selected database.
- FInally, click on **the table** and then select the **OK button**.

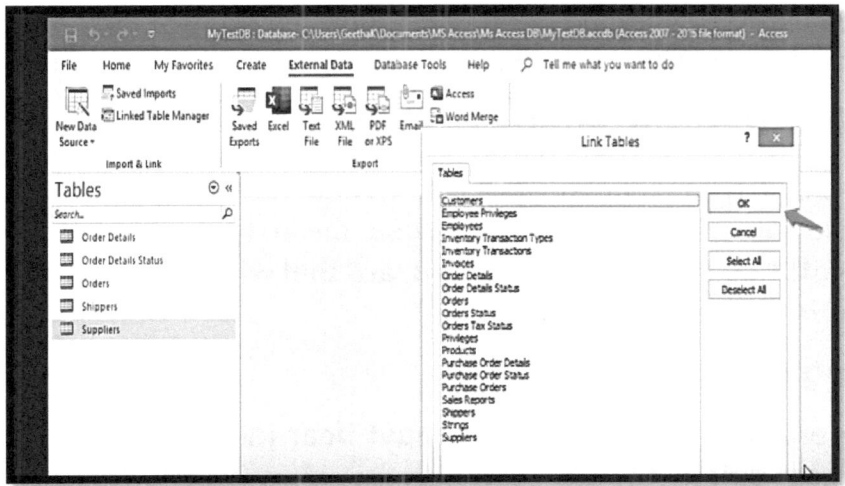

You are free to link more than one table at a time by choosing various tables before you click on the Ok button in the Link Tables dialog box. When you choose the **Select All buttons,** all the tables will be chosen. Once you have chosen all the tables, you can then choose some sections of the table if there is a need to deselect them.

## Linking to ODBC data sources

One major advance that has to do with sharing of data is the establishment of the Open Database Connectivity (ODBC) standard by Microsoft and some other vendors. ODBC is a specification widely used by software vendors in the creation of various database products.

With this specification, Access applications can work with data in a standard fashion across diverse database platforms. If you write any application that conforms to the specifications of ODBC, your application will definitely be able to make use of any ODBC-compliant back end.

The most common way often used in the accomplishment of this requirement is to make use of the SQL Server ODBC driver. When you must have developed the application, and you notice that an organization you have an affiliation with would also like to make use of the application too but their database host is Oracle.

If your application has conformed closely to ODBC syntax, you should then be able to make use of the same application with Oracle by simply getting an Oracle ODBC driver. Not only do vendors supply drivers for their own products, but there are also software vendors now who create and also supply ODBC drivers.

## Linking to non-database data

There is also a need for you to link non-databases like Excel, HTML, and also text files. Whenever you choose these types of data sources, **Microsoft Access will run a Link Wizard that will prompt you through the entire process;**

### Linking to Excel

**Below are the main things you must bear in mind in order to link with Excel data;**

- An Excel workbook file might java various worksheets. There is a need for you to make a choice of the particular worksheet within the workbook file you would like to link except in terms of you making use of named ranges.
- You might choose to link to named ranges that are in the Excel worksheet. Each range will then become a different linked table in Microsoft Access.
- Excel columns might have just about any type of data. The fact that you have linked the Excel worksheet successfully doesn't mean that your application will be able to make use of all the data that is in the worksheet. Since there is no limit to the types of data that can be contained in an Excel worksheet, it is very possible that your application also encounters different types of data within just one column of a worksheet that is linked.

This simply means that there is a need to include a code or get some other strategies for working around the different types of data that are in an Excel worksheet.

**Follow the steps below to link to an Excel spreadsheet;**

- In the database, click **on Import & Link > New Data Source>From File>Excel** on the External Data tab of the Ribbon.
- Choose the **Link to the Data Source option** by creating a Linked Table and then click on the **Browse option.** Note that the same

Get External Data dialog box is used for both import and link operations, ensure you choose the right operation before you continue.

- Find and open **the Excel file**.
- Click on **OK** when you get to the **Get External Data- Excel Spreadsheet dialog box**.
- Choose the **Products worksheet**.
- The Link Spreadsheet Wizard will take you through various screens where you can indicate details like First Row Contains Column headings and also the type of data to be applied to each of the Excel worksheets. The last screen of the Link Spreadsheet will then ask for the name of the table that has just been linked.
- Finally, click on the **Finish button**. The linked table is then created and you will be taken back to the Access environment.

## Linking to HTML files

There are so many limitations imposed by Access as regards linking to HTML files. For instance, Access cannot get data from an arbitrary HTML file except if the data is presented as an HTML table in a row-and-column format and the data also has to be very clean.

More problems might arise if more than one HTML table is being displayed on the page or if the data is shown in a hierarchical manner. It is much better to link with an HTML document that has been specifically prepared as a data source for your Access application than for you to try to work with HTML files that are arbitrary.

**Follow the steps below to link HTML data, note that the process is quite similar to that of Microsoft Excel;**

- Choose the **Import & Link > New Data Source > From File > HTML Document** on the External Data tab of the Ribbon.

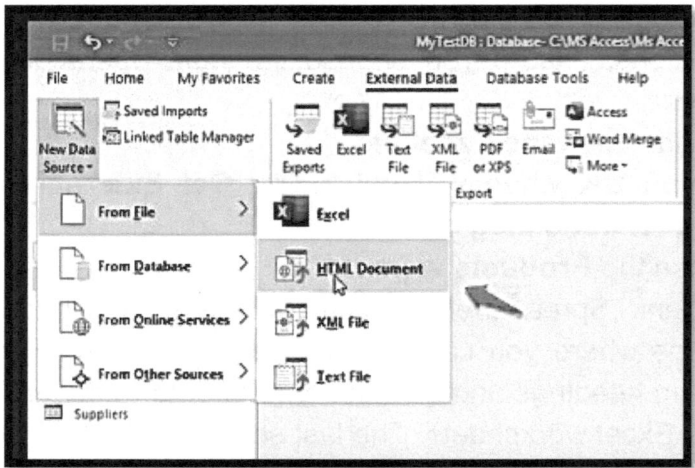

- Choose the **Link to the Data Source** by establishing a Linked Table option, and also click on the **Browse option**.

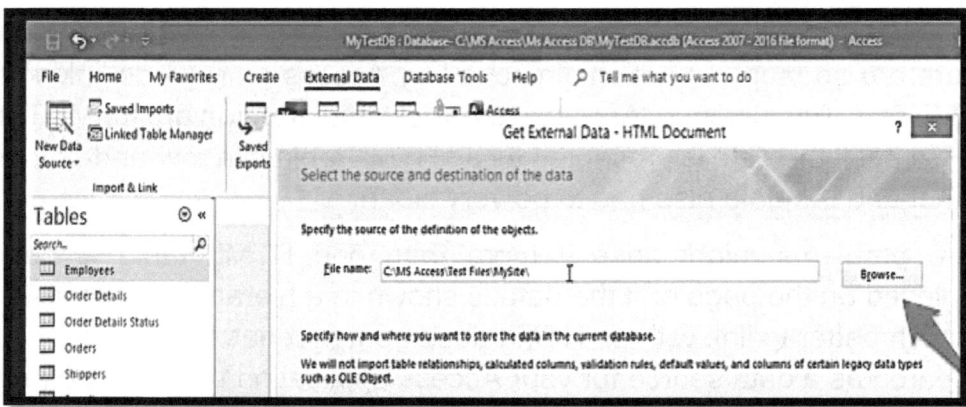

Once you have completed the steps above, the remaining steps are similar to linking to other types of files. **If you will need to provide the field names,**

- Click on the **Advanced button** in order to get to the Link Specification dialog box.

## Linking to text files

More common is a situation wherein you have to link to data stored in plain text files. Most of the applications which include Word and Excel are able to publish data in various text formats.

**The most common formats you might come across are;**
- **Fixed Width**: In a fixed-width text file, each of the lines shows one row of a database table. Each of the fields within a line also has the same number of characters as the corresponding field that are in the lines over and beneath the current line. Each of the data fields is padded with spaces to the right in order to fill out the width that has been given to the field.
- **Comma-separated values (CSV)**: these are rather more complex and quite technical to comprehend than the fixed width. Each of the fields is separated by a comma character ( ) and each of the fields also occupies as much space needed in order to be able to absolve the data. Basically, there is no blank space existing between fields in a CSV file. The advantage of CSV files is that data can be contained in a much smaller file since each field has only the space needed for the data.

## Working with Linked Tables

Once you have linked to an external table from another database, simply use it as you would an Access table. Most features of an external table can be altered any time you are making use of them. Features such as renaming the tables, setting links between the tables, and also setting view properties can all be changed.

Note that when you provide a different name for the table inside Access, it doesn't change the name of the file that is linked to that application. The name Acres refers to that linked table that will still be maintained with the application and doesn't in any way affect the physical table that is linked.

## Setting view properties

As earlier explained above, you can change the view properties of the table linked with Access but you cannot change the structure of the table. **Below are the various properties you can choose to set for the field:**
- Decimal places
- Format
- Caption
- Display control

- IME sequence mode

**To have these properties changed simply;**

- Open the **linked table** in the Design view. When you do this, Access will send a warning that it cannot be altered. Simply ignore the warning then proceed to make the modifications.

# Setting relationships

With Access, you can set permanent relationships at the table level between linked non-Access tables and the native Access tables with the use of the Relationship window. Although you will be unable to set referential integrity between linked tables or between linked tables and internal tables.

When you link to an external Access table, it helps to keep the relationship that might be in existence between the external tables. Hence when you are linking to a backend database, the relationships that have been created in the backend along with any validation and default values are well known by the front-end Database. This is very good because it means that the rules that have been defined will then be enforced without having to pay attention to the number of front ends created to use the tables.

# Optimizing linked tables

When having to work with linked tables, Access will have to get records from an external file. This process can take quite a while and might even be a much longer process if the table is on a network or in a SQL database.

**Whenever you are working with an external data ensure you optimize performance by taking into consideration the rules below;**

- **If records are added to externally linked tables, design a form and have the Data entry property configured to true**: With this option, it makes the form an entry form that begins with a blank record each time you have to run it. Data entry forms are usually not pre-populated with data from the bound table. With the use of a much more dedicated data entry form, you can be sure that it

will be more efficient than having to build a normal form, populating it with data from the linked source, and then having to move to the end of the data in order to include a new record.
- **Avoid multiple movements in datasheets**: All you should do here is to view the data needed alone in a datasheet. Ensure you totally avoid moving up and down the page and also jumping from the first or the last record in all the large tables.
- **Reduce the number of external records that should be viewed**: build a query with the use of a criterion that reduces the number of records from an external table. You can then make use of the same query with other queries, forms, or reports.
- Avoid the use of functions in query criteria: This is very true for aggregate functions like DTotal or DCount which often get records from the linked table before beginning to perform the query operation.

## Deleting a linked reference

There are basically three steps that are involved with deleting a table from a database.

**Below are the steps;**

- Locate the **navigation pane** then choose the **linked table** you would like to delete.
- Click the **Delete key**, or you can also choose to right-click and choose the **Delete option** from the shortcut menu.
- Click on the **OK button** in the Access dialog box in order to delete the file.

## Viewing or changing information for linked tables

Whenever you rename, modify tables, or relationships associated with linked tables, make use of the Linked Table Manager to update the links. **To do this simply;**

- Choose the **External Data tab** of the Ribbon and then choose the **Linked Table Manager** option.
- Select the **check box** close to a linked table and then click on the **OK button**.

- Locate the **missing file** and link it again to Access. Note that if all of the files happen to be linked already when you click on the **OK button**, Access will ensure it verifies all the links that are associated with all the tables that were chosen.
- If you happen to know all of the linked data sources that must have been moved, choose the **Always Prompt for New Location checkbox** and then click on the **OK button**. With this, Access will then prompt you for the new location and with a batch process, link all the tables. The batch process is quite faster than having to link the tables one after the other. If all of your tables happen to come from different sources, the Linked Table Manager will still need you to choose each source one after the other.

## Refreshing a data source and its linked tables

Refresh a data source and also it's linked tables so as to ensure that the data source is accessible and the linked tables are working normally. **Follow the steps below to refresh linked tables;**

- Choose **External Data** then click on **Linked Table Manager**.

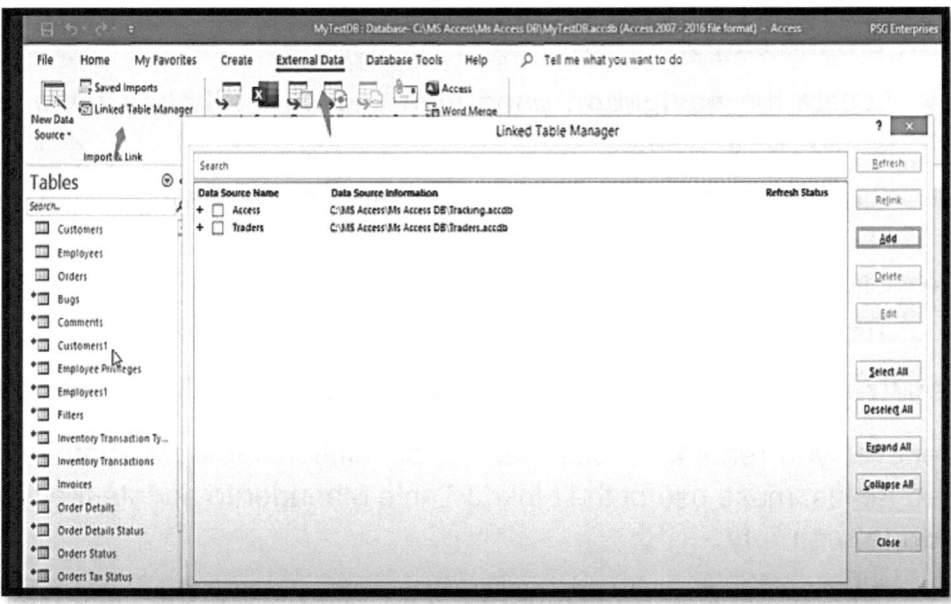

- When you are in the **Linked Table Manager dialog box**, choose a data source or individual linked tables. When you choose a data

source it will automatically select all the tables linked to it. Expand the entries in the Data Source in order to choose individual linked tables.
- Choose the **Refresh option**.

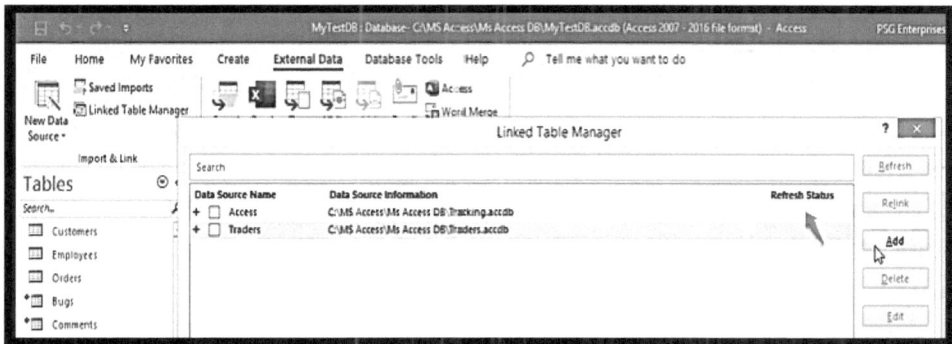

- If there happens to be any problem with the data source location, insert **the location** that is correct if you are prompted to or you can also choose to Edit the data source as an alternative.
- **Ensure that the status column is visible and then check properly to view the results;**
    - **Success**: this will be displayed when the linked tables have been refreshed successfully.
    - **Failed:** this will be displayed if one or more linked tables have a problem. The most common reasons for a failed status include: when there are new credentials, or when there is a change to the name of the table. To have this problem fixed, relink the data source or the linked table.
- Click on the **Refresh option** again until you are sure you have fixed all of the failed linked tables and the Status column shows "success".

## Splitting a Database

The same way tables can be linked to a database, they can also be split. Splitting a database means having to create two different ACCDB files from one with one called backend and the other front-end. The backend contains only relationships and tables while the front end contains macros, code, queries, and UI elements like reports and forms. The front end also has links to all the tables in the back end.

## The benefits of splitting a database

There will definitely be at least one good reason for you to have to split your Access database. When you split a database, you will have it reorganized into two different files which are back end database and front end database. Each user will interact with the data with the use of a local copy of the front-end database. To split a database, you have to make use of the Database Splitter Wizard. When you must have finished splitting the database, ensure you share the front-end database with every one of your users.

**The benefit of a split database includes;**

- **Improved performance**: There is always an increase in the performance of the database since it is only the data that is sent across the network. When a database is not split, the database objects such as the queries, tables, forms, reports, macros, and modules are sent across the network and not just the data alone.
- **Greater availability**: Since it is just the data that is sent across the network, database transactions like record edits will be completed faster leaving the data more available to edit.
- **Enhanced security**: if you happen to store the back-end database on a computer that makes use of the NTFS file system, you can make use of NTFS security features to help with the protection of your data. Since users access the back-end database with the use of linked tables, it is less likely that some intruders will get unauthorized access to the data by stealing the front-end database or by disguising themselves as unauthorized user. If you are not sure of the file system your server is using, ensure you ask the system administrator and if you have administrator privileges on the file server, you can choose to run the msinfo32 command in order to determine the file system by yourself.
- **Improved reliability**: if a user comes across a problem and the database closes in an abrupt manner, any database file corruption is always limited to the copy of the front-end database that the

user must have opened. Since the user only gets access to the data in the back-end database with the use of linked tables, the back-end database file might not be corrupted.
- **Flexible development environment:** since each user gets to work with a local copy of the front-end database, each user can also independently produce queries, forms, reports, and some other database objects without adversely affecting other users. Also, you can develop and share a new version of the front-end database without having to disrupt access to the data that is saved in the back-end database.

# Knowing where to put which objects

The local ACCDB has all the UI objects which include forms, reports, macros, queries, and modules.When you keep the UI components on the local machine, it has a way of improving its performance. There will be no need for you to move forms, queries, or reports across the network, these objects can be more managed with ease on the local machine than when it is accessed across the network.

All of the shared tables ought to be placed in the back-end database and also kept on the server with all the relationships that exist between those tables. The tables in the server database are linked to the front-end ACCDB on each user's desktop.

With more than one person making use of the data in a table, the same record might end up being edited by the same users, The Access database engines will also take care of this problem by locking a record as it is edited by a user. A lock contention will also take place when there is an attempt for more than one user to try to update the same record. Only a user will have "live" access to the record; all the other users will either be locked or have their changes held up until the record holder has completed all the changes necessary.

## Using the Database Splitter add-in

The Database splitter helps to split an application into both front-end and back-end databases. With the use of this Wizard, you will be able to build and also test your database and then have the burden of having to prepare for the application for the multi-user access lightened.

**Follow the steps below to make use of the Database Splitter;**

- Begin the **Database Splitter** by choosing the **Database Tools tab** of the Ribbon then select the **Access Database button** in the Move Data group.
- This action will then open the wizard screen which will inform you of the action of the Database Splitter and also bring suggestions that you ought to create a backup of the database before you proceed.

The only information that Database Splitter needs is where you would like to have your back-end database.

# PART III
# WORKING WITH ACCESS QUERIES

The chapters in this part will enlighten you more about the basic analytic tools and techniques that are available for use in Access. It will also better inform you on how to work with queries.

Queries get various data sources together and also present the combined information in very useful views. With queries, you can synthesize raw data in Access tables to give a very meaningful analysis.

# CHAPTER 8
# SELECTING DATA WITH QUERIES

Queries cannot be overlooked in any database application. They are used to get data from various tables, combine the data and then present the data in a meaningful way to the user(s) as a form, datasheet, or a printed report. Queries are basically used to bring data sources together and also present the combined information in a manner that users will be able to work with the data with ease.

## Introducing Queries

In a database that is well designed, the data that you have a need to present through a form or report is usually found in various tables. With the use of a query, you can get information from different tables and then bring them together in order to display them as a form or as a report. A query can either be a request for data results from your database or can be used for action on the data, it can also work both ways.

With the use of a query, you can have answers to a simple question, perform some simple calculations, combine data from various tables, and add, change, or delete data from a database.

## What Queries can do

With queries you can combine data and also analyze them effectively. **Below is a list of things you can do with queries;**

- **Make changes to data in tables:** With the use of queries, you can alter various rows in the underlying tables as just one operation. Most times, action queries are often used to maintain data like updating specific fields, appending new data, or deleting a piece of information that is no longer in use.
- **Show query data on forms and reports**: The record set created from a query might just have the right fields that you need for a report or a form. When you make a report of form to be dependent on queries, this simply means that each time you have a need to print the report or open the form, you will be seeing the most current information in the tables.

- **Create tables**: You can create an entirely new table based on the data that the query returns.
- **Perform some calculations**: You can use queries to perform some simple calculations like average, totals, or simply counting of data that are in a record.
- Sort records: With the use of queries, you can sort records. For instance, there might be a need for you to see the contacts of a customer that has been sorted either by the last name or by the first name.
- **Choose tables**: Information can be gotten from one table or from various tables that are related to each other by some data. If you have an interest in seeing the name of a customer and also some items the customer bought. With the use of several tables, MicrosoftAccess can combine the data as just one record set.

## What Queries return

Microsoft Access combines a queries report and when it has executed it, shows the query in the Datasheet view. The set of records that are returned by a query is known as a record set. A Recordset object shows the records in a database or the records that emanate from executing a query. Recordset objects are often used to manipulate data at the record level.

When DAO objects are used, you end up having to manipulate data while almost making use of the whole Recordset objects. All Recordset objects are created with the use of records(rows) and fields(columns).

**There are basically five types of Recordset objects.**

Note that the record set returned by a query is not usually stored in the database except if you have instructed Access to build a table from those records.

Each time you run a query, the read ensures it reads the underlying tables and then re-creates the record set. Since recordset in themselves are not usually stored, a query will automatically show any changes that are made to the underlying tables since you last ran the query even if you are in a real-time multiuser environment.

You can view a query's record set in the form of a datasheet, a report, or a form depending on how best it suits you. Anytime you choose to base a form or report on a query, the record set of the query will be recreated and bound to the form or report every time you open it. The recordset of a query can also be used in macros and VBA procedures in order to help drive any number of automated tasks.

## Creating a Query

**Once you have created a query, you are then set to begin work. To create a query follow the steps below;**

- Click on the **create tab on the Ribbon**.
- Click on the **Query Design button** in the queries group. This will then open the query designer. In the dialog box that is then displayed afterward, ensure that you add the tables needed for the query.

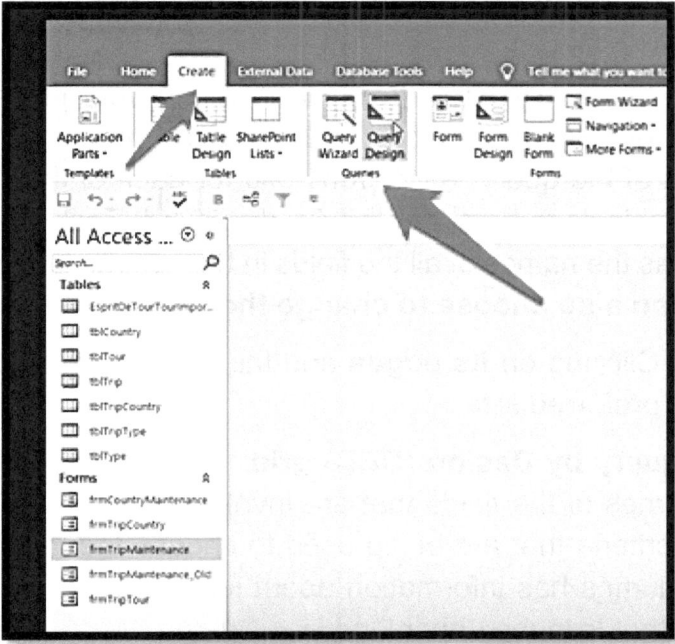

**If you would like to include tables to the query simply;**

- Right click on **anywhere** in the upper part of the **Query Designer** and choose **Show Table** from the shortcut menu that is being displayed.

- With the Show Table option opening, you will then be able to choose **all the table**s and query objects you might be in need of to successfully build your table.

Another fast and easier method can be to simply drag the tables or queries from the navigation pane to the upper part of the Query Designer. You can make use of it very quickly if you have already taken off the Show Table dialog box and you need to quickly include a table or an object to your query.

**The query design window has about three primary views which are;**
- **Datasheet view**: which shows all of the records that are returned by the query.
- **SQL view**: which shows all of the SQL statements behind the query.
- **Design view**: this is the very location where you build a query.

**There are also about two different sections in the Query Designer, they are;**
- **The table/query pane (top):** This is the very place where the tables or queries and the fields in them are included with the design of the query. A different field for each of the lists for each of the objects to be added will be displayed. Each of the field lists also has the names of all the fields in the various tables or queries. **You can also choose to change the size of the field list by**
    - Clicking on **its edges** and then moving the edges to your preferred size.
- **The Query by Design (QBD) grid**: The QBD grid helps to hold the names of the fields that are involved in the query and in any other criteria that are being used to choose the records. Each of the columns has information about just one field from a table or query that is in the upper lane.

**The QBD grid has about six rows that are labeled, they are;**
- **Field**: This is where the names of the field are either labeled or inserted.

- **Table**: This row displays the table the field is from. This is also quite useful in queries that have various tables.
- **Sort:** This row allows the sorting of instructions for the query or queries.
- **Criteria**: This row contains the criteria that filter the records that are returned.
- **Or**: this is the first of the number rows in which you include various query criteria.
- **Run**: This helps to execute the query. It shows a select query's datasheet which serves just the same function as choosing the Datasheet view from the view button. Note that when you are working with action queries, the run button performs the operations that are indicated by the query.
- **Select**: When you choose this option the opened query will be changed into a select query.
- MakeTable, Append, Update, Crosstab, and Delete: Each of the buttons listed above indicate the type of query that you are about to create. Most times you change a select query into an action query when you click on one of these buttons.
- Show table: this button opens the Show Table dialog box.

# Adding fields to your Queries

There are various ways in which fields can be added to a query. You can choose to add fields one at a time or you can also choose to add more than one field or choose all the fields in the field list at once.

## Adding a single field

**You can add a single field in various ways.**

- You can choose to click **twice** on the name of the field in the table that can be found in the top pane of the Query Designer.

- You can also choose to **move a field** from a table in the top pane of the Query Designer and then drop it on a column in the QBD grid. This action will have the other fields pushed to the right side.

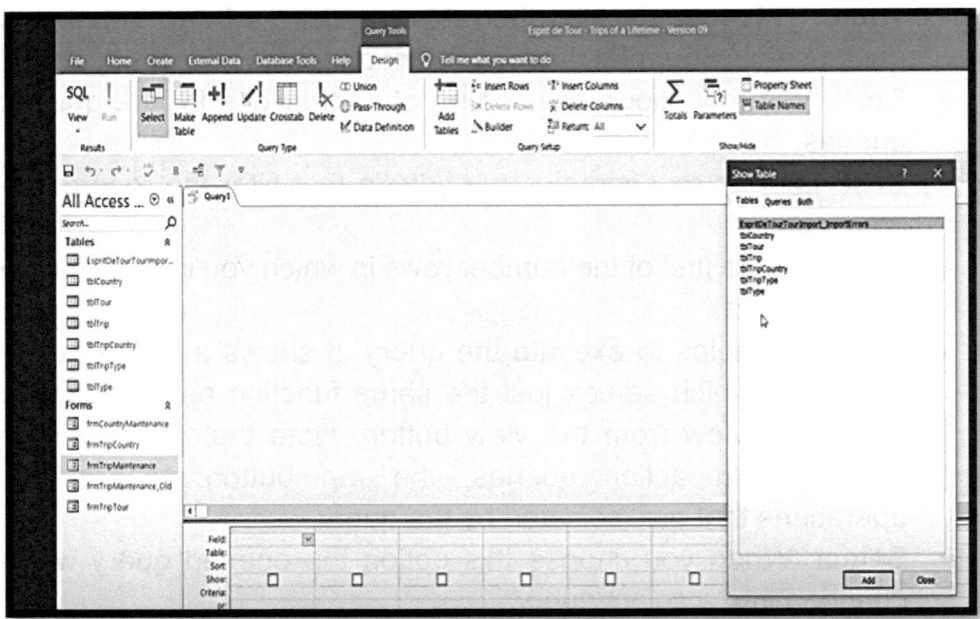

## Adding multiple fields

**You can include more than one field by simply;**

- Choosing the **preferred files** from the field list window and then moving them to the QBD grid. It is not compulsory that the fields are in sequence, you can hold down the ctrl key and choose the various fields as you wish.
- As an alternative, you can also choose to **click and move the asterisk**(*) from the field list to the QBD grid or click **twice on the asterisk** in order to include it in the QBD grid. Though the use of this action does not include all the fields in the QBD grid, the asterisk ensures it directs Access to add all the fields in the table in the query.

The negative side to making use of the asterisk in indicating all the fields that are in a table is that the query will take back all of the fields that are in the table without considering if the field is used on a form or it is used on a report. Getting back data that is not used can be quite an inefficient process. Most often, performance problems can be linked to the asterisk taking back more fields than needed for either a form or a report. You will also be unable to gain control over the order in which the fields are shown in the datasheet.

## Running your query

**Once you have finished choosing your preferred fields, you will then need to execute the query by;**

- Clicking on the **Run button** located on the **Query Tools Design Ribbon.**

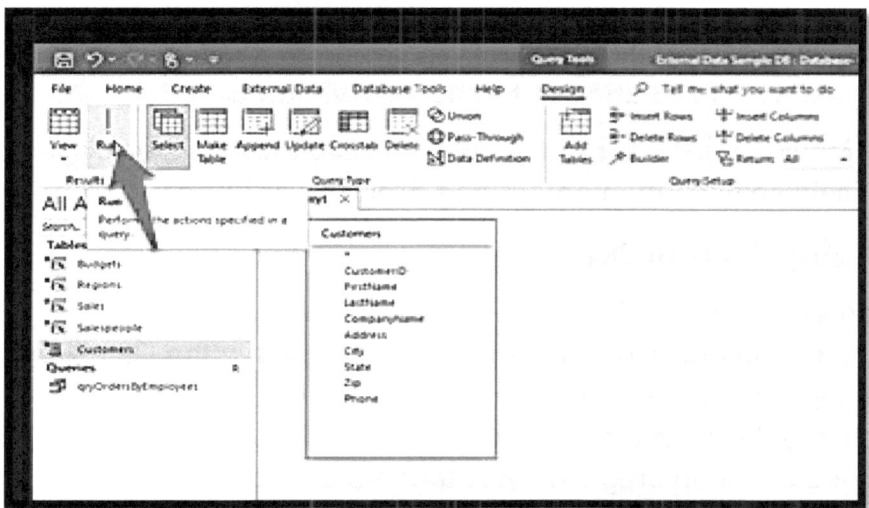

**If you would like to go back to the QBD grid, simply;**

- Locate the **Home tab** and then click on the **View option > Design view**.

**As an alternative, you can also choose to;**

- Right-click on the **tab header** for the query then choose the **Design view option**.

## Working with Query Fields

With the query fields there are times when you might need to work with the fields that you have already chosen, have their order re-organized, include a new field or you might even have a need to delete a field that already exists.

When you add a field without necessarily having to show it allows you to sort on the fields that are hidden or to make a choice to make use of the hidden field as a criterion.

## Selecting a field in the QBD grid

To move the position of a field you have to choose the field first and to do that you have to make use of the field selector.

The field selector is the thin gray area that can be found at the top of the columns in the QBD grid at the lower part of the Query Designer. Each column signifies a field.

**If you would like to choose the category simply;**

- Move **the pointer** until a little selection arrow is displayed in the field selector then **select and drag the column**.

## Changing field order

The order in which the fields are displayed in the QBD grid also determines the order in which they are displayed in the Datasheet view. There might be a need to move the fields in the QBD grid to get a new sequence of fields in the result of the query. Once you have chosen the fields, you can then drag the fields that are on the QBD design by simply moving them to another position entirely.

**To change the field order,**

- Left click on the **field selector bar** and when you are holding down the left button of the mouse, move the field to the preferred position on the QBD grid.

## Resizing columns in the QBD grid

There are about 8-10 fields in the QBD grid in the viewable area. The remaining fields are viewed when the horizontal scroll bar is moved.

There might be a need for you to make some fields smaller in order to be able to view more columns in the QBD grid. You can make some adjustments to the column width to make them smaller by moving the pointer of the mouse to the margin that is between the fields and then moving the column resizer to either the left or the right side.

Note that the width of a column in the QBD grid has no effect on the way the data in the field is being displayed in either a datasheet, form, or report. The column width in the QBD grid is simply a convenience to you as a developer.

## Removing a field

**To take a field off the QBD grid simply;**

- Choose **the preferred field** you would like to remove and then press the delete button.

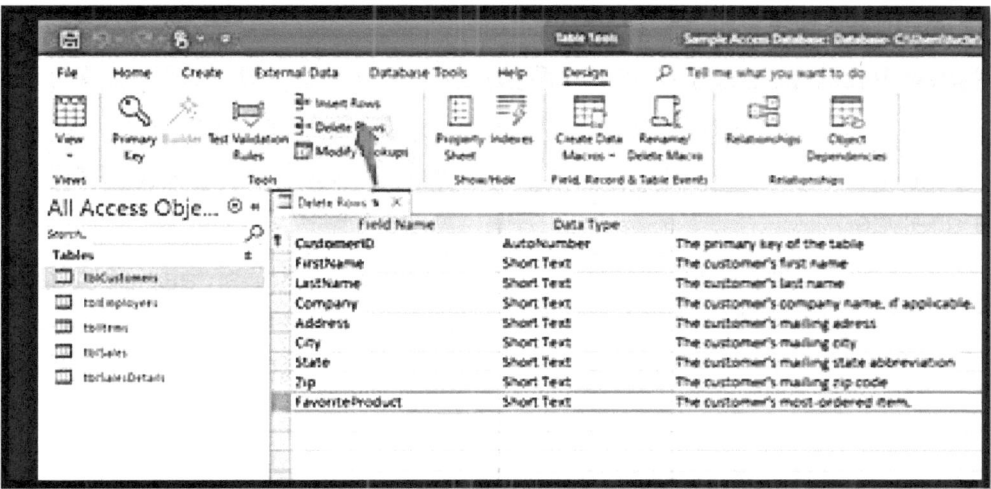

As an alternative, you can also choose to **right-click** on the selector bar of the field and click on the **cut option** from the shortcut menu.

## Inserting a field

**To insert new fields into a QBD grid simply;**

- Drag **a field** from the list of fields that is within the QBD grid and place it in the column in the QBD grid. The new column will then be on the left on which you dropped the field. When you click twice on a field in the field list, it will add the new column to the right side of the QBD grid.

## Hiding a field

There might be a need for you to sometimes hide a field when a query is being performed.

**To hide a field all you have to do is to;**

- Uncheck the **specific field** you want to hide in the Show Check box in the State column.

One other common reason why a field is usually hidden is if the field is used either for sorting or as criteria but the value of the field is not needed in the results of the query.

## Changing the sort order of a field

Anytime you are viewing a record set, there might often be a need for you to show the data in sorted order in order to make it much easier for it to be analyzed.

When you sort records, it places the records in either an alphabetical or numerical order. You can choose to sort on either a single field or multiple fields. The sort order can also either be ascending or descending order.

**To have a sort order specified, take the steps below;**

- Place **the cursor** in the Sort cell in the specific field you want to sort.
- Click on the **drop-down list** that is displayed in the cell and then choose **the sort orde**r option you would like to apply.

Note that fields do not only just appear in the data sheet in a left-to-right manner, they are also sorted in that same order. This order is known as the Sort order precedence. To the farthest left of the field is the sort criteria which is usually sorted first and the right is sorted next.

# Adding Criteria to Your Queries

Almost every user prefers to work with records that conform to some criteria. If this isn't done lots of records might have to be returned by a query which can lead to very serious problems as regards performance. With Microsoft Access, it is very easy to have your data specified.

## Understanding selection criteria

Selection criteria are basically the rules that are applied to data as they are retrieved from the database. With the selection crteria, Access will know the records you want to look at in the record set. With the selection criteria, you can also place a limit on the number of records that will be returned by a query.

It is important to know how to use query criteria as it is quite critical to the success of the Microsoft Access database. Oftentimes, the users have no idea of the data that is stored in the table of a database and will just accept whatever is displayed on a form or report as a true representation of the database. When a criter on is poorly chosen, it affects the information as it can hide it from the application's users which can lead to the users making a bad decision business-wise.

## Entering simple string criteria

The criteria that will be applied to a field is often always based on the Text-type field. The character of the text you want to extract is what you will enter into the field. Note that when inserting the character, Access is not always case sensitive; you can insert the character just as you like.

Generally, when you have to work with character data you should insert equalities, inequalities, or at the very least, a list of values that can be accepted.

**If you have a reason to remove the criteria that you have inserted into the cell, all you have to do is;**

- Choose **the contents** and press **the delete button** or you can choose **the contents** and then **right-click** on the cut option from the shortcut menu that is d splayed.

## Entering other simple criteria

You can also choose to specify criteria for Numeric, Date, and also for Yes/No. All you have to do is insert the value in the criteria field in the same manner as you have done for the text. Most times Access immediately understands the criteria you insert and automatically adjusts in order to apply the criteria correctly to the fields of tre query.

## Printing a Query's Recordset

When you must have created your query, you can then print all the records with ease on the recordset. Although there is no way you can indicate a particular type of report, you can choose to print a simple matrix-type report of the record set created by your query.

There is an amount of flexibility in printing a record set.

**Follow the steps below to indicate some of the options you might prefer;**

- Execute **the query** you have just crested.
- Click on the **file option** then choose the **print** option. You will then be presented with three different options; you can choose to print without having to specify any options, you can print with the use of some specific print settings or you can choose the print preview option so as to check out how the printing will turn out before eventually printing it.
- Make **a choice** of the print options you want in the dialog box that is displayed and click on the **OK button**.

## Saving a Query

You can always save your query so you can get back to it any time you have a need to.

**To save a query simply;**

- Click on the **Save button** on the **Quick Access Toolbar** located at the top of the screen. Access will ask for the name of the query if it is the first time you are saving the query.

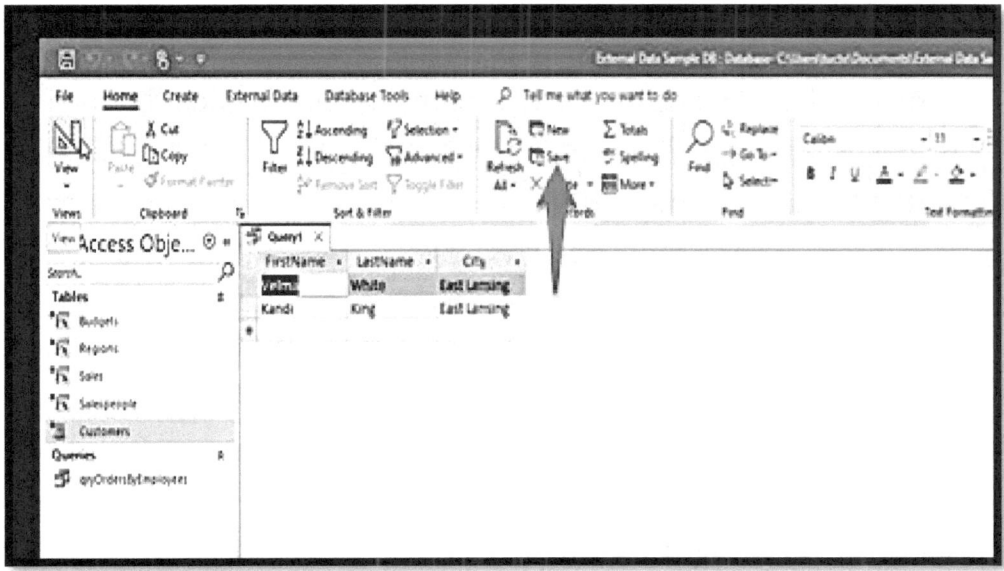

Once you have saved the query, Access will take you back to the mode in which you were working before.

## Creating Multi-table Queries

It is now very common to make use of a query to get information from a table though oftentimes you will have a need for information from various tables that are somewhat related.

Once you have created a table and you have specified how the tables should be related to one another, you are then ready to create more than one table query in order to retrieve information from various tables that are related.

**In creating a multi-table the first step to take is the addition of tables to the query design window;**

- Create a **new query** by clicking on the **Query Design button** on the **Create tab of the Ribbon**.
- Add the tables you want to obtain information from by double-clicking on **each of the names of the table** in the Show Table dialog box.
- Finally, click on the **close button**.

You can add fields from more than one table also, simply follow the same procedure as you have with the single table. Anytime a field that has a common name in various tables is chosen, Access will add the name of the table and then include the period sign and then the name of the field.

## Viewing table names

Whenever you are working with more than one table in a query, the names of the fields in the QBD grid can be very confusing. Automatically, Access keeps the name of the table associated with each of the fields displayed in the QBD grid.

## Adding multiple fields

Adding multiple fields in a multi-table query is quite similar to adding multiple fields in a single-table query. When adding fields from various tables, it must be from one table at a time. The simplest method of doing this is to choose various fields and then move them together towards the QBD grid.

**To choose multiple sequential fields simply;**

- Click on **the first field** that is in the field list then hold down **the shift key** and run through to the last field. You can also choose to select **non-sequential fields** by **pressing down the ctrl key** and then choose **the individual fields** you prefer.

## Recognizing the limitations of multi-table queries

When a query with various tables is built, there are certain limits to which each of the fields must be edited. Generally, you can change data in the record set of a query and your changes will also be automatically saved in the underlying tables.

The main exception in all of this is the primary key of the table, the value of the primary key cannot be edited if referential integrity is in effect and the field is also part of a relationship.

There are times when there might be a need to make a manual edit to the records retrieved from a query. With Microsoft Access, you might not be able to update the records in your table always.

**Below are rules for updating queries;**

| Type of Query or Field | Updateable | Comments |
|---|---|---|
| One table | Yes | |
| One-to-one relationship | Yes | |
| Results contain Long Text field | Yes | Long Text field is updateable if the underlying query is not based on a many-to-many relationship |
| Results contain a hyperlink | Yes | Hyperlink is updateable if the underlying query is not based on a many-to-many relationship |
| Results contain an OLE object | Yes | Ole object will be an updateable if the underlying query is not based on a many-to-many relationship. |
| One-to-many relationship | Usually | Restrictions based on design methodology |
| Many-to-many relationship | No | Can update data in a form or data access page if Record Type = Recordset |

| | | |
|---|---|---|
| Crosstab | No | Creates a snapshot of the data. |
| Two or more tables without join line | No | Must have a join in order to determine update ability |
| Unique Value property is Yes | No | Shows unique records only in a snapshot. |
| Totals query (Sum, Avg, and so on) | No | Works with grouped data creating a snapshot |
| Calculated fields | No | They will be calculated automatically. |
| SQL-specific queries | No | Union and pass-through work with ODBC data |
| Read-only fields | No | If opened read-only or on read-only drive(CD-ROM) |
| Permissions denied | No | Insert, replace, or delete not |
| Locked by another user | No | Cannot be updated when a field has been locked by another field. |
| ODBC tables with no unique identifier | No | Unique Identifier must exist |

| Paradox table without a primary key | No | Primary key file must be in existence. |

## Overcoming query limitations

As you can see from the table above, shows that there are some instances that which queries and fields that are in tables will not be updated. Anytime your query has more than one table and some of the tables have a one-to-many relationship, some of the fields might not be updateable; this also depends on the design of the query.

## Updating a unique index (primary key)

If a query makes use of a table that is involved in a one-to-many relationship, the query must have the primary key from the "one" table. It is compulsory Access has the primary key value, this will help it locate the records that are related in the two tables.

## Replacing existing data in a query with a one-many relationship

Primarily all the fields that are in a "many" table can be updated in a one-to-many query. Furthermore, all the fields in the "one" table can also be updated with the exception of the primary key. This can be used for most database application purposes.

## Updating fields in queries

If there is a need for you to add records to two tables of a one-to-many relationship, ensure you add the foreign key from the "many" table and then display the field in the datasheet. When you must have done this, begin with either the "one" or "many" table. The primary field of the "one" table will be copied automatically to the "many" tables that join the field.

If there is a need for you to include records to multiple tables in a form ensure you add all the fields from the two tables else there will be no complete set of the records data on your form.

# Working with the Table pane

The table pane of the Query designer has information that is of great importance to your query. When you have a perfect understanding of the table pane and how you can work with the field list you will be able to build complex queries with ease.

## Looking at the join line

The line that connects tables in the Query Designer is known as a join line. It also connects the primary key in one table to the foreign key in another table. The join line helps with the representation of the relationship that exists between two tables in the Access database.

If the referential integrity happens to the set on the relationship, Microsoft Access will make use of a kind of thicker line for the join that connects the table in the Query Designer. A one-to-many relationship is shown by an infinity symbol (∞) on the "many" table end of the join line.

**Anytime the conditions below are met, Access will join two tables automatically;**

- The two tables have fields at the same time.
- The fields that have the same data type also have the same data type( text, numeric, and so on). Note that the AutoNumber data type is basically the same as the Numeric(Long Integer).
- One of the fields is a primary key in its table.

Whenever you have to work with so many tables, these join lines can be very confusing as they can overlap. When you scroll through the table, the line will become visible after some time and the field it was linked to will also become very obvious.

## Moving a table

The field list can be moved around the Query Designer when you take the title bar of the field list window with the mouse and move the field list. You can also choose to change the size of a field by simply clicking on its border and then making some adjustments to the height and the width of the field.

Access also tends to save the arrangement when you have the query saved and closed. Basically, the field list will show in the same configuration the next time the query is opened.

## Removing a table

**There might be a need for you to remove tables from a query. With the use of the mouse,**

- Choose **the table** you want to remove at the top pane of the query design window
- Press the **Delete key**.

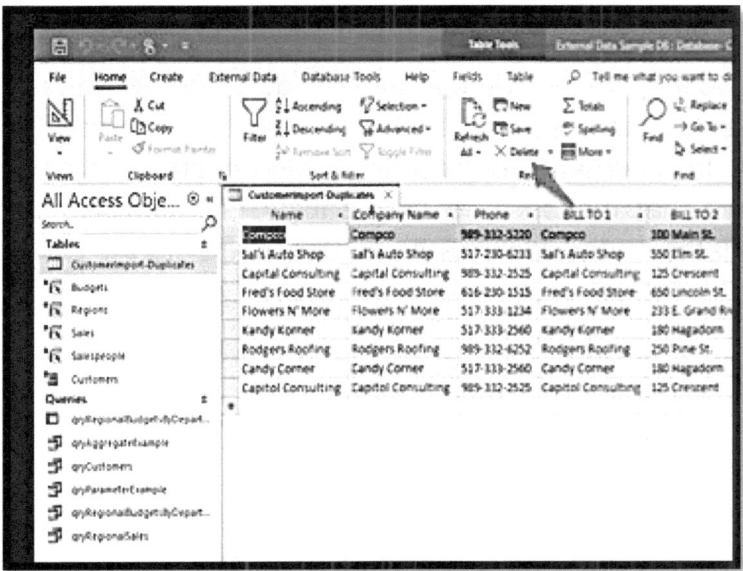

As an alternative, you can also choose to right-click on the field list window and then select the **Remove Table option** from the shortcut menu.

## Adding more tables

While working you might delete a table by mistake and seek to add the table again.

**To add a table simply follow the options below;**

- Click on the **Show Table button** located on the **Query Setup group in the Design Ribbon** option. When this is done the Show Table dialog box will then be displayed.

## Creating and Working with Query Joins

When you include tables to a query, Microsoft Access builds joins that are dependent on relationships that have been defined between tables. You can choose to create joins in queries manually even if they do not represent relationships that have been defined already. If you make use of other queries as a source of data for a query, joins can be created between the source queries and it can also be created between the queries and any table that is used as a source of data.

Joins behave in quite the same manner to query criteria in the sense they create rules that the data must match in order to be included in the query operations. In contrast to criteria, joins also ensure they indicate each pair of rows that makes sure they satisfy the join conditions will be brought together in the record set and how to create the joins.

Joins are to what queries what relationships are to tables: and an indication of how data in both sources can be combined depending on the values they both have in common.

## Understanding joins

There are basically four different types of joins they are; inner joins, outer joins, cross joins, and unequal joins. Cross joins and unequal joins are both advanced join types and they are not commonly used but you ought to know about them to have a complete understanding of how joins work.

### Inner joins

This is a type of join that Access makes includes data from a table if there is a corresponding data in the related table, and vice versa. Oftentimes, inner joins are mostly used. When a join is created and you do not indicate the kind of join it is, Access will assume that you have created an inner join. Inner joins are quite useful since they allow for the combination of data from two different sources based on shared values hence you will only see the data when the picture is complete.

## Outer joins

This type of join is almost the same as an inner join but it includes the rows that are left from one of the tables. Outer joins are quite directional; a left outer join has all the records from the left table-the the first table that is in the join- and a right outer join which also has all the records from the right table-the second table in the join.

## Full outer joins

In some systems, an outer join can have all the rows from both tables, with rows being combined when they respond. This is known as a full outer join, and Access does not totally offer support for them. Nevertheless, you can make use of a cross join and criteria to get the same effect.

## Cross joins

Oftentimes, a cross join is usually a side effect that emanates when two tables are added to a query and they are not joined. Microsoft Access will read this to mean that you have a need to see all the records from one table combined with all the records from the other table. Since there can be no combination of data, this kind of join does not often give any kind of results although there are some very extreme cases where you might be in need of a cross join.

## Unequal join

Unequal employs the use of an operator as against using the equality sign in comparing values and determining if and how the data should be combined. Unequal joins are not supported explicitly, but you can choose to make use of a cross join criteria in achieving the same effect.

## Leveraging ad hoc table joins

An ad hoc table is one that is formed when some tables are added to the query. Tables are not always joined together automatically in a query if they have not been joined already at the table level, if they don't have a common named field for a primary key, or if the Enable Auto join option is turned off.

## Specifying the type of join

The main problem encountered with the specification of joins is the fact that they show inner join behavior as the query is being executed.

**To specify a join all you have to do is to;**

- Right-click **on the line** that joins the two tables together then choose the Join properties to command from the shortcut menu.

Once this is done, it will **open the Join Properties dialog box** which will enable you to indicate an alternate join between the tables.

## Deleting joins

**If you want to delete a join that is between two tables;**

- Choose **the join line** and click on **the Delete key**.

# CHAPTER 9
# USING OPERATIONS AND EXPRESSIONS IN ACCESS

This chapter deals solely with the use of operators and expressions in calculating information, having values compared, and displaying data in a much different format- making use of queries to build examples.

## Introducing Operators

With operators you can compare values, put strings together, format data, and also take up a lot of tasks. With the use of operators, you can tell Access to perform a certain action against one or more operands. The combination of operators and operands can be known as an expression.

Each time you have a need to create an equation in Access, you will make use of the operator. For instance, operators can help indicate data validation rules in table properties, build calculated fields in forms and reports, and also indicate criteria in queries.

## Types of operators

**Operators can be divided into the following types as seen below;**

- Mathematical
- Comparison
- String
- Boolean(Logical)
- Miscellaneous

## Mathematical operators

Mathematical operators also known as arithmetic operators are used for performing numeric calculations. By definition, they are used to working with numbers in the form of operands. When you work with mathematical operators, numbers can be any numeric data type. The number can be a constant value, the value of a variable, or a field's contents. These numbers can be combined together or used individually in the creation of rather complex expressions.

**There are basically seven basic mathematical operators;**

- **Addition**

**If there is a need for you to create a calculated field in a query for the adding of a value, you will make use of this operator.**

- **Subtraction**

**The subtraction operator(-) does the work of very basic subtractions.**

- **The multiplication operator**

You can use the multiplication operator when there is a need to calculate several items. All you have to do is to create a query to show the number of items purchased and then the price for each of the items.

- **The division operator**

**This operator is used in dividing two numbers.**

- **The integer division operator**

The integer division takes up any two numbers, rounds them up or down to integers then divides the first by the second then drops the decimal portion leaving just the integer value. Note that Access uses the principle of banker's rounding or round half to even. Rounding is always done to the nearest even number.

- **The exponentiation operator**

This operator raises a number to the power of an exponent. This simply means multiplying a number by itself. For example, **3^3** means **3x3x3**.

- **The modulo division operator**

The modulo operator takes up any two numbers and rounds them either up or down to integers then divides the first by the second after which it returns the remainder.

The very dicey aspect of modulo division is that the value that is returned is usually the remainder after integer division has been performed on the operands. Oftentimes the mod is used in the determination of a number if it is either even or odd by performing modulo division with the divisor as 2.

## Comparison operators

These operators help with comparing two different values or expressions in an equation.

**There are basically six comparison operators;**

- Equal =: which returns true if both expressions are the same.
- Not equal <> : simply the opposite of the equal operator.
- Less than < : returns a logical True value if the left side of the equation is less than the right side.
- Less than or equal to < = : this returns true only if the operand on the left side of the equation is either less than or equal to the right side operand.
- Greater than > : it is also the opposite of the less-than operator. It returns True when the left side operand is greater than the operand on the right side.
- Greater than or equal to >=: this returns true if the left side is greater than or equal to the right side.

## String operators

There are basically three-string operators for working with strings in Access.

**The string operator is designed basically to work with string data:**

- & Concatenates operands
- Like Operands are similar
- Not Like Operands are dissimilar

## Boolean(logical) operators

Think of Boolean logic as a very simple way of comparing individual inputs and expressions. In order to make those comparisons, it makes use of what are called logical operators. Note that Boolean logic is a form of logic that helps with the reduction of all values to either True or False.

**Boolean operators include the following;**

- And returns True when the two expressions are True.
- Or returns True when any one of the two expressions is true.
- Not returns True when the Expression is not true.
- Xor returns True when either of the two expressions is true but not the two of them.
- Eqv returns True when both of the expressions are true or both are false.
- Imp this does the bitwise comparisons of bits that are identically positioned in two different numerical expressions.

## Miscellaneous operators

**Microsoft Access has about three useful miscellaneous operators which are;**

- Between….. And Range
- In List comparison
- Is Reversed word

## The Between……And operator

This operator helps to determine if the value of an expression falls within the range of values. If the value of the expression happens to fall within value 1 and value 2, or they both have the same value, the result is True if not then it is False.

## The In operator

This operator helps to determine if the value of an expression is the same as any value that can be found within the list. The general syntax of In is

   Expression In (value 1, value 2, value 3)

If the value of the expression is found right within the list, the result then is True; otherwise the result is false.

## The Is operator

**This operator is generally used with the keyword Null in order to determine if the value of an object is null:**

expression Is Null

Within the VBA operator, the Is operator can be used to make certain comparisons with different objects to ascertain if they represent the same entity.

It is very important to note that this operator applies to objects and objects variables alone. You cannot make use of this operator with simple variables like strings or numbers.

## Operator Precedence

Anytime you have a reason to work with complex expressions that have a lot of operators, Access will ensure it determines the operator that will be evaluated first and the operator that will be evaluated next. There is an in-built predetermined order in Access for mathematical, logical, and Boolean operators which are known as operator precedence.

Microsoft Access will always follow this order except if you make use of parentheses to override this default behavior.

Oftentimes operations within parentheses are executed before operations outside parentheses. Within parentheses, Microsoft Access ensures it takes after the default operator precedence.

**The operator ranked by order of precedence is:**

- Mathematical
- Comparison
- Boolean

## The mathematical precedence

**The order of precedence mathematical operators follow is;**

- Exponentiation
- Negation
- Multiplication and /or division(left to right)
- Integer division
- Modulus division
- Addition and/or subtraction (left to right)
- String concatenation

## The comparison precedence

**The order of precedence comparison operators follows include;**

- Equal
- Not Equal
- Less than
- Greater than
- Less than or equal to
- Greater than or equal to
- Like

## The Boolean precedence

**The Boolean operators go after this order of precedence;**

- Not
- And
- Or
- Xor
- Eqv
- Imp

# Using Operators and Expressions in Queries

Building of complex query criteria is one of the most common uses of operators and expressions. When you properly have a complete understanding of how all of this works it can help to ease the process of building queries that are very useful.

It is extremely very important for you to know how to indicate criteria and also how to effectively write queries. Even though queries can be used against just one table for one criterion, various queries retrieve information from various tables with the use of criteria that are more complex. Due to this complexity, your queries can extract only the data that you are in need of and also in the very order that you are in need of it. With the use of operators and expressions, you will be able to create complex select queries in order to limit.

## Using query comparison operators

Whenever you have to work with queries, there might be a need for you to indicate one or more criteria in order to limit the scope of the information that was displayed. All you have to do to indicate criteria is to make use of comparison operators in equations and calculations.

The various categories of operators are mathematical, relational, logical, and string. In select queries, operators can be used either in the field cell or the Criteria cell of the Query by Design (QBD) grid.

**With the use of these operators, you can sort out groups of records such as;**

- A range of products like all the sales made between March and April.
- Product records that have a picture.
- All records that do match a value.

## Understanding complex criteria

Complex query criteria are built with the use of any combination of the operators. For most queries built, complex criteria have a series of Ands and Ors, complex criteria can also oftentimes be created by inserting example data into different cells of the QBD pane. Nevertheless, it is quite important for you to note that the use of Boolean operators is not the only way by which records can be chosen based on multiple criteria.

The And/Or operators are one of the most widely used operators when having to work with complex criteria. The operator takes into consideration two different expressions and then determines if the expressions are either true or false. Once this has been done, the operators will then compare the results of the two expressions against each other for logical true/false answers.

Anytime the result of an And/Or operation is True, the overall condition is also said to be true, and the query also shows the records meeting the true condition. Note that the result of an And operation can only be true when the two sides of the expression are true, whereas the result of an Or operation is true when any of the sides of the expression is true. In fact, one side can be a null value and the result of the Or operation will still be true if the other side is true. This is the basic difference there is between the And/Or operators.

## Using functions in select queries

A query function can be described as a mathematical expression evaluated against each item returned by a query, and whose output is also stored in a dynamic, temporary field generated at query time.

Whenever you work with queries, there might be a need for you to make use of the in-built Access functions to show information. For instance, you might want to display information like the day of the week for sales dates. This information can be displayed when you create calculated fields for the query.

## Referencing fields in select queries

It is best to have referenced field names in an enclosed bracket ([]). Microsoft Access needs brackets around any field names that have spaces or punctuation marks. If by mistake you fail to add the brackets around a field name in the QBD grid. Access might have a quote placed around the field name and then treat it as literal text rather than treating it as a field name.

# Entering Single-Value Field Criteria

While working, you will definitely come to a point where you might have a need to limit the query records returned on the basis of one single field criterion. The queries will have a need for a single value criterion which is just about the entry of only one expression in the QBD grid.

Note that your criteria expressions can be specified for just about any data type: Text, Numeric, Date/Time, and so on. OLE Objects and calculated field types can also have their criteria specified.

## Entering character (Text or Memo) criteria

Character criteria are used basically for Text or for Memo data-type fields. They are neither examples nor patterns of the contents of the field.

**If you would like to create a query that returns customers that live in California for instance, take the steps below:**

- Open a **new query** in Design view based on the customer's table and include the company, phone, and state fields to the QBD pane.
- Click on the **Criteria cell** for the State field.
- Enter **CA in the cell**. Once you have done this, click on the **Datasheet View button** in the Home Ribbon's view group in order to check the result of the query.

There is no need for you to type quotes around CA. Access usually assumes that you are using a literal string CA and will automatically include quotes for you.

## The Like operator and wildcards

You can make use of the Like operator to locate values in a field that matches the pattern that has been indicated. For patterns, you can choose to indicate the complete value or you can decide to make use of wildcard characters in order to locate a range of values.

In an expression, you can make use of the Like operator in the comparison of a field value to a string expression. For instance, if you insert Like "C*" in an SQL query, the query will return all the field values that start with the letter C. In a parameter query, you can prompt the user for a pattern to locate.

Make use of the Like operator in the Criteria cell of a field to perform wildcard searches against the contents of the field. Microsoft Access looks for a pattern in the field; you can make use of the question mark **(?)** to show just one character or the asterisk **(*)** for various characters. The question mark **(?)** denotes any single character that is in the same position as the question mark in the example expression. An asterisk **(*)** also stands for any number of characters in the same position in which the asterisk is located.

Wildcards can be used alone and they can also be used in conjunction with one another. They can be used various times within the same expression.

## Specifying non-matching values

If you would like to indicate a non-matching value, you can simply make use of either the Not or the <> operator at the front of the expression that there is no need to match.

**Follow the steps below to specify non-matching values;**

- Open a **new query** in **Design view** and include the customer table.
- Include **Company and State** from the customer table.
- Click **anywhere** in the Criteria cell of State.
- Enter **<> CA** in the cell. With this Microsoft, Access will automatically add quotation marks around CA if you do not add it yourself before leaving the field. The query will choose all of the records except for customers that live in the state of California.

## Entering numeric criteria

Make use of numeric criteria with either numeric or currency data-type fields. You can simply insert the numbers and the decimal symbol if need be then followed by the mathematical or comparison operator but ensure you do not make use of commas.

The criteria added to numeric fields oftentimes include comparison operators like less than <, greater than >, or equal to =. If there is a need for you to indicate a comparison different from equal, you must also insert the operator too as the value. Note that Access will set the default to equal when you are executing the chosen query.

## Entering true or false criteria

True and False criteria are used basically with Yes/No type fields. There is no use of the Not and the <> operators to show the opposite, but the Yes/No data also has a null state that might be worthy of consideration. Microsoft Access understands lots of forms of true and false.

**Hence, rather than typing yes, you can insert any of the following in the Criteria;**

On, True, Not No, <> No, <No, or -1. Note that a Yes/No field can have about three states: Yes, No, and Null. The Null occurs when no default value was fixed in a table and the value has not been inserted yet. When checking for Is Null, it shows just the record that contains the Null in the field, and checking for Is Not Null regularly shows all records with Yes or No in the field. Once a Yes/No box has been checked, it can never return to Null again. It must either be Yes or No (-1 or 0).

## Entering OLE object criteria

You can choose to indicate criteria for OLEobjects: Is Null or Is Not Null. Note that the Is Not Null option is the right syntax, you can also make use of the Not Null option in the QBD grid, Access will then provide the Is operator for you.

## Using Multiple Criteria in a Query

This section entails having to work with various criteria based on just one field. You can make use of the QBD when you are in this instance. It can help to indicate criteria for various fields in a select query. When you make use of multiple queries, for example, you can determine the products that were sold for the past 60 days.

### Understanding an OR operation

The Or operator is used when there is a need for a field to meet either of two conditions. For instance, there might be a need for you to see all the records wherein the customer has an address in either California or San Francisco. This simply means that you would like to see where a customer has addresses in CA, S.F, or probably both. If either of these expressions happens to be true, the answer will also be true.

**Consider the points below to help clarify the point;**

- Customer 1 has an address in CA: the expression is true.
- Customer 2 has an address in S.F: the expression is true.
- Customer 3 has an address in both CA and S.F: the expression is also true.
- Customer 4 has an address in LA: the expression is false.

## Specifying multiple values with the Or operator

The Or operator can be used in the specification of various values for a field.

**To perform this operation, follow the steps below;**

- Open a **new query** in Design view and then add for examples table for customers and tables for sales.
- Add **company** and state from the customer's table ad sales date from the sales table.
- Select the **criteria cell** of the state.
- Insert either **CA or S.F** in the cell.

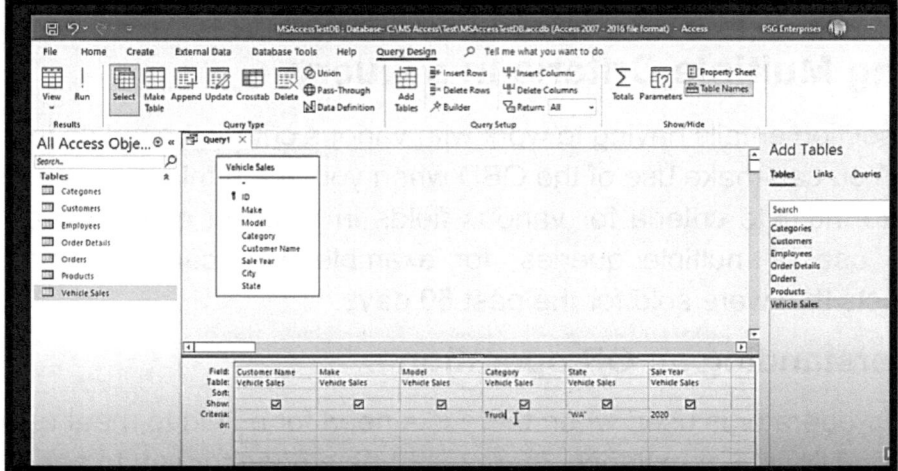

## Using the Or cell or the QBD pane

Apart from making use of the literal Or operator as just one expression on the Criteria row underneath the State field, you can also choose to provide individual criteria for the field vertically on different rows of the QBD pane. Whenever a query is built with the use of "vertical" or criteria, Microsoft Access will optimize the SQL statement at the back of the query by placing all the criteria into just one expression.

## Using a list of values with the In operator

An alternative method you can make use of in indicating various values of just one field is the use of the In operator. The In operator searches for a value from a list of values. The list of values that are embedded in the parentheses will then become an example criterion.

## Using And to specify a range

Oftentimes, the And operator is used in fields that have numeric or date/time data types. It is sparingly used with text data types, though it can be this way in certain situations.

The And operator is used when there is a need for a field to meet two or more conditions. As against the Or operation that has various conditions for which it can be true, the And operation is true only when the two sides of the expression are true. When an And operator with just one field is used, it sets a range of acceptable values in the field. Hence, the main purpose of an Ad operator in just one field is to set a range of records that will be viewed.

## Using the Between… and And operator

You can ask for a range of records with the use of another method which is the Between….And operator. With this method, you can search for records that meet a range of values. Note that the operands for the Between….And operators are inclusive.

## Searching for null data

A field might be empty for various reasons. The value might not be known at the time when the data entry was being made or the person who entered the data might just have forgotten and ended up omitting that particular field. Note that if a value is not specified in the table design, the field will simply remain empty. Logically, a null field is either true or false. It doesn't mean that the field means zero. Simply a null field is one that doesn't have any value.

There are basically two special operators by which you can work with the null value fields in Access. They are Is Null and Is Not Null. These operators are used to place a limit to the criteria based on the null state of a field.

# Entering criteria in multiple fields

This section entails having to work with criteria across more than one field. When there is a need for you to place a limit on records based on the various field conditions, you do this by configuring criteria in each of the fields that you will make use of for the scope. Note that the queries will also need that criteria to be placed in various fields and also on various lines.

## Using And and Or across fields in a query

In order to make use of the And operator and the Or operator across various fields, ensure you place the example or pattern data in the Criteria cells for the And operator and also for the Or cells of one field that is relative to the placement in a different field.

Whenever there is a need for you to make use of the And operator between two or more fields, simply place the example or pattern data you want to work with across the same row in the QBD pane. Furthermore, when there is a need for you to make use of the Or operator between fields, the criteria should also be placed on various rows in the QBD pane.

## Specifying Or criteria across fields in a query

Although the Or operator is not used across all fields as often as the And operator, seldom the Or operator is also very useful. For instance, there might be a need for you to see some customer records regardless of the state wherein the customer lives.

**To create this kind of query, follow the steps below;**

- Add **the customer's table, sales table, and also products** table to a query that has just been created.
- Include **Company and State** from the customer's table and also the Description and the Category from the products table.
- Insert **CA** as the criteria for states.
- Insert **the produc**t in the or cell under Category.

Note that when a criterion is placed on a different row in the QBD grid, Microsoft Access will interpret this as an Or between fields. This query will also return customers who either live in California or happen to have purchased a product.

## Using And and or together in different fields

After you must have worked with And and Or separately, then you must now be ready to build a query with the use of And and Or in various fields. This section is simply about combining the two operators in the dame field. Ensure that the query is logical when you are doing this.

## A complex query on different lines

The use of And s and Or s across different fields can be said to be a complex query. Note that Access always interpreted dates based on the region and language settings in the Windows Control Panel. The settings can inform Access on how it should interpret short dates as mm/dd/yyyy or dd/mm/yyyy. Ensure that you account for all of these regional differences when having to work with dates. Note also that Access interprets two-digit years from 00 to 40 as 2000 to 2040, this is why the use of four-digit years when entering data is always a good idea.

# CHAPTER 10
# GOING BEYOND SELECT QUERIES

Using a select query to display and retrieve records is a core part of data analysis with Microsoft Access. The scope of data analysis is quite a broad one which includes comparing and grouping data, deleting and updating data, shaping and reporting data, and so on. There are some in-built tools in Access that have some special functionalities which are basically designed to take care of this task.

This chapter contains various in-depth knowledge on tools that are available for use in Access and how they can help you go past just select queries.

## Aggregate Queries

An aggregate query can be defined as a method of getting group and subgroup data by analysis of a set of individual data entries. This term is often used by database developers and also database administrators.

With the use of a select query, you can retrieve records alone as they are being displayed in the data source but with the use of an aggregate query, you can retrieve a summary snapshot of all your data that shows averages, totals, counts, and lots more.

## Creating an aggregate query

You can sum a column of numbers in a query with the use of a type of function known as an aggregate function. Aggregate functions do the calculation on a column of data and return just one value. Microsoft Access offers a variety of aggregate functions which includes sum and count. Avg, Min, and Max. You sum data by adding the sum function to your query and you count data by making use of the count function etc.

In addition, Microsoft Access offers various ways to add sum and other aggregate functions to a query.

**You can simply;**

- Open **your query** in the datasheet view and add **a Total row**. The Total Row Which is a feature in access enables you to make use of an aggregate function in one or more columns of a query set without necessarily having to make changes to the design of your query.
- **Create a totals query**: A totals query calculates subtotals across a group of Records; a total row calculates grand total for one or more columns of data. For instance, if you want to subtotal all sales by City or by quarter, you make use of a total query to group your records by the desired category and you then sum the sales figures.
- **Create a crosstab query**: A crosstab query Is a unique type of query that shows its results in a grid that looks like an Excel sheet. crosstab queries help to summarize your values and then drop them by two sets of facts - one set down the side and the other set of facts across the top.

# About aggregate functions

There are various aggregate functions and it is expedient for you to know a particular function that best fits your data analysis.

## Group By

The Group By is an aggregate function in Access that helps with the combination of records that are identical in the indicated field into just a single record. A summary value will then be created for each of the records if you add an SQL aggregate function like Sum or Count in the SELECT statement.

**There are a couple of things that you should have in mind when you are making use of the Group By aggregate function;**

- Access performs the Group By function in your aggregate query first before it performs any other form of aggregation. If you are performing a Group By along with some other aggregate function, the Group By function will be done first.
- Access organizes each of the groups by field in either ascending or descending order. If your query happens to have more than one group-by-fields, each of the fields will also be sorted in ascending order and it will start with the leftmost side of the field.
- Access treats various group-by-field as one unique item.

## Sum, Avg, Count, StDev, Var

All of these aggregate functions perform mathematical calculations on the records in the field you have chosen.

**Bear in mind that these functions do not include any records that are configured to null.**

- **Sum**: this function helps to calculate the total value of all of the records in the designated field or grouping. This function works only with data types such as; Currency, AutoNumber, Date/Time, and Number.
- **Avg**: this function helps to calculate the average of all of the records in the chosen field or grouping. This function works

with data types like; AutoNumber, Currency, Date/Time, and Number.
- **Count**: This function simply helps in counting the number of entries within the chosen field or grouping. This function is very unique too as it works with all types of data.
- **StDev**: this function helps to calculate the standard deviation across all of the records within the designated field or grouping. This function will also work well with the following data types; AutoNumber, Currency, Date/Time, and Number.
- **Var**: this function does the job of calculating the amount by which all of the values that are in the chosen field or grouping vary from the average value of the group. This function also works alone with data types such as; AutoNumber, Currency, Date/Time, and Number.

## Min, Max, First, Last

These functions in this section help to evaluate all of the records in the designated field or grouping and then returns just one value from the group.

**Min**: This helps to return the value of the record with the lowest value in the chosen field or grouping. This function works with data types like; AutoNumber, Currency, and Date/Time. Number, and Text.

**Max**: This option returns the value of the record that has the highest value in the chosen field or grouping. This function will also work alone with data types like; AutoNumber, Currency, Date/Time, Number, and Text.

**First:** this function returns the value of the first record that is in the chosen field or grouping. This function is also a unique one as it works with all of the data types.

Last: this function helps to return the value of the last record in the chosen field or grouping. It is also a unique one as it works with all of the data types.

## Expression, Where

Expressions can be used for a number of tasks in Microsoft Access like performing mathematical calculations, combining or extracting text, or validating data.

**Expressions can be used in the following ways;**

- **Calculate values**: you can use expressions in the calculation of values that are not necessarily in your data. You can calculate in fields in tables and queries, and you can also choose to calculate in controls on forms and reports. A column in a table or a query that emanates from a calculation as such is known as a calculated field. You can create a calculated field that combines two or more table fields.
- **Defining a default value**: expressions can be used to define a default value for a table field or for a control on a form or report. These default values are displayed anywhere you open a table, report, or from.
- **Create a validation rule**: with the use of an expression, you can create a validation rule that can help to control what values users can insert in a field or control.
- **Define query criteria**: you can use expressions to create a limit results to a subset that you desire. You can choose to insert criteria to define a skate range, and Access will only return the rows that match the criteria. Anytime you include criteria to the query and then run the query, it will return only the values that match the dates that have been indicated.

Where is a clause that enables you to include a criterion to a particular field that cannot be found in your aggregate query, effectively applying a filter to your analysis. Finally, note that fields that are tagged with the where clause cannot be shown in an aggregate query, if you happen to check the Show checkbox of a field with a where clause, you will immediately get an error message which will state that you cannot show the field for which you inserted Where in the Total row. .

# Action Queries

In Microsoft Access and some other database management systems, queries can do so much more than just showing data, they can also perform various actions on the data in your database. Action queries are queries that have the capacity to add, alter or delete different records at once.

With the use of action queries, you can choose to increase your productivity and also reduce the chances of errors by ensuring you carry out all your analytical processes within Access. Think of an action query in just the same way you would a select query.

Just like a select query, an active query helps to extract a data set from a data source based on the definitions and criteria that are passed to the query. The main difference is that when an action query sends back results it will not show a data set, rather, it will perform some action on those results. The action it performs is often dependent on its type. There are about four types of action queries and they will be discussed in the section.

## Make-table queries

A make-table query creates a new table that has data from an already existing table. The table that is created has records that must have met some definitions and criteria of the make-table query.

This simply means that when you must have created a query and there is then a need to have the results of your query captured in its own specific table, you can choose to make use of the make-table query to build a hard table with the results obtained from your query. Once this has been done, you can make use of your table in some other analytical process.

Note that the data in a table that is made by a make-table query is not linked to its source data at all. This then means that the data in your new table will not be updated when data in the original table has been changed.

**To create a make-table query simply follow the steps below;**

- Have a **query created** in the Query Design view.
- Choose **the Design tab** of the Ribbon then select the **Make Table button**. The Make Table dialog box will then be displayed.

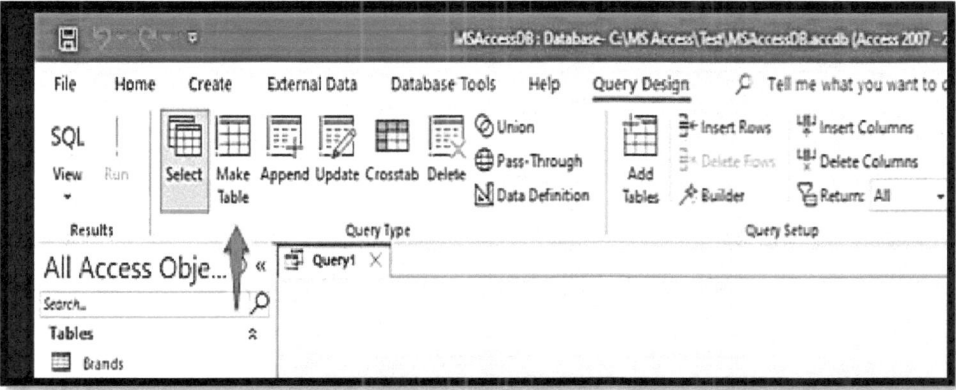

- In the **Table Name field**, insert **the name** you would like to give your new table. Ensure you do not insert the name of a table that you already have in your database as if you do that it will be overwritten.
- Select **the OK button** in order to close the dialog box, then you choose **the Run command option** to execute your query.

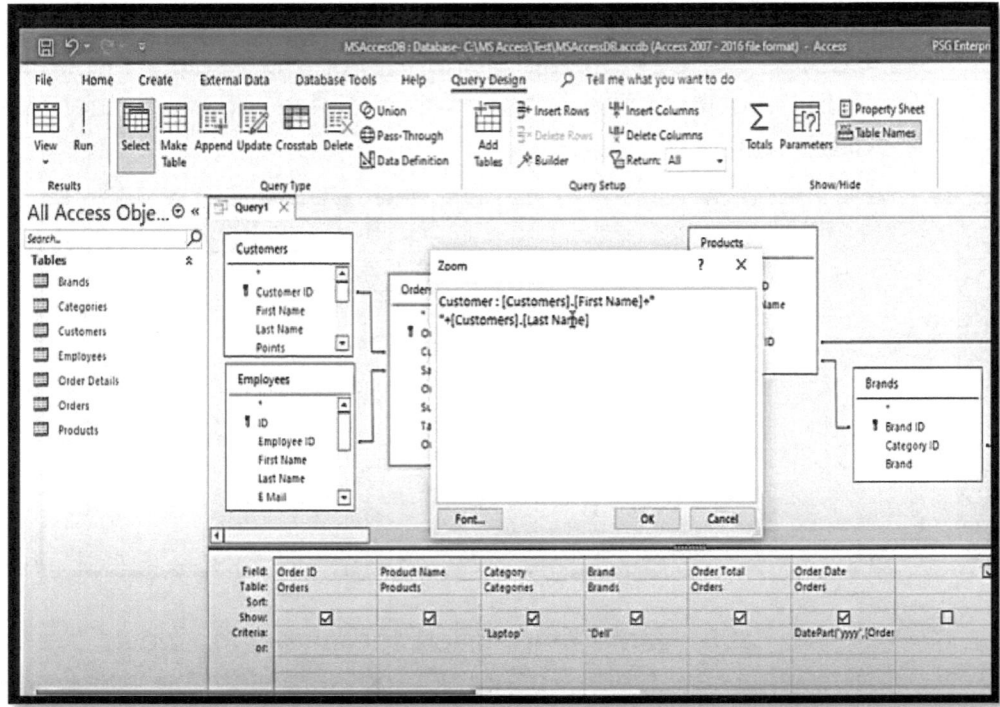

- Click on the **Yes button** in order to confirm and then create **your new table**. Once your query has been executed, you will find a new query in your Table objects.

## Delete queries

A delete query is one that records from a table based on the definitions and the criteria indicated. This means that a delete query can affect a group of records that meet a particular criterion that has been applied. Although you can delete records manually, making use of a delete query is quite more efficient. Delete queries are also best used if there is a need for records to be deleted from a table based on a comparison to another table.

Note that queries that have been deleted can in no way be recovered hence it is best for you; to make a backup of your database before you execute the delete query.

## Append queries

An append query chooses records from one or more sources of data and then copies the chosen records to an existing table. For example, assume that you have a database that has a table of potential new customers, and that you already have a table in your current database that also stores this same kind of data. There will be a need to have the data stored in just one place hence the decision to copy it from the new database to the existing table.

In order to avoid inserting the new data manually, you can simply make use of an append query in copying the records.

**When you make use of an append query, you can;**

- **Append more than one record in one pass**: if you happen to copy data manually, you must have a course to perform multiple copy/paste operations. When you use a query, you choose all the data at once and then copy it.
- **Review your selection before you copy it**: With the use of append, you can view your selection in Datasheet view and then make the necessary corrections as needed before you copy the data. This can be very useful especially if your query includes criteria expressions and there is a need for you to attempt various times just in a bid to get it right. Append query can not be undone, if you make a mistake, you must either restore your database from a backup or correct your error either manually or by the use of a delete query.
- **Make use of criteria in refining your selection**: For instance, there might be a need for you to append the records of the customers who live in your city alone.

Note that not all the record you think is being appended actually makes it to the table, you should also be wary of running the same append query more than once so that the data won't end up being duplicated. Records during append can be lost due to two popular reasons which are key violation and type conversion failure.

**The following are the basic steps to following in creating an append query;**

- Create a **select query**.
- Change the **select query** to an append query.
- Make a choice of the destination fields for each column in the append query.
- Preview and then **execute** the query in order to append the records.

## Update queries

The main reason why you should make use of an update query is to ensure you save time. There isn't any other easier method to edit large amounts of data at once than with the use of an update query.

As with almost every other action query, there is a need for you to always take precautions in order to ensure that you are not in a situation where you cannot undo the effects of an update query. Always ensure you have a backup created before executing your query. As an alternative, you can execute a select query in order to show and then alter the query into a make-table query; execute the make-table query in order to create a backup of the data that you are about to update then execute the query once again in form of an update to have the records overwritten.

**Note that your update query will not be successful if any of the following applies;**

- Your query is making use of a join to another query. To provide solutions to this issue, build a temporary table that you can make use of instead of the joined query.
- You have your query based on a crosstab query, a union query, or a subquery that has aggregate functions. In providing solutions to this issue, build a temporary table that you can make use of instead of having to make use of the query.
- Your query is based on three or more tables and there is a many-to-one-to-many relationship. To provide a solution to this problem, build a temporary table that you can make use of without the relationship.
- Your query is based on a SQL pass-through query. If you would like to have your way around this, build a temporary table that you can make use of instead of the query.

- You have your query based on a table in a database that is already opened as read-only or can be found on a read-only drive. To have your way around this problem, all you have to do is to obtain written access to the database or drive.

## Crosstab Queries

A Microsoft Access crosstab query shows summary information in a compact form that is quite the same as a spreadsheet. These types of queries can show a large amount of summary data in a format that is much simpler to analyze than having to view the information in a database form.

The anatomy of a crosstab is quite simple. There is a need for you to have a minimum of three fields in order to create the matrix structure that will much later become your crosstab. The first field makes up the row headings, the second field makes up the column headings and the third field is made up of the aggregated data which is always located at the center of the matrix.

There are basically two different methods that can be used in creating a crosstab query. You can make use of the Crosstab Query Wizard or you can create a query manually with the use of the query design grid.

## Creating a crosstab querying using the Crosstab Query Wizard

**Follow the steps below to make use of the Crosstab Query Wizard in the creation of a crosstab query;**

- Choose the **Create tab** of the Ribbon then click on **the Query Wizard button**. This will then open the New Query dialog box.
- Choose the **Crosstab Query Wizard** from the selection list then choose the **OK button**.

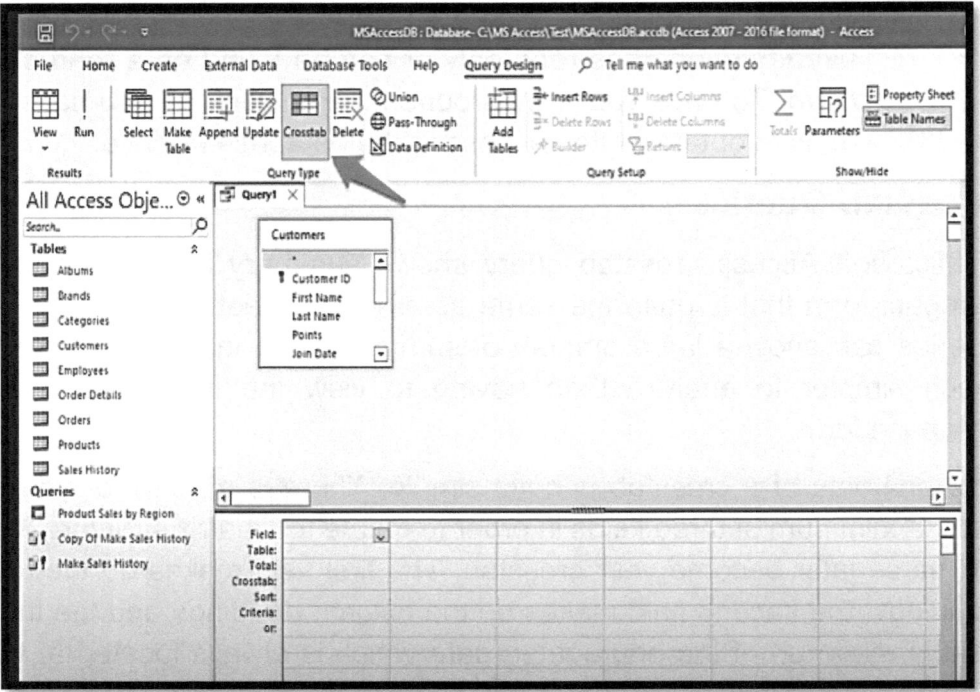

- Choose the **Dim_ Transactions** option then choose the Next button. The next step then is to identify the fields that you would like to make use of the row headings.
- Choose the **ProductID field** and then choose the **button** with the >symbol on it to move it to the Selected Fields list. Note that you have the option to choose up to three fields to include in your crosstab query as row headings. Bear in mind that Access treats each combination of the headings as a special item. This simply means that the combination is grouped before the records in each of the groups are aggregated.
- Click on **the Next button**. In the next step, all you have to do is to identify the field you would like to use as the column heading for your crosstab query. Bear in mind that there can only be one column heading in your crosstab.
- Choose the **OrderDate field** from the field list.

If your Column Heading is a date field, as the OrderDate you will then see a step in which you will have the option of specifying an interval to group your dates by.

- Choose **Quarter** and notice that the sample diagram at the lower part of the dialog box updates as it should.
- Choose **the LineTotal field** from the Fields list and then choose Sum from the Functions list.
- Give your **query a name** you can also view **your query** or modify the design.
- Lastly, you can view your query results then simply clicking on the **Finish button**.

## Creating a crosstab query manually

Though the Crosstab Query Wizard makes it much easier to build a crosstab in just a few clicks, it does have its own limitations that might **inhibit your effort on data analysis:**

- You can choose just one data source on which your cross tab will be based. What this means is that there is a need for you to crosstab data residing across various tables, there will also be a need for you to build a temporary query to use as your own data source.
- There is no way you can filter or place a limit on your crosstab query with criteria from the Crosstab Query Wizard.
- You are limited to just three-row headings.
- You will not be able to explicitly define the order of your column heading from the Crosstab Query Wizard.

## Using the query design grid to create your crosstab query

**Below are steps used in creating a crosstab query with the use of the query design grid:**

- Create an **aggregate query**
- Choose **the Design tab** of the Ribbon and then click **on the crosstab button** with this a row called Crosstab has been added to your own query grid.
- Under each field in the Crosstab row, choose if the field will be a row heading, a value, or a column heading.
- Run **the query** in order to see your crosstab in action.

## Customizing your crosstab queries

Although the crosstab is very useful on its own, there is a need for it to be tweaked a little. The section below explains some ways by which we can customize your crosstab queries to meet your needs.

## Defining criteria in a crosstab query

### To have your filter defined for your crosstab query simply;

- Insert **the criteria** as you normally would for just any other aggregate query.

## Changing the sort order of your crosstab query column headings

By default, crosstab queries often sort their column headings in alphabetical order. You can choose to indicate the column order of a crosstab query by simply changing the Column Headings attribute in the Query Properties.

### To locate the Column Headings attribute:

- Open **the query** in the Design view

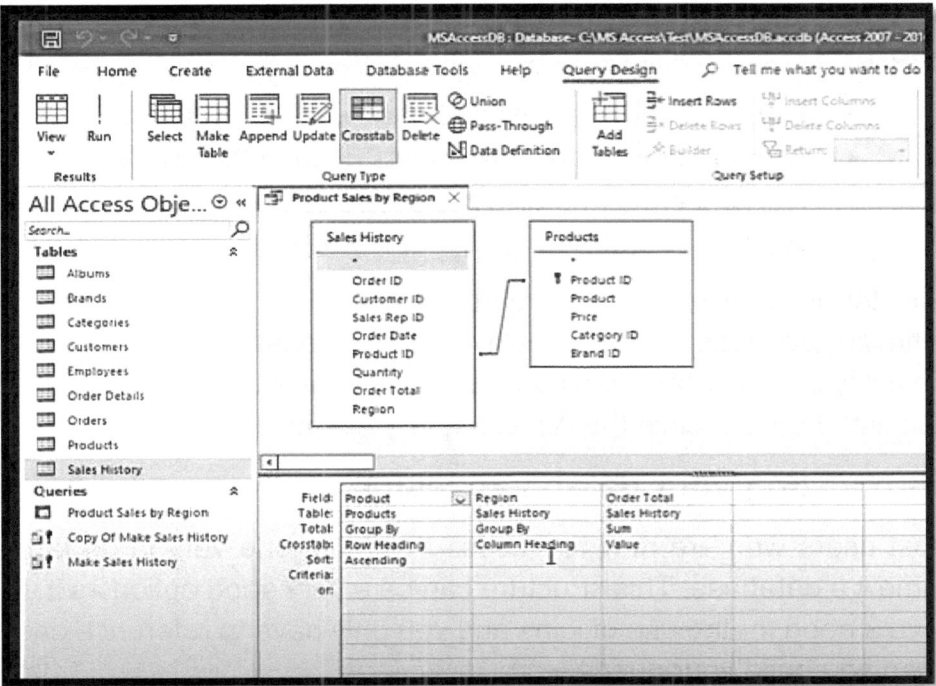

- Right-click **in the gray area** above the white query grid and then choose the Properties option.
- Enter **the order** in which you would like to see the column heading by changing the Column Headings attribute.

## Optimizing Query Performance

With analyzing a considerable amount of data, all are expected to run smoothly but when you have thousands of records, performance can become quite an issue. There are certain steps you can take in order to optimize query performance and also reduce the time t takes to execute your large analytical processes.

Access has an in-built query optimizer. This optimizer is charged with the task of creating a query execution strategy. The query execution strategy can be defined as a set of instructions given to the Access database engine (ACE) that instructs it on how to execute the query in the fastest, most cost-effective way possible.

**Access query optimizer bases its query execution on the factors below:**

- Whether indexes exist in the tables used in the query.
- The number of tables and joins used in the query.
- The presence and also the scope of any criteria or expression used in the query.

The terms garbage-in and garbage-out also apply to the Access optimizer because its functionality is largely based on the makeup and the utility of your tables and queries, tables that are not well designed can also limit how effective the Access query optimizer is.

## Normalizing your database design

Most users who are new to Access build just one very large table and name it a database. This structure can be a very good option as it doesn't have a need for the use of joins and you only have to reference one table when you build your queries.

When you choose to normalize your database to take on a relational structure, you will end up breaking your data into various smaller tables.

## Using indexes on appropriate fields

When you run a query in which you have to sort and filter on a field that has not been indexed, Access has to scan and then go through the whole data set before it can return any result. By contrast, queries that sort and filter on fields that have been indexed run much faster since Access makes use of the index to check positions and restrictions.

You can build an index on a field in a table by simply moving into the Design view of the table and then making some adjustments to the Indexed property.

## Optimizing by improving query design

**Take a look at the steps below to help speed up your queries and also optimize your analytical processes;**

- Ensure **you avoid** sorting or filtering fields that are not indexed.
- Avoid **creating queries** that select from a table.
- There might be a need for you to add more fields in your query design only in order to set the criteria against them.
- Do not use **open-ended ranges like > or<** rather you can make use of the Between…And statement.
- Avoid **making use of calculated fields** in subqueries or domain aggregate functions. When you make use of calculated fields in them it compounds the query's performance loss to some extent.

## Compacting and repairing the database regularly

There might be some changes to your database over a long period of time such as an increase or decrease in the number of tables, you might have added or removed various tables and queries that are temporary or you might have closed the database in an abnormal manner. Access will regenerate table statistics and also re-optimize your queries anytime you make some repairs to your database; this way they will also be recompiled the next time the query is executed.

**To repair your database simply;**

- Choose **the Database Tools tab on the Ribbon**.
- Click on **the Compact and Repair Database command**.

**You can choose to set your database to repair automatically anytime you close it by doing the following;**

- Locate **the Ribbon** and then choose **the File option**.

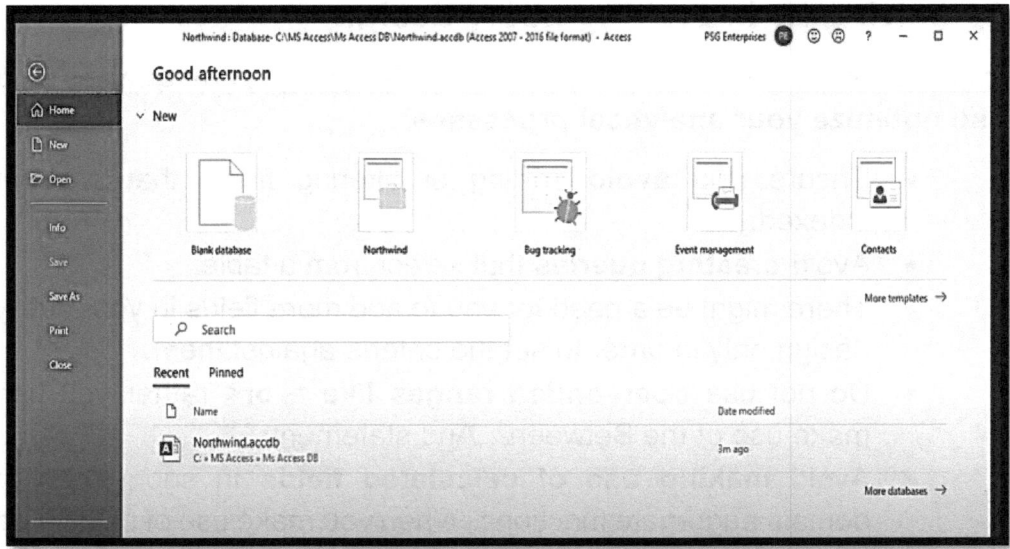

- Click on **Options** then the **Access Options dialog box** will then be displayed.
- Choose the **Current Database** to show the configuration settings for the current database.

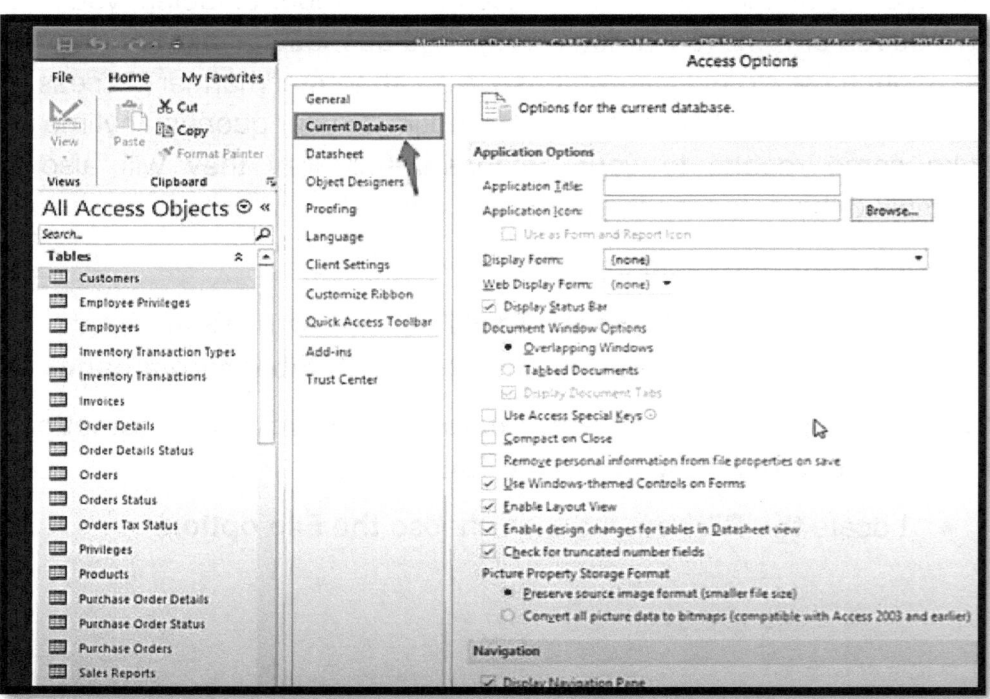

- Place a **checkmark** close to **Compact** on Close and then click on the **OK button** in order to confirm the change.

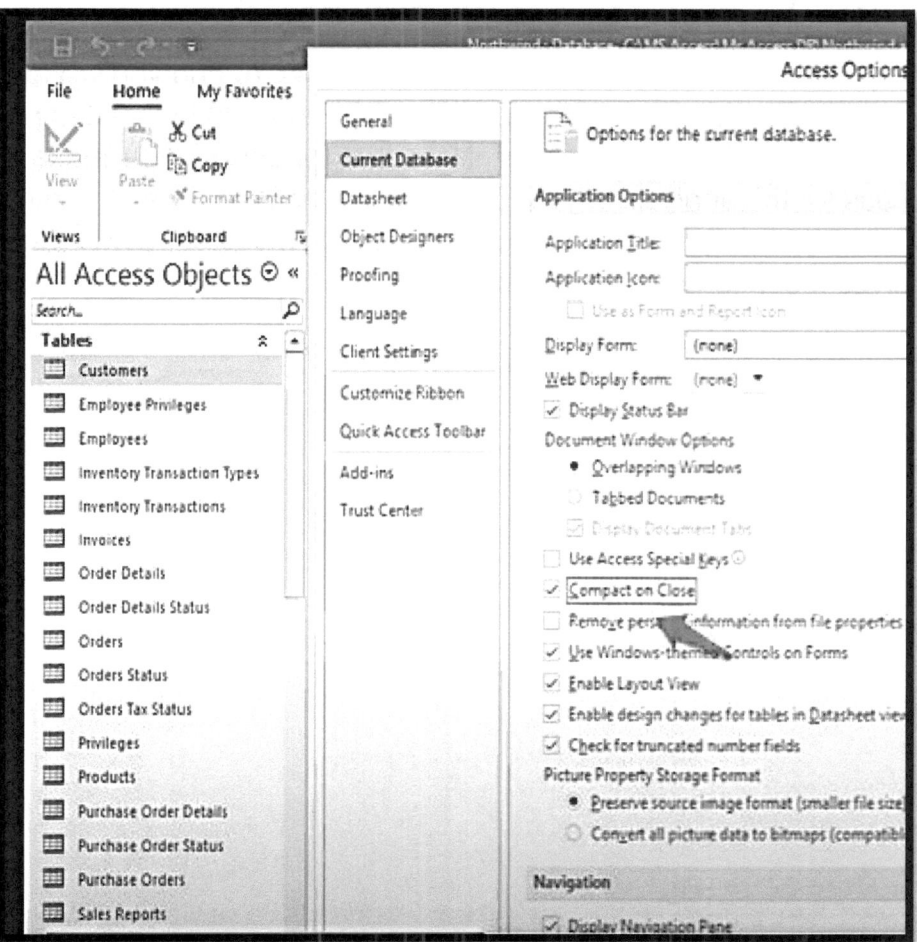

# PART IV
# ANALYZING DATA IN MICROSOFT ACCESS

This part covers chapters 11 through to chapter 16 and you will learn the various tools and various functionalities in Access 2022 that can promote more meaningful data analysis. Note that whenever you make use of Access for the analysis of your data you can help with the streamlining of your analytical processes, increase your own productivity and also analyze much larger sets of data.

# CHAPTER 11
# TRANSFORMING DATA IN ACCESS

The transformation of data generally has to do with various actions that should help with cleaning certain actions like creating a table structure, taking duplicates off, cleaning text, and standardizing data fields. There are definitely times when you will receive data that is totally unpolished and you will have to perform some kind of data transformation before meaningful analysis of the data that is in this state can be done.

In this chapter, you will learn how to make use of some techniques in Access which will make it quite easy for you to clean and transform your data without having to turn to Excel.

## Finding and Removing Duplicate Records

When you have duplicate records it can be really detrimental as it can kill any form of data analysis. Hence, there is a need for you to take off duplicate records each time you receive a new set of data.

### Defining duplicate records

It is important for you to note that when you have two records that have the same value in a column it doesn't really mean that you have a duplicate record. To properly have duplicate records there is a need for you to have a clear and perfect idea of the field that best makes a unique record in your table, with this you can test your table for duplicates with so much ease when you must have configured them as either a primary or combination key.

### Finding duplicate records

If you have checked your records properly and you are very sure that your data contains duplicates it is necessary for you to locate and have a review of the duplicate records before having to remove them. When you do this you will be sure you will not be making any mistakes as a duplicate record and take them off from your analysis.

**The easiest way to locate duplicate records in your data is to execute the Find Duplicates Query Wizard:**

- Choose **the Create tab** option of the Ribbon and then choose the **Query Wizard button**.
- Choose **Find Duplicates** Query Wizard and then select the **OK button**.
- Choose the **specific data set** you will like to make use of in Your Find Duplicate query then click on the **Next option**.
- Locate **the field or combinations of fields** that best defines a unique record in your data set then choose the **Next option**.
- Specify any **additional fields** that you would like to see in your query.
- Give your **query a name** then click on the **finish button**.

## Removing duplicate records

Removing duplicates can be very easy when you are dealing with a small set of data but if you are working with a large set of data, your Find Duplicates query may actually become more difficult for you to handle in regards to deleting records.

**To remove lots of data at once, follow the steps below;**

- Right-click on the **LeadList table** and then choose the **Copy option**.
- Right-click **one more time** and choose **the paste option** which will then display the paste As dialog box.
- Give your new table **a name** and choose **Structure only** from the paste option that is displayed in the dialog box.
- Open your **new leadlist_NoDups table** in the Design view and choose the **appropriate field or combination of fields as the primary key**.
- Design **an append query** that will append all of the records from the LeadList table to the LeadList_NoDups table.

Note that Access in no way tries to determine logically to see if records are duplicated. It will process the result directly. For example, if you make a mistake while typing an address or phone number this would mean that rows that are duplicated will be allowed since there is already a mistake in one.

# Common Transformation Tasks

This section deals with the types of common transformation tasks that might be needed by unpolished sets of data;

## Filling in blank fields

Oftentimes you might be presented with fields that have null values and you will have to fill in the blank fields with some sort of logical code that will serve as an indication of the missing value. Having to fill the null fields in your data set is as simple as executing an update query.

However, it is very important to note that there are about two types of blank values of a text field which are null and empty strings. Whenever you have to fill the blanks values ensure you add the empty strings as a criterion in your update query; with this, you will be sure you won't be missing any field.

## Concatenating

There is no need for you to export data out of Access to Excel simply because you want to concatenate. Concatenation can be done in Access by simply updating the query.

## Concatenating fields

As earlier established, concatenation in Access is all about updating the query. Note that when executing an update query that does the job of concatenation you must ensure that the field you are trying to update is wide enough to accept the concatenated string. For instance, if the length of your concatenated string is about 50 characters and the field size of the field you want to update is 25 characters, your concatenated string will be cut short without you receiving any warning.

# Augmenting field values with your own text

You can choose to augment the values that are in your fields by simply adding your own text. All you must do to make this work as it should is to ensure that you must enclose the text in quotes. Although you can concatenate numbers without having to include quotes.

## Changing case

Should it be lower or uppercase? Always ensure that the text in your database has the right capitalization. Access has some in-built functions that can help with changing cases with ease. For example, if you have values in the Address field, you can make use of the StrConv function which is a type of function that helps to convert a string to a special case. The string that will be converted will simply be the field you are working with. When in a query environment you can make use of the name of the field to indicate that you are converting all of the row values of that particular field.

The type of conversion chosen will let Access know if you want to convert the specified text to all uppercase, all lower case, or a proper case.

**Take a look at the explanation below;**

- **Conversion type 1**: this option helps to convert the text indicated to uppercase characters.
- **Conversion type 2**: this option helps to convert the indicated text to lowercase characters.
- **Conversion type 3:** this option helps to convert the text indicated to a proper case(the first letter of every word is an uppercase) character.

Note that you can also make use of the Ucase and the Lcase functions if you want to convert your text to uppercase and lowercase respectively.

## Removing leading and trailing spaces from a string

Leading and trailing spaces in data can result in some abnormalities most especially when you have a need to append values with leading and trailing spaces to other values that are clean. You can get rid of the leading and trailing spaces with the use of the Trim function. The Ltrim function will get rid of the Leading spaces while the RTrim function will get rid of the trailing spaces.

## Finding and replacing specific text

Imagine that you have included a particular text in all the addresses of the customers on your table which is later deemed to be an infringement and you have to take it off. Going to all of the addresses one after the other can be rather time-consuming and also very hectic, this is where the replace function can come in very handy.

**Note that there are basically three arguments that are deemed required and three that are deemed optional in a Replace function:**

- **Expression (required):** this is the full string you will be evaluating. When in a query environment, you can make use of the name of a field to indicate that you are evaluating all the row values of that particular field.
- **Find (required):** this is the very substring that you need to find and replace.
- **Replace (required):** this is the substring that is used as a replacement.
- **Start (Optional):** this is the position that is within a substring from which the search can be started.
- **Count (optional):** this is the number of occurrences that should be replaced.
- **Compare (optional):** this is the kind of comparison that should be used. You can choose to either have a binary comparison, textual comparison, or the default comparison algorithm.

# Adding your own text in key positions within a string

In the course of transforming data, there might be a reason for you to include your own text in key positions with a string. This editing can be done with the use of the Right function, Left function, and the Mid function and they can also be used with each other.

**For instance, the Right, Left, and Mid functions enable you to retrieve portions of a string beginning from different positions:**

- The Left function helps in returning a specified number of characters from the leftmost character of the string. The arguments that are required for the Left function are simply the text that you are evaluating and the number of characters that should be returned.
- The Right function returns a specified number of characters beginning from the rightmost character of the string. The required

arguments for the Right function are the text that is being evaluated and the number of characters that should be returned.
- The Mid function returns a specified number of characters beginning from the specified character position. The required arguments for the Mid function are the text that is being evaluated beginning with the position, and the number of characters that should be returned.

## Parsing strings using character markers

The parsing string is often used when there is data that is in a field and is separated by commas. For example, having the three names of a contact in the field in the form of Last name, First name, and Middle name. This string of data will need to be parsed into three separate fields. Parsing is not done by just adding spaces, you will have to make use of the Instr function. This function will search for a specified string in another string and then return its position.

### Query 1

The first query will parse out the last name in the ContactName field and then update the Conatct_LastName field. It will then also update the Contact_FirstName field with the strings that are left. When the LeadList table is opened, you will be able to see the impact of your first update query.

### Query 2

The second query will update the Contact_FirstNmae field and the Contact_MI field. Once you have successfully executed your second query, you can then open your table and view the results.

# CHAPTER 12
# WORKING WITH CALCULATIONS AND DATES

More often, organizations usually have a need to carry out some calculations before the very big picture of the data analysis is presented. In this chapter, you will learn about the tools Access provides and also the in-built functions it has and uses in making calculations and dates possibly to work with.

## Using Calculations in Your Analyses

When having to work with Access or any database environment, it is best you keep data separate from the analysis.

**With this, you will be able to store a calculation in your data set although the use of tables to store data can be somewhat problematic for a number of reasons;**

- Stored calculations have a need for constant maintenance as the data in the table might change from time to time.
- Stored calculations have the data configured to a particular analytical path.
- Stored calculations take up valuable storage space.

Rather than having to store calculated results as data, it's better to perform the calculation when there is a need for it. With this, you are guaranteed to have a current and accurate result and you will not be tied to just one analytical path.

## Common calculation scenarios

In Microsoft Access, calculations are performed with the use of expressions. An expression is simply a combination of values, operators, or functions that are evaluated to give back a different value to be used in the following process. For example, 3+3 will return a single integer 6 which you can use in subsequent analysis. You can make use of expressions almost everywhere in Microsoft Access to get various tasks completed in reports, forms, data, and even tables to a certain aspect.

## Using constants in calculations

A constant can be said to be a value that is static. i.e it doesn't change. In almost all calculations, you will have a need to make use of constants or hard-coded numbers.

## Using fields in calculations

You won't have a need to always indicate the constant you are making use of in every calculation, most of the calculations that you might have a need to perform on data are already in fields in your data set.

With the use of fields, you can perform any type of calculation, it doesn't matter if it is formatted either as currency or as a number. When working with fields oftentimes, your calculation will be performed with the use of values in each record dataset which is more like the referencing cell values in the Microsoft Excel formula.

## Using the results of aggregation in calculations

By using the results of aggregation you would be able to perform various analytical steps in a single query.

### Note that the query will be executed in the order;

- The query will start by grouping records.
- The query will calculate the count of orders if the table has to do with purchasing of items
- The query will then assign the aliases that you must have defined respectively.
- The query will then use the aggregation results for each of the tables as expressions.

## Using the results of one calculation as an expression in another

Bear in mind that you can always have more than one calculation in a query. Furthermore, you can choose to make use of the result of a particular calculation as an expression in another calculation.

## Using a calculation as an argument in a function

When the calculation in a specific query returns a number with a fractional part, this can simply mean that it will return a number that has a decimal point followed by various trailing digits. It is however best to have a round figure returned avoiding decimals as this will make the data much easier to read and understand.

With the use of the Int function, you can force the results of your calculation into an integer. The Int function is a mathematical function that helps to take away the fractional part of a number after which it will then return the resulting Integer. Take note that calculations that result in a number in any function that accepts a number can be used as an argument.

## Constructing calculations with the Expression Builder

Expression builder is another function in Access that can help with the construction of an expression with just a few touches on the mouse. This is very easy as all you have to do in order to create an expression is to choose the functions and data fields that are important.

**Before using the expression builder, there is a need for it to be activated. To do this;**

- Click **inside the query** grid cell that has the expression then right-click and choose Build.
- You can right-click **anywhere** (control properties form, control properties reports, etc) you would like to write an expression to activate the Expression Builder.

There are about four panes in the Expression builder: the upper pane is where you insert the expression, and the lower pane shows the various objects that you have at your disposal. Here you can also make use of the plus icons in order to make the database objects bigger.

- To make use of any function in Access all you have to do is to click **twice** on the function and Access will insert the function automatically in the upper pane of the Expression builder.

# Common calculation errors

It doesn't matter how perfect you are or how solid the platform you are using is, you are prone to making mistakes sometimes. Microsoft is yet to produce any function in Access that can help you prevent errors during analysis, however, there are some fundamental actions you can make use of in avoiding some of the most common calculation errors.

## Understanding the order of operator precedence

Similar to BODMAS in mathematics, There are basic rules to follow if you want to ensure you avoid common errors. Whenever you are making use of expressions and calculations that have to do with multiple operations, each of the operations will be evaluated first and then resolved in a predetermined order. You have to be conversant with the operator precedence in Access because if you build an expression in an incorrect manner, it can give rise to a problem.

**Below are the order of operations for Access:**

- Evaluate the items in parentheses first.
- Perform exponentiation.
- Perform negation.
- Perform multiplication and division.
- Perform addition and subtraction at equal precedence.
- Evaluate string concatenation.
- Evaluate comparison and pattern matching operators.
- Evaluate logical operators in the order; Not, And, Or.

If you do not follow the above precedence in any given calculation, you might be getting the wrong answer. Ensure you follow this precedence at all times.

## Watching out for the null values

Null value simply means there is no value given. When an item in a table is empty such is considered to be null.

Whenever Access comes in contact with a null value it doesn't assume the value to be zero it will simply return the value as null.

Null calculation errors can be avoided by making use of the Nz function which allows you to change any null value that you come in contact with to a specified value.

**The Nz function takes up two arguments;**
- **ValueIfNull**: this simply means the value that should be returned if the variant is null.
- **Variant**: this is the data you are working with at the moment.

## Watching the syntax in your expressions

Making some basic mistakes with syntax in your calculation expressions can also lead to errors.

**Below are guidelines to follow in order to avoid any form of slip-ups;**
- Avoid the use of illegal characters like period(.), square brackets([]), etc in your aliases.
- When you are adding an alias to a calculated field, ensure you don't inadvertently make use of a field name from any of the tables that are queried.
- Ensure the names of the fields are well spelled.

# Using Dates in Your Analyses

With Microsoft Access, all the possible dates that begin from December 31, 1899, are stored as a positive serial number. The system of storing dates as serial numbers are commonly referred to as the 1900 system which is also the default for all office applications like ExcelWord and PowerPoint.

## Simple date calculations

For dates to be well calculated, they must be in a field that is formatted as a Date/Time field. If you insert a date into a Short Text field, the data will seem like a date even to you but Access will treat it as a string which will then result in the failure of any calculation done on dates in this kind of format. Make sure you have all dates in fields that are formatted as Date/Time.

## Advanced analysis using functions

Access 2022 has about 25 in-built date/time functions. Though you might not make use of all of the functions, it is necessary for you to know how to make use of the very important ones.

**Below are a few of the functions that you might need to use on a daily basis.**

## The Date function

The is a function in-built into Access that helps to return the current system date i.e today's date. With this function, there will be no need for you to make use of a constant as today's date when you are calculating.

You can make use of this function in filtering out records when you include a criteria expression. There is also a Round function with which you can round the number of years. Furthermore, ensure you wrap your calculations in the Int function this way you are sure that your answers will be clean and void of fractions.

## The Year, Month, Day, and Weekday functions

The Year, Month, Day, and weekday functions are usually used basically to return an integer that shows their respective parts of a date. All of these functions need a valid date as an argument.

Note that the weekday function will return the day of the week from a date. The weekdays in Microsoft Access are always numbered 1 to7 of which the day starts on Sunday. Hence, if the weekday function returns 4, which means the 4th day of the week counting from Sunday it is simply saying Wednesday. You can always change the first day of the week as it suits you with the use of the FirstDayOfWeek argument. The argument will help to specify the day you want to count as the first day of the week.

## The Date add function

Most organizations make use of analysis that helps to add a certain date that the benchmark will be reached. For example in terms of payment of salaries, most organizations have a benchmark date for this.

**There are about three required arguments in the DateAdd function;**

- Interval (required): this is simply the interval of time that should be used.

**The intervals are:**

- "yyyy": Year
- "q": Quarter
- "m": Month
- "y": Day of year
- "d": Day
- "w": Weekday
- "w": Week
- "h": Hour
- "n": Minute
- "s": Second
- **Date (required)**: this is simply the value of the date you are working with.
- **Number(required)**: this is simply the number of intervals that should be added. A positive number brings back dates in the future while a negative number brings back dates in the past

## Grouping dates into quarters

Grouping of dates is always needed if you have to analyze your data on a quarter-over-quarter basis which will need you to convert dates into quarters.

Although there is absolutely no function in Access that allows you to group dates into quarters, you however have the Format function.

With the Format function which belongs to the Text category of functions, you can convert a variant into a string based on formatting instructions. **There are basic valid instructions you can pass to a format function to ensure it is able to group to quarter:**

- Format (#01/31/2019#,"yyyy") which returns 2019.
- Format (#01/31/2019#,"yy") returns 19
- Format (#01/31/2019#, "q") returns 1

Note that the value that is returned when a date is passed through a Format function is a string that you shouldn't make use of in subsequent calculations.

## The DateSerial function

With the DateSerial function you can build the date of your choice by combining given year, month, and day components. This function is best used in the conversion of disparate strings that both represent a date into an actual date.

**There are basically three arguments with the DateSerial function:**

- **Year (required):** this is simply any number from 100 to 9999.
- **Month (required)**: simply any number.
- **Day (required):** any number or expression.

# CHAPTER 13
# PERFORMING CONDITIONAL ANALYSES

Conditional Analysis is one that depends on a predefined set of conditions. It is quite different from your normal straightforward method of simply having to build a query, include some criteria, and calculations, and then execute the query. There are some tools that allow the building of Conditional Analyses like parameter queries, the IIf function, and the Switch function.

In this chapter you will be enlightened on how to make use of these tools and functions in organizing your analytical processes, enhancing your analyses, and also saving time in the process.

## Using Parameter Queries

With the parameter Queries you can be informed of criteria before you execute the query. A parameter query can come in very handy when you have a need to query various questions with the use of different criteria anytime you perform an execution.

When you make use of a parameter query, you will be able to build conditional analysis which is one that is based on various variables you choose to indicate each time the query is executed.

**To build a parameter query all you have to do is;**

- Replace **the hard-coded** criteria with text that you must have enclosed in square brackets.

When you execute a parameter query, it will force open the Enter Parameter Value dialog box and prompt it to ask for a variable. Note that at this point, the text you must have typed inside the square brackets will be displayed in the dialog box.

## How parameter queries work

When you run a parameter query, Microsoft Access attempts to change any text to a literal string by enclosing the text on quotes. Note that if you place squares in brackets around the text, Microsoft Access will assume it is a variable and will attempt to bind some variable to the variable with **the use of the following series of tests:**

- Microsoft Access will check if the variable field inserted is a name. If it is identified as a field name, the field will then be used in the expression.
- If the variable is not a field name, Access will check to be sure that the variable is a calculated field. If Access determines the expression is a calculated field it will carry out the mathematical operation.
- If the variable is then not a calculated field, Access will check to see if the variable is referencing an object like the control on an open form or an open report.
- If all of the above options fail, the option left will then be to ask the user what the variable is, with this, Access will display the Enter Parameter Value dialog box, displaying the text you inserted in the Criteria row.

## Ground rules of parameter query

**Parameter queries also have their own ground rules that should be followed so you can make use of them properly;**

- The name of a field cannot be used as a parameter. If this is done, Access will replace your parameter with the current value of the field.
- There is a need to place square brackets around the parameters. If this is not done, Access will automatically change text into a literal string.
- The number of characters in your parameter must be limited. When you insert a parameter prompt that is too long it might result in the prompt being cut off in the Enter Parameter Value dialog box.

## Working with parameter queries

It is actually very innovative for you to get around with your parameter queries and learn how to make the best use of them, it will be very useful and will better help to solve your data analysis properly. This section throws more light on the various ways in which you can make use of the parameters in your queries.

## Working with multiple parameter conditions

You are free to work with as many Parameters as needed in a query. When you execute a query you will be prompted to insert some information that will enable you to filter on two different data points without the need to rewrite your query.

## Combining parameters with operators

Combination of parameter prompts can be done with the use of any operator that you normally would use in a query. When parameters are used in conjunction with standard operators it enables you to either expand or contract the filters in your analysis without having to recreate your query.

## Combining parameters with wildcards

One of the major problems often encountered with the use of a parameter query is that anytime the parameter is left blank when the query is being executed, the query will not return any records.

A proven method to solve this issue is the use of wildcards, this way even if the Parameter is blank, all records will be returned. Note that when you use the *wildcard alongside a parameter, it allows users to insert an initial parameter and still get results.

## Using parameters as calculation variables

Parameters can be used at any point where a variable is used and not only using it as criteria for a query. Parameters can also be of great importance when it has to do with calculations.

## Using parameters as function arguments

Parameters can be used as arguments functions. When the query that has the parameter is being executed, you will be promcted to a start date and an end date. Those two dates will in turn be used as arguments in the DateDiff function. You can also choose to indicate new dates anytime you run the query without having to recreate the query.

Note that the values inserted into your parameters must be a perfect fit with the data type that is needed for the function's argument.

# Using Conditional Functions

There are built-in functions in Microsoft Access that enable value comparisons, data validation, and conditional evaluation. Two of such functions are the IIf function and the switch function. These functions also known as the program flow functions are designed to test for various conditions and also offer outcomes that are dependent on the results of those tests. The sections below will widen your knowledge of how you can control the flow of your analyses with the use of the IIf and Switch functions.

## The IIf function

The IIf function can be used anywhere expressions can be used. This function can be used to determine if another expression is either true or false. If the expression is true, IIf will return a single value, if the expression is false it will return another value. You are in control of the values it will return either true or false.

IIf will always evaluate both the true part and the false part even though it will return just one value of the two. Due to this, it's best you are on the lookout for side effects that might be undesirable. You can make use of the IIf function on a form, report, in complex expressions, and in a query.

## Using IIf to avoid mathematical errors

The IIf function can help you avoid some errors, all you have to do is perform a conditional analysis on your data set with the IIf function and then evaluate the field that should be calculated just before you calculate.

## Saving time with IIf

Steps can be saved with the use of the IIf function which will also lead to you saving ample time. Rather than having to run two queries or more the IIf function can help shorten such procedures and you will still end up with an accurate result.

## Meeting IIf functions for multiple conditions

Nested IIf functions which means IIf functions in another IIf function can come in very handy whenever you have to test for conditions that are too complex to be handled by a basic IF....THEN....ELSE structure.

Note that anytime an IIf function delivers a true or false answer, the condition used can be expanded by setting the false expression to a different IIf function rather than to a hard-coded value. There is absolutely no limit to the amount of nested IIf functions that you can make use of.

## Using IIf functions to create crosstab analysis

Most data analysts make use of the IIf function in building custom crosstab analysis. An advantage of building a crosstab analysis without the use of a crosstab query is the ability to add more than one calculation in the crosstab report.

## The switch function

The switch function argument has pairs of expressions and values. The expressions are evaluated from left to right and the value associated with the first expression to evaluate to True is returned. If the parts are not well paired, a run-time error will occur.

**The switch returns a null if value:**

- None of the expressions is True.
- The first True expression has a value corresponding to Null.

The switch ensures it evaluates all of the expressions, though it will only return one of them. Hence, it is important you are on the lookout for side effects that might be undesirable. For instance, if the evaluation of any expression results in a division by zero error, an error will occur. It's also important to bear in mind that there is no limit to the number of expressions that can be evaluated with the use of the switch function.

## Comparing the IIf and switch functions

Although the IIF function is a very effective tool that can deal with almost all conditional analyses, the fact remains that the IIf function has a certain number of arguments that limits it to a basic IF....THEN...ELSE structure. With this limitation, it can be extremely difficult to evaluate complex conditions without having to make use of nested IIf functions. Though there is absolutely nothing wrong with having to nest IIf functions, there are however some analyses that ought to be evaluated so as to make building a nested IIF impractical at best.

The problem that might exist with the use of the IIf function is that there are certain situations that might warrant the use of hefty nesting. This means that there will be a need for you to make use of the IIf expressions to deal with the easy layer of probable conditions.

Note that the use of the switch function is oftentimes more practical than using the nested IIf function.

# CHAPTER 14
# THE FUNDAMENTALS OF USING SQL

Structured Query Language (SQL) can be described as a language that relational database management systems like Access make use of when having to perform different tasks. If you are to instruct a DBMS like Access to take up any task, you will have to pass your message across via SQL.

This chapter will briefly inform you on the role that SQL plays in you using Access and you will also learn how to deal with statements developed by SQL when building queries. The things you learn here will help you to perform better and be able to find your way around any database management system you come across.

## Understanding Basic SQL

If you have been used to using Access for a very long time, you might have limited knowledge about the use of SQL because Access is more user-friendly and also does most of its actions in a quite user-friendly environment that does reveal the main work that goes on behind the scenes. With the mode of user-friendly interface that Access provides there is no basic need for you to really know the SQL doing all the main tasks behind each of the queries. That being said, if you really want to harness the real power that exists in dealing with data analysis with Access, there is a need for you to have a perfect understanding of the fundamentals of SQL.

## The SELECT statement

The SELECT statement is the core part of SQL which is used to collect records from a set of data. The basic syntax of a SELECT statement is;

> SELECT column_name(s) FROM table_name

For perfect results, the SELECT statement is often used with a FROM clause which helps with the identification of the tables that make up the source for the data.

## Selecting specific columns

With the use of the SELECT statement and properly defining your data set, you can get back the very columns from your data set.

Note that any column in your database that has a name that contains a non-alphanumeric character or number has to be in brackets when you are writing your SQL statement.

## Selecting all columns

The use of the wildcard has been briefly described in the previous chapter. I will also add here that when you make use of the *wildcard, you will be able to choose all the columns from a set of data without you having to specify all the columns separately.

## The WHERE clause

The WHERE clause can be used to sieve your data set in a SELECT statement. Oftentimes, the WHERE clause is used with an operator like; equal =, greater than >, less than <, greater than equal to >=, less than equal to <=.

## Making sense of joins

Joins are often used to bring two or more tables that are related together in order to achieve the desired result. There are different types of joins available and the very type of join used will also determine what the result will be.

## Inner joins

Inner joins instruct Access to only choose the records from the tables whose values match. Records that have values in the joined field will not be displayed in the two tables that have been omitted from the results of the query.

## Outer joins

An outer join chooses all of the records from a particular table and then chooses the records in the second table that are a match to the records in the first table it has chosen records from. The outer join can be further broken down into two which are; the right joins and the left joins.

With the right joins, records are chosen from the second table without having to consider if the records match or not, and only the records from the first table whose records match the values of the joined field are also selected.

The left join chooses records from the first table without also considering if the records match and it also chooses records whose values match the joined field from the second table.

# Getting Fancy with Advanced SQL Statements

With the SQL statement you can do more than just the basics such as SELECT, FROM, and WHERE statements. The section below tells you more about SQL and other things you can accomplish with it.

## Expanding your search with the Like operator

The Like operator is quite similar to the equal = operator. To get the most out of the Like operator is best used with wildcard characters, this will help expand the scope of your search such that it will add any record that matches a pattern.

**Below are some wildcard characters that can be used in Access;**

- *: this is used in representing any number and type of characters.
- []: with the bracket, you can pass just one character or lots of characters to the Like operator. Values that are of the same match with the character values that are embedded in the brackets will also be added to the results.
- ?: this sign is a representation of any single character.

## Selecting Unique values and rows without grouping

With the use of the DISTINCT predicate, you can retrieve only the unique values from chosen fields in your set of data. While performing this operation, if your SQL statement happens to choose more than one field then the combination of values from all the fields must also be unique so that a given record will also be added to the results.

If there is a need to have the whole row unique, you can then make use of the DISTINCTROW predicate. With this, you will be able to retrieve just the records which make the whole row unique. This means that the combination of all of the values in the chosen fields isn't a match for any other record in the data set returned.

## Grouping and aggregating with the GROUP BY clause

The GROUP BY clause in Microsoft Access helps with the combination of records that have identical values in the indicated field list into just one record. A summary value will also be created for each of the records if you add an SQL aggregate function like Sum or Count in the SELECT statement.

Note that GROUP BY is optional. Summary values are always omitted if there happens to be no aggregate function in the SELECT statement. Null values in GROUP BY fields are often not omitted. Nevertheless, Null values are often not evaluated in any SQL aggregate function.

If it doesn't contain Memo or OLE object data, a field in the GROUP BY field list can actually refer to any field in any table that is listed in the FROM clause, even if the field isn't included in the SELECT statement as long as the SELECT statement has at least one SQL aggregate function. Note that the Microsoft Access database engine cannot group on Memo or OLE Object fields.

## Setting the sort order with the ORDER BY Clause

The ORDER BY clause in Access helps in sorting the resulting record of a query on a particular field or fields in either an ascending or descending manner. ORDER BY is also optional. Nevertheless, if you have a need to show your data in sorted order then you have to make use of the ORDER BY.

If you have a field specified which contains Memo or OLE Object data in the ORDER BY clause, an error will occur. Microsoft Access database engine usually doesn't sort on fields of these types. Note that ORDER Y is usually the last item in an SQL statement. You can choose to add additional fields in the ORDER BY clause. Records are sorted first by the first letter in the field after ORDER BY. Records that also have equal values in the field will then be sorted by the value in the second field listed and so on.

# Creating aliases with the AS clause

With the AS clause, you can add aliases to your columns and tables. Aliases are often used either when you have a reason to work with more than one instance of the same table and you need a way to help refer to one instance or the other or you have to make the names of columns or tables shorter and much easier to read.

## Creating a column alias

A column alias can be described as a temporary alternate name for a column. Aliases are often indicated in the SELECT clause to name or rename columns for the table's result to be clearer and easier to read. Column aliases are optional and each column name in the SELECT clause can have an alias. Once you assign an alias to a column, you can then make use of the alias to refer to that column in any other clause. Note that for the maximum portability of the SQL code that is used outside of the Access SQL procedure, it is best to avoid writing code that refers to column aliases in a WHERE clause, GROUP BY clause, or HAVING clause.

## Creating a table alias

With the use of a table alias, you can use another name to refer to a table in a SELECT statement in your FROM clause. A table alias is simply a name that is assigned to a data source in a query when you make use of an expression as a data source or you use it to ensure the SQL statement is easier to type and read. This can be very useful if the name of the data source is rather too long or quite difficult to type especially when multiple fields with the same name from various tables are involved.

# Showing only the SELECT TOP or SELECT TOP PERCENT

When a SELECT query is executed, all records that meet the definitions and criteria that have been stated will be retrieved. Executing the SELECT TOP statement or a top values query simply means you are instructing Access to help filter the data set that has been returned to display only a specified number of records.

## Top values queries explained

If there is a need for you to create tables and have records from the tables created prioritized, the Top value query can come in handy here. With a Top Value query, you have the option to indicate either a value or a percentage which shows a fraction of the total number of records that are found in the record set and it is very simple to perform in Microsoft Access when you are building the query.

## The SELECT TOP statement

When using the SELECT TOP statement, it is very important for you to indicate the sort direction very accurately since it can make all the difference between choosing the biggest ten results or the smallest ten results. Bear in mind that you can choose to sort on a field without having to show that field.

## The SELECT TOP PERCENT Statement

This statement works just the same way as the SELECT TOP, the only exception is that the records that are returned in the SELECT TOP PERCENT statement show the nth percent of total records as against the nth number of records. Note that the SELECT TOP PERCENT statements offer you only the top or bottom percent of all the records that are returned in the set of data and not the percent of the total value in your records.

# Performing action queries via SQL statements

Building an action query is the same as building a SQL statement that is targeted toward that same action. The SQL statement will also make it possible for you to do more than just choose records only.

## Make-table queries translated

Make-table queries make use of the SELECT …..INTO statement in order to make a hard-coded table that has the results of your query.

## Append Queries translated

With the append query, you can make use of the INSET INTO statement to insert new rows into a specified table.

## Update queries translated

Update queries make use of the UPDATE statement and SET in order to change the data in a data set.

## Delete queries translated

Delete queries make use of the DELETE statement to delete rows in a set of data.

## Creating Crosstabs with the TRANSFORM statement

With the TRANSFORM statement you can create a crosstab set of data that shows data in a more compact view.

**For you to get the best of the TRANSFORM statement it needs basically three components which are;**

- The field to be aggregated.
- The SELECT statement that determines the row content for the crosstab.
- The field that will make up the column of the crosstab.

# Using SQL-specific queries

SQL-specific queries are basically action queries that you cannot execute with the use of the Access query grid. These particular queries must be executed either in SQL view or through code( VBA or macro). There are various types of SQL-specific queries with each one of them performing a specific action.

## Merging data sets with the UNION operator

As the word UNION implies, this operator is used to bring together two SQL statements that are compatible to give rise to one read-only set of data.

Anytime you have to bring together two different sets of data to create an analysis that will display the details and also show the totals in just one table, the UNION operator is the best to use.

Note that when you execute a union query, Access will match the column from the two sets of data by their respective positions in the SELECT statement. This simply means that your SELECT statement must have the exact number of columns and the order of columns in both SELECT statements is equally very important. Once the columns have matching data types, Access will produce a union of the two tables making use of the position of each of the columns.

## Creating a table with the CREATE TABLE statement

There are times when there will be a need for you to create temporary tables with which you can group, manipulate, and also hold data. This is where the CREATE TABLE statement comes in handy as it allows you to do that with the use of just one SQL-specific query.

Records are not returned with the CREATE TABLE statement, it allows for only the creation of the structure and the schema of a table.

### If you would like to make use of the CREATE TABLE simply;

- Begin **a new query.**
- Change **to SQL view**
- Define **the structure or schema** for the table.

## Manipulating columns with the ALTER TABLE statement

You can choose to make some adjustments to the structure of a table with the use of the ALTER TABLE statement. There are various clauses that can be used with the ALTER TABLE statement some of which are very useful in the analysis of data in Microsoft Access. These classes are ADD, ALTER COLUMN, ADD CONSTRAINT, and ADD CONSTRAINT.

Note that you cannot undo the changes to any action that was performed with the use of the ALTER TABLE statement.

### Adding a column with the ADD clause

The ADD clause allows you to include columns in tables that are already existing.

### To use the ADD statement simply

- Start **a new query** in SQL view then define the structure for your new column.

## Altering a column with the ALTER COLUMN clause

With the ALTER COLUMN, you can specify an already existing column in an existing table. With this clause, you can change the data type and field size of a specific column.

**To make use of the ALTER COLUMN statement simply;**

- Begin **a new query** in the SQL view and then **define changes** for the particular column.

## Deleting a column with the DROP COLUMN clause

With the use of the DROP COLUMN, you can delete a particular column from a table that exists.

**To make use of the DROP COLUMN simply;**

- Begin **a new query** in the SQL view and then **specify** the structure for your new column.

## Dynamically adding primary keys with the ADD constraints clause

Most analysts make use of Access as an easy-to-use extract, transform, load(ETL) tool. This simply means that Access gives room for you to extract data sources and then reformat the data into consolidated tables. Analysts also automate the ETL process with the use of macros that helps to start off some queries.

That being said, there are however sometimes when an ETL process needs primary keys to be included in temporary tables so that the data can be normalized during this processing. Most people seek to make use of other alternatives but with the use of the ADD CONSTRAINT clause, you can create primary keys dynamically.

**To use the ADD CONSTRAINT clause simply;**

- Start **a new query** then define the primary key you would like to implement.

## Creating pass-through queries

A pass-through query is one that helps to send SQL commands directly to a database server. Most times, these database servers are known as the back end of the system, and Access is regarded as the front end or the client tool.

The major advantage of making use of the pass-through queries is that the parsing and the processing are often done on the back-end server, not in Access. This makes them quite faster than queries that emanate from linked tables, especially if the table linked is quite large.

**Follow the steps below to create a pass-through query;**

- Locate **the Create tab** of the Ribbon then click on **the Query Design Command**.
- Close the **Show Table dialog box**.
- Click on the **Pass-Through** command on the **Query Tools Design tab**. This will then display the **SQL design window**.

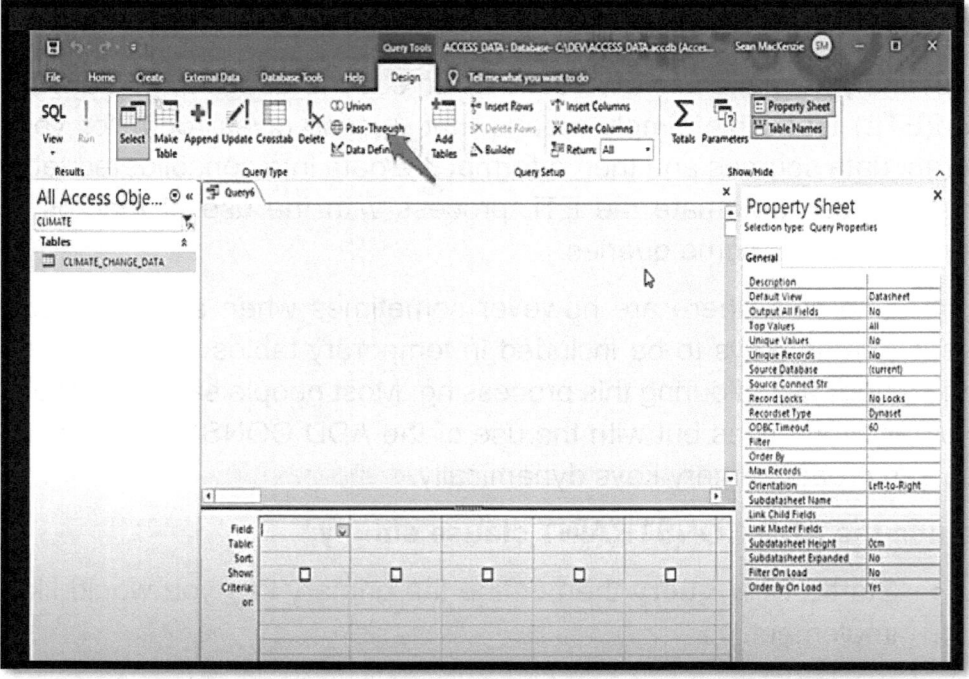

- Insert a **SQL statement** that suits the target database system.

- Locate **the Query Tools Design tab** and click on the **Property Sheet command**. This will also display the Property sheet.

- Insert the **appropriate connection** string for your server
- Finally click **on the Run button**.

# CHAPTER 15
# SUBQUERIES AND DOMAIN AGGREGATE FUNCTIONS

One of the things you will do in Access is to carry out analyses in layers with each layer of analysis being built on the previously existing layer. **When it has to do with layering analyses, there are basically two things in common and they are;**

- Layering of analyses needs the creation of temporary tables or transition queries, overloading your database with the table and query objects that might lead to a very confusing analytical process and also a database that easily expands.
- Layering of analyses helps to add a step to your analytical processes. Note that there is a need to execute every query so that you can also feed another query or all the temporary tables that have been created so that you can make advancements in your analysis.

With Subqueries and domain aggregate functions, you will be able to build multiple layers into your analyses within just one query while removing any need for temporary tables or transition queries.

## Enhancing your Analyses with Subqueries

A subquery can be described as a SELECT query statement inside another query. As you are dragging fields and typing expressions in the query design, Microsoft Access will write a sentence that will describe what it is you are asking for.

This statement will be in SQL which is the most common relational database language. If SQL happens to be a foreign language then you can choose to mock up a query like a subquery that you need, change it to SQL view and then paste it into SQL view in your main query. There will actually be some cleaning up to do, but this is the easiest way to have a subquery created.

With subquery, you can choose to answer various parts of a question, indicating criteria for more selection or defining new fields to be used in your data analysis.

Since the subquery is one that has another query embedded in it, this simply means that the main idea behind a subquery is to have it executed first and then make use of the result in the outer query as a criterion, an expression, a parameter, etc.

## Why use Subqueries?

You might be in the know that subqueries oftentimes execute slower than a standard query that makes use of join especially if they have to deal with a large data. Are you then wondering why you should then make use of them?

Subqueries are best used if you want to have a streamlined procedure and an optimized analytical process. They are also best used with on-the-fly queries so as to save time and also run the execution smoothly.

## Subquery ground rules

**There are quite a few rules that you need to adhere to when making use of subqueries.**

**They are;**

- Subqueries must be enclosed in parentheses.
- They must have a SELECT statement and a FROM clause in their SQL string.
- Subqueries can be used as an expression as long as it returns a single value.
- You can make use of the ORDER BY clause in a subquery only if the subquery is a SELECT TOP or SELECT TOP PERCENT statement.
- You can make use of the DISTINCT keyword in a subquery that has the GROUP BY clause.
- You must establish table aliases in queries in which a table is made use of in both the outer query and also the subquery.

## Creating Subqueries without typing SQL statements

Having to write a SQL statement can be a very challenging task. In fact, most Access users do not create their SQL statements from scratch. Most of them make use of the in-built functionalities provided in Access to save a whole lot of stress and time too.

**To create these Subqueries without having to type SQL statements, follow the steps below;**

- Create **a query**.
- Change over to the **SQL view** and then copy the **SQL statement**.
- Create **a query** that will specify basic criteria.
- Right-click in the **criteria row** and then choose **the Zoom optio**n. This function of the Zoom dialog box basically is to help you see the text clearly and at a glance.
- With the **Zoom dialog box opened**, you can then paste the **SQL statement** that has been copied previously into the white input area.
- Complete **the query** by inserting **a greater than > symbol** at the front of the subquery then alter the GROUP BY of your preferred criteria to a WHERE clause. Click on the **OK button** to save the changes that have been made.

The more you make use of SQL, you will discover that you can create Subqueries manually without encountering any problems at all.

## Using IN and NOT IN with Subqueries

You can effectively run two different queries in one with the use of the IN and NOT IN operators. The basic idea behind this is that the subquery will be executed first and then the resulting sets of data will be used by the outer query in sieving out the final output.

## Using Subqueries with comparison operators

As the name implies, a comparison operator like (=, <,>,<=,>=,<>) does the comparison of two different items and returns True or False. Whenever a subquery is used with a comparison operator this implies that you are telling Access to compare the resulting data set of the outer query to that of the subquery.

The subquery will be executed first, giving a single value with which Access will use to compare the resulting data of the outer query's data set.

Note that for this to be done accurately a single value must be returned when a subquery is used with a comparison operator.

## Using Subqueries as expressions

You can choose to make use of a subquery instead of an expression in the field list of a SELECT statement or in a WHERE or HAVING clause.

In a subquery, you make use of a SELECT statement in making a set of one or more specific values to evaluate in the WHERE or HAVING clause.

Make use of the ANY or SOME predicate in order to get records in the main query that satisfies the comparison with any record that is retrieved on the subquery.

The use of the IN predicate is to retrieve only the records in the main query that satisfies the comparison with all of the records retrieved in the subquery. Then use the IN predicate to retrieve only the records in the subquery that have an equal value.

NOT IN cannot be used to retrieve only the records in the main query for which no record in the subquery has an equal value. Make use of the EXIST predicate in true/false comparisons the determination of if the subquery will return any record. You can also choose to make use of the table name aliases in a subquery to refer to tables that are listed in a FROM clause outside of the subquery.

Some Subqueries can also be used in crosstab queries basically as predicates. Subqueries as outputs are though not allowed in crosstab queries.

## Using correlated Subqueries

A correlated query can be described as a query that refers back to a column that is in the outer query. The uniqueness of a correlated query is that it has to be evaluated more than once, each being for the rows processed by the outer query.

## Uncorrelated Subqueries

You can denote an SQL statement using an uncorrelated subquery when the subquery is evaluated one time to provide you with the average for the whole set of data.

## Correlated Subqueries

You can denote a SQL statement using a correlated subquery when the subquery is reaching back to the outer query. The end result of such will be a dataset that shows the average for just a part of the whole data set.

## Using a correlated subquery as an expression

Correlated Subqueries run just once for each row that is chosen by an outer query. It also has a reference to a value from the row chosen by the outer query. It can also be used to determine the variance between the criteria chosen.

## Using Subqueries with action queries

Action queries can fit well with Subqueries just as select queries can also fit well too. Below are ways a subquery can be used in an action query.

## A subquery in a make-table query

The example below shows how to make use of a subquery in a make-table to design a new table that contains data for all employees that have been hired before March 1996.

SELECT E1.Employee_Number, E1.Last_Name, E1.First_Name

INTO OldSchoolEmployees

FROM Employee_Master as E1

WHERE E1.Employee_Number IN

(SELECT E2.Employee_Number

FROM Employee_Master AS E2

WHERE E2.Hire_Date <#1/3/1996#)

## A subquery in an append query

**The example below makes use of a subquery in an append query to include new customers to the customer master table from the LeadList:**

INSERT INTO CustomerMaster (Customer_Number, Customer_Name, State )

SELECT CompanyNumber, CompanyName, State

FROM LeadList

WHERE CompanyNumber Not In

   (SELECT Customer_Number from CustomerMaster)

## A subquery in an update query

The example below makes use of a subquery in an update query to increase all the prices in the PriceMaster table by 5% for just the branches that are in the North region.

   UPDATE PriceMaster SET Price = [Price]*0.5

WHERE Branch_Number In

   (SELECT Branch_Number from LocationMaster WHERE Region = "North")

## A subquery in a delete query

The example below makes use of a subquery in a delete query to delete customers from the LeadList table if they already in existence in the CustomerMaster table;

 DELETE *

FROM LeadList

WHERE CompanyNumber In

   (SELECT Customer_Number from CustomerMaster)

# Domain Aggregate Functions

A domain aggregate function is one that conditionally acts on the record of a field in order to give a statistical value. As against normal SQL aggregate functions that are always a part of the SQL, domain aggregate functions belong to Microsoft Access and are usually used to help locate a value based on the conditions you must have specified.

Every domain aggregate has an appropriate name which is also known as the function name. The expression argument can be the name of the column that contains the value on which the function will be applied. It can also be a calculation-based expression.

The domain argument can be the name of a table or query that has no need for an external value. The optional condition argument can be used to specify the condition to which a specific record is chosen. It will act like a WHERE condition. Hence, a domain aggregate function is more like a function formula of a SQL statement as follows;

SELECT expression FROM domain WHERE condition

# Understanding the different domain Aggregate function

**There are about 12 different domain aggregate functions in Access with each of them performing different operations.**

## DSum

This function returns the total sum value of an indicated field in the domain.

## DAvg

The DAvg function returns the average value of an indicated field in the domain.

## DCount

The DCount function returns the total number of records in the domain.

## DLookup

The lookup function helps to return the first value of an indicated field that matches clearly the criteria defined in the DLookup function. If a criterion isn't supplied or the one supplied does not identify a unique row well enough, the DLookup function will return a random value in the domain.

## DMin an/d Dmax

The DMin and DMax function helps to return the minimum as well as the maximum values in the domain respectively.

## DFirst and DLast

The DFirst and DLast functions seek to return the first and the last values respectively in the domain.

Note that you might just get a random value if you fail to make use of an ORDER BY clause to sort the field used in your DFirst or DLast function.

## DStDev, DStDevp, DvarP

You can make use of the DStDev and DStDevP functions in returning the standard deviation across a given population sample and also a population respectively. Also, you can make use of the Dvar and the DVarP functions in returning the variance across a population sample and a population.

## Examining the syntax of domain aggregate functions

The syntax to make the Domain Aggregate function work is quite unique as it varies based on the scenario involved. Below are sections that can help you build your domain Aggregate function properly.

## Using no criteria

When using the no criteria option, you can simply sum up all the values in the desired field(s). Note that the names of your field and the set of data must always be embedded in quotes. It is also generally a good practice to always make use of brackets in the identification of either a field, a table, or a query.

## Using text criteria

With the use of the text criteria it is essential that when specifying the criteria that are textual or s string, your criteria must be wrapped in single quotes. Furthermore, the whole criteria expression must also be wrapped in double-quotes.

## Using domain aggregate function

Domain aggregate functions are best used in specialty analyses with subsets of data that are quite smaller than being used in performing large-scale data and have to deal with very large sets of data. Oftentimes this function can be found wherein you have predictable datasets. The section below takes you through some basic examples of how you can make use of domain aggregate functions in order to accomplish tasks that are quite common.

## Calculating the percent total

Calculating the percent total in any table is always a worthwhile analysis, you can always make it much easier and faster to calculate including a column that would produce the percent total per each record. The DSum function can also be very useful in this kind of calculation.

## Creating a running count

To create a running count you can make use of the DCount function which in terms of sales of a product can help to return the number of invoices that have been processed on each of the invoice days.

## Using a value from the previous record

The DLookup function can help you to return a value from the previous record. It will help to search the records and return the value needed based on your specified criteria.

# CHAPTER 16
# RUNNING DESCRIPTIVE STATISTICS IN ACCESS

With descriptive statistics, you can easily simplify a large amount of data such that it will be very easy to understand. It is quite important to note that descriptive statistics are only used to profile a data set and also to enable comparison that you can make use of in other analyses. Basically, you can use descriptive statistics to summarize the survey results for all customers and also describe the data with the use of metrics that can be easily understood.

## Basic Descriptive Statistics

This section will enlighten you on certain basic steps you can perform with the use of descriptive analysis.

### Running descriptive statistics with aggregate queries

By now you must have executed some aggregate queries as we have discussed in previous chapters. Running an aggregate query is almost the same as creating descriptive statistics, the simplest descriptive query can be generated with the use of an aggregate query.

### Determining rank, mode, and median

Ranking records, and calculating mode and median are all the tasks performed by a data analyst. However, you will have to devise a means to get this data as there are no built-in functions in Access to help carry this function out.

### Ranking the records in your data set

You will definitely come across situations that will warrant you ranking records in your data based on a specific metric like revenue. Ranking of records is very key, especially in the aspect of having to calculate records like the mean, median, percentile, and quartile. The easier way to rank records in a set of data is through the use of correlated subquery.

## Getting the mode of a data set

The mode of a set of data is often described as the number with the highest occurrence. For example the mode of (6,3,3,3,3,1,6,5,7) is 3.

With Access, there is no in-built function to help calculate the mode hence you have to carry this operation out yourself. The easy way to calculate the mode of a large set of data is to employ the use of a query which will help count the occurrences of a certain data item and then have it checked for the highest count.

## Getting the median of a data set

The median of a set of data is simply the number that is found to be in the middle after the numbers must have been ranked. For example, the median (9,8,7,6,5,4,3,2,1) is 5 as it is the number in the middle after the numbers have been ranked in descending order.

Access also as with mode has no in-built function to determine the median of a data set, this will have to be done on your own.

**Follow the steps below to determine the median by building a query in two steps;**

- Create **a query** that will help to sort and rank your records.
- Identify **the record** that is really in the middle in your set of data by counting the total number of records and then dividing the number gotten by two. With this, you will have a middle value. The idea behind this is that since the record has been sorted and also ranked, the record with the same value as the middle value will automatically be the median.

## Pulling a random sampling from your data set

Random sampling as it were is the basis for statistical analysis. There are so many ways random sampling of data can be created in Access but the easiest is to make use of the Rnd function. This function helps to return a random base that is based on an initial value.

The clear idea behind this is to build an expression that makes use of the Rnd function to a field that has numbers and then put a limit to the records that have been returned thereby setting the Top Values Property of the query.

Note that the End function won't work if the fields have text or have some null values. The Rnd function will work with fields that have all numerical values even if the field is formatted as a Short Text field. However, if your table happens to be made up of fields that have only text, you can include an AutoNumber field to use with the Rnd function.

# Advanced Descriptive Statistics

This section will describe statistics that can be used for more advanced statistical analyses.

## Calculating percentile making

Percentile rank shows the standing of a particular score against the normal group or standard scores. Percentile the word implies is often used in terms of percentage especially when it has to do with scores and results.

Percentiles are often used in the analysis of data as a means of measuring the performance of a subject in relation to the group as a whole.

Note that calculating a percentile ranking for a set of data is basically a mathematical operation.

**For the step below to complete this operation;**

- Build **your preferred query**.
- Add **a field** that will produce a count of all the records in your data set.
- Create **a calculated field** with the expression ([RCount]-[Rank])/[RCount].
- Once you have successfully completed the above steps you can then execute the query.

## Determining the quartile standing of a record

A quartile can be described as a statistical division of a data set into four equal groups with each of the groups making up 25 percent of the data set. The first quartile is the top 25 percent of the data set and the bottom 25 percent is known to be the fourth quartile.

You don't need a mathematical operation to establish the quartile; it simply has to do with the comparison of data. This means all you have to do is compare each of the record's rank values to the quartile benchmarks for the data set.

A much easier way to get this done swiftly is to create the Rank and RCount fields in your query, you can then make use of the fields in a switch function such that it will tag each of the records with the appropriate quartile standing.

## Creating a Frequency distribution

The frequency distribution can be described as a kind of analysis that organizes data based on the count of occurrences wherein a variable assumes a rather specified value attribute.

The easiest way to get this done is to make use of the Partition function. This function will locate the range that a particular number falls into which will help to indicate where the number occurs in a well-calculated series of ranges.

**The Partition function needs the following arguments to fully function well;**

- **Number(required)**: This has to do with the number you are evaluating. In a query environment, you will basically use the name of a field to indicate that you are evaluating all the row values of that particular field.
- **Range Start (required)**: this is a whole number that will be the overall range of numbers. Note that this number must not be less than zero.
- **Range Stop (required)**: this is a whole number that will be the end of the overall range of numbers. Note that this number cannot be equal to or less than the Range Start.
- **Interval (required)**: this is a whole number that is to be the span of each range in the series of Range Start to Range Stop.

# PART V
# WORKING WITH ACCESS FORMS AND REPORTS

Forms and reports are very basic components that you cannot do without in Access. With Access forms you can build user interfaces at the top of database tables, providing a robust rapid application development platform for a lot of organizations.

The basic thing Access does is to easily integrate your database analysis with polished PDF-style doing the reporting of functionality, complete with grouping, sorting, and conditional formatting.

# CHAPTER 17
# CREATING BASIC ACCESS FORMS

A form can be defined as a database object that can be used to create a user interface for a database application. They can also be used for switchboards, dialog boxes that control the flow of the system, and also for messages. This chapter also discusses the various types of forms in Access.

Note that the forms added to the Access database are an integral aspect of the application you design. The integrity of a database data is well managed by the tools that can be found in forms. Since forms have VBA code or macros, a form can verify data entry or confirm deletions before such can occur. A form can also provide default values or perform calculations based on input by the user or retrieved from a database table.

## Working with Form Views

Forms though an object has its own views. These views are ways by which users interact with forms. You can also choose to place a restriction on the views that are made available.

**To have a change in the view of forms simply go through the following steps below;**

- Make use of **the View drop-down** list that is located on the Home Ribbon. Choose among the various views available;
  - **Form view**: this is the most common way users interact with forms. There is no design or layout done in the form view and only interacts with data.
  - **Datasheet view**: this view also allows users to interact with data. It looks almost the same as the Datasheet view but it is not often used as the form view.
  - **Design view:** as the name implies, this view is where most of the design is done. It has major areas such as header, footer, and detail.

- **Layout view:** this can be described as a combination of the form view and design view. This view brings to you the data as it would be displayed on your form. In this view, you have a restricted ability to move controls around and change control's properties.

**If you would like to switch views at any point in time,**

- Locate the **View control** on the Home Ribbon.

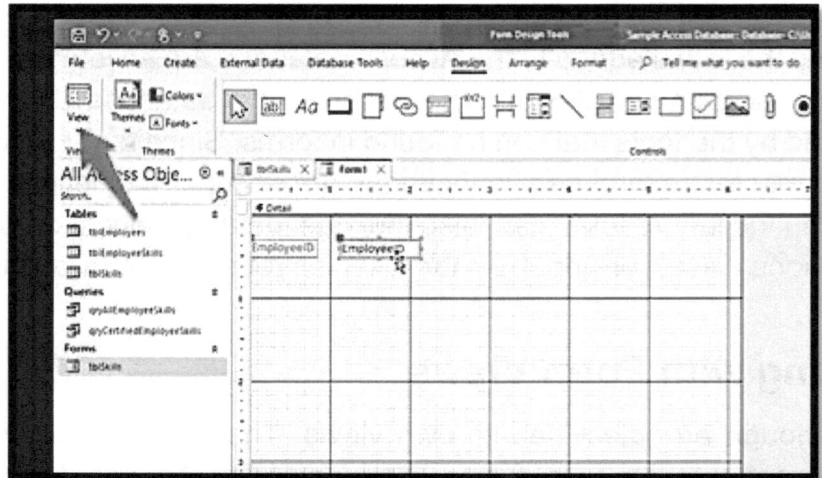

- Right-click **the form title ba**r if it is opened or you can as an alternative choice right-click **on the icon** of the form in the Navigation pane if the form is not opened.

## Understanding Different Types of Forms

With Microsoft Access, you can create forms that do a lot of tasks which include adding and changing information that is stored in the database. You can create forms to work for your organization's basic needs. A complete understanding of the different kinds of forms in Access will aid your decision in choosing the right one for whatever it is you want to do.

There are basically two kinds of forms in Access. The first kind is known as a bound form. Bound forms are forms that contain data that has a connection between the form and the database in Access. Note that these two are dependent on each other which means that when there is a change of data in the bound form, this change will also be implemented in the database that it is bound to.

Unbound forms on the other hand do not make any form of updates or make changes to the database in this manner but they are still very much useful in some other ways.

## Switchboard Form

With the use of the switchboard forms, you can create menus for a database. The switchboard Form is a type of an unbound form since changing data in the switchboard form has no effect on the same data that is in the database. Switchboards can also be used to easily open or close databases. The form can also be swiftly used in accessing data from any other forms that are related to your database.

## Dialog Box form

This form can be used in Access to show results for a search that is conducted by end-users. It can also be used by the end-user to choose certain conditions to retrieve data. Similar to the switchboard form, the dialog box form is unbound since it also cannot change data in the Access database when the dialog box is used.

Dialog boxes are a great choice when you want to make finding data from a database much easier for your end-users.

## Data Entry Form

This kind of form can be used to change data in an Access database; this means it is a bound form. This form allows you to have your end-user insert some very vital information like a different name or address and also have this information update both the form and also the relevant information contained in the database at the same time. With this form, customers have the liberty to enter the information and then make adjustments to it when need be.

## Record Display Form

This type of form is also a bound form in that it shows data from a spreadsheet based on the criteria that have been indicated. Note that with this form you can also create forms that show various records also.

# Creating new forms

**There are so many ways forms can be created in Access. The easiest is to;**

- Choose **a data source** like a table
- Click on **the Form command option** on the Create tab of the Ribbon.

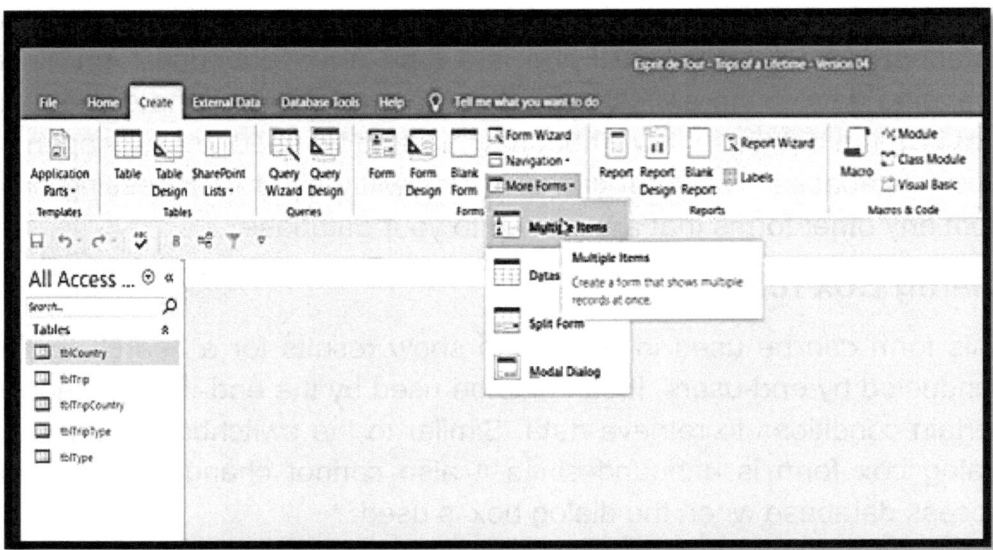

## Using the Form command

You can also choose to make use of the Form command in the Forms group of the Ribbon to automatically create a new form that is based on the table or query that has been chosen in the Navigation pane.

Using this option will open the new form in the Layout view which has lots of controls with each of the controls being attached to a field in the underlying source of data.

## Using the Form Wizard

You can also make use of the form wizard in the creation of a form. The form wizard will ask lots of questions about the form you intend to create after which it will help create the form automatically. The form wizard is quite flexible and gives you so much control also as it allows you to choose the fields you would like to have on the form and the form layout which includes Tabular, Datasheet, or Justified.

The main benefit of making use of the form wizard is the fact that it ensures the new form is bound to a data source and also adds certain controls for the selected field.

## Looking at special types of form

In this section we will be looking at the various types of special forms we have in Access as the word form, especially when it has to do with Microsoft Access, can mean a lot of things based on the context in which it is used. The sections below discuss various ways in which forms are used in Microsoft Access.

## The navigation forms

Navigation contains several tabs that offer instant access to other forms in Access in either a form or subform arrangement. Subforms are simply forms that are presented in another form.

## Multiple-item forms

This is a type of form which is also known as the continuous form, which permits users to show information in more than one record at a particular time. The data will be organized in rows and columns which is quite similar to a datasheet, and multiple records will then be shown at a time.

Nevertheless, since it is a form, it has rather more customization options than what is obtainable with a datasheet. Features that can be added to this form include; graphical elements, buttons, and other controls. A multiple-item form can also look like a datasheet when it is first created.

**To create multiple forms simply;**
- Locate **the navigation pane** then click **on the table or query** that has the data that you would like to see on the form.
- On the **Create tab option**, in the forms group, click on **Multiple items**. If multiple items are not available, click on **More forms** then click on **multiple items**.

- If you would like to start making use of the form, change to Form view.

## Split forms

A Split form provides two different views of your data at the same time- a form view and a Datasheet view. These views are linked to the same data source and are also synchronized with each other at all times. When a field is chosen in a particular part of the form, the same field will also be selected in the other part of the form. You can choose to include, edit or even delete data from either part of the view.

**To create a split form simply;**

- Locate **the navigation pane**, and choose the table or query that has the data you need on your form. Or you can also choose to **open the table or query** in the Datasheet view.
- Locate **the Create tab** in the Forms group, **choose More forms** and then click on the **split forms option**.

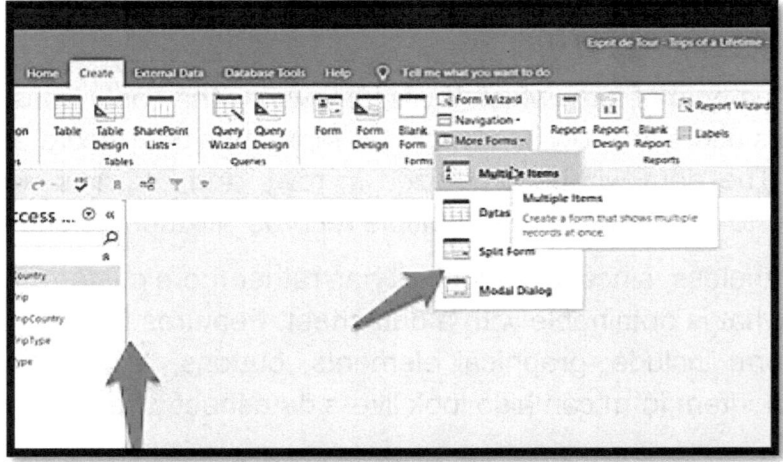

## Datasheet forms

A datasheet form is one that enables you to display information from more than one record at a time. The data in the form is organized in rows and columns and more than one record is displayed at a particular time.

A datasheet is also said to be the visual representation of the data contained in a table, or of the results that are being returned by a query.

It shows the fields for each record from a table or query result in a tabular format.

**To create a datasheet form simply;**

- Locate the **navigation pane**, click **on the table or query** that has the data which you would like to see on the form.
- Locate **the Create tab option** in the forms group and click on the **More forms option**, then cl ck on **Datasheet**.

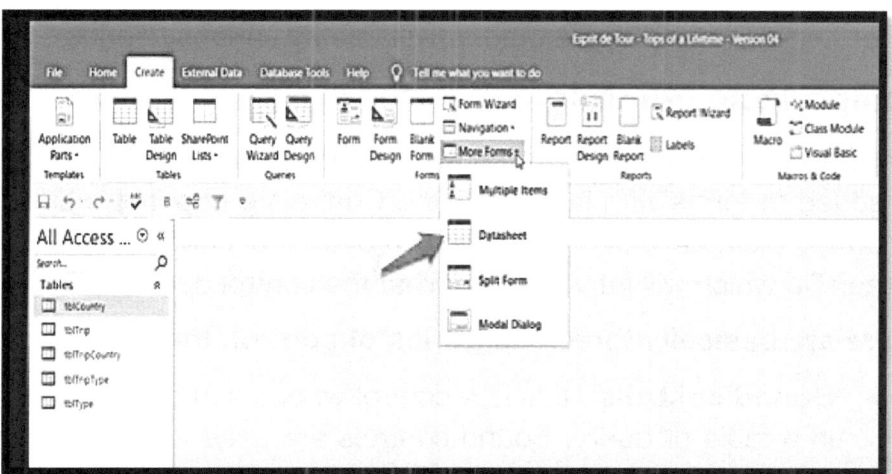

## Resizing the form area

You can simply add controls to the form from the areas with gridlines that are in the design view.

**You can have the size of the form adjusted by simply;**

- Placing **the cursor on any part** of the border and then **dragging the border** of the area to e ther enlarge or decrease it.

## Saving your form

**Saving forms is as easy as simply;**

- Clicking on the **Save button** in the **Quick Access toolbar**.

When you click on the Save option you will be prompted to give the form a name, ensure you give it a name that is meaningful and you can recollect with ease later on. Note that if you work on a form and fail to say the form, you might lose all the records in the form.

# Working with Controls

The core part of a form or a report is simply Controls and Properties. Control is just an object on a form or report like a label or text box.

Data can be entered into controls and you can also show data with the use of controls.

Not all controls are built into Access, some are developed separately and are known as ActiveX controls. ActiveX controls extend the basic feature set of Access and they are made available by various vendors.

## Categorizing controls

There are various controls embedded in forms and reports. Controls can be added to forms with the use of the Controls group in the Design tab. When you place your mouse arrow over the control it will show a ScreenTip which will let you know what the control does.

**There are basically three categories of control, they are;**

- **Bound controls**: this is a control whose source of data is a field in a table or query. Bound controls are used to show values that are from fields in the database. These values can either be text, dates, numbers, Yes/No values, pictures, etc.
- **Unbound control**: this is a control that has source data. Unbound controls are used to show information, pictures, lines, or rectangles.
- **Calculated controls**: this is a control whose source of data is an expression rather than being a field. The value to be used will be specified as the source of the data in the control by defining an expression. An expression can be a combination of operators, control names, functions that return just one value, and constant values.

## Adding a control

**To add a control follow the steps below;**

- Click **on any button** in the Controls group on the **Design tab of the Ribbon** and then draw a new unbound control on the form. You can also drag a field from the field list to add a bound control to the form. When this is done Access will automatically choose a control that is appropriate for the field's data type and then bind the control to the field that has been chosen.

## Using the Control group

You can make use of the buttons in the Controls group to add a control, this process is very flexible as you have the freedom to choose the particular type of control you would like to use for each field. The control added isn't unbound and it will have a default name. Upon the creation of the control, you can then decide the table field you would like to bind the control to, insert text for the label, and then set any property of your choice.

## Using the field list

The field list as the name implies shows a list of fields from the table or query the form is based upon.

**You can open a field list by simply;**

- Clicking on **the Add Existing fields** button in the **Tools group** which is located on the **Design tab of the Ribbon**.

Note that fields are not static, they can be moved either singly or in groups. Though multiple fields can only be dragged to a form that is already bound to a data source.

- Simply **drag a field** to move it and then click on **the key** or the **shift key** to move more than one field.

Whenever you drag fields from the field list window, the first control will be placed where you release the mouse button. Ensure that you have a lot of space on the left side for the controls of the labels. If you don't have enough space, the labels will move behind the controls.

## Selecting and deselecting controls

To change the size of a form you have to select the form first. Based on the size a selected control might have about four to eight handles around the control- at the corners and also mid-way along the sides. The moving handle is used in moving the control and the other handles are used to size the control.

## Selecting a single control

**You can select a single control by;**

- Clicking **anywhere** on the control.

When you click a control, the sizing handles will also be displayed and if the control also has an attached label, the move handle for the label will also be displayed in the upper-left corner of the control.

## Selecting multiple controls

**Multiple controls can be chosen in the following ways;**

- Hold down the **shift key** and then click **each of the controls**.
- Move the **point around** the controls you would like to select.

## Deselecting controls

**The easiest way to deselect a control is by**

- clicking an **unselected part** of the form that has no control. When this is done, the handles will disappear from any selected control. When you select another control it will also deselect a control already selected.

## Manipulating controls

After adding controls to a form there might be a need to move them and properly size them. Controls can be manipulated in the Arrange tab of the Ribbon.

## Resizing a control

Resizing a control can be done easily with the use of the smaller handles in the upper, lower, and right edges of the control. The handles in the control corners let you either increase or decrease the control in both width and height.

- Once the mouse arrow is placed on the corner sizing handles, it becomes a diagonal double arrow with which you can drag the sizing handle until you have your preferred size of controls. Double-clicking **any of the size handles** will make Access change the size of the control in such a way that it will fit perfectly the text contained in the control.

## Sizing controls automatically

There are various commands on the Size/Space drop-down on the Sizing & Ordering group of the Arrange tab of the Ribbon.

- **To Fit**: this helps to adjust the height of the control for the font of the text that is in them.
- **To shortest**: this makes the chosen controls control the height of the shortest selected control.
- **To Tallest:** this makes the chosen controls control the height of the tallest selected control.
- **To Grid**: this moves all of the sides of the chosen controls in or out to meet the closest points on the grid.
- **To Widest:** this makes the chosen controls control the height of the widest selected control.

## Moving a control

**Once you have clicked on a particular control, you can easily move that control by making use of any of the listed methods below;**

- Click and **move the handle** in the upper-left corner of the control. This is totally different from all of the other methods in the sense that it will independently move the control or its label.
- Click once to **choose the control** then drag the mouse over any of the edges that have been highlighted

## Aligning controls

Aligning controls makes them more orderly and well organized.

**The Sizing & Ordering group's Align gallery on the Arrange tab of the Ribbon has the following alignment commands;**

- **To Grid**: this helps to align the top-left corners of the chosen controls to the nearest grid point.
- **Left**: this helps to align the left edge of the chosen controls with the left-most chosen control.

- **Right**: this helps to align the right edges of the chosen controls with the right-most chosen control.
- **Bottom**: this helps to align the bottom edge of the chosen controls with the most bottom chosen to control.

To align any number of chosen controls all you have to do is choose the Align command button. When you do this, Microsoft Access will use the control that is the closest to the preferred selection as the model for the alignment.

## Modifying the appearance of control

**To make some changes to the way control is displayed,**

- Choose the **control** and then click on **the commands** that modify that control like the options in the Font or Controls group.

## Grouping controls

If you often make changes to the properties of various controls there might be a need for you to group such controls.

**To group controls together simply;**

- Choose **all the controls** by holding down the shift button and clicking on each of these controls.
- Once you have **chosen your preferred controls**, choose the **Group command** from the Size/Space gallery on the Arrange tab of the Ribbon.

## Copying a control

You can make different copies of any control by simply copying it to the clipboard and then pasting the copies wherever you want them. If you have a control for which you have inserted many properties or specified a certain format, you can choose to copy it and change only the properties to make it an entirely different control.

## Deleting a control

**You can always delete a control by simply;**

- Choosing the **particular control** in the forms **Design view** and then pressing the **Delete key**. This will make the control and any label attached disappear.

Controls don't have to be deleted one after the order, you can choose to delete more than one control at a particular time.

**All you have to do is**

- choose **all of the controls** while pressing **the shift key** then click on **the delete button**.

## Reattaching a label to control

**To have a label reattached to control simply follow the steps below;**

- Choose **the Label button** located on the **Controls group**.
- Place **the mouse pointer** in the **Form Design** window the mouse will then be in the form of the capital alphabet A.
- Select and hold down **the mouse button** where you would prefer the control to begin from; move the mouse to close up the control.
- Type **Description** and then choose **outside the control**.
- Choose the **Description label control**.
- Choose **the Cut option** from the clipboard group on the Home tab of the Ribbon.
- Choose the **Description text box control**.
- Click on the **paste option** from the Clipboard group on the Home tab of the Ribbon in order to attach the label control to the text box control.

# Introducing Properties

Properties are known as attributes of controls, fields, or database objects that can be used in the modification of the characters of control, field, or object. Certain examples of these attributes are the color, appearance, or name of a certain object.

Properties are used widely in forms and reports to change the characteristics of controls. Each of the controls on the form has properties. The form in itself also has properties as with each of its sections.

When you set properties you can do so much like moving and changing the size of controls, and changing fonts and colors.

## Displaying the Property Sheet

Properties are always displayed in a property window or property sheet window.

**To show the Property sheet for the Description text box, follow the steps below;**

- Drag the **Description of the preferred form**.
- Click on the **Description text box** control to choose it.
- Click on the **Property Sheet command** in the Tools group located on the **Design tab of the Ribbon** or as an alternative press **the F4 button** in order to show the Property Sheet.

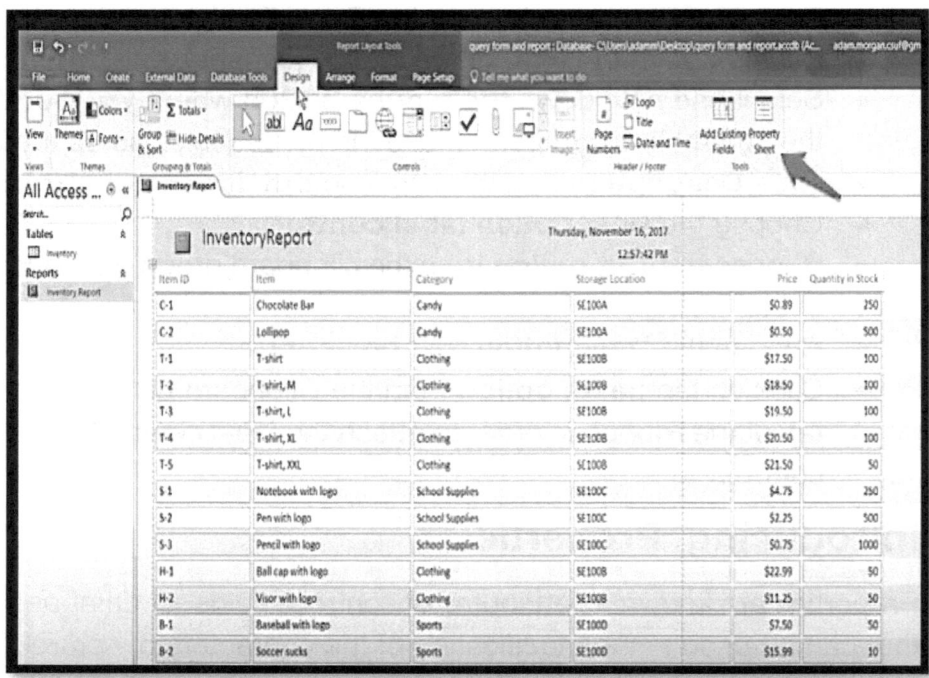

## Getting acquainted with the Property Sheet

The Property sheet has an All tab with which you can see all the properties for a control.

**The basic tabs and groups of properties are as follows;**

- **Format**: these properties determine what a value or label will look like. Here you will determine things like font size, color, special effects, and scroll bars.
- **Data**: these properties affect how a value will be shown and the source of data it is bound to like the input masks, validation, default value, and other data type properties.
- **Event**: Event properties are simply known as events like clicking **the mouse button, adding a record,** or **pressing a key** for which you would be able to define a response.
- **Other**: Other properties display some other characteristics of the control like the name of the control or the description that is shown in the status bar.

## Changing a control's property setting

**There are various methods by which property settings can be adjusted and they are;**

- By changing the control itself like changing its size.
- Insert or choose the **preferred value** in a Property Sheet.
- Make use of **inherited properties** from the bound field or from the default control of the property.
- Change label text style, size, color, and also alignment with the use of the Ribbon commands.

You can also change a control's properties by simply clicking on a property and then typing the preferred value.

## Naming control labels and their captions

By default, the label's Caption property is the same as the text box's Name property. The text box's Name property is almost always the name of the table field which is shown in the Control Source property. There are times when the label's Caption is quite different since a value has been inserted into the Caption property for each of the fields that are in the table.

Whenever you are creating controls on a form, it is a very nice idea to make use of standard naming conventions when you are setting the control's Name property.

Note that you can always find a complete, well-established naming convention online.

# CHAPTER 18
# WORKING WITH DATA ON ACCESS FORMS

An Access application's client interface is made up of forms. Forms show and alter data, acknowledge unused data, and associate with the client. Forms pass on a lot of the identity of an application, and a carefully outlined client interface drastically decreases the preparation required of new clients.

## Using Form View

The form view is where you view and make certain changes to data. The data in the Form view is the same data that is displayed in a table or query's Datasheet view with just a slight difference in presentation. Form view displays the data in a more friendly format which can be created by you.

**Follow the steps below to create a new form:**

- Select **your preferred table** in the Navigation pane.
- Click on the **Create tab on the Ribbon**.
- Select the **Form command** in the Forms group.
- Choose the **Form View button** in the **Views group** of the Home tab to change from **Layout view to Form view.**

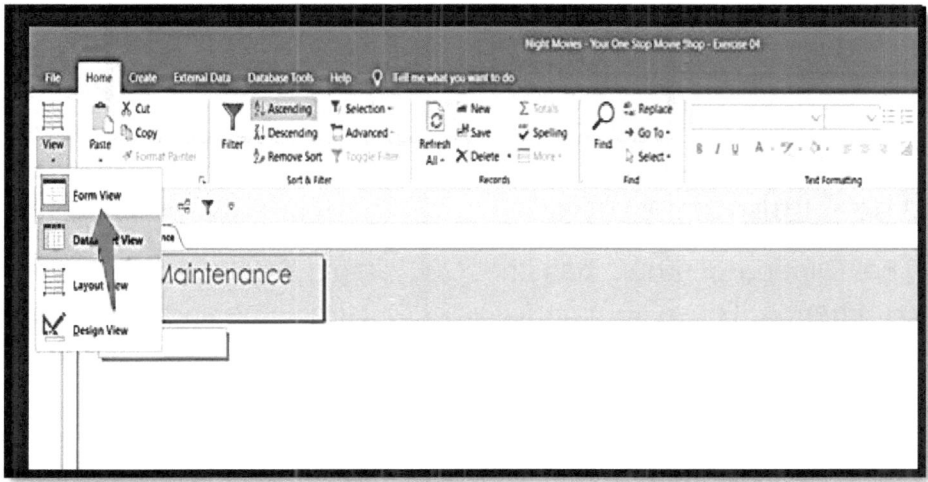

# Looking at the Home tab of the Ribbon

The Home tab of the Ribbon tab offers a way to work with the data. The Home tab has some objects you are already used to on it as they can also be found in some other applications owned by Microsoft, as well as some new ones. This section offers an analysis of the Home tab.

## The views group

**To the far left of the Ribbon is the view group which enables you to change to any view you prefer which you can view by clicking on buttons or the drop-down arrow.**

- **Form view**: enables you to make changes to data on the form
- **Datasheet view**: displays the data in the row-and-column format.
- **Layout view**: enables you to modify the form's design while also viewing data at the same time.
- **Design view**: enables you to modify the form's design only.

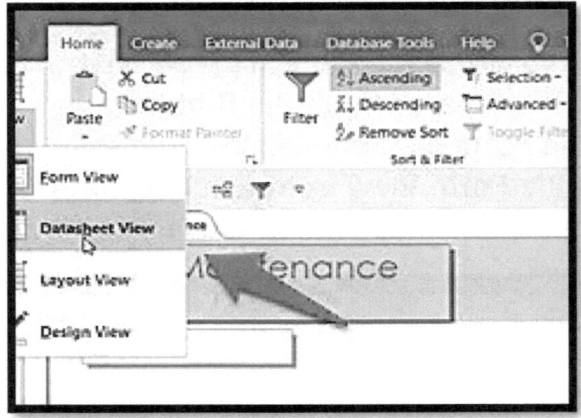

## The Clipboard group

The Clipboard group has the Cut, Copy, Paste, and Format Painter commands. These commands work just the same as in other applications (such as Word and Powerpoint). You can cut and copy items and some objects and have them pasted in Access, note that you can however not copy an Excel spreadsheet and paste it in Access form in the Form view since the view cannot work with an Excel spreadsheet.

There are three different options with the paste command which are;

- **Paste:** with this option, you can insert whatever item has been copied to the Windows Clipboard into the current location in Access. Based on whatever you're working on, the pasted item can be a text, a control, a table or form, or any other object.
- **Paste Special:** with this option, you can paste the contents of the Clipboard in different formats such as text, CSV, records, and so on.
- **Paste Append:** with this option, you can paste the contents of the Clipboard as a new record as long as a record with a similar structure has been copied to the Clipboard.

## The Sort & Filter group

With the Sort & Filter group, you can make changes to the order of the records and also limit the records shown on your form(based on your criteria).

## The Records group

You can save, delete or add a new record to your form with the use of the record group. It also has commands that show totals, freezes, and hides columns and also makes changes to the width and height of the cell while the form is being displayed in the Datasheet view.

## The find group

Finding replacing data can be done with ease with the use of the find group. Make use of the Select command option to choose a record that should be found.

## The Window group

**There are two controls in this group;**

- **Size to Fit Form:** there are certain instances when the user is working on a form and has a need to enlarge the form for easy access. When this has been done and the user has finished working on the form, the Size to Fit Form can be used to return the form back to its original dimension.

- **Switch Windows**: You can see all objects with ease in the Switch Windows, you can also choose to change to another object from the drop-down list that is displayed when you click on Switch Windows.

## The Text Formatting group

The Text Formatting group allows you to alter the look of the datasheet in the Datasheet view or Design view. Use these commands option to change the font, font size, color, and so on, use the Align Left, Align Right, and Center commands to arrange the data in the selected column. Click the Gridlines option to toggle grid lines on and off.

## Navigating among fields

Navigation within forms is quite similar to moving in a datasheet. You can move around with ease by simply clicking on the controls and making the desired changes.

| Navigational Direction | Keystrokes |
| --- | --- |
| Previous field | Shift+Tab, left-arrow (←) key or up-arrow (↑) key |
| Next field | Tab, right-arrow (→) key, down-arrow (↓) key |
| First field of current record | Home |
| Last field of current record | End |
| Next page | PgDn or Next Record |
| Previous page | PgUp or Previous Record |

## Moving among records in a form

The easiest way to move between records in a form is to make use of the navigation buttons which can be found at the bottom left corner of the Form window. The record number shown in the Navigation controls is simply an indicator of the current record position in the record set, it is not constant as it might change when the records are filtered or sorted.

## Knowing which controls you can't edit

**Not all the controls in a field can be edited, the controls you cannot edit in a field are;**

- Controls that show AutoNumber fields.
- Fields that are locked or disabled.
- Calculated controls.
- Controls in multi-user locked records.

## Working with pictures and OLE objects

OLE objects also known as Object Linking Embedding objects are those objects that are not a member of the Access database. Oftentimes, OLE objects contain pictures but they can also be any number of data like audio files or Word documents.

A picture or OLE object cannot be viewed in a Datasheet view without gaining access to the OLE server, however, you can size the OLE control area to be large enough to show a picture, chart, and other OLE object in the design view.

## Entering data in the Long Text field

LongText fields are fields that have up to 1GB of characters. Clicking on the textbox will display a vertical scroll bar which enables you to see all the data in the control. Furthermore, to make the text larger you can change the size of the form in the Design view.

## Entering data in the Date field

The date field has been configured in such a way that it only accepts and shows date values.

Below is an instruction on how to operate in this field;

- When you click **on the inside of the text box,** a Date picker icon will be displayed next to it automatically and when you also click on the Date Picker it will show a calendar from which you can pick a date.

## Using option group

With the option group you can choose just one value from a number of possibilities. You have checkboxes, toggle buttons, and option buttons in an option group.

**To create an option group;**

- Change to the **Design view** and choose the **Option Group button** from the Design tab's Control group.

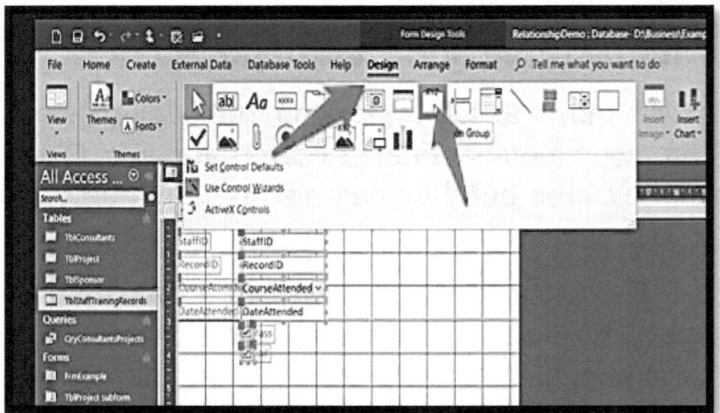

## Using combo boxes and list boxes

Access has two types of controls which are list boxes and combo boxes and are used for showing lists of data from which a user can choose. The list box usually shows as much of the list as possible, and the combo box has to be selected to open the list. A combo box can be described as a combination of a text box and a list box. The text box portion of a combo box can always be seen, and the user can insert text into it just as with any other text box. The user can also choose the drop-down arrow to show the list box portion of the combo box and choose an item rather than having to type it.

**To design a combo box;**

- Change to the **Design view** and choose the **Combo Box command** from the controls group of the Design tab. Ensure that the Use Control Wizards command has been chosen.

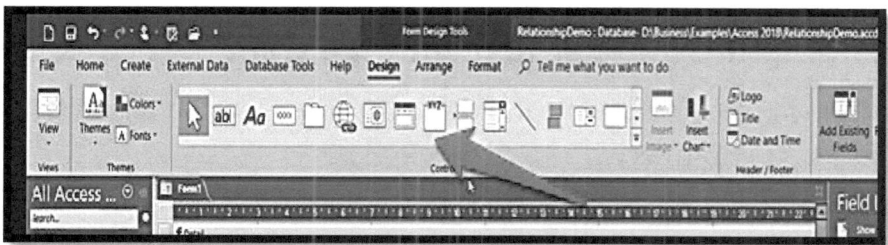

## Switching to Datasheet view

**To change to a Datasheet view, ensure that a form is opened then make us of any of the options below;**

- Choose the **Datasheet View command** in the Home tab's Views group.
- Click on the **Datasheet View button** in the View Shortcuts section which is located at the bottom-right of the Access window.
- Right-click the **form's title bar** or any blank area of the form and click on **Datasheet View from the shortcut menu.**

### Saving a record

Records in Access are saved automatically when you leave a particular record and move to another.

**Alternatively, you can also;**

- Press the **Shift + Enter button** or click on the **Save option** on the **Quick Access toolbar** to save the record without having to leave.

## Printing form

Printing a form is very easy, you can print a form as it is being displayed on the screen.

**The easiest way to print a form is to;**

- Press the **Ctrl +P buttons** and the print dialog box will be displayed with options like print range which will print a chosen page or the whole form, and copies which determine the number of copies that will be printed, and collate which also determines if the copies should be collated or not.

## Changing the title bar text with the Caption property

The form's Caption property indicates the text shown in the title bar when the form is in Form view.

**Follow the steps below to change the title bar text:**
- Choose **the form selector** to be sure the form itself is selected.
- Select the **Property Sheet button** in the Design tab's Tools group, or you can also **press F4 t**o open the Property Sheet.

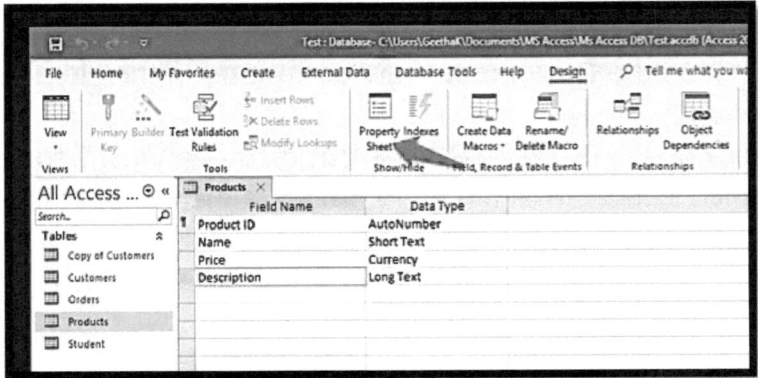

- Click on the **Caption property** in the Property Sheet and insert Products in the property's text box
- Click any **other property** or press **Enter** to move off of the Caption property.
- Change to **Form view** to see the form's new title bar text.

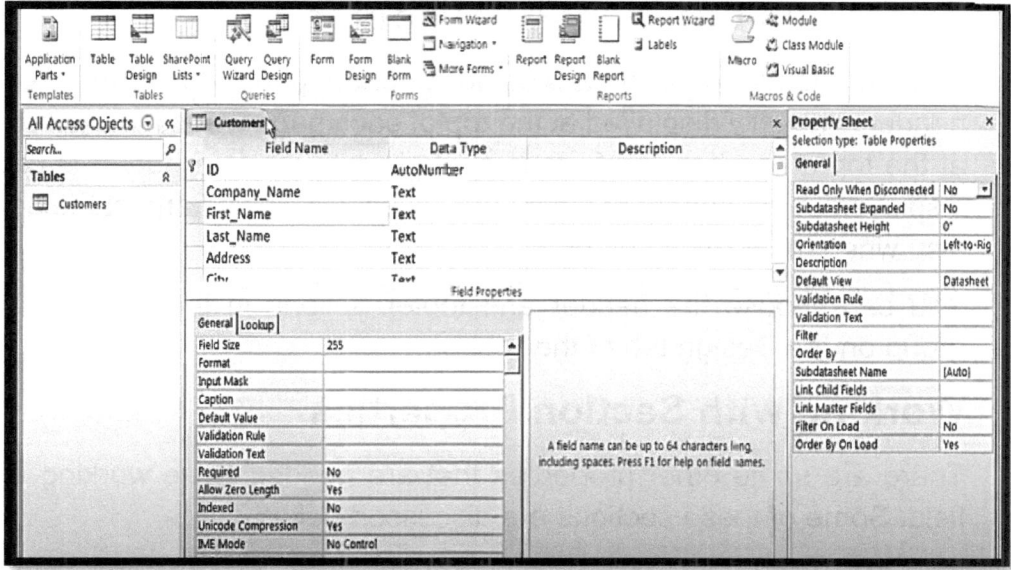

## Creating a bound form

A bound form automates the update of data in the bound source when the user moves to another record in the form. This form has a direct link to a data source such as a table, SQL statement, or query. Note that before you can create a bound form you must indicate a data source in the forms record source.

## Specifying how to view the form

Microsoft makes use of various properties to decide how a form should be viewed. Forms can be viewed either as Single form which shows a record per time, continuous form which displays more than one record at a time, datasheet, and split form which provides two different views of the same data at the same time.

## Removing the Record Selector

The record selector property decides if the record selector should be displayed or not. The record selector is very important when it has to do with dealing with various record forms or datasheets since it points to the current record.

- To remove the record selector simply **change the form of the Record Selector** property to No.

# Adding a Form Header or Footer

The form header or footer is also an important part of the form. The form header is usually displayed at the top of each page when it is viewed and at the top also when the form is printed while the form footer is usually displayed at the bottom of each page when it is viewed and at the bottom also when the form is printed.

You can choose the header and footer options in the Header/Footer group on the Design tab of the Ribbon.

# Working with Section Properties

There are some other properties that are needed while working in the field. Some of these sections are discussed below

## The Visible property

This section is basically a Yes/No property as it helps the form to decide if it should be hidden or visible.

## The Height property

This property is also used in showing how tall the section is. The easiest way to change the height of the section is to make use of the mouse in dragging either up or down to either increase or decrease the height.

## The Back Color property

The Back Color property determines the color of the background of the controls. You can change the BackColor property by using the drop-down control on the Property Sheet.

## The Special Effect property

The Special Effect property can be configured to be Flat, Raised, or Sunken. The flat is the default value and Raised and Sunken offer a rounded effect at the edges of the section.

## The Display When property

The Display When property can be configured to Always, Screen Only, or Print Only. This enables you to hide or show a section when printing.

# The printing properties

The section properties left like Auto Height, Can Grow, and Can Shrink, are more applicable to reports than forms. With these properties, you can control the height of sections based on the data those sections contain. They have no effect on how your form is shown on the screen and are also not used frequently.

# Changing the Layout

**To change the layout of a form simply follow the steps below;**

- Open **a form** in the layout view.
- Choose **the Arrange tab option** in the Form Layout Tools area of the Ribbon. You can then begin to make the changes in accordance with your preference.

### Changing a control's properties

**You can change the properties of the control in the layout view by following the steps below;**

- Choose **the Property Sheet command** in the Form Layout Tools Design tab's Tools group to show the Property Sheet for the chosen control.

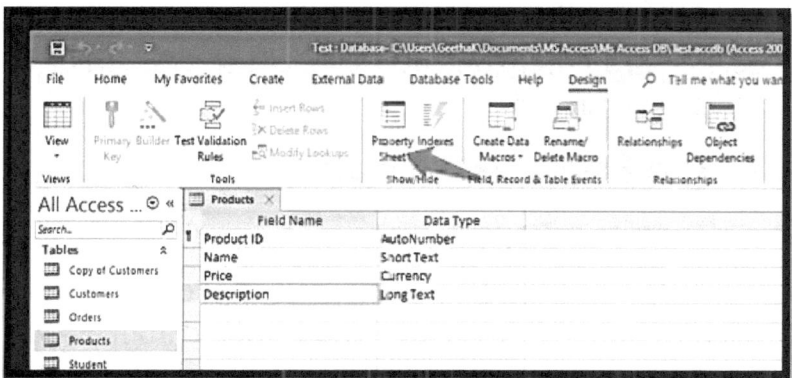

# Setting the tab order

The tab order of the form is the order in which the focus moves from one control to another as you press Tab. Moving controls around the form mean there will be a need for you to make certain changes to the tab order of the form.

- Choose **the Tab Order** from the Design tab's Tools group when you're in the Design view to show the Tab Order dialog box. The dialog box will then display the controls in the manner in which they are arranged in the tab order in view. There are several buttons in the tab order with which you can arrange the tab order if it appears disorganized.

## Modifying the format of text in a control

**To change the formatting of text within a control;**

- first select it, then choose **a formatting style** to apply to it.

You can find some more commands for making changes to the format of control on the Format tab of the Ribbon.

## Using the Field List to add controls

The Field List section of the form shows a list of fields from the table or query that the form is built on. If the Field List is not currently accessible, use the Add Existing Fields button on the Design tab to open it.

- To **add bound** controls to the form, **drag fields** from the Field List to the form's surface.

- Select and **drag them** one at a time, or use **the Ctrl or Shift keys** to select several fields.

# Converting a Form to a Report

**To convert a Form to a Report;**

- Open the **form in the Design view** and choose **File Save As** to save it as a report. The report is then created from the whole form. The report's Header and Footer parts are based on the form's headers and footers. Page headers and footers are used as the report's Page Header and Page Footer sections if the form provides them. You may now use the report in Design view, which allows you to add groups and other features without having to recreate the overall structure.

# CHAPTER 19
# WORKING WITH FORM CONTROLS

This chapter helps you to understand forms and subforms better and all that has to do with the control of forms. You will also learn how to create forms from scratch.

## Setting Control Properties

Controls which are the building blocks of Access is in the controls group which is located on the Design tab of the Ribbon. It houses different types of controls which include option groups, checkboxes, combo boxes, list boxes, and some other controls.

Each of these controls has a set of properties that decides how the control is displayed and how it also behaves. With the Property sheet opened you can click on any control in the form to show the property settings of the control.

**If you would like to display the properties of the form in the property sheet when you must have shown the properties of the control;**

- Click on a **totally blank area** in the form design window.

## Customizing the default properties

When you design a control from the Ribbon, the control will also be created by default with a set of property values.

**If you would like to control defaults,**

- Choose **a tool** in the Controls group of the **Design tab** and then configure the properties in the Property Sheet without adding the control to the form.

Setting the default properties is also the same as setting the default properties for that same type of control for the current form in use.

## Looking at common controls and properties

In this section, the most commonly used controls that are mostly used in the Access application and the properties that control their appearance and behavior.

## The Text Box control

Text, numbers, dates, times, and note fields can all be shown using text box controls. A text box can be linked to a field in an underlying table or query. You can modify the value in a field in the underlying table or query by entering a new value in a text box that is tied to a field. A text box can also be used to display calculated values.

## The Command Button control

To initiate a macro or a Visual Basic process, use command button controls. When a user hits the button, Access opens a hyperlink address that you define.

## The Combo Box and List Box controls

Use a combo box control to display a list of possible control values as well as an editable text box. Values for the Row Source attribute of the combo box can be entered to generate the list. You may also make the values in the list come from a table or a query. In the text field, Access shows the currently selected value. Access displays the values in the list when you click the arrow to the right of the combo box. To reset the value in the control, select a new value from the list. If the combo box is bound to a field in the underlying table or query, you can modify the field's value by selecting a new option.

To hold a list of possible values for the control, use a list box control. The values for the list can be entered into the list box's Row Source attribute. As the source of the values in the list, you may also specify a table or a query. List boxes are constantly open, and the presently selected value in the list box is highlighted in the list box. To reset the control's value, you choose a new value from the list.

If the list box is bound to a field in the underlying table or query, changing the value in the field is as simple as selecting a new value from the list.

When you link the list box to a multi-value field, Access shows a list with checkboxes so the user can choose numerous values. You can tie multiple columns to the list, and by setting a column's width to 0, you can conceal one or more of the columns in the list.

## The Checkbox and Toggle Button controls

To hold an on/off, true/false, or yes/no value, use toggle button controls. When you click a toggle button, its value changes to -1 (which stands for "on," "true," or "yes"), and the button seems to be pressed in.

When you click the button again, the value changes to 0 (which stands for off, false, or no), and the button returns to its original state. A toggle button can be included in an option group and given a unique numeric value. Selecting a new toggle button in a group with several controls clears any previously chosen toggle button, option button, or check box in that group (unless other buttons or checkboxes in the group also have the same value).

To hold an on/off, true/false, or yes/no value, use a check box control. When you pick a check box, its value changes to -1 (which stands for "on," "true," or "yes"), and a checkmark appears in the box. When you choose the check box again, its value changes to 0 (off, false, or no), and the check mark vanishes from the box. In an option group, you can include a check box and give it a unique numeric value. Selecting a new check box in a group with several controls clears any previously chosen toggle button, option button, or check box in that group (unless other buttons or checkboxes in the group also have the same value).

- If the check box is bound to a field in the underlying table or query, clicking the **check box** toggles the field's value.

## The Options Group control

To hold an on/off, true/false, or yes/no value, use an option button control (also known as a radio button control).

- When you choose **an option button**, its value changes to -1 (which stands for on, true, or yes), and a filled circle appears in the button's center.

- When you choose **the button again**, its value changes to 0 (which stands for off, false, or no), and the filled circle vanishes. An option button can be included in an option group and given a unique numeric value.
- Selecting **a new option button** in a group with several controls clears any previously chosen toggle button, option button, or check box in that group (unless other buttons or checkboxes in the group also have the same value).

If you link the choice button to a field in the underlying table or query, you may use it to change the value of that field.

## The Web Browser control

To display the content of online pages directly inside a form, use a web browser control. A web browser control can be used to display a map of an address entered in a table, for example. The Control Source property of the web browser control can be used to connect the control to a field in the record source of your form. A bound web browser control cannot be used in the Detail section of a continuous form.

## Creating a Calculated Control

To display the results of a calculation, you can utilize calculated controls on forms and reports in Access databases. If you have a report that shows the number of products sold and the price of each unit, for example, you can add a calculated text box that multiplies those two fields to show the overall price.

To get the result, the computed text box's Control Source property contains an equation that multiplies two fields (the number of items times the unit price).

**To create a calculated control simply follow the steps below;**

- Right-click **on the form** of the report in the **Navigation pane** then click on **the Design View.**

- On the **Design tab**, in the **Controls group**, click on **the tool** for the type of control you would like to create.
- Place **the pointer** where you would like the control to be located on the form or the report then choose to **insert the control**.
- If a control wizard should start, choose the **Cancel option** to close it.
- Choose the control then **press F4** to show the property sheet then insert an expression in the Control Source property box.
- Change to the **Form view** or the **Report view** and then indicate the calculated control should work just how you would want it to.

# Working with Subforms

Subforms is essential for showing data from two separate tables or queries on the same screen. Subforms are typically utilized when the record source of the main form has a one-to-many relationship with the record source of the subform that is, many records in the subform are associated with one record in the main form.

The Subform control's LinkMasterFields and LinkChildFields attributes are used by Access to determine which records in the subform are associated with each record in the main form. Access automatically queries the subform whenever the value in the main form's link field changes.

You might want to display subform aggregate information in the master form while generating a subform. It's worth noting that you have to find the value of aggregate data in the subform before you can put it in the master form.

# Form Design Tips

In the section below are various form design tips that might be very useful to you. Study carefully and apply to bring the best out of your form.

# Using the Tab Stop property

There are times when you might place a control on a form that is intended to cause a trigger which will produce a fairly drastic result like printing a very long report or deleting such a report. If you would like to control the effect this kind of control might have it is best you make use of the Tab Stop property which indicates if you can make use of the Tab key to move the focus to the control.

## Tallying check boxes

This option is usually used when there is a need to count the number of True values in a Check Box control.

## Setting up combo boxes and list boxes

A list of values or options is displayed in the list box control. The list box holds rows of data and is normally sized so that numerous rows can be seen at once. One or more columns can appear in each row, with or without titles. If the list contains more rows than the control can display, Access displays a scroll bar in the control. The user's options are limited to those in the list box; there is no way to type a value into a list box.

The combo box control presents a list of options in a more compact format; the list is concealed until you click the drop-down arrow. You can also use a combo box to input a value that isn't on the list. The combination box control combines the functionality of a text box with a list box in this way.

**To create a Listbox or a combox with the use of the wizard, simply follow the settings below;**

- Right-click **the form** in the Navigation pane and then click on the **Design View option**.
- On the **Design tab** which is located in the **Controls group**, make sure that the Use Control Wizard option is chosen.

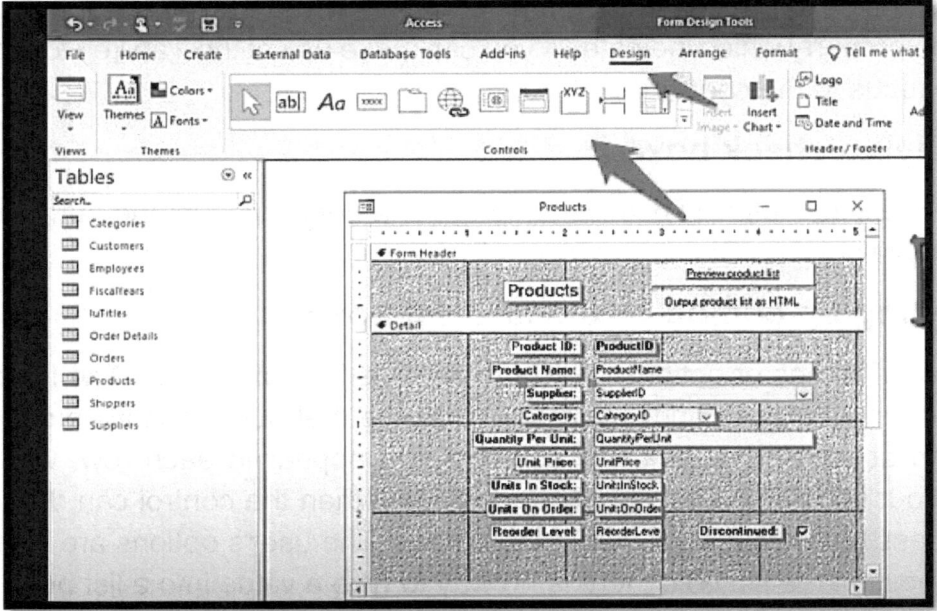

- Choose either the **List Box tool or the Combo Box too**l.
- On the form, click on **the very place** you would prefer to put the list box or the combo box.
- When **the wizard prompts** a query asking how you want to get the values for the control, choose your preferred option.

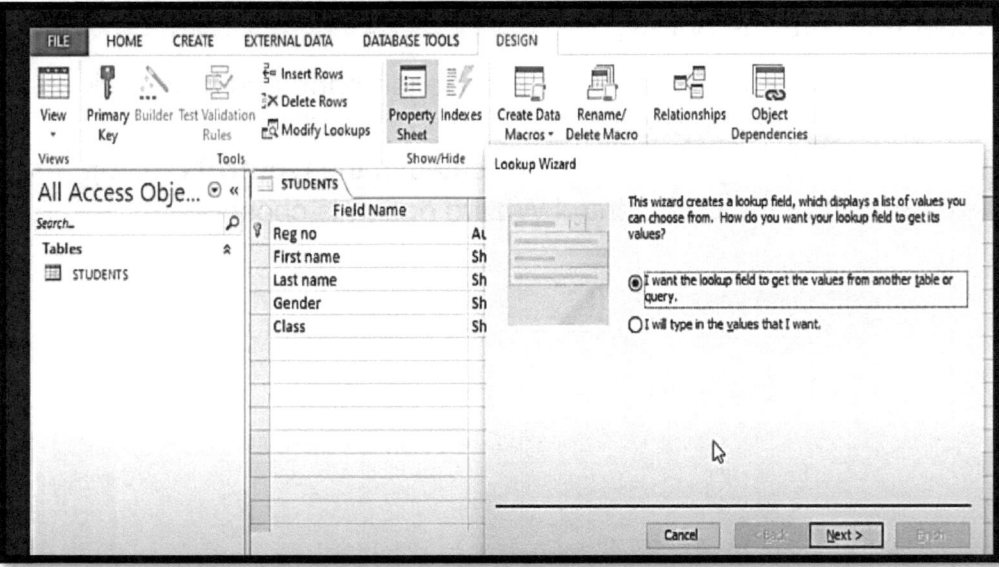

- Follow through on the instructions indicating how the values will be displayed.
- Click on the **Next button** and **type a label** you would like to use for the control. This label will be shown next to the control.
- Click on the **Finish button**.

# Tackling Advanced Forms Techniques

This section discusses the various features that have been in Microsoft Access for quite a while but have not been discovered by lots of developers.

## Using the Page Number and Date/Time controls

The current date and time are frequently included on forms. With the Date and Time command in the Header/Footer group on the Design tab of the Ribbon, Access makes this process of inclusion easier.

The Date and Time dialog box opens when the Date and Time command is selected, asking how you want the date and time formatted. Access adds a form header providing the date and time formatted as you asked after you make your selections and click OK. Other commands in the Header/Footer group allow you to add a logo (almost any image file) and a title to the form header section. Using the Header/Footer controls in an application ensures that all forms have the same look.

## Morphing a control

The requirement to define the control type when a control is added to a form is undoubtedly one of the most aggravating issues when creating Access forms. You can alter the type of control in Access to any other kind that works.

**Simply;**

- Right-click **on the control** and choose the **Change To Command option** from the shortcut menu in order to have the options displayed.

## Using the Format Painter

Access contains a Format Painter that works similarly to Word's Format Painter. When constructing a form, you set the appearance of control and then copy the properties to a special internal buffer by

- clicking the **Format Painter** button on the Font group on **the Design tab of the Ribbon**.

The aesthetic characteristics of the control that has been chosen and placed in the internal buffer will be passed to the second control whenever you click on another control of the same kind.

## Offering more end-user help

ScreenTips note that appear when you hover the mouse over control or button in Microsoft Office products. You should use ScreenTips consistently across an application.

## Adding background pictures

Forms that are appealing to the eye are always a good addition to Access apps. In the same way that a watermark can show on pricey bond paper, Access makes it simple to add a graphic to the backdrop of a form. The picture can be integrated into the form or linked to an external file and is defined by the form's Picture property. If the image is linked, the graphic on the form will update whenever the external file is modified.

**If you would like to include a picture on your form,**

- Open **the form** in the Design view and then display the Property Sheet. If the Property Sheet is not displaying the properties of the form already, you can choose Form from the combo box.

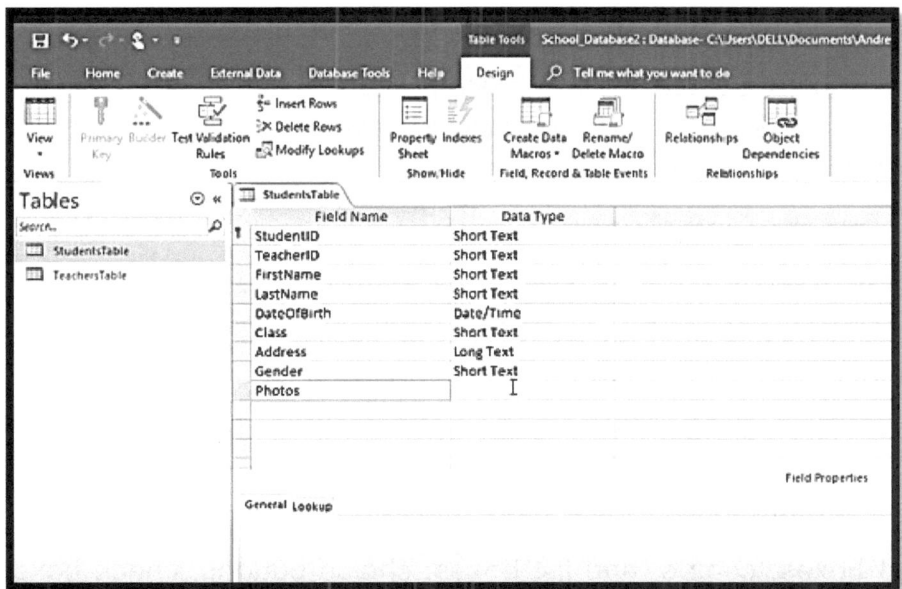

- Click on **the builder button** for the Picture property to choose **the picture** you would like to add to the form.

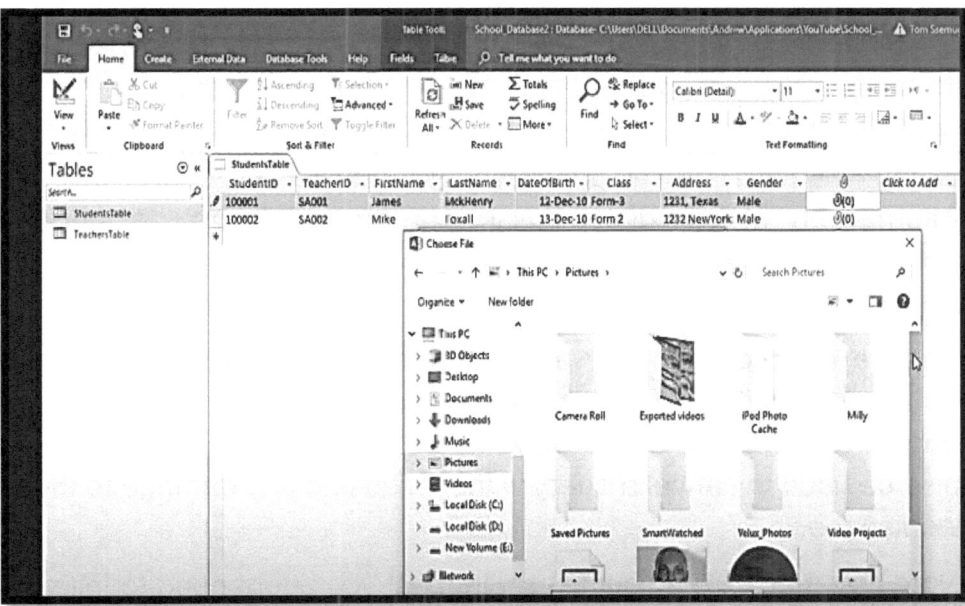

- Change **the Picture Tiling**, and **Picture Size Mode properties** to show the picture in various ways.

## Limiting the records shown on a form

The Record Source property usually determines how many records a form displays, but if you want to show fewer records, simply change the underlying query or SQL expression.

## Using the Tab Control

A Tab control displays a number of pages, each of which can be accessed using a tab at the top, bottom, or side of the dialog box. A Tab control is made up of several tabs.

- The quickest and easiest way to add or delete a page from the user interface is to right-click **the control** and select **the relevant command** from the shortcut menu.

Text boxes, combo, and list boxes, choice buttons, check boxes, and OLE objects are all examples of controls that can be found in a Tab control. Although a form can have numerous Tab controls, overloading the user with more than one Tab control is typically not a good idea.

## Using Dialog Boxes to Collect Information

Typically, dialog boxes capture a specific sort of data, such as font properties or hardcopy parameters. Without cluttering the main form, dialog windows are a great way to prefilter or qualify user input. Alternatively, utilize a dialog box to allow the user to provide query criteria before running a query that populates a form or report, or to collect data for a report's header or footer area.

Despite the fact that they are forms, dialog boxes rarely resemble or behave like other forms in the application. Dialog boxes frequently appear on top of the user's work. When used correctly, dialog boxes can also be used to cancel a query without causing any damage to the user's workspace.

Note that there are a couple of rules that you might need to follow in the construction of the dialog boxes. These rules ensure that your dialog boxes adhere to the generally accepted behavior for Windows dialog boxes.

## Designing the query

**Queries are always designed in order to focus on a specific set of data. Simply follow the steps to create a query;**

- Choose the **Create option** then click on the **Query Wizard**.
- Choose the **Simple Query option** then click on the **OK button**.
- Choose **the table** that has the field then include the Available Fields you want to Selected Fields and then click on the **Next button**.
- Decide if you would like to have the query opened in the Datasheet view or change the query in the Design view and then click on the **Finish button**.

## Setting up the command buttons

When you add a command button to a form, Access displays a wizard to assist you to define the button's behavior. The Execute Query action will be selected for the Run Query button, and qryDialog will be selected as the query to run on the wizard's following screen. As a result, when the button is pressed, the query will run and the form's text box will be used as a criterion.

## Adding a default button

If the user clicks the Enter key while the dialog box is open, a button on the form should be immediately selected. The default button does not need to be selected by the user to be triggered; when the user taps the Enter key, Access automatically fires the default button's Click event. Note that the button that should be chosen should be one that won't cause any harm if accidentally it is pressed as the default for a form.

## Setting a Cancel button

If a user presses the **Esc key** while the form is open, the Cancel button on the form is immediately selected. In most circumstances, the dialog box ought to close if the user presses the Esc key while it's open.

## Removing the control menu

You won't need the control menu button in the upper left corner of the form after you've assigned the default and Cancel buttons. To conceal the control menu button, set the Control Box property on the form to No. The user will have to use the Cancel or Run Query buttons to remove the form from the screen once the control menu box has been removed.

## Designing a Form from Scratch

This section explains how a form can be created from scratch, here you will need to apply all you must have learned in previous chapters.

## Creating the basic form

Any table in your database can be used to construct a form in Access. Any form you generate from a table will allow you to view existing data in the table as well as add new data.

**After you've generated a form, you can customize it by adding new fields and design elements such as combo boxes.**

> Locate the **Navigation pane** then choose **the table** you would like to make use of in creating the form. There is no need for you to have the table opened.

- Choose the **Create tab option**, find the Forms group and then choose the **Form command.**
- Your form will then be opened in the Layout view.
- Save **the form** by clicking on the **Save command** on the **Quick Access toolbar**. When there is a prompt, include a name for the form and then click on the OK button.

## Creating a subform

**A subform is a datasheet form that shows linked records in a table-like format.**

**To create a subform;**

- Locate the **navigation pane**, right-click and then choose the **Design view option**.

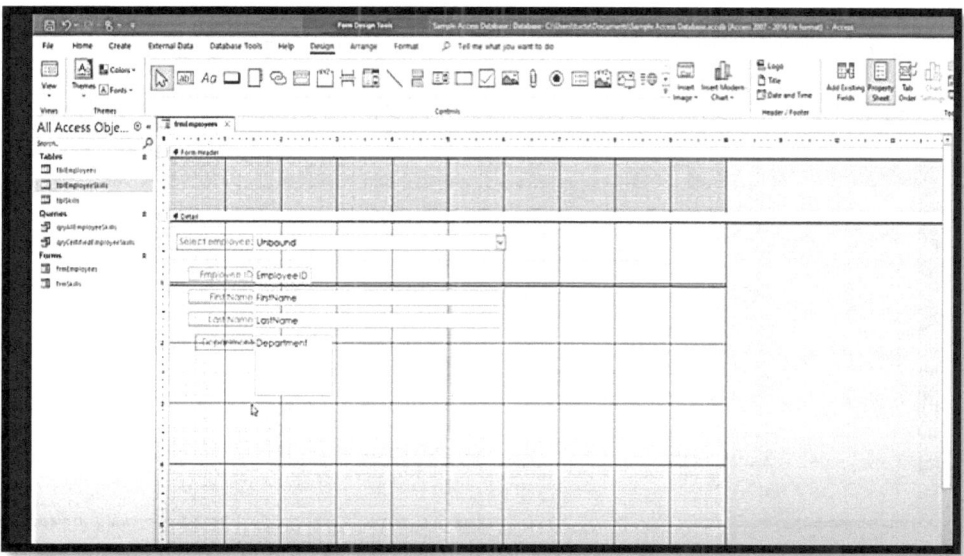

- Locate the **Controls** on the **Toolbar in the Design tab** then click on the **downward arrow** to expand the control's toolbar.
- Click on the **subform.**

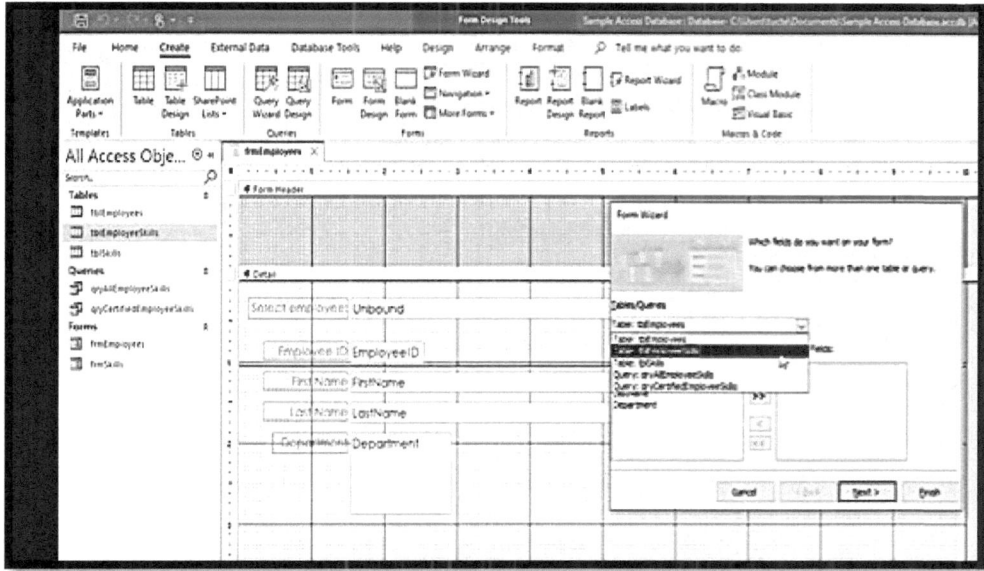

- Choose the **exact location** you would like to have the subform.
- Once you have chosen the **location** click on the **Next option** where you will choose the field that you would like to show in your subform.

- Link the **subform** to the access form and then click on the **Next button**.
- Name your **subform** and then click on the **finish button**.

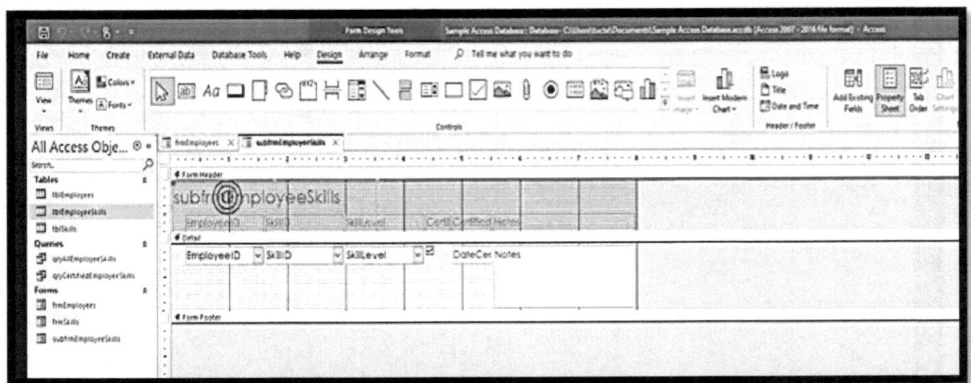

- The subform will then be saved as a separate form.

## Adding the subform

**To add a subform;**

- Open the form.
- Expand the **controls Toolbar**
- Choose the **Subform option**.
- Choose the **Data Source** to use for the subform
- Choose the **fields**
- Choose the **linking fields**
- Make some modifications if need be.
- Click on the **finished button**.

## Changing the form's behavior

In this section you have to change some of the properties of the form and also its controls so you can get the behavior that you want.

### Setting the form's properties

**Make changes to the form properties below to the values given;**

- **Caption: New**: Invoice Entry
- **Allow Datasheet View**: No
- **Allow Layout View**: No

- **Record Selectors**: No
- **Navigation Buttons**: No
- **Control Box**: No
- **Data Entry**: Yes
- **Cycle**: Current Record

## Looking up values during data entry

You can choose to look up values either from the subform or from the main form, where you basically have more fields.

## Saving the record

**To create a command button that will save the record simply follow the following steps below;**

- Locate the **Controls group** of the **Design tab of the Ribbon** then choose the **Button control** and put it on the form.
- Locate the **command button Wizard** first screen then choose the **Record Navigation** option and locate the **Next Record option** then click on the **Next option**.
- On the screen that follows in the wizard, check on the **Show All Pictures checkbox** and then click on the **Save Record** picture and then click on the Next option.
- On the Last screen of the wizard, include a name for the button then click on the **Finish button**.

## Changing the form's appearance

The final stage is to make the form look nice. Change the width and placement of the controls on the main form, and set the command buttons in the bottom right. You are quite free to play around here such that you can make the form appear just the way you would like it.

# CHAPTER 20
# PRESENTING DATA WITH ACCESS REPORTS

Reports are an excellent tool for seeing and printing data from your database. You can display information that is extremely summarized, detailed, or somewhere in between, and you can read or print it in a variety of forms. A report can include multilayer totals, statistical comparisons, and images and graphics.

In this chapter, you will learn how to create reports and also make use of the Report Wizard.

## Introducing Reports

Reports are ways in which data can be presented. You can either print a report or view it on the screen. Pictures and other images, as well as memo fields, can be used in reports.

### Identifying the different types of reports

**There are various types of reports in Microsoft Access. Some will be discussed in the section below;**

### Tabular reports

Data is printed in rows and columns with groupings and totals in these reports. Summary and group/total reports are examples of variations. To divide information, these reports frequently use page numbers, report dates, or lines and boxes. Color and shading may be used in reports, as well as photos, graphs, and memo fields. A summary tabular report has all of the features of a detail tabular report but does not include record details.

### Columnar reports

Columnar reports display data in the same way that a data entry form does, but they're only used to examine data, not to enter it. They usually display reports with one or more records per page and in a vertical format.

## Mailing label reports

Mailing reports are a type of report for which Access has a Label Wizard to assist in their production. You can choose from a variety of label styles with the Label Wizard. Access provides a report design that is accurate based on the label type you choose. The report can then be opened in Design mode and customized as desired.

## Distinguishing between reports and forms

A form is a database object that can be used to design a database application's user interface.

Forms make it possible to see real-time data from a table. It is primarily used to make data entering and editing easier.

A report is a type of item found in desktop databases that are used to format, calculate, print, and summarize data. You can even decide to change the design and feel of the report. A report can repeat anything you can do with a form, except input data. You can even save a form as a report and then tweak it in the Report Design box.

# Creating a Report from Beginning to End

The process involved in creating a report in Microsoft Access is quite simple. Note that the main purpose of a report is for you to transform raw data into information.

**Below are the processes involved in creating a report;**
- You begin with **defining** the layout of the report.
- Bring the **data that will be transformed together**.
- Create the **report with the use of the Access Report Wizard**.
- Print the report (hard copy) or you can decide to simply view it on the screen.
- Save **the report**.

# Defining the report layout

Consider how the data should be sorted (for example, chronologically or by name), how the data should be grouped (for example, by invoice number or by week), and how the data will be constrained by the quantity of the paper used to print the report when setting up a report.

## Assembling the data

This is the next step after you must have concluded with the layout of the report.

**Microsoft Access makes use of data from two main sources;**
- A single database table
- A record set produced by a query

## Creating a report with the Report Wizard

Creating a report with the use of the report wizard makes it easier to create some type of report. The report wizard can provide you with a basic layout for your report which you can then customize to just how you would like it to be.

## Creating a new report

**To create a new report begin by;**
- Clicking on the **Report Wizard button** which will then display the first screen of the Report Wizard.

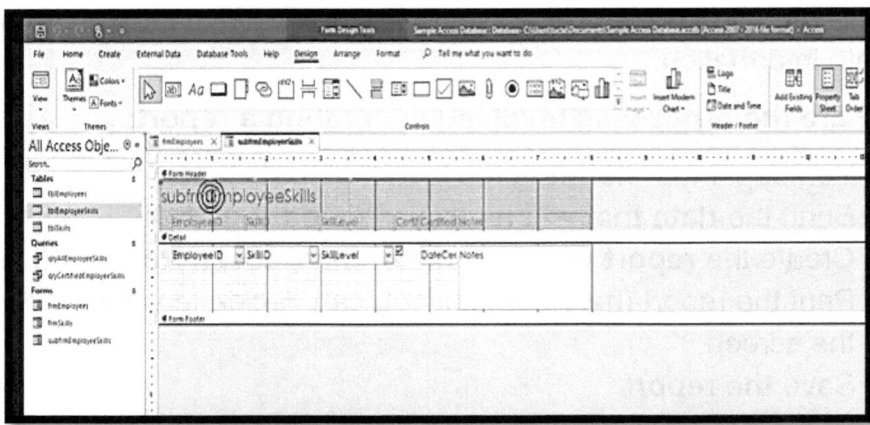

- Choose **the table** for which you would like to create a report in the navigation pane.

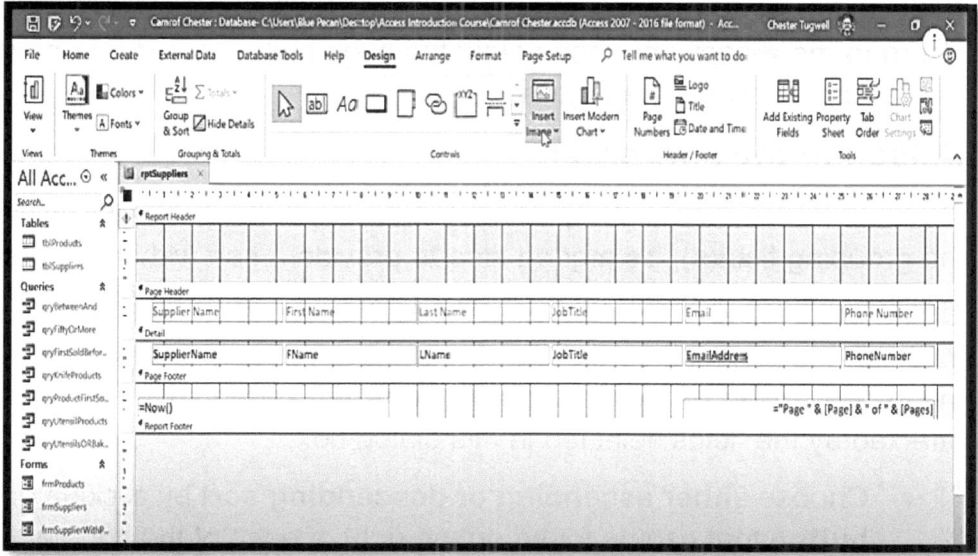

- Beneath the drop-down list of the table are fields wherein you would find the data.
- After you must have chosen your data, click on the **Next button** to move to the next step in the Wizard.

## Selecting the grouping levels

In this dialog box, you will be able to choose the fields you would like to make use of for grouping data. The manner in which data is displayed is dependent on the field that is chosen for grouping, the grouping field will also be displayed as group headers and footers in the report.

Note that with the use of the Report Wizard, you can choose as many as four group fields in your report.

## Defining the group data

### Once you have chosen your preferred group field(s);

- Click on the **Grouping Options** button which can be found at the bottom of the dialog box in order to help show the **Grouping intervals dialog box** which will allow you to define how you would like the group to be displayed on the report.

Once you have shown the Grouping Intervals dialog box, you can then return to the wizard and then select the Next button in order to move to the sorting screen of the wizard.

## Selecting the sort order

Although Access sorts grouped records in a meaningful order based on the grouping field(s), it's a good idea to provide a sort within each group because the order of the records within the group can't be guaranteed.

You can only choose sorting fields that haven't been grouped yet. Only the sorting order of the data displayed in the report's Detail section is affected by the fields selected in this dialog box.

- Choose **either ascending or descending sort** by clicking on **the button** that can be found on the right of each of the sort fields.

## Selecting summary options

A Summary Options button may be found near the bottom of the Report Wizard's sorting screen.

- When you click **on the button** it will display the **Summary Options dialog box** which offers more display options for numeric fields.
- Once you have completed this when you click on the **OK button** in the dialog box, it will return you to the sorting screen of the Report Wizard from which you can click on the Next button to move to the next screen.

## Selecting the layout

The Layout area enables you to determine the basic layout of the data. The Layout area provides three layout choices that tell Access whether to repeat the column headers, indent each grouping, and add lines or boxes between the detail lines.

- As you select **each option**, the picture on the left changes to show how the choice affects the report's appearance.
- You can choose between **Portrait and Landscape layout** for the report in the Orientation area. Finally, the Adjust **the Field Width**

**So All Fields Fit** on a Page check box enables you to compress a lot of data into a little area.

Once you have done the above, you can then click on the Next button in order to move to the next wizard screen.

## Opening the report design

A text box on the final Report Wizard screen allows you to give the report a title. This title appears only once, at the start of the report, rather than at the top of each page. The report title also serves as the new report's name. The default title is the name of the table or query you selected as the report's data source when you first created it.

**Once you have done that, select one of the option buttons at the bottom of the dialog box:**

- Preview **the report**
- Make **some changes** to the design of the report.

## Adjusting the report's layout

If you have a need for you to make changes to the layout of the report, you can choose to do this in the Layout view wherein you can choose to work with the controls in this view which is the same as working with the Layout view for a form.

## Choosing a theme

For Access 20022 forms and reports, a theme determines the color scheme, font face, font colors, and font sizes. In Access 2022, themes are a crucial notion. When you move your mouse over the theme icons in the gallery, the report in the Layout view underneath the gallery changes to show you how the report would look with the chosen theme. Each theme is identified by a name, such as Office, Facet, Organic, or Slice. When you wish to refer to a specific theme in the application's documentation, or in an e-mail or other contact, theme names can be useful.

## Creating new theme color schemes

Access 2022 comes with a number of pre-installed themes, each of which includes a set of complementary colors, fonts, and font attributes. Using a custom color theme to apply a company's corporate color scheme to forms and reports in an application is a wonderful method to do so.

**To create a new theme color scheme, have the report or form opened in the Design view then follow the steps below;**

- Choose the **Colors button** in the **Themes group on the Design tab of the Ribbon**.
- Choose the **Customize colors command** at the bottom of the list of color themes.
- Once you are done with the customization choose a name for the custom color theme then click on the **Save button.**

## Using the Print Preview window

**If you would like to open a report in the Print Preview,**

- Right-click **on the report** in the Navigation pane and click on **the Print Preview option**.

This view shows your report's fonts, shading, lines, boxes, and data as they will appear when printed to the default printer. The view can be toggled between a zoomed view and a complete page view by using the left mouse button on the report's surface.

Controls for altering the size, margins, page orientation (Portrait or Landscape), and other printing parameters may be found on the Print Preview tab of the Ribbon. The Print Preview tab also has a Print button for printing the report and a Close Print Preview button for returning to the previous view of the report (Design, Layout, or Report view).

## Publishing in alternate formats

An amazing feature of the Print Preview tab in Access 2022 is its ability to print the Access report in certain formats which include; PDF, XPS, HTML, and others.

- All you have to do is to click on **the PDF or XPS button** in the Data group on the Print Preview tab of the Ribbon which will then open the **Publish as PDF or XPS dialog box**. This dialog box offers various options for outputting in standard PDF format or in a condensed version.

## Viewing the report in Design view

### To view the report in Design view,

- Right-click on the **title bar** of the report then choose the **Design view option**.

## Printing or viewing the report

Printing is the final step when it has to do with creating a report.

## Printing the report

**There are various by which you can print your report one of which is;**

- Click on **File** then choose the **Print option** in the main Access window which will display various options for you to choose from.
- Click on the **Print button** on the **Print Preview tab of the Ribbon**.

## Viewing the report

A report can be seen in four different ways: design, report, layout, and print preview.

You can see the relative placements of the controls on the report's surface, as well as the margins, page headers and footers, and other report elements, in the Layout view.

The biggest limitation of the Layout view is that you can't fine-tune the design of a report until you go to the Design view. The layout view is designed for adjusting the relative placements of controls on the report; it is not intended for moving individual controls around the report.

## Saving the Report

### You can save the report design by;

- Choosing the **file option** then clicking **on save** then clicking on the **save as option**. The first time you will click on the **save as option**, you will be prompted to insert a name.

# Banded Report Design Concepts

In Access development, the banded report design is a crucial notion. Data is processed one record at a time in an Access report. Individual fields can be placed in various locations on a report, and they can even appear more than once if necessary.

The design view is aimed to let you determine how each row is set out on the printed page because Access processes report data one record at a time. The design view also displays features like a page's header and footer, as well as sections inhabited by group headers and footers. Each control region has an impact on the report's appearance when printed.

## The Report Header section

A Report Header section is frequently used as a cover page, a cover letter, or for information that needs to be delivered just once to the report's user.

- Set the **Force New Page** to attribute in the Report Header section to the After Section to use the Report Header section as a title page. The controls in the Report Header section will be printed on their own page as a result of this.

## The Page Header section

Most often controls in the Page Header area printed at the top of each page. If the first page's report header isn't on its own page, the information in the Page Header section prints right below the report header information.

In group/total reports, page headers usually incorporate column heads. A title for the report that appears on every page is frequently included in page headers.

## The Group Header section

The name of the group is usually displayed in the Group Header section. When the name of a group changes, Access recognizes that all of the records in the group have been displayed in a Detail section. It's worth noting that group headers and footers can have many levels.

## The Detail section

Each value is printed in the Detail section, which processes every record in the data. Calculated fields, such as profit, are usually found in the Detail section and are the outcome of a mathematical equation.

## The Group Footer section

To calculate summaries for all the detail entries in a group, go to the Group Footer section. You can change the way summaries are calculated in the Report Design window by changing the Running Sum property of the text box.

The default setting for a Running Sum is No, which just displays the value of the current record. The amounts for that control will be accumulated for every record in the group if the value of Over Group is used. Over All collects the values for that control across all records in the report.

## The Page Footer section

Page numbers or control totals are normally seen in the Page Footer section. The date and time the report was printed can also be provided. The page number text box can be found in the Page Footer section.

## The Report Footer section

After all of the detail records and group footer sections have been printed, the Report Footer section is printed once at the end of the report. Grand totals or other data (such as averages or percentages) for the whole report are often displayed in report footers.

# Creating a Report from Scratch

This section throws more light on the creation of tables from scratch, most of the time, you'll build a report using the Report Wizard or one of the other shortcuts, which you may then customize to fit your needs.

## Creating a new report and binding it to a table

### Follow the steps below to create a new report;
- Choose the **Create tab** option of the Ribbon.
- Select **the Blank Report** button in the Reports group.

- Right-click **on the title bar** of the report and choose **the Design View** from the shortcut menu.

## Defining the report page size and Layout

Consider the page layout qualities, as well as the type of paper and printer you wish to utilize for the output, as you plan your report. Several dialog boxes and settings are used to make adjustments as you make these options. These requirements work together to get the intended result.

The Page Setup page contains choices for changing the report's paper size, orientation (Portrait or Landscape), margins, and other features. When you select Size or Margins from the drop-down menu, a gallery of popular settings for each of these parameters appears.

**If the margins you require for your report aren't listed in the Margins options,**

- Open the **Page Setup dialog box** by clicking **Page Setup** in the **Page Layout group**. The margins, orientation, and other page layout criteria can all be specified in this dialog box.

## Placing controls on the report

**Placing control on a report is quite easy. Follow the steps below;**

- Select the **Add Existing Fields button** in the **Tools group** on the **Design tab of the Ribbon.**

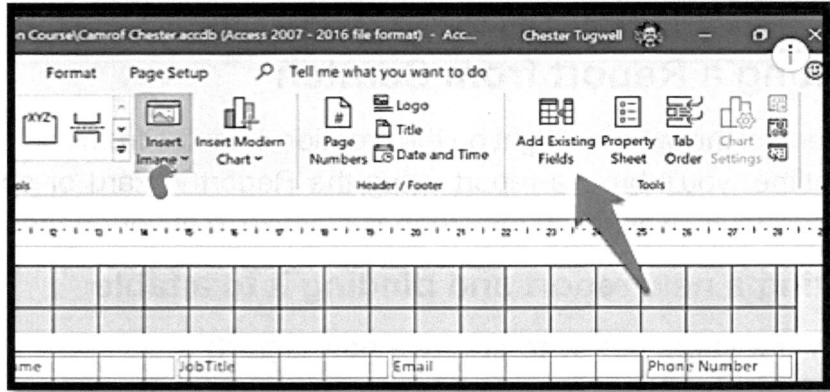

- Select **control** in the **Controls group on the Design tab** if there is a need for you to use something other than the default control types for the fields.

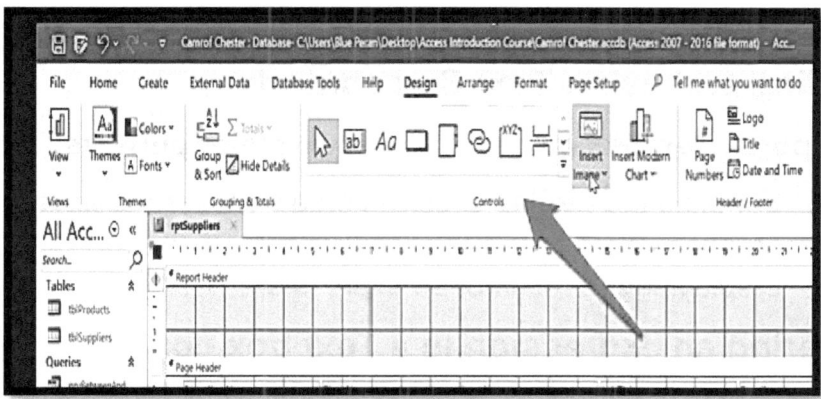

- Choose each of the **fields** that you would like to have on your report and then move them to the **appropriate part of the Report Design window**.

For information to be displayed in the page header section, controls are required. But first, you'll need to alter the page header to make a place for them.

## Resizing a section

There is a need for you to resize a section if you have to make room for the title information in the page header. You resize simply by dragging the bottom of the piece you wish to resize with your mouse. When the mouse pointer is over the bottom of a report section, it transforms into a vertical double-headed arrow. To make the portion smaller or larger, drag the section border up or down.

## Modifying the appearance of a text in a control

To change the appearance of the text in a control, select it and then click the relevant option on the Format tab to apply a formatting style to the label.

# Working with Text BOX controls

Unbound text boxes are another sort of Text Box control that is commonly used in reports to hold phrases such as page numbers, dates, or a computation.

## Adding and using Text Box controls

**In reports, TextBox controls serve two major purposes, which are;**

- Enabling the display of stored data from a specific field in a query or table.
- Displaying the result of an expression.

## Entering an expression in a Text box control

You can use expressions to produce values that aren't existing in a database or query. They might be as simple as a page number to as complicated as complex mathematical computations.

## Sizing a Text Box control or Label control

By clicking on a control, you can select it. The mouse cursor becomes a double-headed arrow when it is moved over one of the side handles. When the pointer changes, click and drag the control to the desired size.

When you double-click one of the sizing handles, Access resizes the control to fit the text in it. If you increase the font size and subsequently realize that the text no longer matches the control, this option comes in useful.

## Deleting and cutting attached labels from Text Box controls

**In a report, you may easily delete one or more associated controls.**

- Simply **choose the controls** you want to delete and press Delete.

If you wish to move the label to the Page Header area (rather than just deleting it), you can cut it instead of deleting it.

## Pasting labels into a report section

Cutting labels from controls and pasting them into the page header is just as easy as deleting labels and also creating new ones in the page header. You can choose to make use of the shortcut buttons; cut (ctrl + x ) and paste (ctrl + v).

## Moving Label and Textbox controls

An associated label is automatically generated when a Text Box control is combined with a compound control. When one of the controls in a compound control set is moved, the other control moves with it. This means that if you move the label or the text box, the linked control will move as well.

Select one of the pairs of controls with the mouse to move both controls in a compound control. The mouse cursor transforms into a hand when you move it over any of the objects. Drag the controls to their new location by clicking and dragging them. A compound control outline moves with your pointer as you drag.

## Modifying the appearance of multiple controls

**The instructions below will show you how to change the appearance of text in numerous Label controls:**

- By selecting **each Label control** at the bottom of the Page Header section one at a time while holding down the Shift key, you can select all of them.
- On the Format tab, select the **Bold option**.

## Changing Label and Textbox control properties

To change the properties of a Text Box or Label control, open the Property Sheet for that control. The Property Sheet allows you to view and update the properties of a control. The property settings of control can also be changed by using tools on the Format tab of the Ribbon, such as font dropdowns and text formatting buttons.

## Growing and shrinking Text Box controls

Access provides the option for allowing control to grow or shrink vertically based on the exact contents of a record when you print or print preview controls with varying text lengths. They Can Grow and Can Shrink attributes dictate whether or not a Text Box control's vertical dimension is resized to accommodate the quantity of text in its bound field. These characteristics can be used for any text control, but they're particularly useful for Text Box controls.

# Sorting and grouping data

By combining the data in interesting ways, you may often make the data on the report more valuable to users.

## Creating a group header or footer

When you group on a field in the report's data, you get two new sections: Group Header and Group Footer.

**Follow the steps below to create a group header or footer.**

- Choose **the Group & Sort button** in the Grouping Totals group on the Design tab of the Ribbon.
- Select the **Add a Group button in the Group, Sort, and Total area**.
- Choose the **Category option** from the Field List.

## Sorting data within groups

Sorting allows you to choose the order in which records appear on the report based on the values of one or more controls. When you wish to view the data in your tables in a different order than your input, this order is crucial.

Although you can sort data in a table by primary key or in a query by any field, there are several advantages to doing so in the report, one of which is that the report will remain in the right order if the query or table is changed.

## Removing a group

**If you would like to remove a group,**

- Simply **display the Group, Sort, and Total area**, select the **group or sort** specifier to delete, and then click on the **Delete key**. Any controls in the group header or footer will be removed.

# Hiding a section

Microsoft Access also provides ways by which we can hide a section. **Follow the steps below to have a section hidden;**

- Select **the section** you would like to hide.
- Show **the Property Sheet of the section**.
- Choose the **Visible property option** and then click on the **No button** from the drop-down list in the text box property.

# Sizing a section

Upon the creation of the group header, there might be a need for you to put some controls in the section, move some controls around, or even move controls between sections. Before you start manipulating controls within a section, you should make sure the section is the proper height.

To make changes to the height of a section, drag the top border of the section below it. You can make a section larger or smaller by dragging the bottom border of the section.

# Moving controls between sections

You can move one or more controls across sections by dragging them from one section to another with your mouse or by cutting and pasting them from one section to another.

# Adding page breaks

You can use Access to add page breaks depending on groups. Except for the Page Header and Page Footer sections, you can also insert breaks within parts.

You might want to add a page break now and then, and not just because of a grouping. The Page Break control in the Controls group of the Ribbon is the solution.

# Improving the Report's Appearance

You usually add a few graphic components like lines and rectangles, as well as potentially some special effects like shadows or sunken sections, to make a report more visually appealing. You want to make sure that each part has different portions that are separated by lines or colors.

Make sure the controls aren't in contact with one another. Ensure that the text is aligned with the text above and below it, as well as both to the right and left.

## Adjusting the page header

The page header features multiple enormous labels that are spaced far apart. The column headers are small and appear to float. They could be enlarged by one font size. A horizontal line should separate the full page header from the Detail section.

**To add this line simply follow the steps below;**

- Choose **the Line tool** in the Controls group of the Ribbon.
- Move **the line** below the page header.
- Click **on the line and change the Border Width property** to 2 pt on the line of the Property Sheet.

## Creating an expression in the group header

**To create an expression in the group header simply follow the settings below;**

- Choose **the Category control** in the Category Group Header section and show the Property Sheet for the control.
- Make changes to the **Control Source property to =" Category: " & [Category].**
- Then finally, change the **Name property to textCategory**.

## Creating a report header

Features like the report's title, a logo, and the print date and time should all be included in the report header. The inclusion of this information in the report header allows any user of the report to quickly learn what's in it and when it was printed.

The Ribbon contains a Design tab when the report is in the Design view. A number of controls on the Design tab's Header/Footer group allow you to add crucial features to the report's header and footer. Explore the Design tab and play around with the controls to check out what will best fit your report header.

# CHAPTER 21
# ADVANCED ACCESS REPORT TECHNIQUES

The last chapter, you created some very useful reports by following the basic steps highlighted. This chapter will enlighten you more on reports that you cannot build with just the use of the default Access reports only, you will also learn some tips on how to avoid blank reports.

## Grouping and Sorting Data

Having a data group well-sorted is very important as it will make your data look well organized. Grouping data that is quite similar can make the specific data you might be looking for easier to find and will also reduce the amount of data presented.

## Grouping alphabetically

The main essence of having a report group in alphabetical order is to ensure that the data is well arranged and orderly. For example, if you are to present the data of sales of a product by different customers, such data might be very clumsy and difficult to understand if it is not grouped but when you group such data, you will be able to understand the data and also pick out the information you need with ease. You can also choose to group the data in a table.

**To add a text box containing an alphabetic character, go through these steps;**

- Right-click on **the title bar** of the report and then click on **the Design view**.
- Choose **Group &Sort** from the **Design tab of the Ribbon.**
- Add a **group name** for the desired field.
- Click **on the More option** and make sure that the With a Header Section option has been selected. Once this is done, it will add a band for a group based on the field you have chosen.
- Choose the **By First Character option** rather than choosing the **By Entire Value option**.

- Expand the **group header** of the field you have chosen and include an unbound text box to the group header of your desired field.
- Configure **the Control Source property text box** to your preferred expression.
- Delete **the label** and ensure you set the other properties of the text box like font and font size properly.
- While grouping make sure that the names in the field are well sorted.
- Finally, **include a sort for the records** in the field you have chosen.

## Grouping on date intervals

There is so many reports that might have to be grouped according to dates. There is a feature in the Access report engine which can help Group and sort data according to dates.

**To make use of this report simply;**

- Open the **Group, Sort, and Total pane** again and then build **a group for the OrderDate field**.
- Choose **the with a Header Section** option from the header drop-down.
- Once the option above has been completed, you can then choose **any of the options** such as Year, Quarter, Month, Week, and so on. Note that there is still a need to sort the whole value of the OrderDate to make sure that they are in sequential order within the week option.

## Hiding repeating information

When information that appears to be repeated is reduced to the barest minimum it appears to help to make the tabular report quite more efficient.

**To hide reports that appear to be repeating simply:**

- Open the **report in the Design view**.
- Locate **the Detail section** and then choose **the field** that has the information that might be repeating.

- Open the **Property Sheet** for the name of the field.
- Change the **Hide Duplicates property to Yes**. Note that this step is quite important as the default is No.
- Change to **Print Preview mode** and view the new report layout.

Note that the Hide Duplicates property option is always applied to only records that are displayed in a consecutive manner on the report. Once Access places a particular name on a particular report, such a name will not be repeated again all through the entire report.

## Hiding a page header

You don't necessarily have to always show the page header in your reports.

**If you would like to hide the header after the first page;**

- Include **an unbound Text Box control** to the report with its Control Source property set to the expression = HideHeader ().
- **Delete the label of the text bo**x. The HideHeader () will then return a null string which will make the text box invisible.

## Starting a new page number for each group

Most of the time, reports usually have a number of pages for each group of data. For each group to have its own numbering, there might be a reason for you to reset each of the page numberings to 1 so that each of the groups will print on its own. This can be done with the use of the Report Page Property. This simply means that you can choose to configure the page at any time as the report is being printed. You can also choose to make use of the group header format even to reset the page property of the report to 1.

# Formatting Data

Reports can be made to be quite more useful when you format them so as to add certain information to them. If you would like to make your report look distinct, you can choose to number the bullet points and also make use of lines or spaces to separate certain parts of the report. Furthermore, it is quite good to have the data in your report presented in a lovely and accurate manner and the manner in which the elements are positioned can be a determining factor as to if your report will be well presented or not.

## Creating numbered lists

By default, the items that are listed in the Access report are usually not numbered. The settings in the Group, Sort, and Total pane determine the manner in which the items are listed. The use of number count makes a listing of items in the report more unique and it can also aid in easy identification of items in the list.

With the use of the Access Running sum feature, you can have a number assigned to all the items that are in the list on an Access report. Even though much of all of this work can be done with the use of the VBA which can help to programmatically sum the values which are returned by the query or a SQL statement in the report's Record Source property, it is always best to allow the Access query engine do all of the aggregate functions. Note that there is always an automatic optimization of the Access queries when the queries are saved.

## Creating bulleted lists

Bullet characters can be added to a list instead of adding numbers if you would prefer that option. Rather than making use of a different field for containing the bullet, you just concatenate the bullet character control to the control's Record Source property which is said to be a much more easy solution. The bullet is usually added by making use of exploiting Windows features.

Note that anytime you are using proportionally spaced fonts like Arial it can sometimes be different to get the actual alignment between report elements. When the data in a text box is concatenated, t helps to remove any problems that might be associated with spacing characters. Although, if the amount of text that s in the text box goes beyond just one row, the rows that follow subsequently will not be indented.

The only constraint you might encounter on the characters used in an Access report is that the font used in the text boxes on the report must have indicated characters.

## Adding emphasis on the run time

You can choose to either hide or show control for a specific record by configuring the setting to Visible property. This can be very useful if only you have a need to show a field in some conditions and hide it in other conditions. Design time is best to hide a control when you configure the Visible property to either False or No. The Visible property can be configured to True only when you have a need to make use of the information that is contained in the control.

## Avoiding empty reports

If Microsoft fails to look for valid records to enter into the Detail section of a particular report, all that will be displayed is a blank detail section when the report has been printed. This seems much like a problem but it can be avoided when you add code to the report's NoData event that shows a message and then cancels the print event if it does not locate any record.

The NoData event is usually triggered when Microsoft Access attempts to create a report and can find data in the report's underlying record set. Since the NOData event is attached to the report itself, there is no need for you to look for it in any of the sections of the report. All you have to do is to add this code as the NoData of the report event procedure with this, your users will never wonder why they are looking at a blank report.

## Inserting vertical lines between columns

With the height of a report section being fixed, you can easily include a vertical line. The inclusion of a vertical line that can grow in height is more difficult.

Though most of the controls are usually added at the time of design, there are times when you have to draw control as the report is being prepared for printing. The best way to go about this is to make use of the line method in the report to include vertical lines at run time. Line methods usually need four different arguments which are X1, X2, Y1, and Y2 which help to indicate the top and the bottom of the coordinates of the line. Note that you can also make use of the same procedure in drawing the horizontal lines. Note that when you make use of the Line control any time the height is fixed helps to draw the lines for each of the sections faster.

## Adding a blank line

When records are fused together without adequate spacing, it can make records extremely difficult to read and comprehend; it can also make it very easy to have records lost. Just as when you are writing in Microsoft Word which you can add blank spaces to make the words you are typing much easier to read, it will also be quite easier when a blank line is added to data in a report.

Though Access does not offer a way to insert a blank row in the middle of a detail section, you can however with the aid of some programming and some hidden controls add a blank row.

## Even-odd page printing

There is quite a difference when a report is printed on an even or an odd page. When the report is on the odd-numbered page, the page ought to be displayed on the right edge of the page while on the even-numbered side, the page number will be displayed on the left side of the page.

How can you then follow this format? You can make use of the page footer's Format in the Page Footer section event to decide if the current page is either even or odd and then have the text aligned to the left or the right side of the text box accordingly. With the Format event, you will rest assured you can always decide where the text will be aligned regardless of where the Text Align is configured to whether it is Right or Left as at the time of design.

## Using different formats in the same text box

There might be a need to make use of different formats in certain fields on the report. Unfortunately, a control in a Detail section of a report can have just one specified format in its Property Sheet. There is however a trick that can be used to set the format property at run time. This trick has to do with the use of the flex format function which is usually stored in the MFunctions module and also used in the rptFlexFormat, using the 1 Decimals argument to return a string that indicates the specified format.

The string format will also return the text that has 1 Decimal number of characters and also all the characters will be zero.

## Centering the title

It can be quite difficult to center the title of a report in the middle of a page. The best way to ensure that the title is centered is to stretch the tile from the left margin to the right margin and once you are done simply click on the Center button in the Text Formatting group of the Home tab.

## Aligning control labels

It can sometimes be very difficult to keep text boxes and their labels properly aligned on reports. Due to the fact that a text box and its label can be moved differently, there is a need to always adjust the position of the label in order to bring it to alignment with the text box.

Text box labels can be removed totally when you add the label text as a part of the record source of the text box. Note that once this has been done, any time you have a need to move the text box, the label, and the bound record source will move together as a single unit. The only issue with this technique is that you must always make use of the same format for the text box and its label.

## Micro-adjusting controls

The easiest way to make adjustments to the size or position of controls on a report in quite little increments is to hold down either the **Shift or the Ctrl key** and then click **on the arrow keys** according to how you want to make the adjustments.

# Adding Data

In this section, you will learn how to increase the confidence users have in a report by adding some touches to the report such that it will help the user know when the report was printed.

## Adding more information to a report

Page and pages are both report properties that are made available at run time and can be added to the report. To do this you should also take into consideration the value of adding some other report properties to the report. Most of the report properties can be included in unbound text boxes so long as the property is in square brackets.

## Adding the user's name to a bound report

When there is an unbound text box that has its control Source configured to an unresolved reference, it can lead to Access requesting certain information to complete the text box. Access shows a parameter dialog box for each parameter in a parameter query. The text which is entered into the text box will then be displayed on the report.

You can also choose reference with the use of other controls on the report, the unbound text box on the report. The Enter Parameter Value dialog box will then be displayed before the report is ready for printing, which also means that the data you insert into the dialog box can be used in calculations or the VBA code that is at the back of the report.

# Adding Even More Flexibility

This section talks more about features and some more techniques that can make your report much more flexible for users.

## Displaying all reports in a combo box

The MSysObjects system table has all of the names of all the top-level database objects saved in it. You can always run a query against MSysObjects just the same way you run queries against any other table in the database. To perform this operation,

- Choose **Table/Query as the Row Source** Type for the list box and put the SQL statement in the RowSource of your list box to fill up the box with a list of all reports that are in the database.

Note that reports do not have to be opened before you can make use of this technique. MSysObjects knows all the objects in the database, hence no reports will run away from being noticed when using this technique.

If you happen to be making use of a naming convention for the objects in your database, make use of a prefix to display only the reports that are needed. Since MSysObjects saves the names of all the database objects, you can simply take back the names of the other top-level database objects also.

**View the MSysObject table by;**

- Choosing **the Show System Objects** check box in the Navigation Options dialog box and you can get there by right-clicking on **the Navigation panes title bar** and then choosing the **Navigation Options** from the shortcut menu.

You don't have to make MSysObjects visible for this trick to work.

## Fast printing from queried data

Reports and forms do not use the same recordset hence it can take a very long time to print a report that is based on a query when a user finds the correct record on a form, it will have to run the query over again before it will be able to print the record on the query.

To solve this problem, you can design a table that has all of the fields that will be printed on the report. This way, when the user locates the correct record on the form, copies the record from the form to the table, and then opens the report. You only have to run the query once to have the result populated. Since the report is now based on a table, it will open very fast and is then ready to be printed immediately after the report is open.

## Using snaking columns in a report

Snaking columns is a very popular feature in Microsoft Access that is basically used by advanced users. Snaking columns in Microsoft Access can be found in Access reports and also helps in the consumption of all of the spaces left on the page hence leading to much fewer prints and a faster process. There is often a need to have some text printed which can be accommodated with ease in less than half or just basically half the page. When you are faced with such a situation, you can choose to make use of the snaking columns and then make full use of the space on your page.

When you are making use of snaking columns to print text, you will obtain documents in the form of data stored in phone books or in dictionaries. This will not just save paper, it can be done faster also it is also more comprehensive and pleasing aesthetically.

If you are making use of a query that provides you with a lot of information, you can also make use of snaking in order to be able to comprehend all of such information. If you would like to print a very lengthy report, ensure you java it previewed in various layouts hence you will be able to see the very one that best suits you along with snaking columns. With this, you will have the perfect idea about the layout that best suits your report and you will also have an insight into how pleasing your report can look when it is created with the use of snaking columns.

## Exploiting two-pass report processing

The main benefit of making use of a two-pass report is that your reports can have expressions that basically rely on information available anywhere in the report. Another benefit of making use of the two-pass report is that you will be free to make use of the aggregate functions based on the reports of the underlying record source. Information that cannot be known yet can be in Group headers and footers till all the record sources is being processed.

## Assigning unique names to controls

If you make use of the Report Wizard or drag fields from the Field List when designing your reports, Access will assign the new text box the same names as the fields in the recordset underlying report.

There is a need for you to make changes to the Name property of the control to something like txtDiscount so that Access can state the difference between the name of the control and the underlying field.

# PART VI
# MICROSOFT ACCESS PROGRAMMING FUNDAMENTALS

# CHAPTER 22
# USING ACCESS MACROS

A macro can be described as an automated input sequence that imitates keystrokes or mouse actions. A macro is typically used to change a repetitive series of keyboard and mouse actions and is used in spreadsheets and also some database applications.

As Access evolved as a development tool, the Visual Basic for Applications (VBA) programming language became the standard automating Access database applications. The macros in previous versions of Access lacked variables and error handling which has made a lot of developers leave macros. Today, this feature has been embedded in macros which is a much more viable alternative to VBA than in previous versions.

## An Introduction to Macros

A macro is defined as a tool that enables you to have tasks automated in Access. With the use of Access macros, you can perform certain defined actions and then include functionality in your forms and reports.

Designing macros have to do with choosing some actions from the drop-down list and then filling the arguments of the action. With macros, you can choose actions without writing one line of VBA code. The macro actions are a part of the commands VBA provides. Oftentimes, people find it quite easier to build a macro than to write VBA code. Assuming you want to build the main form with buttons that can open the other forms in your application. You can choose to add a button to the form, build a macro that will open another form in your application then add this macro to the button's Click event.

### Creating a macro

**If you want to build a new macro simply;**

- Click **on the Macro button** on the Macros & Code group on the Create tab of the Ribbon.

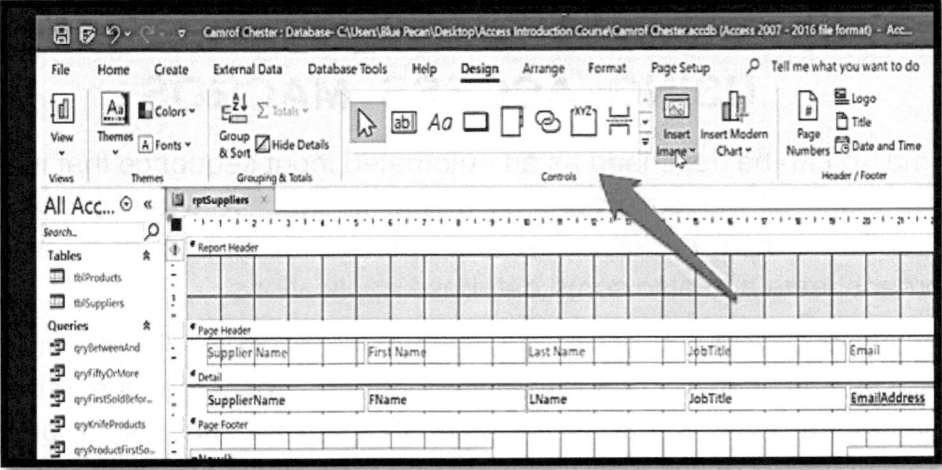

- Click on the **Macro button** which will in turn open the macro builder which contains a drop-down list of more macro options.

To the right side of the Macro Builder is an Action Catalog which contains different macro options and information about the action that should be used for a particular task.

- Click on **MessageBox** from the drop-down list in the macro builder. The macro builder will then change to show an area where you include the arguments like the message, beep, type, and title which are associated with the messagebox action.

To run the macro, click on the Run button in the Tools group of the Design tab of the Ribbon. When you create a new macro, you will be prompted to save the macro and this must be done before Access will execute it.

**Note that macros can also be executed from the Navigation pane.**

- Close the **macro builder** and then show the display group on the Navigation pane.
- You can then click **twice** on the mcrHelloWorld macro to execute it.

When the Hello World! Macron has been displayed and you are satisfied with the view.

- click on **the close button** in the upper-right corner of the macro builder to go back to the main Access window.

## Assigning a macro to an event

Macros are strictly used for the automation of applications without having to write a VBA code. For it to be quite easy to use an application, it is best for your macros to the event of an object.

The button click event is the most common event you can choose to assign a macro to.

**Go through the steps below in order to build a button that runs the mcrHelloWorld;**

- Choose the **Create tab** on the Ribbon and then click on the Form Design button in the forms group.
- On the Form Design Tools Design tab of the Ribbon, deselect the **Use Control Wizard's** option in the controls group.
- Choose the **Button control** and draw a button on the form.
- Configure **the name** of the button property to cmdHelloWorld.
- Configure **the caption property** of the button to Hello World!
- Choose the **drop-down list** in the click event of the button's property and choose mcrHellowWorld from the list.

## Understanding Macro Security

Not all macros are harmless. There is almost nothing you can do in a macro that cannot be done in the Access user interface. Certain things like executing a delete query can give rise to an unexpected data loss. Access has got you covered as it has a built-in security environment with which you can prevent unwanted and harmful macros from being executed.

Access makes use of the Trust Center to determine commands that are safe when objects such as forms, macros, and queries are being executed. The Trust Center assumes macros and VBA code as "macros' and hence it does not recommend that they should be trusted by default. If commands that are not safe are allowed to be executed they can possibly be a threat to the computer, change the configuration of the computer, or can totally damage the workstation all through the network environment.

## Enabling sandbox mode

Sandmode box can be described as a security feature that prevents Access from running some expressions that can be termed as unsafe, These so-called unsafe expressions are usually blocked not regarding if the database has been trusted.

The registry key is used to indicate if Access should be executed in the sandbox mode or not. By default, the sandbox mode is enabled, and the registry key is misconfigured to enable sandbox mode when Access is installed on a computer. If there is a need for you to allow all expressions to be executed, you can choose to alter the registry key value to disable sandbox mode.

**To enable the sandbox mode simply follow the steps below;**

- Open Access, click on the **File button** and then choose **Options**.
- Click on the **Trust Center tab**, and then click on the **Trust Center Settings.**
- Choose the **Macro Settings tab.**
- Select either **Disable All Macros without Notification** or **Disable All Macros** with Notification.

A digital signature is a security file that is encrypted and accompanies a macro or document. It confirms that the author is a trusted source for the macro or document. Digital signatures are basically implemented in large organizations that are willing to fund the expense of purchasing and maintaining digital signatures. Make sure you do not sign your Access project until the application has been well tested and you are not expecting any changes to it. Modifying any of the code in the project will invalidate the digital signature.

## The Trust Center

The Trust Center is where you can get security and privacy settings for Access.

**If you would like to show the Trust Center;**

- Click on the **File button** then click on **Options** in order to open the Access Options dialog box.

- Choose the **Trust Center tab** and then click on the **Trust Center Settings**.

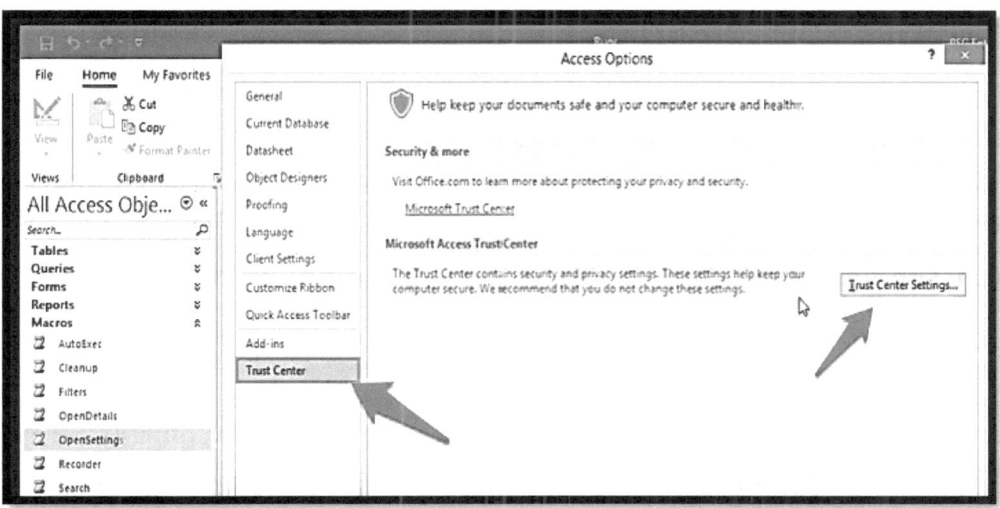

**Below is a description of each section in the Trust Center Settings and what it controls;**

- **Trusted Publishers**: it shows a list of trusted publishers. If you would like to remove a publisher from this list, choose the publisher and then click on the **Remove option**. Trusted publishers must have a valid digital signature that has not expired.
- **Trusted Locations**: this shows the list of trusted locations on the computer network. From this part, you can choose to add, remove or make changes to folders on your computer that will always have a trusted file. A trusted file can be opened in a trusted location without necessarily being checked by the Trust Center.
- **Add-ins**: this allows you to set up the manner in which Access deals with add-ins. You can decide that add-ins should be signed digitally from a trusted source and also decide if you should show a notification for add-ins that are not digitally signed yet.
- **ActiveX Settings**: this allows you to control the level of security for Active X controls.
- **Macro Settings**: this gives you the option of setting the security for macros that are not in a trusted location.

Other sections include; the message bar, privacy options, and trusted add-in catalogs.

## Multi-action Macros

The true demonstration of macros is when it is able to take up various actions when the click of just a single button. Creating a macro that runs more than one query is better than clicking twice on each action query in the Navigation pane.

**If all the action is not being displayed in the Action drop-down list,**

- Choose the **Show All Actions command** in the Show/Hide group on the Macro Tools Design tab of the Ribbon.

Some macro actions need a well-trusted database or an enabling macros environment through certain security settings. Furthermore, some macro actions are known to be unsafe since they alter data in the database or perform actions that might lead to causing harm to the application. There is a warning icon always indicated for macro actions that are considered to be unsafe in the macro designer. By default, Access will only show trusted macro actions that execute not regarding the security settings.

## Submacros

A sub-macro statement in Access defines a different macro in the Macro Designer window. You can choose to run the actions stated in sub macros from a different macro with the use of the RunMacro action.

**In the Macro Name argument of the RunMacro action, you can make use of the syntax below to execute the sub macro;**

<macro name>.<submacro name>

A sub macro statement can also be used in the definition of an error handling set of actions within a macro.

**To implement a macro with the use of sub macros;**

- Create a **form** with three buttons then configure the **On Click event properties** of these buttons.

With the Sub Macros, you can reduce the number of macros that are being displayed in the Navigation pane and manage more macros with more ease.

## Conditions

With sub macro, you can add various single macro objects into just one group but then a condition indicates certain criteria that must be met before the macro will perform the action. Note that the IF macro action takes a Boolean expression also if the expression evaluates to False, No, or 0, the action will not execute. If the expression evaluates to some other value, the action will be performed.

### Opening reports using conditions

To show conditions and the IF macro condition, using the example of a Report Menu which has three buttons and a frame control with two different button options which are Print and Print Preview.

- When you click on the **Print option**, it will set the value of the frame to 1 and when you click on the **Print Preview option** it will set the frame value to 2. The macro that will be opening the report will make use of the sub macro as well as the If macro action.

### Multiple actions in conditions

If there is a need for you to execute various conditions based on a particular condition, add multiple actions within the If and End If actions. The If macro will then allow you to execute certain actions based on the values that are in your applications. Make use of the If macro action to reference controls on forms or reports and some other objects and then decide on the actions that should be executed.

## Temporary Variables

In the previous versions of Access before this, you could only make use of variables in VBA codes. With the creation of Access 2007, about three new macro actions were designed which were; RemoveTempVar, SetTempVar, and RemoveAllTempVars which allow the creation and use of the temporary variables that are in your macros. These variables can be used in conditional expressions in order to control the actions that should be executed or to pass data to and from forms or reports. You can also choose to gain access to VBA in order to communicate data to and from modules.

## Enhancing a macro you've already created

When you have a need to enhance a macro that has already been created, you can make use of any of the above-discussed macro actions to get a value from the user and then show it in the message box. The SetTempVar action has two arguments which are Name and Expression. The name is just the name of the temporary variable and the expression is what the value of the variable should be. Other actions have their own specifications and can be used just in accordance with how you would want to have the macro enhanced.

Note that temporary variables are global, once you create them you can make use of them in just any VBA procedures, queries, macros, or object properties.

## Using temporary variables to simplify macros

With the use of temporary variables, you can make the use of macros quite easier by eliminating certain steps like the need to create a structure of multiple OpenForm or OpenReport actions. You can also choose to make use of more than one variable in a macro.

## Using temporary variables in VBA

You can begin with the use of macros to get your application automated but with time, you can start making use of the VBA code to automate and also add some functionalities to other areas. If you have some temporary variables that you have already implemented with macros you don't have to leave them you can also make use of them directly in your VBA code.

Note that any VBA created is also always available for use in macros and vice versa. Variables which you also remove in VBA are no longer available for use in your macros and vice versa. When you make use of temporary variables, your macros and VBA code will no longer be independent of each other.

# Error Handling and Macro Debugging

The fact that there is no error handling in macros is one major reason most developers make use of VBA rather than macros in order to have their applications automated. Anytime there is an error in macros, it can lead to the macro seizing operation and being inactive for long hours till the error is fixed. When you have error handling added to your macros it will enable you to choose what you would like to do anytime an error occurs while a macro is still running.

## The OnError action

With the ONError action you can make your decision on what you would like to do when you encounter an error in your macro. Basically, there are two arguments in this action which are the Go to argument and the Macro Name argument.

**One of the simplest ways to have error handling to a macro is to**

- Make the OnError the first action and then configure the **Go to the argument** as the Next. Once this has been done, your macro will keep running non-stop but you will not know the actions that are running and the ones that are not.

## The MacroError object

The macro error object has information about the last error that occurred. It also keeps this information until another error occurs or the last one has been cleared with the use of the ClearMacroError action. This object has some read-only properties like ActionName, Arguments, Condition, Description, MacroName, and Number.

You can make use of the MarcoError object as a debugging tool or to show messages to the user who in turn can pass the information to you. Make use of the Object that is within an If action to customize the actions that are running based on the error that occurred. When the object is also used in combination with the OnError action, it will give you more functionality with the handling of errors, showing useful messages, and also offering information to both you and the user.

## Debugging macros

With the use of the OnError action and also the MacroError object, debugging Access macros can be a lot easier.

## Embedded Macros

An Embedded macro is put away in an event property and is the portion of the object to which it has a place. Once you adjust an embedded large-scale object, you do not need to stress any other controls that might utilize the large scale since each inserted large scale is free. Inserted macros aren't obvious within the navigation pane and are as they were available only from the object's Property Sheet.

Embedded macros are well trusted. They will always run even if your security settings do not allow the code to run. With the use of embedded macros, you can always share your application as a trusted application since embedded macros are always prevented automatically from performing operations that are not safe.

# Macros versus VBA Statements

In Access, macros regularly offer a perfect way to require care of numerous subtle elements, such as running reports and forms. You'll be able to create applications and allot activities quicker employing a macro since the arguments for the macro activities are displayed with the macro. You do not have to keep in mind complex or troublesome language structures.

There are lots of actions you can achieve with the use of VBA statements that are better suited for macros.

**The actions below tend to be more efficient when they run from macros;**

- Using macros against the whole record with action queries.
- Running reports
- Opening and closing of forms.

## Choosing between macros and VBA

Although oftentimes macros have proven to be the solution, VBA is the tool to beat at other times.

**You will most often want to make use of VBA other than macros when you want to:**

- Create and make use of your own functions.
- Make use of automation in communication with other window applications or to run system-level actions.
- Make use of existing functions in external Windows Dynamic Link Libraries.
- Work with records one after the other.

## Converting existing macros to VBA

After you've gotten comfortable with composing VBA code, you'll need to rework a few of your application macros as VBA methods. As you start this process, you rapidly realize how rationally challenging the exertion can be as you survey each macro in your different macro libraries. You can't just cut the macro from the macro builder and add it into a module window. For each condition, activity, and activity contention for a macro, you must analyze the task it finishes and after that compose the identical articulations of VBA code in your method.

Fortunately, there is a tool in Access that can change macros to VBA code automatically. Locate the Tools group of the Design tab of the Ribbon and you will find a Convert Macros to Visual Basic button. With this option, you can change a macro to a module in just a few seconds.

# CHAPTER 23
# USING ACCESS DATA MACROS

For a very long time, macros have always been said to be inferior to VBA in terms of handling the logic of an application. Access macros have encountered some basic problems like; difficulty in keeping track of the effect of macro on a particular form, difficulty in trapping or handling errors in macros, and inability to work with code. This chapter discusses Access data macros in full which is why Microsft Acess 2022 is now the most preferred version.

## Introducing Data Macros

Data macros are overseen from the Table tab while seeing a table in Datasheet view and don't appear under Macros within the Navigation Pane. Among other things, you'll be able to utilize Data macros to approve and guarantee the exactness of information in a table. There are two fundamental sorts of Data macros those that are activated by table events (moreover called "event-driven" Data macros), and those that run in reaction to being called by title (too known as "named" Data macros).

## Understanding Table Events

There are about five various macro programmable table events which are BeforeChange, BeforeDelete, AfterInsert, AfterUpdate, and AfterDelete. In this section, these events will be briefly described.

### "Before events

The before events(BeforeChange and BeforeDelete) is quite easy and straightforward and also offer support for just a few macro actions.

The BeforeChange event is comparative to the BeforeUpdate event connected to forms, reports, and controls. As its name infers, BeforeChange fires just before the information in a table is changed by the client, an inquiry, or VBA code. Furthermore, with BeforeChange, you have the opportunity to take a look at new values in the record currently in use and then make some alterations if need be.

The BeforeChange event can't hinder the client with a message box or halt the record from upgrading within the fundamental table. All BeforeChange can do is set a field's value or set a local macro variable's value before the record is added or upgraded within the table.

### "After" events

The after events which include the AfterUpdate, AfterInsert, and AfterDelete options are quite bigger than they are before equivalents. Each of the above-listed events provides support for all the family of data macro actions which means that these events might be used more often as the basis of data macros.

The AfterInsert data macro is usually executed when a record is added to the table. Comparatively, you can choose to add the data macros to the table's AfterUpdate and AfterDelete in order to log other changes to the table.

## Using the Macro Builder for Data Macros

Data macros utilize the same macro builder utilized to form implanted and client interface macros. Once you ace the macro builder, you'll utilize it for all macro advancement and macro administration. The essential contrast is that the Activity Catalog (depicted within the other segment) contains distinctive activities, depending on the setting.

Adding data macros to a table is very simple. In reality, an Access table doesn't indeed ought to be in the Design view you can include data macros to a table shown as a datasheet if you would prefer that.

The data macros you develop for a table are in effect promptly, so you'll be able effortlessly to work on a macro and watch how well the macro works without compiling or exchanging between the Design view and Datasheet view. With your table in the Design view, you can get to the data macro builder with ease by just choosing the Create Data macros command from the Design tab.

## Understanding the Action Catalog

The Activity Catalog on the right side of the macro builder serves as the store of macro activities you include in your data macros. The contents of the Activity Catalog depend completely on which table event has been chosen, so its appearance shifts impressively whereas you work with Access macros.

## Program flow

At the very top of the Action Catalog is some program flow constructs that can be added to your macros. When you are making use of data macros, the only program flow constructs that can be used are comments, groups and If blocks.

## Data blocks

If you check under the Program Flow constructs properly, you will find Data Blocks. Each of the data block constructs has an area that is used to include one or more macro actions. All of the macro actions can be done by the data block construct as part of its operations.

The data blocks macro actions include; CreateRecord, EditRecord, ForEachRecord, and the LookupRecord.

## Data actions

The following bunch of activities within the Activity Catalog is the Data activities; these are the activities a data macro can take. You've as of now read that a data macro comprises one or more activities that are executed as a single unit in reaction to a table event. You would like a great understanding of the variations of macro activities accessible to data macros.

## Creating Your First Data Macro

**Now that you have some prior knowledge about macro builders follow the steps below to create your first Data Macro.**

- Open the **preferred table** in the Datasheet view
- Choose the **Table tab option** the Ribbon then click on the **BeforeChange event**.
- Click **twice or move the Group program flow action** to the design surface of the macro.

- When in the newly created group, click **twice** on the Comment program flow action to add a comment to the design surface of the macro.
- Click twice on **the If program** flow action to add a new logic check on the design surface of the macros.
- If the condition specified evaluates to true, the record should then be edited by clicking twice the Setfield action button.
- If you have taken the processes up to this stage, the logic for macro is complete. All you have to do next is to click and **save commands**.

## Managing Macro Objects

This section tells you what you can do in managing macro objects once you have added them to a macro's design.

### Collapsing and expanding macro items

Collapsing items can be of great help especially when there is a need for you to have a review of large macros and view just a subset of the macro at a particular time. Note that you can also choose to collapse/Expand commands that are found in the Ribbon.

### Moving macro items

Macro items can be moved from one place to another with the use of the copy and paste function, as an alternative you can also choose to drag the items with the use of the mouse button.

### Saving a macro as XML

A totally covered-up feature of Access data macros is the capacity to duplicate them from the macro builder and paste them into a content editor as XML. Access internally stores macros as XML, and replicating a macro really implies replicating its XML representation.

## Recognizing the Limitations of Data Macros

Although Data macros are very powerful, they cannot do everything. For instance, they have no user interface, cannot display a message box, and cannot open a form or report. They are basically meant to run invisibly with the highest performance.

Data macros cannot work on multi-value or attachment fields. If you have to make use of logic in the control of these data types then you must make use of traditional user interface macros or VBA.

Data macros cannot call VBA procedures. Making them very portable to SharePoint when an application was upsized to a web application was one of the main objectives. Data macros do not support transactions. All the field and record updates are immediately executed and there is no way multiple table changes can be rolled back.

# CHAPTER 24
# GETTING STARTED WITH ACCESS VBA

Most Access designers utilize macros almost every time. In spite of the fact that macros give a speedy and simple way to mechanize an application, composing Visual Basic for Applications (VBA) modules is the most perfect way to form applications. VBA gives data access, looping and branching, and other features that macros essentially do not support. In this chapter, you learn how to utilize VBA to expand the control and value of your applications.

## Introducing Visual Basic for Applications

Microsoft Access incorporates a number of features to permit database engineers to make data entry forms, reports, and queries that can direct users in questioning existing data within the database and entering unused data. Different inquiry builders and wizard devices ease this development process. However, with these devices, be that as it may, there may be circumstances where the designer would like to include even more functions not as of now given by the MS Access advancement tools. For instance, the engineer may wish to automatically redress awful data before it is saved within the database. The way to achieve such customization is by including code utilizing the Visual Basic for Applications programming language.

VBA is a key component in most proficient Access applications. Microsoft gives VBA in Access since VBA gives critical adaptability and control to Access database applications. Without a full-fledged programming language like VBA, Access applications would have depended on a somewhat limited set of actions being provided by Access macros. In spite of the fact that macro programming moreover includes adaptability to Access applications, VBA is much less demanding to work with when you're programming complex data-management features or advanced user-interface necessities.

## Understanding VBA Terminology

**Below are terms that are often used with VBA;**

- **Keyword**: This is simply a word with special meaning in VBA. For example, the word Now in VBA refers to the name of a built-in function that sends back the current date and time.
- **Statement**: this is a single VA word or group of words that build an instruction to be performed by the VBA engine.
- **Procedure**: this is a group of VBA statements put together to take up some task. The two basic types of VBA procedures are Subroutines and Functions
- **Module**: procedures are often stored in modules. A module has one or more procedures and some other elements which are put together as just one entity within the application.

## Starting with VBA Code Basics

There are an interminable number of distinctive VBA programming statements that seem to appear in an Access application. For the most part, be that as it may, VBA statements are reasonably simple to study and get it. Most frequently, you will be able to understand the reason for a VBA statement based on the keywords. Each VBA statement is an instruction that is processed and also executed by the VBA language engine which is built into Access.

## Creating VBA Programs

Access incorporates a wide assortment of devices that empower you to work with tables, queries, forms, and reports without ever having to type in a single line of code. A few operations can't be fulfilled through the client interface, even with macros.

For circumstances such as these, you need the drive of a high-level programming language such as VBA. VBA is an advanced, organized programming language that offers lots of the programming structures accessible in most programming languages. VBA is extensible (capable of calling Windows API schedules) and can be associated through ActiveX Information Objects (ADO), Data AccessObjects (DAO), and with any Access or VBA data type.

## Modules

Modules are containers wherein procedures are stored. There are basically two different types of modules. They are the standard module and classic module.

Standard modules are free from other Access objects, like shapes and reports. They are utilized to store code that's utilized from any place inside your application. These strategies are frequently called global or public since they're open to all components of your Access application. Use public strategies all through your application in expressions, macros, occasion methods, and other VBA code. To utilize a public method, you basically sort its title in another method in your application.

Class modules state the behavior of an object. You can choose to build your own class module but the class module widely used is one that is bound to a form or a report. For class modules that are bound to a form or report, the module is made naturally by Access at whatever point you include VBA code to the form or report. The foremost vital distinction between standard modules and class modules is that class modules bolster events. Events react to client activities and run VBA code that's contained inside the event strategy.

## Procedures and functions

The next step you completed after making a module to hold your strategy was to make the strategy itself. It's a straightforward method that does a little straightforward math and shows the result. Each statement is organized concurrently to the language's syntax, meaning that the spelling of keywords and the order of the words within the statement are critical.

A function is exceptionally comparative to a subprocedure, with one major exemption: a function returns a value when it closes. A straightforward case is the built-in VBA Now() function, which returns the current date and time. Now() can be utilized essentially any place your application ought to utilize or show the current date and time. An example is having Now() in a report header or footer so that the client knows precisely when the report was printed. Now() is just one of a few hundred built-in VBA functions. In addition to built-in capacities, you might include custom capacities that return values required by your applications.

## Working in the code window

Utilize the Code window to type in, show, and alter Visual Basic code. You'll be able open as many Code windows as you have got modules, so you'll be able to effortlessly see the code in numerous forms or modules, and duplicate and paste

between them.

### White space

In the wide world of programming, indentation and certain blank lines are known as white space. With exceptionally few exemptions, VBA overlooks white space. In a few programming languages, white space is imperative and important. That isn't the case for VBA. The reason for white space is to make your code clear. Diverse software engineers arrange their code with white space in several ways.

Whatever formatting conventions you select to utilize, the foremost imperative thing is to be steady. Consistency in organizing will assist you in examining and understanding your code more effectively, even if you're perusing months or a long time afterward.

### Line continuation

The line continuation characters are a space taken after by an emphasis. When the VBA compiler sees space and an emphasis at the conclusion of the line, it knows that the other

line may be a continuation of the current one. Make use of the line continuation characters in breaking long statements into various lines. With this, you will be able to view the whole statement.

## Multi-statement lines

Another way to make strides in the clarity of your code is by putting two or more statements on one line. VBA uses the colon to isolate statements on the same line. If you have some brief statements that are taking up a part of vertical space within the code sheet, you'll be able to put a number of them on the same line to clean up the code.

## IntelliSense

There are about four different features in Access collectively known as Intellisense and they are used to help you locate the proper keyword to be used and they also determine the right parameters as each line of code is being created. These features are complete word, Auto List Members, Auto Quick Info, and Auto constants.

## Compiling procedures

After writing a code, it should then be compiled in order for the development process to be completed. The compilation step changes over the English-like VBA syntax to a binary format that's effectively executed at run time. Moreover, amid compilation, all your code is checked for erroneous syntax and other mistakes that will cause issues when the client works with the application.

In the event that you do not compile your Access applications amid the improvement cycle, Access compiles the code at whatever point a client opens the application and starts utilizing it. In this case, blunders in your code might prevent the client from utilizing the application, causing a lot of burden to everybody included.

## Saving a module

**Modules are saved by saving the database and reacting to the prompts that Access shows.**

- Within the VBE, select **File** then click on **Save** to save the database. You will be prompted to save all unsaved modules and other unsaved objects.

You aren't prompted to save modules that have as of now been saved, nevertheless in case they've been changed. Those modules are basically spared with the name you gave previously. Class modules that are connected to a frame or report are saved when the form or report is saved.

# Understanding VBA Branching Constructs

A programming language is best known for its ability to make a decision that is dependent on a condition that might be somewhat different each time the user makes use of the application. There are primarily two methods by which the procedures can be executed in VBA;

## Branching

Branching in VBA can simply be described as the ability of an application to view a value and based on that same value, decide the code it will run.

## The If keyword

The If keyword can be utilized in some diverse ways, but they all check a condition and, based on the assessment, perform an activity. The condition must be assessed to a Boolean value (True or False). In the event that the condition is True, the program moves to the line taking after the If statement. If that condition is False, the program skips to the statement taking after the Else statement, If present, or the End If explanation statement If there's no Else clause.

## The Select case...End Select statement

VBA provides the Select Case statement to check for various conditions. **Below is the general syntax for the Select Case statement;**

>Select Case Expression

Case Value1

>[Action to take when Expression = Value1]

Case Value2

>[Action to take when Expression = Value2]

Take note that the syntax is comparative to that of the If...Then statement. Rather than a Boolean condition, the Select Case articulation employs an expression at the top. At that point, each Case clause tests its value against the expression's value. When a Case value matches the expression, the program executes the block of code until it comes to another Case statement or the End Select statement. VBA executes the code as if it were one matching Case statement.

## .Looping

Looping in VBA is simply the ability to run just one statement or a group of statements multiple times. The statement or group of statements executed will also be repeated until some of the conditions are met. There are two types of looping constructs VBA offers which are the Do….Loop and the For….Next. Do…Loop constructs are used basically when you have a need to repeat a statement and you don't know the number of times you would have to repeat the statement while the For…Next constructs are used when you also have a need to repeat a statement but you already know the number of times the statement will be repeated.

## The Do... Loop statement

Do…Loop is utilized to repeat a bunch of statements until a condition is true. This statement is one of the foremost commonly utilized VBA looping constructs. Do…Loop has various alternatives. The While clause causes the VBA statements inside the Do…Loop to execute as long as the condition is true. Execution drops out of the Do…Loop immediately the condition assesses to false. The Until clause on its own doesn't work in the same manner, it works such that the code within the Do….Loop will only be executed when the condition is false.

## .The For... Next statement

The For Next statement is used to repeat a statement block a couple of times. Most of the time, a For…The next loop checks upward, beginning at an initial value and increasing the counter variable by the sum indicated by the step value. In a few cases, be that as it may, you might require a loop that begins at a high beginning value and steps descending to conclusion esteem. In this case, utilize a negative number as the step value. The Step keyword is required when looping in reverse. If you overlook it, the For statement will see that CounterVariable is more noteworthy than End and the loop won't be executed.

## Working with Objects and Collections

VBA offers various constructs designed primarily to work with objects and collections of objects. In spite of the fact that VBA for Access isn't entirely an object-oriented language, it's frequently alluded to as object-based. Numerous of the things you work with in Access are objects and not fair basic numbers and character strings. For the most part, an object is a complex substance that performs a few kinds of work inside an Access application. Access uses collections to bring together objects as a single bunch.

Collections are ordinarily named by taking the name of the objects they contain and making them plural. The Forms collection contains the Form object. The Reports collection contains the Report object. There are exemptions, be that as it may, such as the Controls collection. While the Controls collection does contain Control objects, each Control object is additionally another sort of object. A Control object can be a Textbox object, a Combobox object, or any one of a few more particular object sorts.

## Properties and methods

**Objects also have properties and methods which are also discussed in the sections below;**

### Properties

With properties, you can choose to change some values that are the characteristics of that particular object. Properties also can return some other objects.

### Methods

Methods are quite different from properties in that they do not return a value.

**Methods basically can be in two categories which are;**

- Methods with the ability to change more than just one property at once.
- Methods that can perform an action external to the object.

### The With statement

The With explanation allows you to get to an object's properties and methods without writing the object's name over and over. Any properties or methods utilized between With and End With naturally allude to the object indicated within the With statement. Any number of statements can show up between the With and End With statements, and With statements can be settled. Properties and methods will refer to the protest within the deepest With a piece that contains them.

In any case, when working with enormous sets of information, the With explanation might contribute to overall execution. In any case, the With explanation decreases the wordiness of the subroutine and makes the code much simpler to read and understand. It moreover spares tons of writing when you're changing a part of the properties of an object

## The For Each statement

The For Each statement can be used to transverse the controls collection. It ensures it goes through every member of the collection and ensures it is available for examination or manipulation.

# Exploring the Visual Basic Editor

In this section you will learn more about the features of the Visual Basic Editor and how to effectively make use of them.

## The Immediate window

The duty of the immediate window is to allow you to give your procedure a trial without you necessarily having to leave the module.

**You can execute the module and also check variables.**

- Click on the **Ctrl+G buttons** to see the immediate window or click on View then Immediate window when you are in the VBA code editor.

## The Project Explrer

This is a window that is within the VBE that shows all the modules that are in your project. It also offers a much easier method of moving modules without having to go back to the main Access application.

**To view the Project Explorer;**

- Press the **Ctrl+R buttons** or click on **View** then Project Explorer from the menu of the VBE.

# The Object Browser

With the Object Browser which is also a window in VBE, you can see all the objects, properties, methods, and events that are in your project. The object browser can be very useful especially when you are looking for properties and methods, the Object browser can help show all the elements that are in a particular string also.

## VBE options

Below are some of the other options that are available for use within the VBE;

## The Editor tab of the Options dialog box

This box has lots of very important settings that influence how you deal with Access as you include code in your applications.

**You can access these by**

- clicking on **Tools** and then **Options** from the VBE menu.

## The Project Properties dialog box

Access takes charge of the code in your application by ensuring it keeps track of all the code objects that are contained in the project which is basically different from the code that is included in the application as runtime libraries and as wizards.

All the projects in Access have some very important options, The project Properties dialog box has some settings that are also quite important for developers.

Open the Project Properties dialog box by clicking on Tools then choose Project Name Properties assuming "project name" is the name given to your database project.

# CHAPTER 25
# MASTERING VBA DATA TYPES AND PROCEDURES

A variable may be a value, merely pronounced in your code and thus it is saved in your computer's memory and stored there. You've got to name your variable and it's a great practice to pronounce the data type of your variable. After you announce the Data type, you're telling the program, the sort of information that must be put away by your variable. You will utilize the variable in your code, and the program will also gain access to your variable. The real value of your variable can alter while your code is still being executed.

The variables you make use of having a lot of effect on your applications. You have some other options as regards the establishment and use of variables in your Access programs. The inappropriate use of a variable can slow down the proper execution of an application or result in a loss of data.

This chapter has all that you need to know about the creation and use of variables, the information here will also help you to make the most efficient use of data types while also avoiding the well-known problems that are related to VBA variables.

## Using Variables

A variable may be a transitory capacity area for some value and is given a name. You can utilize a variable to store the result of a calculation, hold a value entered by the user, or read from a table, otherwise, you can make a variable to create a control's value accessible to another procedure. To refer to the result of an expression, you employ a variable's name to store the result. To allow an expression's result to a variable, you employ the = operator.

### Naming variables

Almost every programming language has its own defined fuels that it uses in naming variables.

**In VBA, the conditions a variable name must meet are as follows;**

- The name must be unique with a mix of both upper and lower case.
- There must be no space in the names or punctuation characters.
- It must start with an alphabetical character.
- It must not be longer than 255 characters.

## Declaring variables

There are basically two ways by which variables can be added to your application. The first method is known as the implicit declaration which is the method described when VBA automatically creates the variable for you. This isn't a very good idea as it can lead to issues with performance and problems debugging.

The second method is the explicit declaration. This method uses a keyword when declaring. The keywords include; Dim keyword, Static keyword, Private or Public keyword. Note that the choice of keyword used will always have an effect on the scope of the variable within the application and it will also be a key determinant of where the variable can be used in the program.

Though VBA doesn't need you to declare your variables before you make use of them, it offers several declaration commands. Note that it is a very good practice to always have your variables declared. When a variable is declared it simply means there is a certain type of data that can be assigned to it which most of the time is usually a numeric value or characters alone.

## The Dim keyword

In declaring a variable, it's best to make use of the Dim keyword. When you make use of this keyword ensure that you provide the name of the variable. In declaring a variable note that the name of the variable will always follow the Dim statement. Furthermore, when naming a variable, make use of the use As Data Type for the indication of a particular data type for the variable. This data type is basically the type of information that will be stored in the variable, the default data type is variant as it can hold any type of data.

You can also declare variables in the declarations part of the module after which all the procedures in the module will be able to gain access to the variable. The procedures on the outside of the module in which the variable has been declared will however not be able to read or make use of the variable.

## The Public keyword

If you would like to make all of the modules in the application available then you should make use of the Public keyword. The best method of declaring a public variable is to have them declared in just one standard module that is used to store public variables alone. When all the publicly declared variables are located in just a single place it can be very easy to find them.

## The Private keyword

There isn't so much difference between the Dim keyword and the Private keyword technically but making use of the Private keyword at the module level in declaring variables that are available only to that module's procedure is a very good idea. The private keyword will make sure that all the procedures in the module can access the variable but not all procedures in the other module can.

# Working with Data Types

When you declare a variable you ought to specify the data type for each of the variables also. Each variable has its own data type and the data type will also determine the type of information that will be stored in the variable. For example, a string variable will only be able to hold a data type of string that can be typed on a keyboard.

## Forcing explicit declarations

Access gives a straightforward compiler order that forces you to continuously pronounce the variables in your applications. The Option Explicit statement, when inserted at the top of a module, tells VBA to require an explicit declaration of all variables within the module.

Since explicit declaration is such a great thought, it may not come as a shock that Access gives a way to naturally guarantee that each module in your application uses explicit declaration.

## Using a naming convention with variables

One way to ease the burden of overseeing the code and objects in an application is through the utilization of a naming convention. A naming convention applies a standardized strategy of providing names to the objects and variables in an application.

The default common naming convention utilized in Access applications uses a one- to four-character prefix (a tag) joined to the base name of the objects and variables in a VBA application. The tag is for the most part based on the sort of control for controls and the type of data the variable holds or the scope for variables.

The names used for variables often follow a similar pattern. The strong variable which contains the name of a customer can be named sCustomer and a Boolean variable that is indicating if the customer is active or not would be named bActive.

## Understanding variable scope and Lifetime

A variable is more than just a basic information store. Each variable could be a dynamic portion of the application and may be utilized at diverse times amid the program's execution. The declaration of a variable sets up more than just the title and data type of the variable. Depending on the keyword utilized to declare the variable and the situation of the variable's statement within the program's code, the variable may be very visible to large portions of the application's code. Then again, a different placement may extremely restrain where the variable can be referenced within the strategies inside the application.

## Examining scope

The visibility of a variable or strategy is called its scope. A variable that can be seen and utilized by any strategy within the application is said to have public scope. A variable that's accessible to any strategy in one module is scoped private to that module. A variable that is usable by a single method is said to have a scope that is local to that strategy.

Misconception variable scope may be a major cause of genuine bugs in numerous Access applications. It's totally conceivable to have two same-named variables with diverse scopes in an Access VBA project. When uncertainty exists, Access continuously uses the "closest" declared variable.

## Determining a variable lifetime

The same manner in which their visibility is decided by the location of their declaration, their lifetime is decided by their declaration as well. A variable's lifetime decides when it's available to the application. By default, local variables are always in existence only while the procedure is being executed. Immediately after the procedure finishes, the variable will be taken off the memory and will not be available again.

## Deciding on a variable's scope

To decide on the scope of a very all you need to do is to limit the scope of your variables to the barest minimum. With this, most of your variables will be just at the procedure level and declared with the use of the Dim keyword. When the scope is limited, it will also reduce the number of locations a variable can change and this can make it extremely easy to note problems as soon as they occur.

## Using constants

There is one major difference between constants and variables which is the fact that a constant does not change values. If you at any point attempt to change the value of a constant after it has been declared, it will result in an error.

## Declaring constants

**Constants are declared with the use of the const keyword. The format for the declaration is as follows;**

> [Public | Private] Const constname [As type] = constvalue

When you make use of contestants, it can help make your code easier to read and it also helps to aid in error-proofing your code if you happen to make use of the same value in more than one place. Note that when constants are declared with the use of a private keyword inside a procedure, they are made available only within that same procedure. It is also worthy to note that the values of constants do not change and as such the static keyword is not in use and totally irrelevant when declaring constants.

## Using a naming convention with constants

It is a very good idea to make use of the same naming convention that is used with variables. When you prefix the name of a constant it allows you to know the scope of the constant easily when you are about to make use of them. You can also make use of a prefix in identifying the data type of the constant as it helps to keep the names of your constant unique and also prevents error. You can declare constants with the use of any combination of both upper and lower case letters. The rules that guide naming variables and procedures also apply to constants.

## Working with arrays

An array is a very special type of variable. Rather than just keeping one block of memory, an array keeps various blocks of memory. The size of an array can be fixed or dynamic.

## Fixed arrays

When a fixed array is declared, the size is also indicated in the Dim statement and that size cannot be changed afterward. The easiest way to declare a fixed array is by fixing the upper bound index in parentheses after the name of the variable.

If you notice at any point in time that you are having certain performance problems or your application appears to be using too much memory check your array to be sure the memory in place is not larger than what you actually need.

## Dynamic arrays

Dynamic arrays are often declared without the use of any indices and their size can be changed much later in the procedure. With the declaration of a dynamic array, no memory is allocated until the array has been initialized by the provision of dimensions. The data type is also configured when the array has been declared and it also cannot be changed. If you don't know the size of the array you will be using until runtime, it's best if you make use of the dynamic array.

## Array functions

VBA offers lots of useful functions that can be used with arrays some of which are; boundary functions, the array function, the split function, the join function,

## Understanding Subs and functions

As earlier stated, the codes in a VBA application are saved in modules and the code within the modules are composed of procedures. There are primarily two types of procedures in VBA and they are called subroutines or subprocedures(commonly known as subs) and functions.

Subs and functions both have lines of code that you can execute. The main difference between a procedure and a function is that when you call it, a function will return a value i.e a value is generated when it runs and makes the value available to the code that called it. A sub on the other hand doesn't return a value.

## Understanding where to create a procedure

**There are two places where a procedure can be created;**

- **In a standard VBA module**: a sub or function is created in a standard module when the procedure will be shared by code in more than one form or report or by an object other than a form or report.
- **Behind a form or report**: if you are certain the code you are creating will be called by just one procedure or form then you should create the sub or function in the form or reports module.

# Calling VBA procedures

VBA procedures can be called from events behind forms and reports or they can be placed in modules and called by simply making use of their name or their Call statement. Subs are called, get their work done, and that the end, only functions get to return values that might be assigned to variables. Note that the syntax used in calling subroutines with parameters can change based on how the procedure is called.

## Creating subs

**Oftentimes, forms are always created in forms. Follow the steps below to create subs;**

- Choose **the location** you would like to create the sub from the Design view.
- Click on **F4** to show the Property Sheet for the control.
- Click on the **After Update event property** in the Event tab of the Property Sheet and choose Event Procedure from the events drop-down list.
- Click on the **builder button** in order to have the VBA code editor opened.
- Close the **VBA window** and go back to the location you chose initially.

## Creating Functions

Functions vary from subroutines in that capacities return a value. Although functions can be made behind individual forms or reports, ordinarily they're made in standard modules.

## Handling parameters

Parameters are usually treated just like any other variable by the procedure. They have a name and a data type and are used as a means of sending information to a procedure. You can also use parameters to get information from a procedure also. You are free to give a parameter whatever name you so desire.

## Calling a function and passing parameters

A function call usually comes from a form or report the event and at other times though rare from another procedure, and the call does well by sending information as parameters.

# Simplifying Code with Named Arguments

Named Arguments is another feature that can be found in Access VBA. Without this feature, the arguments that are passed to procedures must be displayed in the correct left-to-right order. If on the other hand the arguments are named, you will provide the name of every parameter that has been passed to a sub or a function the sub or function will then make use of the argument based on the name as against its position in the argument list.

# CHAPTER 26

# UNDERSTANDING THE ACCESS EVENT MODEL

When dealing with a database system, you may find yourself repeating the same duties. You can use VBA macros to automate the procedure rather than repeating the same steps every time.

To have these activities automated, you can use VBA code across your application. The VBA language provides a comprehensive set of commands for manipulating table records, form controls, and just about anything else. This chapter continues the discussion of working with procedures in forms, reports, and standard modules from the previous chapters.

## Programming Events

An access event occurs as a result of or as a result of a user's activity. When a user moves from one record to the next in a form, dismisses a report, or clicks a command button on a form, an Access event happens. Even simply moving the mouse causes a series of events to occur.

**You can categorize Access events into seven distinct groups which are;**

- Windows events.
- Keyboard events.
- Mouse events.
- Focus events.
- Data events
- Print events
- Error and timing events

## Understanding how events trigger VBA code

When a user performs any of the many varied events that Access recognizes, you can construct an event procedure that runs. Special form and control features allow Access to react to events. Reports include a comparable set of events, which are adjusted to the report's specific demands and requirements.

## Creating event procedures

The event properties of an object in Access are used to perform event processes.

You can utilize event properties in Access to link VBA code to an object's events. The On Open property, for example, is associated with a form or report that appears on the screen.

Select the event property in the object's Property Sheet to add an event method to a form or report. A drop-down arrow and a builder button display in the property's box if there is presently no event procedure for the property.

## Identifying Common Events

Many distinct Access objects can cause certain events to be triggered. Microsoft has gone to great lengths to ensure that these events behave consistently regardless of the object that triggers them. The table below covers some of the most popular events used by Access programmers. The majority of these events are applicable to forms and all of the various controls that you might include in an Access form.

| Event | Event Type | When the Event is Triggered |
| --- | --- | --- |
| Click | Mouse | When the user presses and then releases the left button of the mouse on an object. |
| DbClick | Mouse | When the user presses and releases the left button of the mouse two times on an object. |

| | | |
|---|---|---|
| MouseDown | Mouse | When the user presses the button of the mouse while the pointer is on an object. |
| MouseMove | Mouse | When the user moves the mouse pointer over an object. |
| MouseUp | Mouse | When the user releases an already pressed mouse button while the pointer is on an object. |
| MouseWheel | Mouse | When the user spins the wheel of the mouse. |
| KeyDown | Keyboard | When the user presses any key on the keyboard when the object has focus or when the user makes use of a SendKeys macro action |
| KeyUp | Keyboard | When the user releases a pressed key immediately after using a SendKeys macro action. |

Because the mouse and keyboard are the user's primary way of inputting information and giving guidance to an application, it's no surprise that these events are all linked to them. Not every item responds to each of these events, but when an object does, the event behaves in the same way.

## Form event procedures

When working with forms, you can develop event procedures that are based on events that occur at the form, section, or control level. When you connect an event procedure to a form-level event, the action is applied to the entire form whenever the event occurs (such as when you move to another record or leave the form).

You build an event procedure and connect it to the event property in the form that recognizes the event to have your form respond to it. At the form level, many characteristics can be utilized to activate event operations.

## Essential form events

Many different events trigger access forms. Because of their specialized nature, you'll never develop code for most of these events. However, there are some events that you'll implement in your Access apps over and over again.

| Event | When the Event Is Triggered |
| --- | --- |
| Open | When a form is opened, but the first record is not displayed yet |
| Load | When a form is loaded into memory but not yet opened |
| Unload | When a form is closed and the records unload, and before the form is removed from the screen |
| Close | When a form is closed and removed from the screen |

| Active | When an open form receives the focus, becoming the active window |
|---|---|
| Deactive | When a different window becomes the active window, but before it loses focus |
| Timer | When a specified time interval passes. The interval (in milliseconds) is specified by the TimerInterval property. |

## Form mouse and key-board events

Access forms also respond to some mouse and keyboard events. The table below better describes this;

| Event | When the Event is Triggered |
|---|---|
| Click | When the user presses and also releases the left mouse button. |
| Double Click | When the user presses and releases (clicks) the left mouse button twice on a form |
| Mouse Down | When the user presses the mouse button while the pointer is on a form |
| MouseMove | When the user moves the mouse pointer over an area of a form |

| | |
|---|---|
| MouseUp | When the user releases a pressed mouse button while the pointer is on a form |
| KeyDown | When the user presses any key on the keyboard when a form has focus cr when the user uses a SendKeys macro action |
| KeyUp | When the user releases a pressed key or immediately after the user uses a SendKeys macro action |
| KeyPress | When the user presses and releases a key on a form that has the focus or when the user uses a SendKeys macro |

## Form data events

Access forms are mostly used to display data. As a result, Access forms have a number of events that are directly tied to the data management of the form. Almost every time you work on an Access program, you'll come across event routines built for these events.

After the data on a form is refreshed, the Current event fires. This usually happens when the user switches the form to a different record in the record set that underpins it. The Current event is frequently used to execute computations or format controls based on the form's data.

The BeforeInsert and AfterInsert events are used to move data from a form to an underlying data source. BeforeInsert fires when Access prepares to transmit data, and AfterInsert fires after the record have been committed to the data source. The BeforeInsert and AfterInsert events are used to move data from a form to an underlying data source.

## Control event procedures

Controls can also cause events to occur. Control events are frequently used to alter the control's look or to validate data when the user changes its contents. Control events also affect how the mouse and keyboard interaction with the control when the user is working with it.

The BeforeUpdate event of a control fires as soon as the focus leaves the control (more precisely, before data is transferred from the control to the recordset underlying the form, allowing you to cancel the event if data validation fails), whereas the BeforeUpdate event of a form does not fire until the form is moved to another record. (BeforeUpdate on the form commits the full record to the data source.)

## Report event procedures

Reports, like forms, respond to specific events by using event processes. Events are supported in Access reports for both the overall report and each segment. Individual controls on Access reports do not result in events being triggered.

When you add an event method to a report, it runs code every time it opens, closes, or prints. Events that run when the report is produced or printed are included in each area (header, footer, and so on).

| Event Property | When the Event is Triggered |
| --- | --- |
| Open | When the event is opened before printing |
| Close | When the report is closed and taken off the screen. |
| Active | When the report receives the focus and hence becomes the active window. |
| Deactivate | When a different window becomes active. |
| Page | When the report alters pages |

| Error | When a runtime error is produced in Access. |

Even though users do not interact with reports in the same way that they do with forms, events are nevertheless important in report design. When you open a report with no data, the findings are usually incorrect. A title and no detailed information may be displayed in the report. It may also display #error values for missing data.

## Report section event procedures

Access provides three unique event attributes for usage with report sections in addition to the form's event elements.

| Event | When the Event is Triggered |
|---|---|
| Format | When the section has been pre-formatted in memory before it is being sent to the printer. |
| Print | This is when the section is being sent to the printer. |
| Retreat | This is immediately after the format event but before the Print event. This usually occurs when there is a need for Access to backup previous sections on a page in order to take up several formatting. |

# Paying Attention to Event Sequence

Even a seemingly innocuous move on the part of the user can trigger a cascade of consequences. The KeyDown, KeyPress, and KeyUp events are raised every time the user touches a key on the keyboard, for example. The MouseDown and MouseUp events, as well as a Click event, are all triggered when the left mouse button is pressed. As a VBA developer, you have complete control over which events you program in your Access applications.

Events do not happen at random. Depending on whatever control is raising the events, events fire in a predictable pattern. Keeping track of the sequence in which events occur can be one of the most difficult aspects of working with events. It can seem counterintuitive that the Enter event occurs before the GotFocus event.

## Looking at common event sequences

**Below are the series of events for the most frequently encountered form scenarios;**

- Opening and closing forms
    - When a form opens: Open (form) → Load (form) → Resize (form) → Activate (form) → Current (form) → Enter (control) → GotFocus (control)
    - When a form closes: Exit (control) → LostFocus (control) → Unload (form) → Deactivate (form) → Close (form)
- Changes in focus

    When the focus moves from one form to another: Deactivate (form1) → Activate (form2)

    When the focus moves to a control on a form: Enter → GotFocus

    When the focus leaves a form control: Exit → LostFocus

    When the focus moves from control1 to control2: Exit (control1) → LostFocus (control1) → Enter (control2) → GotFocus (control2)

    When the focus leaves the record in which data has changed, but before entering the next record: BeforeUpdate (form) → AfterUpdate (form) → Exit (control) → LostFocus (control) → Current (form)

When the focus moves to an existing record in Form view: BeforeUpdate (form) → AfterUpdate (form) → Current (form)

- Mouse events

    ○ When the user presses and releases (clicks) a mouse button while the mouse pointer is on a form control: MouseDown → MouseUp → Click

    ○ When the user moves the focus from one control to another by clicking the second control: Control1: Exit → LostFocus Control2: Enter → GotFocus → MouseDown → MouseUp → Click

    ○ When the user double-clicks a control other than a command button: MouseDown → MouseUp → Click → DblClick → MouseUp

## Writing simple form and control event procedures

It's straightforward to write basic methods to check the event sequence of a form or control. Determine which event in your application should be harnessed using the previous information. Unexpected behavior is frequently traced back to an event procedure attached to an event that occurs too late or too early to capture the data required by the application.

Remember that you should only create code for events that are relevant to your app. Access ignores any events that do not include code and has no impact on the program. Furthermore, it's very likely that you'll write the incorrect event for a certain task at some point. You might be tempted to alter the appearance of a control by adding code to the Enter event. (To make it easier for the user to see which control has the focus, many developers alter the BackColor or ForeColor of the control.) The Enter event is an inconsistent indicator of when control has taken focus, as you'll quickly discover.

## Opening a form with an event procedure

To complete the application's business functions, most apps require many forms and reports. An application typically provides a switchboard form to aid users in navigating within the application, rather than requiring users to traverse the database container to find which forms and reports complete which tasks. The switchboard has a series of command buttons that are labeled to indicate the purpose of the form or report that is being opened.

## Running an event procedure when closing a form

When you close or leave a form, you may want to do something with it. For example, you might want Access to keep track of who has used the form, or you might want the Print dialog box to close every time a user closes the main form. Simply utilize the Form Close event to accomplish this. Although it isn't an error to try to close a form that isn't currently open, it's a good practice to check if an object is available before performing an operation on it.

## Using an event procedure to confirm record deletion

Although you may delete a record in a form using the Delete button on the Records group on the Home tab of the Ribbon, providing a Delete button on the form is a better practice. An Erase button is more user-friendly since it shows the user how to delete a record visually.

Furthermore, because you may integrate code to check the deletion before it's done, a command button gives you more control over the delete process. Alternatively, you might need to run a referential integrity check to ensure that deleting the record will not break a link to it in another table in the database.

# CHAPTER 27
# DEBUGGING YOUR ACCESS APPLICATIONS

Fixing an error in VBA or a problem in an application can be tough and time-consuming, just like any other programming language. Tracking down even a little coding error may be a difficult task based on how well organized the code is and whether fundamental practices like providing descriptive names for variables and procedures were followed.

Access, fortunately, comes with a comprehensive set of debugging tools to make life easier. These tools can aid in understanding how the code is structured and how execution goes from procedure to process, as well as saving time by helping you spot where a coding issue occurs.

This will be focusing a lot on those bugs that cause major problems in your application.

## Organizing VBA Code

Avoiding coding problems in the first place is the first step toward troubleshooting your code. This should be unsurprising that the type and amount of mistakes you encounter in your applications are mostly determined by your coding habits. Simple coding conventions can often remove all but the most difficult syntactical and logical mistakes in VBA code.

- **Use a naming convention**

    A consistent naming system can aid in the detection of problems that might otherwise go undetected.

- **Limit scopes for variables**

    By default, variables are created at the procedure level, and the scope is only increased when the logic of your code necessitates it. Keep your variables with a global scope in their own module. Consider modifying your code when the list of global variables grows too long.

- **Keep your procedures short**

    When you have a lot of small procedures instead of a few big ones, your code will be considerably easier to manage.

    If your procedures get too long to fit on a single screen, consider dividing them into smaller procedures and invoking each one from the main procedure.

- **Don't repeat yourself**

    Consider separating the code into distinct procedures and passing arguments from the event procedure if you find yourself repeating the same code over and over. If you need to make a change, you'll only have to make it once, conserving your time and eliminating errors.

- **Compile often**

    Do not wait until the full module or project has been written before compiling it. After you've written or updated numerous lines of code, compile your project. When you're writing your process, you'll have a lot of knowledge about what it does and where it's utilized, so it's the perfect time to identify problems.

## Testing Your Applications

You test your application every time you change the view of a form or report from Design to Normal or exit the VBA Editor to run some code. You're testing the property you've changed every time you modify a property in a form or notify and shift your cursor to another property or control.

Testing is when you check to see if your program works as expected, or even if it works at all. You've discovered a bug when you start an application but it doesn't really work. Debugging is the process of detecting and fixing errors in code.

The majority of issues with a query, forms, and report design are self-evident. When a query returns incorrect data, or a form or report fails to open or displays an error notice as it opens, you know you have a problem. When you execute forms and reports, Access frequently generates an error if it detects something that is clearly erroneous.

However, pinpointing the exact location of a defect in VBA code and determining what to do to fix it can be difficult. When it comes to identifying and resolving errors with VBA code, you're very much on your own. Fortunately, the editor comes equipped with a number of features to assist you.

## Testing functions

Because functions return values, they are considerably simpler to test than other operations. It is best you test your function as it is written will reveal any issues at a time when they are easiest to resolve. It may be more difficult to track down an error in a function that proliferates to a control on a form. Writing tests also forces you to consider the logic of your functions from a variety of perspectives.

## Compiling VBA code

**There is just one way to compile your complete application;**

- Open **the compiler**, then choose **Debug Compile Database Name** from the Modules toolbar in the VBA editor window. To reach the Debug menu, you must have a module open. To ensure that all code is stored in a compiled state, you should always use the Compile Database Name command.

Compiling complex programs might take a long time, so you should compile your Access projects only before delivering them to end-users or performing benchmark tests.

The name of your project appears when you select Debug Compile Database Name. This is the name you gave your database file when you created or saved it for the first time. The project name does not change if you rename the database file later. Choose Tools Properties in the module window to modify the database name; the database Properties dialog box provides the database name setting.

# Traditional Debugging Techniques

Since Access 1.0, two frequently utilized debugging approaches have been offered. The first is to use MsgBox commands to display variable values, procedure names, and other information. Inserting Debug.Print is the second most frequent technique.

## Using MsgBox

The MsgBox keyword stalls code execution and displays a string in a box that must be cleared before the code may proceed. You don't have to have the Immediate window open or flip to the Immediate window to see the message box because it appears immediately on the user interface. The MsgBox statement is simple to use and only requires one line of code.

## Using Debug.Print

The second most commonly used debugging technique is the Debug.Print to output messages to the Immediate window. You don't have to do much to conceal the Debug, unlike the MsgBox statement. Print the user interface's output. Debug.Print only prints to the Immediate window, and since end users never get to see the Immediate window, you don't have to bother about debug messages being displayed to them.

# Using the Access Debugging Tools

Microsoft Access comes with a rich set of debugging tools and other features. These tools are used to track the progress of your VBA code, pause execution on a statement so you may inspect the value of variables at that point in time, and do other debugging chores.

## Running code with the Immediate Window

The Immediate window shows information from debugging statements in your code or commands typed into the window directly.

**To open the Immediate window, click the button below.**

- Select the **Immediate window (CTRL+G)** from the View menu.
- To run code in the Immediate window, press **Ctrl+Enter**.

**In the Immediate window, type a line of code.**

- To run the statement, press **ENTER**.

**Use the Immediate window to do the following:**

- Problematic or newly written code should be tested.
- While an application is running, you can query or modify the value of a variable. Assign a new value to the variable while execution is halted, just as you would in code.
- While an application is running, you can query or alter the value of a property.
- Procedures are called in the same way they are called in code.
- While the program is running, look at the debugging output.

## Suspending execution with breakpoints

You use a breakpoint to halt the execution of a procedure at a certain statement, such as when you think there are problems. When you no longer require breakpoints to interrupt execution, you remove them.

**To set a breakpoint**

- Place **the insertion point** anyplace in a process line where you want the procedure to stop running.
- Choose **Toggle Breakpoint (F9)** from the Debug menu, or click on the **next button** close to the statement in the Margin Indicator Bar (if visible) or the toolbar shortcut:

The line is set to the breakpoint color selected on the Editor Format tab of the Options dialog box, and the breakpoint is added.

When you set a breakpoint on a line with numerous statements separated by colons (:), the break happens at the first statement on the line.

**To get rid of a breakpoint**

- Place **the insertion point** on any line of the method that has a breakpoint.

- Toggle **Breakpoint (F9)** from the Debug menu, or click next to the statement in the Margin Indicator Bar (if visible).
- The breakpoint has been reset, and the highlighting has been deleted.

**To remove all breakpoints from the app**

- Clear **All Breakpoints (CTRL+SHIFT+F9)** from the Debug menu.

## Looking at variables with the Locals window

Dim, Static, or ReDim (arrays only) are used to declare a local variable within a process. A variable called temp can exist in multiple procedures, but because each variable is local to its procedure, it acts independently of the others and can have different values. Local variables declared using the Dim statement are only valid for the duration of the process. Local variables declared with Static are persistent during the application's lifetime. You might want to keep a variable value constant throughout the program, and you'll see an example of how a static variable might help your code.

You can change the values of simple variables (numeric, string, and so on) in the Locals window by selecting the Value column in a variable's row and putting in a new value for the variable. This makes experimenting with different combinations of variable values in your application a breeze.

### Setting watches with the Watches window

As you single-step through your code, the Watches window allows you to define the variables you want to monitor. As the code runs, the value of a monitored variable changes dynamically. (To really see the values, you'll need to be at a breakpoint.) The Watches window has the advantage of not requiring the variables displayed to originate from the local method. The variables in the Watch box, in fact, might come from anywhere in the application.

**Setting a watch involves a few more steps than setting a breakpoint or utilizing the Locals window.**

- Select **View** then click on **Watch Window** to display the Watches window.
- Select **Debug** then click on **Add Watch** or right-click **anywhere** in the Watches window and choose Add Watch from the shortcut menu
- Insert **the name** of the variable or any other expression in the Expression text box.

## Using conditional watches

Although it can be fun to observe variables in the Locals or Watches windows, you can waste a lot of time that can be spent on something more productive trying to see anything unexpected happen.

Setting a conditional watch on a variable and instructing the VBA engine to break when the condition you've created is met is usually far more efficient. Conditional watches can also be used in various ways, for as employing compound conditions (X = True and Y = False) and causing a break anytime a value differs from the value set in the Expression text box.

### Using the Call Stack window

You may see the function or procedure calls that are currently on the stack by utilizing the Call Stack window. The Call Stack window displays the method and function calls in chronological sequence. A call stack is a useful tool for examining and comprehending an app's execution path.

When debugging symbols aren't accessible for a section of a call stack, the Call Stack window may be unable to display the right information for that section of the call stack, instead of displaying.

## Trapping Errors in Your Code

To detect mistakes on an Access form or report, use the Error event. The Error event is triggered, for example, when a user tries to enter text in a Date/Time field. When you add an Error event procedure to an Employees form and then provide a text value in the HireDate field, the Error event procedure fires.

The DataErr integer input is passed to the Error event method. The DataErr input in an Error event function specifies the number of the Access error that occurred. The only way to discover the number of errors that occurred is to check the value of the DataErr argument within the event process.

## Understanding error trapping

VBA raises an error when it discovers an error in your code. When an error occurs, several things happen, the most important of which is that the VBA engine looks for an On Error statement and the Err object is created. When you want VBA to react in a specific way when an error occurs, you use the On Error keywords in your code.

## On Error Resume Next

On Error Resume Next causes execution to resume with the statement that comes after the one that generated the run-time error, or with the statement that comes after the most recent call out of the procedure that contains the On Error Resume Next statement.

Despite a run-time error, this statement allows execution to continue. Rather than shifting control to another area inside the procedure, you can place the error-handling routine where the error would occur. When another procedure is called, an On Error Resume Next statement becomes inactive, therefore if you want inline error handling within that routine, you should execute an On Error Resume Next statement in each called routine.

## On Error Goto 0

On Error GoTo 0 disables the current procedure's error handling. Even if the method comprises a line numbered 0, it does not indicate line 0 as the start of the error-handling code. When a procedure is exited without an On Error GoTo 0 statement, the error handler is immediately disabled.

## On Error GoTo Label

The On Error GoTo label statement starts an error-handling process on the line where the statement is located. Before the first line where an error could occur, enable the error-handling function.

When an error occurs while the error handler is active, execution moves to the line provided by the label parameter. The error-handling routine should begin on the line given by the label parameter.

## The Resume keyword

Resumes can be utilized on their own as well. When Resume is used alone, the program returns to the line that created the error, and the error is raised again. This is beneficial when you want to handle issues but also want to inspect the line that generated the error, but if you're not careful, it can lead to an infinite loop of raising errors and restarting. A resume can also be combined with a label to direct program execution to a different location.

## The Err object

When a user meets an error in your program, he should be given a detailed description of the issue and how to solve it. The Err object gives VBA programmers a simple way to locate and cause Microsoft Windows-specific problems.

The Err (short for error) object, in essence, keeps track of any problems that occur during the current procedure. Properties are used to store this information.

**The following are the most prevalent Err properties:**

- The current error is described in the description field.
- The current error number is contained in the number (0 to 65,535).
- The name of the object that caused the error is found in the source field.

There might be some occasions when your program encounters an error that is identical to that described in an Err description but does not result in the corresponding Err number. The Raise method of the Err object can be used to cause errors to occur. The Raise method displays a dialog box to the user when a certain error condition is triggered. A number is passed as a parameter to the Raise method.

# Including error handling in your procedures

You should provide some type of error handling whenever your software interacts with the outside world to deal with unexpected inputs or outputs. Writing your own error-handling routines is one technique to provide error handling.

Error-handling procedures are your program's traffic cops. These procedures can deal with every type of programming or human-caused error you can conceive of. They should not only detect the issue but also attempt to correct it or at the very least provide the program or interacting humans the opportunity to do so.

**To start error handling in a process;**

- Use the **On Error GoTo statement** to indicate that an error-handling function will be used. This statement can be inserted anywhere in your method, but it's best if it's near the top, just after any procedure-level variable declarations.

Before program execution enters the error-handling method, the Exit Function or Exit Sub commands must be executed. A procedure that executes without errors also performs the error handler if these statements are not present. A procedure that executes without errors also executes the error-handling method if there is no Exit statement.

The first step in handling errors is to type the name of the error handler, followed by a colon. You then create code to respond to the error in the error handler.

# PART VII
# ADVANCED ACCESS PROGRAMMING TECHNIQUES

# CHAPTER 28
# ACCESSING DATA WITH VBA

Although bound forms and reports can be used to create applications, employing Visual Basic for Applications (VBA) code to access and change data directly offers significantly more freedom than a bound application. Any task that can be accomplished with bound forms and controls can be accomplished with a little VBA code that uses ActiveX data objects (ADO) or data access objects (DAO) to retrieve and manipulate data.

This chapter includes detailed examples of working with processes that manipulate database data using DAO, SQL, or ADO.

## Working with Data

ADO is the primary object model for accessing databases among Visual Basic programmers. Although ADO is a great architecture with its own set of advantages, it lacks native database connectivity in the context of Access databases, which is where DAO shines.

Other programming languages, like Visual Basic, Delphi, and others, require explicit connection to the data source they wish to alter, and they must do so every time the data or underlying schema has to be changed. This is due to the fact that, unlike Access, these apps have no built-in link to the data source.

DAO allows you to alter data and structure through an implicit connection that Access maintains with whichever Access database engine, ODBC, or ISAM data source it is connected to.

Because linked tables are a feature unique to Access, DAO is simply the best option for accessing Access databases. In fact, using any other data access model, it is impossible to do so natively.

DAO has evolved in lockstep with Jet and the Access database engine, and it is now the finest paradigm for interacting with and modifying Access database engine objects and structure. DAO enables faster access to Access databases than ADO or the Jet Replication Objects because of its tight connection with Access (JRO).

**This may all sound like marketing hype, but to qualify the advantages of DAO over other models, consider the following:**

- ADO connections are limited to one database at a time, but DAO allows you to link (connect) to several databases at the same time.
- The DAO allows you to open a table while blocking other users from opening the same table with write access using the dbDenyWrite parameter of the OpenRecordset function. The adModeShareDenyWrite constant of the ADO Connection object functions at the connection level, not at the table level.
- The DAO allows you to open a table while preventing other users from doing so using the dbDenyRead parameter of the OpenRecordset method. The adModeShareDenyRead constant of the ADO Connection object can only be set at the connection level.
- DAO allows you to create users and groups, but ADO does not allow you to specify the PID (Personal IDentifier).
- DAO allows you to access an object's implicit rights using AllPermissions attributes, whereas ADO does not have an AllPermissions property, forcing you to enumerate each user's groups.
- Using PrivDBEngine, DAO allows you to run a private session of the Access database engine; ADO does not.
- Using new complex data types, DAO allows you to create multi-value lookup fields. In an embedded record set, a multivalued lookup field is a single field that can store several values.

## Understanding DAO Objects

Working your way down the object hierarchy in code, you refer to objects in the DAO hierarchy.

A collection, as you may recall from our previous session, is a container for a group of items of the same type. Many DAO object collections contain yet more collections, thus you may need to navigate through numerous collections before reaching the item you wish to work on. This approach to accessing data and schema is extremely structured and predictable.

All DAO objects, with the exception of the DBEngine object, are contained within their own collections. Individual items that are named in the plural (ending with the letter s) are collections, whereas collections that are named in the singular (ending with the letter s) are individual objects.

A connection to a database or other data source is represented by the Database object. It belongs to the Databases collection of the Workspace object, which is a container for a collection of Database objects that represent connections to one or more databases.

## The DAO DBEngine object

The top-level object in the DAO model is represented by the DBEngine object, which is a property of the Access Application object. Although the DBEngine object contains all of the other objects in the DAO object hierarchy, you cannot create extra DBEngine instances, unlike many of the other DAO objects. Workspaces and Errors are the two main collections in the DBEngine object.

## The DAO Workspace object

A workspace is a defined user session that incorporates open databases and allows for transactions as well as user and group-level security (depending on the database format). Because you can have multiple workspaces open at the same time, the Workplaces collection is where all of your workspaces are stored.

The Microsoft Access workspace allows you to use the Microsoft Access database engine to access Microsoft Access database engine databases (ACCDB files created in Access 2007), Microsoft Jet databases (MDB files developed in prior versions), and ODBC or installable ISAM data sources. Microsoft Access workspaces support the following collections, objects, and functions.

## The DAO Database object

An open database is represented by a Database object.

**To manipulate an open database, you utilize the Database object and its methods and properties.**

- You can conduct an action query in any database by using the Execute method.
- To connect to an ODBC data source, set the Connect property in order to establish a connection. .
- To limit the amount of time it takes for a query to execute against an ODBC data source, use the QueryTimeout property.
- To find out how many records were affected by an action query, use the RecordsAffected property.
- To run a select query and produce a Recordset object, use the OpenRecordset function.
- To find out which version of a database engine built the database, use the Version property.

When you open a database with linked tables, the linkages to the specified external files are not automatically established. Either open a Recordset object or refer to the table's TableDef or Field objects. A trappable error happens if you are unable to link to these tables. You may also require authorization to access the database, or the database may be open only for another user. Trappable errors arise in these situations.

Local Database instances, as well as any open Recordset objects, are closed when a method that declares a Database object has been completed. Any outstanding updates will be lost, and any pending transactions will be rolled back, but there will be no trappable errors. Before exiting procedures that declare, you should explicitly complete any ongoing transactions or modifications and close Recordset and Database objects. There is no need to indicate the DBEngine object when you make use of the OpenDatabase method.

## The DAO TableDef object

The stored definition of a base table or a linked table is represented by a TableDef object (Microsoft Access workspaces only). A TableDef object and its methods and properties are used to manipulate a table definition. **You can, for example:**

- Examine the field and index structure of any database table, whether it's local, connected, or external.

- To set or return information about linked tables, use the Connect and SourceTableName properties, and to update connections to linked tables, use the RefreshLink method.
- To set or return validation conditions, use the ValidationRule and ValidationText attributes.
- Based on the table definition, use the OpenRecordset method to build a table, dynaset, dynamic, snapshot, or forward–only–type Recordset object.

## The DAO QueryDef object

In a Microsoft Access database engine database, a QueryDef object is a stored definition of a query.

Use the CreateQueryDef method to create a new QueryDef object. If you provide a string for the name argument or explicitly change the Name property of the new QueryDef object to a non–zero-length string in a Microsoft Access workspace, you will construct a permanent QueryDef that will be appended to the QueryDefs collection and stored to disk. A temporary QueryDef object is created by passing a zero-length string as the name parameter or explicitly setting the Name attribute to a zero-length string.

Temporary QueryDef objects are not saved to disk or added to the QueryDefs collection, unlike permanent QueryDef objects. Temporary QueryDef objects are useful for queries that need to be executed repeatedly during the run time but don't need to be saved to disk, especially if the SQL statements are created during run time.

## The DAO Recordset object

The records in a base table or the records returned by a query are represented by a Recordset object.

Recordset objects are used to manipulate data at the record level in a database. When you utilize DAO objects, you nearly exclusively manipulate data via Recordset objects. Records (rows) and fields are used to create all Recordset objects (columns).

**Recordset objects are divided into five categories:**

- **Table-type recordset:** is a coded representation of a base table that can be used to add, edit, or delete records from a single database table (Microsoft Access workspaces only).
- **Dynaset-type Recordset**: the result of a query with updatable records. A Dynaset Recordset object is a dynamic set of records that you can use to add, update, or delete entries from underlying database tables. A Dynaset recordset object can include fields from one or more database tables. An ODBC keyset cursor corresponds to this kind.
- **Snapshot-type Recordset**: a static copy of a set of records that you can use to find data or generate reports. A snapshot-type Recordset object can contain fields from one or more tables in a database but can't be updated. This type corresponds to an ODBC static cursor.
- **Dynamic-type Recordset**: a query result set from one or more base tables in which you can add, change, or delete records from a row-returning query.
- **Forward-only-type Recordset**: identical to a snapshot except that no cursor is provided. You can only scroll forward through records. This improves performance in situations where you only need to make a single pass through a result set. This type corresponds to an ODBC forward-only cursor.

## Navigating recordsets

A record set is a data structure that contains data in the form of rows and columns. Of course, the rows are records, and the columns are fields.

For ease of access, DAO provides methods for traversing a record set. You can use the vertical and horizontal scroll bars or the arrow keys to go up and down, left and right, through the Datasheet view of the recordset while viewing a table or query results as a datasheet.

The idea of a current record pointer is supported by Recordsets. Within a record set, only one record is current at a time. Your code only affects the current record whether you make changes to a record set or navigate through its rows.

## Deleting the record set end or beginning

Using the Delete method, you can remove an existing record from a table or dynaset-type Recordset object. A snapshot-type Recordset object does not allow you to delete records.

The Access database engine deletes the current record without warning or prompting when you use the Delete method. When you delete a record, the following record does not automatically become the current record; you must use the MoveNext method to advance to the next record. You will not be able to return to the deleted record once you have moved away from it.

## Counting records

You could make the mistake of selecting a criterion that yields an excessive number of records, which you can't process efficiently. The RecordCount attribute of the Recordset objects indicates how many records are there in the record set.

RecordCount is a useful tool for determining whether or not a record set contains any records. The only problem with RecordCount is that it penalizes performance on huge recordsets. The Recordset object counts the number of records in its collection, pausing execution until the count is finished.

## The DAO Field objects (recordsets)

A Field object is a representation of a data column with a common data type and set of characteristics. The specifications for the fields represented by Index, QueryDef, Relation, and TableDef objects can be found in the Fields collections of those objects. Field objects in a row of data, or in a record, are represented by the Fields collection of a Recordset object. The Field objects in a Recordset object are used to read and set values for the fields in the Recordset object's current record.

A Field object and its methods and properties are used to manipulate a field in a Microsoft Access workspace.

Data from the current record is displayed in the Field object's Value property when you access it as part of a Recordset object. You don't normally reference the Fields collection directly to change data in the

Recordset object; instead, you indirectly reference the Value property of the Field object in the Recordset object's Fields collection.

## Understanding ADO Objects

ActiveX Data Objects is a programming model, hence, it is not reliant on any particular back-end engine. However, OLE-DB is currently the only engine that supports the ADO model. There are several native OLE-DB Providers available, as well as an ODBC OLE-DB Provider. ADO is used in C++ and Visual Basic programs to connect to databases like SQL Server and others. It also works to connect to a cloud-based Azure SQL Database.

Through an OLE DB provider, Microsoft ActiveX Data Objects (ADO) allow your client applications to access and alter data from a variety of sources. Its main advantages are its simplicity, speed, low memory overhead, and tiny disk footprint. ADO provides essential functionalities for client/server and Web-based applications.

### The ADO Connection object

A Connection object represents a single data source session. It may be equivalent to an actual network connection to the server in a client/server database system. Some collections, methods, or properties of a Connection object may not be available depending on the capability enabled by the provider.

**The Connection and Recordset objects in ActiveX Data Objects (ADO) can be opened in a number of ways;**

- Setting the ConnectionString property to a valid Connect string then calling the Open() method. This connection string is known to be provider-dependent.
- Passing a valid Connect string to the first argument of the Open() method.
- Passing a valid Command object into the first argument of a Recordset's Open method.
- By passing the ODBC Data source name and if necessary, user-id and password to the Connection Object's Open() method.

## The ADO Command object

The ADO command object helps to describe a particular command that you would like to run against a data source. If you would like to query a database and return records in a Recordset object, run a bulk operation, or alter the structure of a database, use a Command object.

Note that some Command collections, methods, or properties may trigger an error when referred, depending on the capability of the provider.

## The ADO Recordset object

The ADO recordset object represents the complete collection of records from a base table or the output of a command. The Recordset object only refers to one record in the set as the current record at any one time.

To manipulate data from a provider, you need Recordset objects. When you use ADO, you virtually exclusively manipulate data via Recordset objects. Records (rows) and fields make up all Recordset objects (columns). Note that some Recordset methods or attributes may be unavailable depending on the capability supplied by the supplier.

# Writing VBA Code to Update a Table

Using a form to update data in a database is simple. Simply set controls on the form for the table fields that need to be updated.

## Updating fields in a record using ADO

When updating fields in a record with the use of the ADO, it saves any changes you make to a Recordset object's current row or a Record object's Fields collection.

Use the Update method to save any changes you've made to a Recordset object's current record since calling the AddNew method or modify any field values in an existing record since calling the AddNew method. Updates must be supported by the Recordset object.

## Updating a calculated control

To display the results of a calculation, you can utilize calculated controls on forms and reports in Access databases. Whenever the user changes the information, the total sales or tax amount must be recalculated.

## Checking the status of a record deletion

Access always confirms user-initiated deletions. A dialog box appears in Access, requesting the user to confirm the deletion. If the user confirms the deletion, the current record is removed from the form's record set and saved in memory temporarily so that the deletion can be reversed if necessary.

## Eliminating repetitive code

When creating the same or very similar code in several event procedures, it's advisable to move it to a standard module and call it from the event procedures, this can help prevent repeating the code often. Don't just put the code into a standard module because it's comparable, note that while it might be comparable, it might not be identical.

## Adding a new record

It's just as simple to add a record to a table as it is to update one. To add a new record to a table, use the AddNew method.

Using the AddNew method to edit record set data is identical to using the Edit method. AddNew is a function that generates a buffer for a new record. You assign values to fields in the new record once you run AddNew. The Update method appends a new record to the end of the record set before inserting it into the underlying table.

## Deleting a record

The ADO method Delete is used to delete a record from a table. The deletion confirmation dialog box is not displayed when records are deleted. Changes to data produced with code are generally not validated because doing so would disrupt workflow. There is no way to revert the modification to the underlying table once the record is destroyed. However, referential integrity is still enforced by Access. You'll get an error if you try to delete a record that violates referential integrity.

## Deleting related records in multiple tables

Before deleting records in multiple tables, you must be aware of the application's relationships while writing code to delete records. It's possible that the table containing the record you're deleting has a one-to-many link with another table.

# CHAPTER 29
# ADVANCED DATA ACCESS WITH VBA

In the previous chapter, you were introduced to DAO and ADO and also how to access data in tables and queries with the use of recordsets. In this chapter, you will bring to play what you have learned and also learn how you can show forms that you have chosen with the use of a combination of various techniques involving forms, Visual Basic code, and queries.

## Adding an Unbound Combo Box to a Form to Find Data

Selecting a value from a list rather than remembering a value to type can be faster and easier when entering data on forms in Access desktop databases. A drop-down menu also aids in ensuring that the value entered in a field is correct. A list control can display fixed values that you enter when you create the control, or it can connect to existing data.

When creating a form in Access, you can include a list box or a combo box that can be used to find a record when a value from the list is selected. Users will be able to find existing records more quickly without having to type a value into the Find dialog box.

The combo box control presents a list of options in a more compact format; the list is concealed until you click the drop-down arrow. You can also use a combo box to input a value that isn't on the list. The combination box control combines the functionality of a text box with a list box in this way.

## Using the Find a Record method

The FindRecord method finds a record in the bound record set of a form. This is the same as using the Ribbon's magnifying glass to locate a record in a datasheet.

**When searching for a datasheet,**

- Start by **selecting the column** you want to search, such as LastName.
- After that, you open the Find and Replace dialog box by clicking the magnifying glass (Find button) on the Ribbon and typing the name you want to find in the record set.
- When you insert the data, Access will move the datasheet record pointer to the row that has the data you must have inserted.

## Using a bookmark

Haven specified that the Find a Record method is a good way to search for data. The Bookmark Method is another lovely way to locate any data you might be in need of. A bookmark is a stationary pointer to a record in a record set. The AfterUpdate is a code that uses a bookmark to find the records in the record set of the form matching the search criteria in the process.

# Filtering a form

Although the FindRecord and FindFirst methods help you to rapidly discover a record that meets your criteria, they nevertheless display all of the other entries in a table or query record set, and they don't always keep all of the records together. Filtering a form allows you to see only the record or collection of records you desire while hiding all other records that don't match.

Filters are useful when you have a huge number of entries to go through and only want to see a subset of them that meet your criteria.

## Filtering with code

You can also choose to filter records with the use of a code. The first line of the code will configure the filter property of the form, which is exactly the same string that is used as the criteria passed to the FindFirst property of the record set. The second line of the code completes the task of turning on the filter. Note that when a filter is turned on, it is best to also provide a way by which you can turn it off. A small button beside the combo box is usually used to turn off the filter.

## Filtering with a query

You might want one form to control the other. Alternatively, you might want a record set to display data based on user-defined criteria. The best method to accomplish this is to utilize a parameter query.

## Creating a parameter query

Any query with criteria that references a variable, a function, or a form control are referred to as a parameter query. Create a select query, specify the query's criteria, then run the query to see that it works before changing the criteria to include the question you want to ask.

## Creating an interactive filter dialog box

Parameter queries have the drawback of being only applicable for simple parameters. Users must know exactly what to type into the parameter dialog box, and if they do so wrong, they will not see the expected results.

Creating a simple form, placing controls on the form, and referencing the controls from a query as parameters is a superior way. This means that the query gets its parameter values from the form's controls.

## Linking the dialog box to another form

The parameter dialog box can do a lot more than just create a value that can be referred to from a query, it also has code to open the form in which it can be found. The Requery method, on the other hand, ensures that the form displays new data if it has already been opened for example, if you use the dialog box to search for another record a second time.

# CHAPTER 30
# CUSTOMIZING THE RIBBON

Access, like all other Office products, has a Ribbon that may be customized. When compared to other Office apps, Access is a one-of-a-kind program. The key distinction is that Access is used to construct apps, whereas Word and Excel are used to create documents.

Access has its own set of customizing options for the ribbon. You'll have an advantage with Access if you've altered the Ribbon in other Office apps because you'll be familiar with the XML. If you're completely new to Ribbon customization, I will be detailed enough so you can understand perfectly.

## The Ribbon Hierarchy

The Ribbon is a hierarchical structure with a complex structure. The tabs that go along the top of the Ribbon are at the top level.

**Each tab is divided into groups, each of which has one or more controls.**

- **Tabs**: Tabs are the highest level of the Ribbon structure. Tabs are used to organize the most basic activities into logical categories.
- **Ribbons**: In the Ribbon hierarchy, groups are the second-highest object. Groups are used to logically divide operations enabled by a Ribbon tab. They can comprise any of a variety of different types of controls.
- **Controls**: On the Home tab, there are a number of controls within each group. The controls in a group are usually related to one another, but this isn't always the case.

## Controls for Access Ribbons

Buttons, text boxes, labels, separators, checkboxes, and toggle buttons can all be found on a ribbon. Access has a number of unique controls that you may utilize on your custom Ribbons. These controls are available in the default Ribbon as well as customized Ribbons you create for your applications.

# SplitButton

A SplitButton in Access is a button that may be divided vertically or horizontally into two separate components. The control's left (or top) side functions like any other button and responds to a single click. The button's right (or bottom) side has an arrow that, when clicked, displays a list of single-select alternatives.

## Menu

In many aspects, the SplitButton and Menu are comparable. When you click them, they both reveal a list and display a list of single-select items. The key distinction is that a SplitButton is divided into two parts (the button that performs the default action and the menu), whereas a Menu simply lowers down the list when clicked.

## Gallery

Access makes significant use of gallery controls to display features like formatting controls and font selection.

## Button

When you click a button, it performs an action. It does not provide menu or gallery options, but it can launch a dialog box with additional settings.

## ToggleButton

The ToggleButton is a unique form of button control that is used to set the application's state or condition.

ToggleButtons can be toggled between two states which are on and off. When a ToggleButton is turned off, it shows on the Ribbon as a regular button. The background color of a ToggleButton change to reflect its state when it is clicked to set the on state, the ScreenTip caption may change also.

## ComboBox

The ComboBox control on a form is quite similar to the ComboBox control on the Ribbon. It's a cross between a text box and a list box in that you can input directly into it or use the control's down arrow to see a list of possibilities.

## CheckBox

A CheckBox control resembles a check box on a form in appearance and behavior. A check mark displays in a CheckBox when it is clicked; otherwise, the box appears empty.

## Special Ribbon features

There are two unique qualities of the Ribbon that are worth mentioning. Some controls include SuperTips, which can increase the amount of data displayed in a ScreenTip.

## SuperTips

A SuperTip is a control that displays the text you define, assisting the user in understanding the control's function.

## Collapsing the Ribbon

On the screen, the Ribbon is constantly open. When users are working with an application, the Ribbon, with all of its buttons and tabs, can get in the way. Ctrl+F1 or double-clicking any tab is the simplest way to collapse the ribbon.

- A **single click** on any collapsed tab restores the Ribbon, but only for a short time; the Ribbon will "auto collapse" until you **double-click** a tab **(or press Ctrl+F1)** to restore it to its pinned state.

# Editing the Default Ribbon

Changes to the Ribbon are saved in Access on the system where they were made, however, the Ribbon Designer has an option to export adjustments.

- To open the Ribbon Designer, **right-click** anywhere on the Ribbon and select **Customize the Ribbon** from the shortcut menu.

Once the menu is opened, you are free to customize the ribbon as you wish.

**Note that if you would like to export the changes you must have made simply;**

- Click on **the Import/Export button underneath the Customize the Ribbon list**, this will then export the changes you have made to the Ribbon in the form of an external file.

It's simple to apply custom Ribbon changes to all users working with an Access 2022 application by using a customization file. It's also an excellent way to save a copy of your changes in case you need to reapply them later. For example, you may customize the Ribbon exactly how you want it to appear to your users, export the customization, and then restore the Ribbon to its original configuration so that you have access to all Ribbon capabilities during your design process.

# Working with the Quick Access Toolbar

The Quick Access toolbar is located right above the File tab in the upper left corner of the main Access screen. The Quick Access toolbar can be completely customized. With the Customize Quick Access Toolbar option, you can hide or show a list of default controls, some of which are hidden.

**The easiest way to add a command to the Quick Access toolbar is to**

- Locate **the command** on the Ribbon, **right-click it**, and then select **Add to Quick Access Toolbar** from the shortcut menu that appears. Access adds the selected item to the rightmost position in the Quick Access toolbar.
- Select **More Commands** from the shortcut menu to open the Customize the Quick Access Toolbar screen for more freedom when changing the Quick Access toolbar.

The Quick Access toolbar gives you a convenient way to control which commands users have access to when using your Access apps. Backing up the current database, converting the current database to another Access data format, inspecting database properties, and linking tables are all functions available through the Quick Access toolbar.

To change an item from the left to the right list, use the Add and Remove buttons in the Quick Access Toolbar Designer. You can't add the same command to the Quick Access toolbar more than once, once it's been added to the Quick Access toolbar.

The Quick Access Toolbar Designer additionally has up and down arrows to the right of the selected list that you can use to reorganize the Quick Access toolbar commands from left to right.

## Developing Custom Ribbons

The Ribbon Designer and Quick Access Toolbar Designer make customizing the Access user interface a breeze. In Access, there is no programmable object model for ribbons. USysRibbons is a special table that contains XML declarations that describe ribbon customizations. The information found in the XML is used by Access to compose and render the Ribbon on the screen.

### The Ribbon creation process

**The process below highlights Ribbon creation:**

- Design **the Ribbon** and compose **the XML** that defines the Ribbon.
- Write VBA callback routines (described in the following section) that support Ribbon's operations.
- Create **the USysRibbons table**.
- Provide **a Ribbon name** and add the **custom Ribbon's XML** to the USysRibbons table.
- Specify the **custom Ribbon's name** in the Access Options dialog box.

## Using VBA callbacks

A callback is a piece of code that is passed to a different object to be processed. Each procedure you develop to support Ribbon operations is given to Access' "Ribbon processor," which executes the Ribbon's activities. This isn't the same as the event-driven code you've been using in Access.

When you click a button on a form, the code in the button's Click event method is instantly triggered. The callback procedure for a Ribbon is linked to the Ribbon, but it is performed internally by Access and does not run in response to a Ribbon click.

## Creating a Custom Ribbon

There are about five steps used in describing the process of creating a custom ribbon.

**These steps are explained in detail in the section below;**

**Step 1: Design the Ribbon and build the XML**

The first step in building a new Access Ribbon, as with other database objects, is to carefully design it. The XML document you create for your Ribbon should be identical to the design you've created. Visualizing how the Ribbon will look based on the XML behind it is maybe the most difficult component of composing the Ribbon XML.

A Ribbon XML document has no visual indications that indicate how the Ribbon will appear when rendered in Access. When it comes to Ribbon customization, the experience will be your best guide and sometimes trial and error is the only way to obtain the desired result. Open your favorite XML editor to build the XML that will define the new Ribbon elements.

**Step 2: Write the callback routines**

You must reference the Microsoft Office 16.0 Object Library in the References dialog box before creating any callback code for Ribbon controls, or the VBA interpreter will have no notion of how to handle references to Ribbon controls.

Callback routines are similar to event procedures, except they do not react to control events directly. Each callback routine has its own "signature" that must be followed in order for the Ribbon processor to discover and use it. Despite the fact that these callbacks support the same onAction control property, the signatures change due to the differences in the controls. To distinguish it from callback processes for other controls, the callback method for control is frequently named after the control.

The declaration of this procedure fits the prototype for the onAction callback procedure of button control. This procedure also includes a comment that specifies the Ribbon control that calls the routine, while it isn't essential.

Callback routines must be declared in a standard module with the Public attribute, or the Ribbon process will not notice them. As long as the procedure's declaration matches the control's onAction signature, you can call callback routines whatever you like. The procedure's name must obviously match the value you set to the control's onAction attribute, and documenting the procedure's link to a Ribbon control is extremely useful when it comes time to change the Ribbon or the callback.

**Step 3: Create the USysRibbons table**

To see if there are any custom Ribbons in the current database application, Access looks for a table named USysRibbons. This table is not present by default; if it is, it contains the XML that defines the application's custom Ribbons.

Since USysRibbons is a table, it's possible that your Access database has the definitions for a variety of custom Ribbons. At any given time, however, only one custom Ribbon can be active.

The ID field in the USysRibbons table just keeps track of the table's Ribbons, RibbonName is a Long Text field that contains the XML that defines the Ribbon, whereas RibbonXML is a Long Text field that contains the XML that defines the Ribbon.

If you change USysRibbons, make sure the three essential fields aren't removed or renamed (ID, RibbonName, and RibbonXML). For your custom Ribbons to work, these three fields must exist in USysRibbons and be labeled correctly.

**Step 4: Add XML to USysRibbons**

You can now put your XML into the USysRibbons database. In the Datasheet view, open the USysRibbons table. Enter rbnMessages in the RibbonName box and then move the pointer to the RibbonXml field.

Copy the XML you prepared in Step 1 and paste it into USysRibbons' RibbonXml field. Open the XML file in XML Notepad and click View

Source to output the XML to Windows Notepad if you're using XML Notepad. After that, copy the XML and put it into USysRibbons.

**Step 5: Specify the custom Ribbon property**

Before restarting the application, go to Current Database Properties, scroll down to the Ribbons and Toolbar Options section, and choose the new Ribbon's name from the Ribbon Name combo box. The names of custom Ribbons in USysRibbons that were in the table when Access started are not included in the combo box's list, nor is the name of the new Ribbon.

The names of custom Ribbons in USysRibbons that were in the table when Access started are not included in the combo box's list, thus it does not include the name of the new Ribbon. You can either type the name of the Ribbon into the combo box or restart the application and let Access find it in USysRibbons.

When you close the Access Options dialog box after selecting a new Ribbon Name, Access warns you that the changes won't take effect until you close and reopen the database.

# The Basic Ribbon XML

The Ribbon (XML) component allows you to use XML to customize a ribbon. If you want to customize the ribbon in a way that the Ribbon (Visual Designer) item doesn't allow, use the Ribbon (XML) item. From the Add New Item dialog box, you can add a Ribbon (XML) item to any Office project.

## Adding Ribbon Controls

**In this section, we will be looking at some Ribbon controls that you can include in your document;**

## Specifying imageMso

The imageMso attribute on most Ribbon controls specifies the picture associated with the control. Each Ribbon control in the Office 2022 applications has an imageMso value connected with it. You put these data in your custom Access Ribbon controls and give them a label that explains what the control is for.

To find the imageMso for a certain Ribbon control, open a specific Ribbon in the Customize the Ribbon window. Then choose the Ribbon category containing the Ribbon command from the dropdown in the upper left of the designer, and hover the mouse over the command's entry in the list.

## The Label controls

The Label control is by far the simplest and most straightforward to incorporate into a Ribbon. A Ribbon label is quite similar to a label added to an Access form. It holds text that is either hardcoded or generated via a callback method.

## The Button control

The Button control is one of the most basic and useful of all the Ribbon controls. A button has only three attributes: a label, an imageMso attribute for setting the button's image, and a onAction attribute for naming the callback procedure.

## Separators

A separator is a visual element that splits a set of things. Separators have no text and appear in a group as a vertical line. They're not particularly intriguing on their own, but they graphically separate controls that would otherwise be too close together within a group.

## The CheckBox control

The CheckBox control is useful for allowing the user to choose from a variety of alternatives. The user can select any of the checkboxes inside a group without affecting other selections, as CheckBox controls are not mutually exclusive.

## The Dropdown control

The DropDown control is more complicated than the previously discussed labels, buttons, and checkboxes. It provides a menu of options from which the user can select. As a result, a DropDown has a variety of appearance-related properties.

The DropDown control requires the user to select an item from the list before displaying it in the control. The user cannot directly alter the value of the DropDown control, despite the fact that it looks like a ComboBox control.

The ComboBox control works similarly to a DropDown, with the exception that the user can alter the value directly in the control and is not confined to the list items. List Boxes and Combo Boxes are similar to DropDown controls and CombBox controls that you might see on a form.

## The SplitButton Control

The SplitButton control comes in handy when the user has a variety of options to choose from, but one option is utilized more frequently than the others. The menu> and /menu> tags hold the items on a SplitButton's list. The SplitButton's list includes any controls that appear within these tags.

## Attaching Ribbons to forms and Reports

You can always see the Ribbon elements you've generated so far. You'll frequently want the Buttons, DropDowns, and Menus you set on the Ribbon to be accessible at all times. However, you can have some Ribbon elements that you only want to show in certain circumstances. When a form or report is active, Access provides an easy way to display Ribbons and this can be done with the use of the RibbonName property that you can configure in either the Property Sheet or the VBA.

## Removing the Ribbon Completely

**You might have a need to remove the Ribbon completely; simply follow the steps below.**

- Build **a new table called** USysRibbons if you haven't already done so.
- If you will be creating the USysRibbons table for the first time, including the three fields: ID (AutoNumber), RibbonName (Text), and RibbonXML (Memo).
- Create **a new record** with the RibbonName set to Blank. It doesn't really matter what you call it.
- Add the following **XML to the RibbonXML column**:
- Restart the **database**.

- Select **the File tab** and then click on the **Options button** in the Backstage.
- Click the **Current Database tab** and scroll to the **Ribbon and Toolbar Options area**.
- In the Ribbon and Toolbar Options area, set the **Ribbon Name to Blank** (the same name you specified for the RibbonName column in the third step).
- Close and have the database reopened.

# CHAPTER 31
# PREPARING YOUR ACCESS APPLICATION FOR DISTRIBUTION

Not only does properly distributing your application make it easier for end-users to install and use it, but it also makes it easier for you, the application's developer, to update and maintain it. This chapter discusses the challenges that come up when it comes to delivering Access apps.

## Defining the Current Database Options

A variety of options exist in Access databases that make the distribution process easier.

**These database parameters can be accessed by**

- Going to **File Options** and then to the Current Database tab.

Database options allow you to configure certain features of your program, decreasing the amount of starting code required. Before you deploy an Access program, it's critical to organize these settings correctly.

## Application options

This section describes the various options that can be explored in the options of an application.

## Application Icon

Your application's title bar and Windows task switcher (Alt+Tab) will display the icon you specify in the Application Icon box. If you don't give an icon for your application, Access will use the default Access icon, therefore you may wish to provide an application-specific icon.

## Display Form

When Access starts, the form you choose in the Display Form dropdown list opens automatically. The Form Load event of the display form fires when the form loads, eliminating the requirement for an Autoexec macro.

## Display Status Bar

- To remove the status bar at the bottom of the Access screen, deselect the **Display Status Bar check box.**

## Document Window Options

In this section you can choose how the forms and reports will be displayed in your distributed application. The options that are available to you include; Overlapping windows which keep the view of the former version of Access, and Tabled documents which make use of a single-document interface that looks much like the recent version of famous web browsers.

## Use Access Special Keys

If you choose this option, users of your application will be able to bypass various security controls by using accelerator keys particular to the Access environment, such as unhiding the Navigation pane.

When distributing the application, choose the Access Special Keys check box to prohibit users from bypassing the options you choose; otherwise, users may accidentally reveal the Navigation pane or VBA code, causing confusion and other issues.

## Compact on Close

When you check the Compress on Close checkbox, Access will compact and fix your database automatically when you close it. While some Access developers prefer to utilize Compact on Close to undertake this maintenance process every time a user interacts with a database, others believe it is unnecessary.

It's important to keep in mind that compacting a huge database can take a long time. Furthermore, Compact on Close has no effect on the backend database. The Compact and Repair Database option may be of little use to your users unless your application uses the front end for temporary tables or other procedures that cause the front end to bloat.

## Remove Personal Information from File Properties on Save

When you check this box, the personal information from the file properties is immediately removed when you save the file. For this modification to take effect, you must close and reopen the existing database.

### Use Windows Theme Controls on Forms

If you check this box, the form/report controls will utilize your system's Windows theme. This option is only available if you are using a Windows theme other than the default.

### Enable Layout View

When you right-click an object tab, the Enable Layout View check box shows or hides the Layout View button on the Access status bar and in the shortcut menus that appear.

## Enable Design Change for Tables in Datasheet View

The Enable Design Changes for Tables in the Datasheet View check box lets you make structural changes to your tables without having to go to Design view.

### Check for Truncated Number Fields

Checking this option makes numbers show as ##### when the column is too narrow to display the whole value. Unchecking this option truncates values that are too broad to be displayed in the datasheet, which means that users see only a part of the column's value when the column is too narrow and might misinterpret the column's contents.

## Picture Property Storage Format

You can specify how graphic files are saved in the database under Picture Property Storage Format.

## Navigation options

You can define parameters that affect how users explore your database as an application in the Navigation section.

### The Display Navigation Pane check box

When the Display Navigation Pane option is deselected the Navigation pane is hidden from the user when the computer starts up.

### The Navigation Options button

When the Navigation pane is accessible at startup, Access 2022 allows you to choose which database objects are shown to users.

- The Navigation Options dialog box appears when you click the **Navigation Options button.** It allows you to change the categories and groups that appear in the Navigation pane.

## Ribbon and toolbar options

When accessing your database as an application, the Ribbon and Toolbar Options section allows you to design custom Ribbons and toolbars. For any of the options in this section to take effect, you must close and reopen the current database.

### Ribbon Name

This option allows you to create a personalized Ribbon. If you don't provide Access a Ribbon name, it defaults to the built-in Ribbon, which may or may not be acceptable for your application.

### Shortcut Menu Bar

The default menu for shortcut menus is changed to a menu bar that you select when you set the Shortcut Menu Bar. It is usually preferable to have bespoke shortcut menus with functionality relevant to your application.

### Allow Full Menus

When the Allow Full Menus box is checked, Access displays all of the commands in its menus rather than just the ones that are often used.

### Allow Default Shortcut Menus

When a user right-clicks an object in the Navigation pane or a control on a form or report, the Allow Default Shortcut Menus setting governs whether Access shows its own default shortcut menus.

### Name AutoCorrect Options

Various developers have run across issues with altering the names of fundamental database objects on a regular basis. In Access 2022, Microsoft implemented the Name AutoCorrect capability to help developers avoid the difficulties that unavoidably arise when database objects are renamed.

## Developing the Application

Defining requirements, establishing database objects and writing code, developing documentation, and testing an application are all common steps in the development process. If you're making an app for yourself, the needs are generally already in your thoughts. You can also not see the necessity to codify the requirements since you're so familiar with the problem you're trying to solve. Consider putting them down anyway to help you clarify your thoughts and spot any potential issues early on in the development process.

### Building to a specification

All databases are designed to help people address a certain problem. The issue could be that they are unable to access or obtain data in the format that they require. The easiest way to ensure success is to plan out the application thoroughly before creating any tables, queries, or forms. Only by following a plan will you be able to determine how successfully the app will handle the user's problem.

# Creating documentation

It is essential to make proper documentation before creating an application, with this you are sure that nothing will go wrong with the application.

## Documenting the code you write

Changes or enhancements to the application may be required over time. Even if you're the one making the changes, the passage of time since you first developed the code may mean you're having difficulty comprehending what it accomplishes. As a result, it's a good idea to have the code you've developed documented.

## Documenting the application

The applications you deliver to end-users should come with documentation that explains how to use them. End-user documentation does not require to include details of the user interface's core structure or logic. It should, however, clarify how the forms and reports function, give printouts of sample reports and identify items users should avoid (for example, modifying current data).

## Testing the application before distribution

Consider how you'll test the various components of your app as you create it. Because you'll still remember the functionalities of the form or report if you plan your tests during the design phase, this is the perfect time to do so. As soon as it's feasible, carry out your test plans. Then run them once more when the project is finished and you're ready to distribute it. The first time you use them, you can be sure you designed the object correctly. Executing them at the end ensures that no bugs are introduced by future changes.

## Polishing Your Application

Spend some time polishing your application after it has been properly tested and appears to be ready for distribution.

# Giving your application a consistent look and feel

The first thing you need to do is to establish some visual design guidelines and apply them to your app. If you want your applications to have a professional look and feel, this stage is critical.

**The following are examples of design decisions you might want to ask yourself;**

- Will the text boxes be elevated, chiseled, flat with a border, flat without a border, or sunken?
- What color should the back of text boxes be?
- What color are the forms going to be?
- To divide related things, will you utilize chiseled borders or a sunken or raised border?
- What size buttons will there be on forms?
- When the form opens, which control will be the center of attention?
- What method will be used to determine the tab order?
- For text boxes, what will your Enter key property be?
- Will you make a visible distinction between multi-select list boxes and those that aren't?
- Will you add a visual indicator when the Limit to List property of combo boxes is set?

## Adding common professional components

Aspects of most professional applications are similar. The splash screen, an application switchboard, and an About box are the most frequent components. These may appear to be minor features, but they can significantly improve the appeal of your application.

## A splash screen

The splash screen not only improves an application's perceived speed but also gives it a clean, professional appearance from the first time a user uses it.

## An application switchboard

An application switchboard is a navigational tool that helps users navigate around the application's functionalities and forms. You may also utilize the switchboard as a navigation form, displaying other forms with the help of buttons.

## An About box

The About box contains information about your organization and copyright, as well as the name of the application and its current version. The About box serves as legal notification of ownership and makes it easier to support your application by providing easy access to version information to your users.

## The status bar

The status bar displays information about the state of the object you're working on by default. The SysCmd function in Access allows you to display messages in the status bar. You can show your own messages on the left side of the status bar using SysCmd. Since it doesn't require any user involvement, the status bar is an excellent area to display non-critical messages.

## A progress meter

In the status bar at the bottom of the main Access window, there is a built-in progress meter. This progress meter is a rectangle that extends horizontally while Access executes a long-running process.

In order to set up and use a progress meter, you must first initialize it, then set the meter to the next value.

## Making the application easy to start

To make an application start with ease it's best to have it pinned to the Windows Start screen. When used correctly, a program icon gives the impression that the application is separate from Access and that it has the same status as Word, Excel, or other task-oriented programs.

# Bulletproofing an Application

Bulletproofing an application entails making it more stable and less vulnerable to problems caused by inexperienced users. Bulletproofing entails catching user-caused problems including improper data entering, attempting to launch a function while the program isn't ready, and allowing users to click the Calculate button before all relevant data has been entered.

## Using error trapping on all Visual Basic procedures

For most data entry errors (for example, characters entered into a currency field), Access has built-in error processing; however, automatic error processing for VBA code errors does not exist. Every VBA procedure should have error handling procedures.

Any untrapped error discovered in your code causes the program to stop completely when executed at run time. Your users will be unable to recover from such a crash, and significant data loss may result. After an application error, your users must restart the program.

## Maintaining usage logs

The user's name or ID, the date, and the time are all captured in usage logs. They provide useful information, especially in the event of an error. Although you can quickly accumulate too much data, a well-designed usage log will allow you to discover whether a particular sort of problem always appears when a specific user interacts with the system or when a specific query is conducted. Usage logs are also a great approach to conducting a postmortem on an application that isn't working properly. Instead of relying on the user's explanation of the error, you can observe exactly what happened at the moment an error occurred if you have logged in each subroutine and function that might fail at run time.

## Separating tables from the rest of the application

Forms, reports, queries, modules, and macros should all be kept distinct from table objects. Separate code and data database files should be used in all properly distributed programs, especially those designed for network use.

## Building bulletproof forms

**Below are the steps to be taken to ensure the forms in your application are virtually bulletproofed:**

- Consider removing the Control Box, Min, Max, and Close buttons from the form at design time.

- Always put a Close or Return button on forms to return the user to a previous or next form in the application.
- Set the ViewsAllowed property of the form to Form at design time.
- Use modal forms where appropriate.
- Use your own navigation buttons that check for EOF (end of file) and BOF (beginning of the file) conditions on bound forms.
- Use the StatusBarText property on every control, to let the user know what's expected in each control.

## Validating user input

Simply validating anything the user enters into the database is one of the most important bulletproofing strategies. Error data input can be captured during data entry, which is a crucial safety to include in your apps.

## Using the /runtime option

When you open a database in Access' runtime mode, all of the interface elements that allow you to edit objects are hidden. In reality, a user is unable to view the Navigation pane while in runtime mode.

If you choose to make use of the runtime option, make sure your app has a launch form that offers users access to any items you want them to see.

## Encrypting or encoding a database

When data security is crucial, one of the first steps you should take is to encrypt or encode the database. The data and contents of Access databases are protected by robust encryption.

**Follow the steps below to have an Access database encrypted;**

- Open an **existing database** exclusively.
- Select the **File button** in the upper-left corner of the screen, then choose the **Encrypt with Password command** on the info tab.

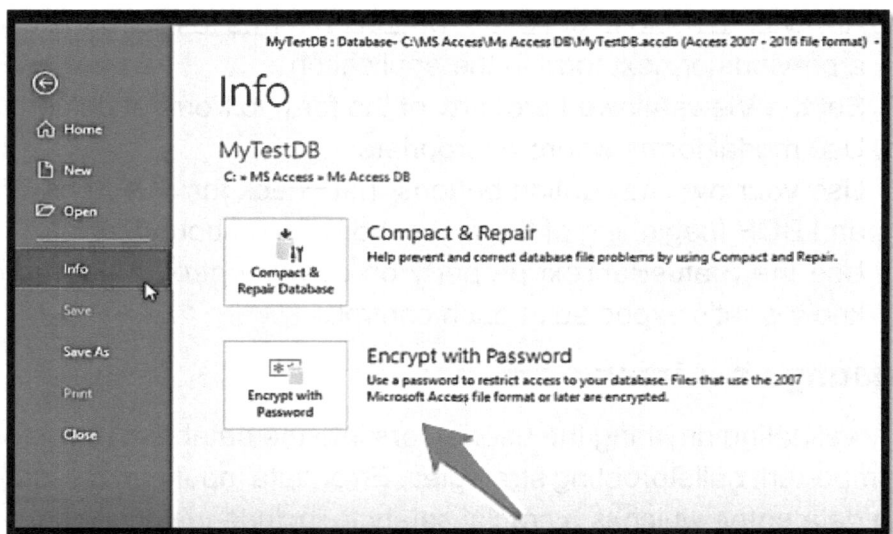

- In the Password field, insert **the password** that you would like to make use of in securing the database.
- Type **the same password again** in the Verify field and then click on the **OK button**.

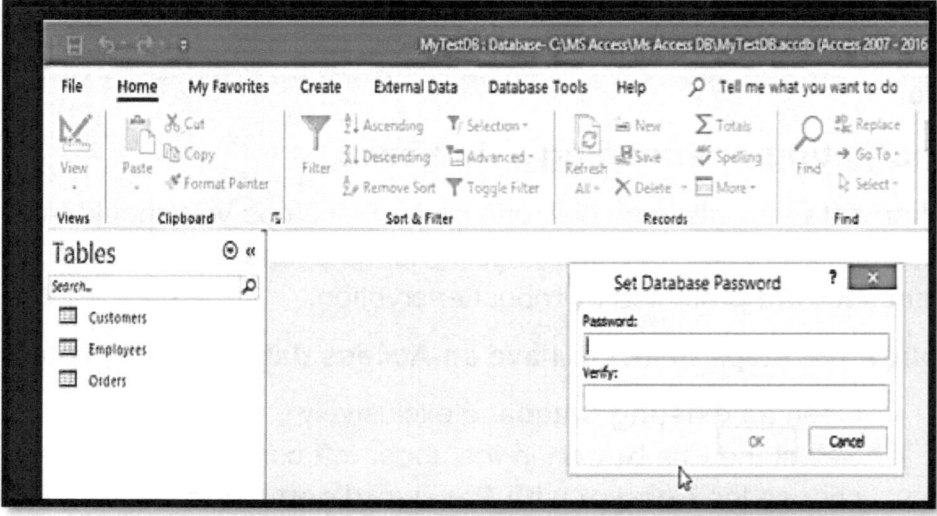

## Removing a database password

Run through the steps below if you would like to remove the password from an encrypted database;

- Open **the encrypted database**.

- Select **the File button** in the upper-left corner of the screen and choose the **Decrypt Database command** on the info tab
- Insert the **database password** and click on the **OK button**.

## Protecting Visual Basic code

By defining a password for the Visual Basic project you want to secure, you can restrict access to the VBA code in your application. Users are requested to input the database password each time they try to see the Visual Basic code in the database when you specify a database password for a project.

Distributing your database as an ACCDE file is a more secure way of safeguarding your application's code, forms, and reports. Access compiles all code modules, eliminates all editable source code, and compacts the database when you save it as an ACCDE file.

## Securing the Environment

Unauthorized users must be kept out of a major Access application. Multiple degrees of security are provided via the built-in user-level security mechanism. Note that only the MDB database format supports user-level security. Other methods of data security, such as password-protected strong encryption, are available in the ACCDB format but are not available in the MDB format.

## Setting startup option in code

The choices you choose in the Access Options dialog box's Current Database tab apply to every user who logs into the database on a global basis There are times when you want to control these options through startup code instead of allowing the global settings to control the application. Almost all of the options in the Access Options dialog box can be changed using code.

You can set or reset any of these properties using VBA code on the splash screen or switchboard form, depending on the username (and password) provided on the login form.

## Disabling startup bypass

Bypassing your startup routines, you'll be able to see the application's design and any items concealed behind the user interface.

Fortunately, the Access designers foresaw the requirement for bulletproofing an application starting by including the AllowBypassKey database property. This parameter disables (or enables) the Shift key bypass at the application starting and takes True or False values.

**The code to implement the AllowBypassKey attribute is as follows:**

```
Public Sub SetBypass(bFlag As Boolean)
  Dim db As DAO.Database
  Dim pBypass As DAO.Property
  Const sKEYNAME As String = "AllowBypassKey"
  Set db = CurrentDb
  On Error Resume Next
    Set pBypass = db.Properties(sKEYNAME)
  On Error GoTo 0
  If pBypass Is Nothing Then
    Set pBypass = db.CreateProperty(sKEYNAME, dbBoolean, Flag)
    db.Properties.Append pBypass
  Else
    pBypass.Value = bFlag
  End If
End Sub
```

## Setting property values

**If a startup property does not exist, the following function sets its value, generating and appending the property to the Properties collection:**

```
Public Function SetStartupProperty(sPropName As String, _
```

```
        ePropType As DAO.DataTypeEnum, vPropValue As Variant) As Boolean
    Dim db As DAO.Database
    Dim prp As DAO.Property
    Dim bReturn As Boolean
    Set db = CurrentDb
    On Error Resume Next
      Set prp = db.Properties(sPropName)
      If prp Is Nothing Then
    Set prp = db.CreateProperty(sPropName, ePropType, vPropValue)
      If prp Is Nothing Then
        bReturn = False
      Else
        db.Properties.Append prp
        bReturn = True
      End If
    Else
      prp.Value = vPropValue
      bReturn = True
    End If
    SetStartupProperty = bReturn
        End Function
```

It's simple to use SetStartupProperty(), but you must know the exact property name and data type of the property before calling it ().

## Getting property values

It's far easier to determine the worth of a property than it is to determine the value of a property. The property is returned by the Properties collection, while the value is returned by the Value property.

**The following is the syntax for getting the value of the AppTitle property;**

    On Error Resume Next

    GetAppTitle = CurrentDb.Properties("AppTitle").Value

# CHAPTER 32
# INTEGRATING ACCESS WITH SHAREPOINT

The option to launch your Access application as a SharePoint website is an exciting feature of Microsoft Access 2022.

**In this chapter,** we'll look at the different methods for converting Access databases to SharePoint. This chapter explains what SharePoint is and how it can be used to help organizations share and collaborate data.

## Introducing SharePoint

SharePoint is a web-based collaboration system that enables corporate teams to collaborate by using workflow applications, "list" databases, and other web elements and security features. SharePoint also allows companies to regulate information access and automate workflow procedures across corporate groups.

SharePoint allows information workers in all verticals, large and small, to boost their productivity and visibility. SharePoint's capabilities revolve around an intranet-based cross-collaboration environment that allows for safe sharing, document management, and workflow collaboration, among other things.

SharePoint is a web-based platform that allows users to submit documents and share them with those who need to access them right away. They can also have their own personal storage space, known as a OneDrive, where no one can see a document or file they upload until they "share" or give other users access to it.

This simplifies the process of allowing a group of coworkers to view a published document but it doesn't have to be. The above-mentioned approval and workflow tools can be used to manage how documents are exchanged and how employees work with data in their businesses.

Email can also be used to send links to shared documents or collaborative areas, making it simple for users to find what they need.

# Understanding SharePoint Sites

**This section provides an insight into the two commonly used SharePoint sites;**

## SharePoint documents

SharePoint is a web-based platform that allows users to upload documents and share them with others that need immediate access. They can also have their own personal storage space, known as a OneDrive, where no one can see a document or file they upload until they "share" or provide access to other users.

This makes permitting a group of coworkers to read a published document easier but it doesn't have to be that way. The approval and workflow technologies listed above can be used to govern how documents are transmitted and how employees work with data in their companies.

Users can also send links to shared papers or collaborative spaces via email, making it easier for them to discover what they need.

From the time files are added to a list until they are removed or deleted, SharePoint keeps track of them. A document can be shared by anyone with written access to a SharePoint site. SharePoint keeps track of when a document is checked in or out, as well as who made the modifications. If required, SharePoint can even be told to roll back document changes to a previous version.

This document-sharing paradigm is most typically used to distribute information across enterprises, allowing users of the SharePoint site to collaborate.

## SharePoint lists

A SharePoint list is one of SharePoint's most powerful and adaptable capabilities, but its potential is sometimes neglected. One reason for this is that lists are frequently thought of as a feature that only IT experts or individuals with significant technical knowledge can utilize, yet SharePoint lists are actually not that difficult for power users and citizen developers to use.

Multiple lists are easily supported in SharePoint, allowing an organization to add as many lists as it needs. Unfortunately, unlike Access tables, SharePoint lists are not relational; there is no mechanism to link data from two different SharePoint lists or to query several SharePoint lists for relevant information. SharePoint lists, on the other hand, can be connected or imported into Access. SharePoint integration

## Sharing Data between Access and SharePoint

Going into an Access program, linking to SharePoint lists, and then building forms and reports based on those linked tables is all it takes to create Access apps with SharePoint data. Access treats a linked SharePoint list like any other linked data source.

### Linking to Sharepoint lists

Access can link to a SharePoint list and use the data as it would any other linked data source.

**To link to a SharePoint list, follow these steps:**

- Click **the New Data Source** then click on **From Online Services >SharePoint List** in the Import & Link group on the External Data tab
- Click on the **"Link to the data source by creating a linked table"** option, and click **Next**
- Insert your **username and password**
- Add a **checkmark** next to each list you want to be linked, and then select **OK**.

## Importing SharePoint lists

When you import a SharePoint list into Access, you may simply take a snapshot of the list and bring the data in as a separate unconnected table. An imported list, unlike a linked SharePoint list, will not be instantly updated with new SharePoint data.

**Follow the steps below to Import a SharePoint list;**

- Choose the **New Data Source** drop-down button in the Import & Link group on the External Data tab.

- Click on **From Online Services >SharePoint List** from the list of online services.
- In the top portion of this dialog box, either select a recently **visited SharePoint site** or enter **a new destination SharePoint URL**; then select the Import option.
- Insert t**he appropriate permissions** to import a SharePoint list.
- Add a **checkmark** next to each list you want to be imported, and then select **OK.**

## Exporting Access tables to SharePoint

Data must occasionally be transferred from Access to SharePoint so that SharePoint users have access to the same information as Access users. **The steps below will show you how to export a table from Access to a SharePoint list.**

- Right-click **the table** you want to export in the Navigation pane, and then **select Export > SharePoint List**.
- Insert or select the **target SharePoint site URL**.
- Choose the **OK button**.
- Select the **Close button** in Access to dismiss the Export to SharePoint dialog box.

## Moving Access Tables to SharePoint

An alternative to just exporting Access tables to SharePoint is to move all of the tables in an Access program to SharePoint in a single export operation and then link the new SharePoint lists back to the Access application. In a single operation, all of the tables in the Access database are migrated to SharePoint and then linked back to Access.

Moving Access Tables to SharePoint has the advantage of allowing you to build out your data model in Access, utilizing all of the simple table creation tools, and then upsize the data model to SharePoint. Any modifications performed in SharePoint will be immediately visible in Access once the data is in SharePoint.

## Using SharePoint Templates

The SharePoint templates in Access 2022 support critical business functions such as Contacts, Tasks, Issues, and Events.

This alternate strategy involves creating fully new SharePoint lists within the Access environment, rather than exporting existing Access tables to SharePoint or linking to SharePoint lists. Access 2022 has SharePoint list templates that include all of the information needed to create SharePoint lists, such as column names, data types, and other list features. This is primarily intended to save time for anyone who needs to quickly create a new list in SharePoint.

## Conclusion

Even if you're not a database expert, Microsoft Access 2022 gives you the tools to get the most out of your data. And, through newly added Web databases, Access 2022 amplifies the power of your data, making it easier to track, report, and share with others.

**Some of the amazing features you are set to experience include;**

- New themes and templates
- Access event model
- Distributing access application
- Larger show table dialog
- Query box to easily locate Access tools and features
- Ability to export linked data source information to Excel

Whether you're a large corporation, small-business owner, nonprofit organization, or if you're just looking for more efficient ways to manage your personal information, Access 2022 makes it easier to get what you need to be done more quickly, with more flexibility and with better results.

# INDEX

## 2

2022 Interface, 27

## A

Access, 1, 2, 4, 5, 7, 8, 9, 10, 11, 13, 19, 21, 22, 23, 24, 25, 26, 27, 28, 29, 31, 32, 33, 34, 35, 36, 37, 39, 42, 43, 44, 45, 47, 49, 50, 54, 56, 63, 69, 70, 72, 73, 75, 76, 77, 78, 83, 85, 97, 98, 101, 104, 108, 109, 112, 116, 119, 121, 122, 129, 130, 134, 137, 139, 140, 141, 147, 148, 149, 150, 151, 152, 154, 156, 157, 158, 159, 160, 161, 162, 163, 164, 165, 166, 168, 172, 173, 174, 175, 176, 177, 179, 181, 182, 183, 184, 186, 187, 188, 190, 194, 199, 200, 201, 202, 205, 206, 207, 208, 209, 211, 212, 213, 215, 218, 219, 220, 221, 223, 225, 227, 229, 230, 236, 239, 240, 241, 242, 244, 245, 246, 247, 248, 251, 253, 254, 255, 256, 257, 259, 260, 265, 266, 267, 268, 269, 271, 273, 274, 276, 278, 279, 282, 285, 286, 290, 291, 292, 293, 294, 295, 297, 298, 299, 300, 307, 308, 309, 311, 312, 313, 320, 321, 322, 323, 324, 325, 327, 328, 331, 332, 337, 340, 341, 342, 343, 344, 348, 349, 351, 354, 355, 356, 357, 359, 361, 362, 363, 365, 366, 367, 368, 369, 370, 371, 374, 375, 376, 377, 378, 379, 381, 382, 383, 385, 387, 389, 390, 391, 393, 394, 395, 399, 400, 401, 403, 404, 405, 406, 407, 408, 409, 410, 411, 413, 414, 417, 418, 422, 423, 424, 428, 430, 431, 433, 434, 436, 437, 438, 439, 440, 441, 442, 443, 444, 445, 446, 447, 448, 449, 450, 453, 454, 455, 457, 458, 461, 463, 464, 465
ACCESS MACROS, 365
ACCESS BUILDING BLOCKS, 3
access data, 56
ACCESS DATA MACROS, 376
Access database, 5, 9, 10, 13, 22, 35, 39, 47, 66, 69, 73, 76, 82, 97, 98, 147, 148, 149, 151, 152, 164, 165, 173, 174, 175, 186, 187, 199, 206, 239, 268, 291, 293, 311, 365, 381, 422, 423, 424, 426, 428, 442, 455, 464
Access Database Engine, 1
Access Database Engine(ACE), 1
ACCESS EVENT MODEL, 400
ACCESS FORMS, 290, 291, 307
ACCESS QUERIES, 188
ACCESS REPORT TECHNIQUES, 354
Access Ribbon, 27, 441, 443
Access tables, 182
ACCESS TABLES, 35, 36, 111
ACE database, 65, 110
ACE database engine, 65, 110
Action Catalog, 366, 377, 378
**ActiveX Settings**, 369
ad hoc table, 209
ad hoc table joins, 209
**Add button option**, 104
**Add column**, 26, 39
**Add column.**, 26
Adding page breaks, 351
Address field's Size, 8
**Advanced button**, 159, 180
AfterInsert, 376, 377, 405
aggregate functions, 183, 226, 227, 234, 241, 276, 282, 283, 284, 357, 363
aggregate query, 225, 226, 227, 229, 237, 238, 285
Aggregating Data, 143
Aligning controls, 301
**Allow Layout View**, 334
AllowZeroLength, 66, 67
AllowZeroLength property, 66, 67
Alphanumeric characters, 46
alter records, 111
ALTER TABLE statement, 272
alternate formats, 342
analysis, 1, 5, 14, 17, 188, 225, 227, 229, 237, 244, 245, 251, 254, 256, 259, 260,

261, 262, 263, 265, 271, 272, 276, 277, 284, 285, 286, 287, 288, 290, 308
**Append Data**, 81
**append query**, 233, 234, 246, 270, 281
Applications code, 11
application-specific integrity rules, 110
Archive snapshots, 11
arithmetic operators, 211
Array functions, 397
AS clause, 269
asterisk button, 118
attachment field, 83, 84
Attachment Fields, 83
Augmenting field, 247
auto number field, 56, 70, 97
Auto number field, 39, 70, 71, 101
AutoNumber, 40, 50, 54, 55, 70, 82, 89, 101, 102, 119, 121, 206, 227, 228, 287, 311, 445
Autonumber field, 119
AutoNumber value, 101
AutoNumbers, 102

# B

background pictures, 328
backstage view, 23, 24, 31
Banded Report Design Concepts, 344
BeforeChange, 376, 377, 378
bitmap files, 83
bitmap image, 83
Bitmap pictures, 122
bix Macros, 1
blank column, 83
**blank database**, 23, 25
Blank Database, 23, 25
blank line, 359
**Blank Report** button, 345
Bold button, 136
Boolean, 211, 213, 214, 215, 216, 217, 371, 386, 394, 458, 459
Boolean logic, 213
Boolean operators, 214, 215, 216, 217
Boolean(Logical), 211
Boolean(logical) operators, 213
**Bound controls**, 298
box's Row Source, 321
Branching, 386

building block, 3
Built-in Date, 60
Built-in dates, 60
built-in Short Date format, 61
bulleted lists, 357
Business graphs, 122

# C

**Calculated controls**, 298, 311
Calibri 11-point font, 135
Cancel button, 331
**Caption**, 57, 64, 181, 305, 314, 334
Categorizing controls, 298
**Category and Filter By Group**, 28
changed layout, 139
character abbreviation, 61
character markers, 250
Check Box control, 325
Checkbox, 322
Checkboxes, 21
**checkmark**, 243, 322, 463, 464
chronological order, 48, 72
City field, 36, 69
**clipboard**, 81, 82, 115, 122, 130, 302, 303
Clipboard, 115, 303, 308, 309
**close button**, 24, 27, 201, 366
code window, 384
color schemes, 341
column alias, 269
column border, 134
column header, 83
column headings, 65, 235, 238
Column Headings attribute, 238, 239
Columnar reports, 336
combination key, 245
combo box, 125, 312, 313, 321, 325, 326, 328, 361, 433, 434, 443
Combo Box, 313, 321, 326, 433
combo boxes, 21, 312, 320, 325, 332, 452
command button, 11, 118, 124, 302, 321, 331, 335, 400, 409, 410
Command Button Wizard, 11
command buttons, 10, 11, 21, 331, 335, 410
command tabs, 31, 33
**Comma-separated values**, 181
Comparison, 211, 213, 215

comparison operators, 213, 216, 217, 220, 278
Compiling procedures, 385
Completed Table, 77
composite primary keys, 71, 72, 103
Concatenates operands, 213
Concatenating, 247
CONDITIONAL ANALYSES, 259
Conditional Analysis, 259
Conditional Functions, 262
**Configuring databases**, 31
contacts table, 69
**Contains Field Names** checkbox, 158
**Control Box**, 332, 335, 454
Control group, 299, 312
Control Wizard option, 325
control's Record Source, 357
conversion issues, 54
conversion mode property, 57
copying, 32, 82, 115, 130, 165, 172, 233, 302
Copying a control, 302
**Create tab**, 25, 39, 89, 201, 235, 246, 274, 294, 295, 296, 297, 307, 332, 345, 365, 367
CREATE TABLE statement, 272
Created Date, 30
Creating subs, 398
Creating tbl Customers, 50
Credit Status, 41
CreditBalance, 41
CreditLimit, 41
criteria, 9, 65, 112, 115, 142, 143, 183, 192, 193, 198, 199, 208, 209, 211, 216, 217, 218, 220, 221, 222, 223, 224, 229, 230, 232, 233, 237, 238, 240, 241, 256, 259, 261, 269, 277, 278, 280, 283, 284, 293, 309, 330, 346, 371, 434, 435
Cross joins, 208, 209
crosstab query, 226, 234, 235, 236, 237, 238, 263
Crosstab Query Wizard, 235, 237
Crosstabs, 271
crucial notion, 341, 344
CSV file, 181
**Currency**, 41, 46, 54, 55, 59, 120, 121, 227, 228
currency field, 59, 454
currency field format, 59

current database, 147, 149, 233, 242, 439, 442, 449
current field, 49, 129, 131, 132, 141
current record, 114, 119, 129, 133, 310, 311, 315, 345, 427, 428, 430, 431
Custom, 28, 59, 60, 440, 441
custom format, 58, 59
Customer data, 20
Customer Data, 18
Customer ID, 82, 98, 106
customer's table, 88
CustomerID, 40, 69, 70
customerID order, 72
Customer-Related Data, 16
**Customers and orders**, 95
customer's table, 88, 94, 219, 222, 224
CustomID field, 69
**Cycle**, 335

# D

DAO objects, 190, 424, 426
Dash Dot, 137
data, 1, 3, 4, 5, 6, 7, 8, 9, 10, 11, 12, 13, 14, 15, 16, 17, 19, 20, 21, 23, 24, 25, 27, 32, 36, 38, 39, 40, 42, 44, 45, 46, 47, 48, 49, 50, 51, 52, 53, 54, 55, 56, 57, 58, 60, 62, 63, 64, 65, 66, 67, 68, 69, 72, 73, 75, 76, 78, 79, 80, 81, 82, 83, 84, 85, 86, 87, 88, 89, 91, 92, 93, 94, 96, 97, 98, 99, 101, 102, 103, 106, 107, 108, 110, 111, 112, 113, 116, 117, 118, 119, 120, 121, 122, 127, 130, 132, 134, 135, 136, 137, 139, 140, 141, 142, 143, 144, 147, 148, 149, 150, 151, 152, 154, 155, 156, 157, 158, 159, 160, 161, 162, 163, 165, 168, 169, 172, 173, 174, 175, 176, 177, 178, 179, 180, 181, 182, 183, 184, 185, 186, 187, 188, 189, 190, 194, 197, 198, 199, 202, 203, 204, 205, 206, 208, 209, 211, 213, 216, 217, 218, 220, 223, 224, 225, 226, 227, 228, 229, 230, 233, 234, 235, 237, 239, 240, 244, 245, 246, 247, 248, 249, 250, 251, 252, 253, 255, 257, 260, 261, 262, 263, 265, 266, 267, 268, 269, 270, 271, 272, 273, 277, 278, 279, 280, 283, 284, 285, 286, 287, 288, 291, 292, 293, 294, 295, 296, 297, 298, 299, 305, 307, 308,

309, 310, 311, 312, 315, 317, 324, 325,
330, 331, 332, 335, 336, 337, 338, 339,
340, 341, 342, 344, 345, 348, 350, 354,
355, 356, 357, 358, 359, 361, 362, 367,
370, 372, 376, 377, 378, 379, 380, 381,
382, 391, 392, 393, 394, 396, 399, 405,
406, 407, 408, 409, 412, 422, 423, 424,
425, 426, 427, 428, 429, 430, 431, 433,
434, 435, 438, 439, 443, 450, 451, 453,
454, 455, 457, 459, 461, 462, 463, 464,
465
Data actions, 378
Data blocks, 378
Data design, 15
Data Entry Form, 293
Data events, 400
data like Social Security, 47
Data macros, 376, 377, 379, 380
Data Macros, 376, 377, 379
data management task, 9
Data Normalization, 87
Data Services, 151
**Data Source**, 150, 152, 154, 157, 159, 162,
164, 167, 178, 179, 180, 185, 334, 463
Data Type, 40, 46, 392
data type column, 51
data types, 38, 45, 46, 47, 56, 57, 58, 68, 147,
159, 162, 163, 223, 227, 228, 272, 380,
391, 423, 465
Database, 1, 4, 9, 20, 31, 32, 77, 82, 104,
117, 121, 147, 151, 152, 155, 164, 165,
166, 175, 176, 177, 182, 185, 186, 187,
188, 241, 242, 413, 424, 425, 429, 443,
446, 448, 457, 458, 459
database applications, 13, 91, 97, 174, 365,
381
database design, 3, 94, 102, 240
database development, 4, 19
Database development, 4
DATABASE DEVELOPMENT, 4
Database Documenter button, 77
database engine, 20, 56, 66, 69, 96, 97, 239,
268, 422, 423, 424, 425, 426, 428
database engines, 20, 150, 187
database management, 1, 2, 4, 5, 147, 230,
265
database management system(DBMS), 1

database objects, 6, 7, 11, 12, 25, 28, 30, 45,
77, 164, 186, 187, 253, 303, 361, 441, 449,
450
Database Objects, 9
database projects elongate, 97
database system, 4, 13, 97, 274, 400, 429
database table, 10, 36, 37, 43, 82, 99, 100,
174, 181, 291, 338, 425, 427
Database Table, 82
Database table relationships, 20
Database terminology, 4
Database Tools, 31, 32, 77, 104, 188, 241
databases, 1, 4, 5, 8, 9, 22, 23, 25, 31, 32, 49,
64, 69, 73, 85, 91, 93, 98, 103, 130, 147,
148, 150, 165, 166, 174, 175, 178, 187,
293, 323, 337, 422, 423, 424, 429, 430,
433, 446, 450, 455, 461, 465
Databases, 4, 8, 85, 424
Data-entry and display forms, 10
datasheet, 7, 9, 27, 49, 53, 56, 57, 65, 82, 83,
84, 111, 112, 113, 114, 115, 116, 117, 118,
119, 122, 123, 130, 132, 134, 135, 136,
139, 142, 144, 145, 146, 183, 189, 191,
193, 195, 197, 205, 226, 295, 296, 297,
310, 315, 332, 377, 427, 433, 434, 448
Datasheet, 26, 27, 39, 33, 111, 112, 113,
114, 115, 117, 123, 125, 126, 136, 137,
140, 142, 143, 146, 160, 168, 190, 192,
193, 196, 219, 233, 291, 295, 296, 297,
307, 308, 309, 310, 311, 313, 331, 334,
376, 377, 378, 427, 442, 448
Datasheet layout, 136
Datasheet view, 26, 27, 39, 83, 111, 115,
117, 143, 146, 160, 168, 190, 192, 193,
196, 233, 291, 296, 307, 308, 309, 310,
311, 313, 331, 376, 377, 378, 427, 442
**Datasheet View**, 115, 117, 219, 313, 334,
448
Datasheet window, 113, 114, 125, 142
Datasheet Window, 112
Datasheets, 111, 112
Date add function, 256
Date function, 256
date intervals, 355
Date/Time field, 37, 48, 255, 417
**DateAdd function**, 256
DateSerial function, 258
DAvg, 282

dBase, 1, 149, 151, 174
DBMS, 1, 4, 265
DCount, 183, 282, 284
Debugging macros, 374
Decimal placeholder, 63
Decimal places, 181
**Decimal Places**, 57
default button, 331
**Default Value**, 57
Delete Rows, 44
Deleting a control, 303
Deleting a field, 52
Deleting relationships, 110
delimited file, 157, 158
Delimited text files, 157
**delimiter**, 157, 158, 160
Denormalization, 87, 91
Description, 18, 40, 44, 125, 224, 303, 304, 373
description column, 49, 51
Descriptive Statistics, 285, 287
DESCRIPTIVE STATISTICS, 285
deselecting controls, 299
Deselecting controls, 300
design a database, 12, 24, 34, 337
Design tab, 42, 52, 70, 74, 89, 104, 109, 231, 237, 274, 275, 298, 299, 304, 312, 313, 314, 316, 317, 318, 320, 324, 325, 327, 328, 333, 335, 342, 346, 347, 350, 352, 354, 366, 367, 370, 375, 377
Design Tips, 324
Design view, 40, 84, 115, 182, 192, 195, 219, 220, 222, 231, 238, 240, 246, 291, 303, 308, 310, 311, 312, 313, 318, 328, 331, 332, 342, 343, 352, 354, 355, 377, 398, 448
**Design View**, 104, 115, 323, 325, 346
Designing the query, 331
Detail section, 323, 340, 344, 345, 352, 355, 358, 359
dialog box, 33, 80, 104, 106, 121, 125, 130, 131, 133, 134, 135, 136, 138, 143, 145, 159, 161, 163, 165, 166, 167, 170, 175, 176, 177, 179, 180, 183, 184, 191, 192, 193, 200, 201, 208, 231, 235, 237, 242, 246, 259, 260, 274, 278, 293, 314, 318, 327, 330, 331, 339, 340, 341, 342, 346, 361, 362, 368, 390, 410, 413, 415, 419,

431, 433, 434, 435, 437, 440, 441, 443, 449, 457, 464
Dialog Box form, 293
dialog boxes, 113, 291, 330, 346
DiscountPercent, 41
Display control, 181
display fonts, 134, 135
DISTINCTROW predicate, 267
**division operator**, 212
DLookup, 283, 284
DMax function, 283
Documenter dialog box, 77
Domain Aggregate Functions, 282
DOMAIN AGGREGATE FUNCTIONS, 276
Dots, 137
double-quotes, 158, 284
**downward arrow**, 133, 142, 333
**drop-down arrow**, 33, 308, 325, 401, 433
drop-down list, 33, 64, 68, 74, 79, 133, 136, 137, 143, 144, 170, 198, 291, 310, 339, 351, 365, 366, 367, 370, 398
drop-down menu, 150, 346, 433
DStDev, 283
DStDevp, 283
DSum, 282, 284
duplicate data, 85
DvarP, 283
DVarP functions, 283
Dynamic arrays, 396

# E

Edit relationships dialog box, 108
ELSE structure, 263, 264
Embedded Macros, 374
Embedding (OLE), 83, 122
employee recruitment table, 90
**Employees and paychecks**, 95
enforcing referential, 104
Enter Parameter, 259, 260, 361
Error and timing events, 400
Error Handling, 373
European language applications., 58
Even-odd page printing, 359
Excel, 1, 4, 9, 27, 56, 85, 92, 93, 115, 122, 148, 151, 154, 155, 156, 158, 162, 169, 172, 174, 178, 179, 180, 226, 245, 247, 252, 308, 436, 453, 465

EXCEL files, 147
Excel worksheet., 27, 56, 178
Exchange Server, 165
**Existing Table**, 81
Exponentiation, 215
**exponentiation operator**, 212
**Exporting**, 148, 150, 163, 165, 166, 168, 464
exporting XML documents, 160
External Data, 31, 32, 147, 151, 152, 154, 157, 159, 160, 162, 163, 165, 166, 168, 170, 172, 175, 176, 178, 179, 183, 184, 463
EXTERNAL DATA, 172
external data source, 151
external files, 47, 147, 149, 172, 425
External Formats, 165

# F

**F6 button**, 51, 68
field description, 49, 113
field Descriptions, 68
**field entry area**, 42, 44
field formats, 59, 62
field input mask, 62
field location, 53
**field name**, 44, 45, 51, 53, 54, 74, 84, 155, 218, 255, 260
Field Name, 40, 45
Field Name column, 40, 45
**field names**, 16, 38, 45, 50, 77, 113, 158, 180, 218
Field names, 45
field order, 51, 134, 196
field properties, 42, 44, 55, 56, 65, 68
**field properties area**, 42, 44
**field selector**, 53, 196
field size, 47, 51, 54, 55, 89, 97, 134, 247, 273
**Field Size**, 42, 56
field size property setting, 97
**Field Validation Rule**, 49
field's data type, 55
fields, 4, 7, 9, 10, 13, 15, 16, 17, 18, 19, 21, 36, 37, 38, 39, 40, 42, 43, 44, 45, 47, 48, 49, 50, 51, 52, 56, 58, 59, 64, 68, 69, 70, 71, 72, 73, 74, 75, 76, 82, 85, 88, 90, 91, 93, 94, 96, 98, 99, 100, 101, 102, 103, 104, 106, 108, 111, 112, 113, 116, 117, 119, 120, 121, 122, 129, 132, 134, 136, 138, 139, 142, 155, 157, 158, 159, 160, 162, 163, 181, 189, 190, 192, 193, 194, 195, 196, 197, 198, 199, 202, 204, 205, 206, 211, 218, 219, 220, 221, 223, 224, 225, 227, 229, 234, 235, 236, 240, 241, 245, 246, 247, 250, 252, 253, 255, 267, 268, 269, 276, 277, 287, 288, 295, 297, 298, 299, 303, 306, 310, 311, 318, 321, 323, 332, 334, 335, 336, 339, 340, 344, 345, 347, 359, 362, 363, 380, 423, 426, 427, 428, 430, 431, 442, 445
file cabinet, 4
File Name box, 24, 26
file server, 12, 186
**file tab**, 24, 25
filtering, 9, 32, 140, 241, 256
Filtering a form, 143, 434
Filtering a selection, 141
**first blank column**, 83
First Data Macro, 378
First normal form, 88
first table, 86, 93, 209, 266, 267
Five-Step Design Method, 13
**fix a checkmark**, 33
Fixed arrays, 396
fixed decimal point, 55
Fixed-width text files, 158
Focus events., 400
**Force New Page**, 344
**foreign key**, 69, 88, 98, 99, 102, 104, 109, 205, 206
foreign key field, 98, 104, 109
foreign key values, 99
Form command, 294, 307, 332
Form design, 21
**form title bar**, 292
Form Wizard, 294
**Format**, 56, 58, 64, 117, 120, 168, 181, 257, 258, 305, 308, 318, 328, 347, 349, 359, 407, 415, 449
format property, 58, 59, 359
formatting, 32, 40, 58, 63, 116, 118, 121, 136, 137, 168, 257, 290, 318, 347, 349, 384, 407, 437
Formatting Data, 356
Former versions, 83

Forms, 10, 21, 29, 152, 290, 291, 292, 294, 296, 307, 315, 327, 328, 332, 337, 388, 448, 454
form's appearance, 335
**Four-Digit Years checkbox**, 160
Freezing columns, 138
Frequency distribution, 288
Full outer joins, 209

## G

**General Date**, 60
**General number**, 59
global temporary tables, 7
good database design, 85
Graphical objects, 21
graphical user interface (GUI), 1
**Gridlines**, 136, 145, 310
**gridlines command**, 116
Group Footer, 345, 350
Group Footer section, 345
group header, 350, 351, 352, 355, 356
Group Header section, 344, 352
group/total reports, 336, 344
Grouping alphabetically, 354
Grouping controls, 302
grouping levels, 339

## H

**Header Section**, 354, 355
help tab, 33
Hiding a field, 198
hierarchical manner, 179
Home tab, 25, 32, 115, 119, 141, 143, 195, 303, 307, 308, 313, 360, 410, 436
Horizontal, 136
**HTML**, 151, 162, 163, 174, 178, 179, 342
HTML Document, 151, 163, 179
HTML documents, 162
HTML file, 162, 163, 179
HTML files, 179
HTML table, 174, 179
HTML template, 163
**hyperlink**, 22, 203, 321
Hyperlink, 47, 203

## I

ID field, 93, 94, 98, 102, 442
Identifying entities, 89
**Ignore Nulls**, 75
IIf function, 259, 262, 263, 264
**IME Mode**, 57
**IME Sentence Mode**, 58
Import Text Wizard, 157, 159, 163
importance of indexes, 73
**Importing**, 1, 25, 147, 148, 150, 151, 152, 154, 156, 157, 160, 162, 163, 164, 463
IMPORTING AND EXPORTING DATA, 147
In operator, 214, 222
incorporate column heads, 344
**Indexed**, 57, 67, 147, 240
Indexes, 44
inner join, 106, 107, 208, 209, 210
Inner joins, 208, 266
input mask, 42, 49, 59, 62, 63, 64, 67, 121
**Input Mask**, 56, 62
input mask property value, 63
input mask wizard, 64
**insert key**, 127
Insert Rows, 43
**insert rows button**, 52
Integer division, 215
Integrity Rules, 96
IntelliSense, 385
invoice data, 20
Invoice Data, 18
Is operator, 214, 215, 221

## J

Jet Database Engine, 1
join line, 204, 206, 210
Join Properties dialog box, 106, 210
**Join Type button**, 106
junction table, 95, 96

## K

Kanji mode, 57
Keyboard events., 400
Keys, 100, 447
Keystrokes, 113, 127, 310

## L

language's syntax, 383
LastSalesDate, 41
**Lawyers to clients**, 96
**Layout view**, 292, 294, 307, 308, 332, 341, 343
Less obvious entities, 89
Line continuation, 384
Line Items, 18
line-item details, 20
**LineTotal field**, 237
Link Spreadsheet Wizard, 179
LinkChildFields, 324
linked reference, 183
Linked Table Manager, 150, 183, 184
**Linking**, 148, 172, 175, 177, 178, 179, 130, 435, 463
LinkMasterFields, 324
List Box controls, 321
Local temporary tables, 7
Looping, 387
lower pane, 65, 253
lowercase equivalent, 62
low-order ASCII characters, 45
Ltrim function, 248

## M

Macintosh applications, 147
Macintosh computers, 150
Macro Builder, 12, 366, 377
Macro Debugging, 373
Macro Designer window, 370
**Macro Settings**, 368, 369
**Macro Settings tab**, 368
MacroError object, 373, 374
Macros and VBA, 1, 11
Macros versus VBA Statements, 374
**Magazine subscriptions**, 96
Mailing label reports, 337
make-table query, 230, 234, 280
Managing Macro Objects, 379
Manipulating controls, 300
manual database systems, 4
manual databases systems, 4
manual system(filling),, 7
Many-to-many, 93, 95, 203

many-to-many relationship, 37, 95, 96, 203
matching field, 97
Mathematical, 211, 215
mathematical operators, 211, 212, 215
mathematical precedence, 215
matrix-type report, 200
maximum length, 65
message box, 65, 372, 377, 379, 414
**MessageBox**, 366
MFunctions module, 359
Micro-adjusting controls, 360
Microsoft, 1, 10, 22, 23, 36, 43, 57, 58, 59, 61, 63, 64, 65, 66, 67, 68, 69, 70, 71, 72, 73, 74, 75, 76, 77, 78, 82, 83, 85, 86, 93, 94, 96, 97, 98, 99, 101, 102, 103, 104, 105, 106, 107, 108, 110, 111, 115, 120, 121, 122, 123, 130, 135, 136, 139, 141, 143, 144, 145, 147, 148, 149, 150, 154, 156, 157, 160, 162, 163, 164, 165, 166, 168, 169, 172, 173, 174, 177, 178, 179, 190, 198, 199, 202, 206, 208, 209, 214, 215, 218, 219, 220, 222, 224, 225, 226, 229, 230, 235, 251, 252, 254, 255, 256, 259, 260, 262, 268, 270, 272, 276, 282, 292, 295, 302, 308, 315, 327, 328, 336, 337, 338, 351, 358, 359, 362, 381, 401, 414, 419, 424, 425, 426, 427, 428, 429, 441, 450, 461, 465
Microsoft Access, 1, 10, 22, 23, 36, 43, 57, 58, 59, 61, 63, 64, 66, 67, 68, 69, 70, 71, 72, 73, 74, 75, 76, 77, 78, 82, 83, 85, 86, 93, 94, 96, 97, 98, 99, 101, 102, 103, 104, 105, 106, 107, 108, 110, 111, 120, 121, 122, 123, 130, 135, 136, 139, 141, 144, 145, 147, 148, 149, 150, 154, 156, 157, 160, 162, 163, 172, 173, 174, 178, 190, 198, 199, 202, 206, 208, 209, 214, 215, 218, 219, 220, 222, 224, 225, 226, 229, 230, 235, 251, 255, 256, 259, 260, 262, 268, 270, 272, 276, 282, 292, 295, 302, 327, 336, 337, 338, 351, 358, 362, 381, 414, 424, 425, 426, 427, 428, 461, 465
Microsoft Access inserts records, 75
MICROSOFT ACCESS PROGRAMMING, 364
Microsoft office suite apps, 130
Mid function, 249, 250
Miscellaneous, 211, 214
Modified Date, 30

473

Modulus division, 215
**monolithic table**, 86
Mouse events., 400
Moving a table, 206
Moving macro items, 379
**MSysObject table**, 362
MSysObjects, 361, 362
Multi-action Macros, 370
multi-language applications, 57
Multiple actions, 371
multiple conditions, 263
multiple controls, 300, 349
multiple coverages., 96
**Multiple items**, 295
multiple OpenForm, 372
multiple parameter conditions, 261
Multiple-field indexes, 74
multiple-item form, 295
Multiple-item forms, 295
**multiplication operator**, 212
Multi-statement lines, 384
multi-table queries, 202
multi-value field, 322

# N

natural order, 72, 73
navigation button, 113
navigation buttons, 114, 119, 311, 455
Navigation buttons, 114, 124, 142
**Navigation Buttons**, 335
navigation forms, 295
navigation pane, 25, 27, 28, 29, 34, 79, 81, 82, 84, 117, 169, 183, 192, 295, 296, 297, 332, 338, 374
Navigation pane, 28, 79, 82, 148, 163, 292, 294, 307, 323, 325, 332, 342, 366, 370, 371, 447, 449, 450, 455, 464
Navigational Direction, 113, 310
Negation, 215
network permissions, 77
new database, 11, 22, 23, 25, 27, 37, 233
new field, 27, 51, 52, 54, 83, 84, 94, 195
new report, 338, 341, 345, 356
New Table, 37, 155
**New Values**, 56
Next field, 113, 310
Next record, 114

non-database, 178
non-image files, 83
non-matching values, 220
normalized relational database, 91
NTFS file system, 186
NULL, 66
Null index value, 75
Null index values, 75
Null keyword, 99
Null value, 98, 99, 254
numeric format, 59

# O

Object Browser, 390
Object Linking, 83, 122, 311
Object Type, 29
object-oriented database, 5
**Object-oriented database**, 5
ODBC, 151, 166, 167, 174, 177, 204, 422, 424, 425, 427, 429
ODBC drivers, 166, 167, 178
**office.com**, 23, 24
OLE field, 122
OLE Object, 46, 122, 268
OLE object field, 122
**OLE objects**, 122, 147, 311, 330
OLE Objects, 218
OLE server, 122, 311
one-many relationship, 205
OnError action, 373, 374
ONError action, 373
One-to-many, 93, 94, 203
one-to-many relationship, 85, 94, 99, 205, 206, 234, 324
One-to-one, 93, 203
one-to-one relationship, 93, 94
Opening a Datasheet, 117
**opening databases**, 31
OpenReport actions, 372
operator and wildcards, 219
Operator Precedence, 215
option buttons, 21, 66, 312, 341
**option under Navigate**, 28
**optional description**, 42
Optional digit, 64
**Options buttons**, 77
Oracle, 1, 147, 150, 174, 177

order tracking database, 94
**OrderDate field**, 236, 355
order-entry clerk, 110
Orders table, 94, 95, 98
OrigCustomerDate, 41
original file, 83
orphaned record, 100
Outer join, 106
Outer joins, 209, 266
overall design, 13
Overtype mode, 127

## P

Page Footer section, 345, 359
Page Header section, 344, 349
page headers, 343, 344
Paradox, 1, 205
parameter query, 219, 259, 260, 261, 361, 435
parameters, 260, 261, 262, 330, 342, 346, 385, 398, 399, 435, 446, 449
parent program, 83
Paste Append, 115, 309
Paste Special, 115, 309
Paste Special option, 115
pasting, 25, 32, 115, 130, 175, 302, 348, 351
Pasting Values, 130
**Patients and appointments**, 95
**Patients and insurance coverage**, 96
PDF or XPS, 169, 170, 342
PDF or XPS formats, 169
PDF reader programs, 171
PDF-style formatting, 11
percent total, 284
percentile making, 287
Percentile rank, 287
**plus sign**, 60, 123, 126, 129
PowerPoint, 4, 255
**preferred HTML** output, 163
preferred location, 53
**preferred name**, 89
**preferred table name**, 104
**preferred template**, 24
Preview window, 77, 146, 342
Previous field, 113, 310
Previous record, 114

primary key, 43, 69, 70, 71, 72, 74, 75, 76, 88, 93, 94, 95, 97, 98, 99, 100, 101, 102, 103, 104, 112, 119, 156, 158, 162, 163, 165, 174, 202, 205, 206, 209, 246, 273, 350
Primary key, 40, 70, 89, 93, 102, 205
Primary Key, 43, 69
**primary key button**, 70
primary key field, 69, 101, 102, 103, 104, 119
primary key value, 100, 101, 103, 205
primary table, 97, 98
Print events, 400
Print Preview tab, 342, 343
**Print Range**, 145
Print Table Definition dialog box, 77
printing reports, 91
**ProductID field**, 236
Program flow, 378
Programming, 11, 400
progress bar, 113
Project Explrer, 389
Property Sheet, 44, 275, 304, 305, 314, 316, 317, 320, 328, 349, 351, 352, 356, 359, 374, 398, 401, 445
**Publish button**, 170

## Q

**QBD grid**, 192, 193, 194, 195, 196, 197, 202, 218, 221, 224
QBD pane, 217, 219, 222, 224
quartile standing, 287, 288
queries, 1, 5, 9, 13, 23, 28, 29, 32, 36, 45, 52, 53, 56, 65, 67, 73, 74, 97, 99, 102, 111, 148, 152, 163, 164, 165, 183, 186, 187, 188, 189, 190, 191, 192, 193, 202, 204, 205, 206, 208, 211, 216, 217, 218, 221, 224, 225, 226, 229, 230, 232, 233, 234, 235, 238, 240, 241, 259, 260, 262, 265, 270, 271, 273, 274, 276, 277, 278, 279, 280, 285, 324, 357, 361, 367, 372, 374, 381, 382, 426, 433, 435, 450, 454
Queries, 9, 10, 29, 152, 188, 189, 190, 193, 198, 201, 216, 225, 230, 235, 259, 270, 331
query criteria., 193
**Query Design button**, 191, 201
Query designer, 206

475

Query Designer, 191, 192, 193, 196, 206
Query Fields, 195
Query Joins, 208
query limitations, 205
Query Performance, 239
Query Properties, 238
**Query Wizard button**, 235, 246
Query's Recordset, 200
Quick Access toolbar, 28, 33, 34, 77, 112, 119, 129, 139, 297, 313, 332, 439, 440
Quick Access Toolbar, 33, 141, 200, 439, 440

# R

Read-only form, 10
real-world object, 36
Record Display Form, 293
record index field, 75
**Record Selectors**, 335
**Record Validation Rule**, 49
**record-number box**, 114
records, 4, 8, 10, 11, 14, 24, 44, 49, 72, 73, 75, 76, 82, 83, 85, 86, 87, 90, 91, 93, 95, 96, 97, 98, 99, 100, 101, 102, 103, 105, 106, 107, 108, 111, 112, 113, 116, 117, 118, 119, 123, 124, 129, 130, 133, 134, 136, 138, 140, 141, 142, 144, 145, 149, 151, 157, 158, 182, 183, 190, 192, 193, 198, 199, 200, 202, 204, 205, 209, 217, 218, 220, 221, 223, 224, 225, 226, 227, 228, 230, 232, 233, 234, 236, 239, 245, 246, 252, 256, 261, 265, 266, 267, 268, 269, 270, 279, 282, 284, 285, 286, 287, 288, 293, 295, 297, 309, 311, 324, 330, 332, 336, 340, 344, 345, 350, 355, 356, 358, 359, 375, 400, 403, 425, 426, 427, 428, 430, 431, 433, 434
Records, 7, 72, 82, 106, 115, 118, 123, 132, 133, 134, 135, 138, 140, 143, 144, 145, 226, 233, 245, 266, 268, 272, 309, 313, 410, 426, 430
Records and Fields, 7
Recordset objects, 190, 425, 426, 428, 429, 430
referential integrity, 1, 97, 98, 99, 102, 104, 107, 108, 149, 182, 202, 206, 410, 431
Referential integrity, 96, 110

**Referential Integrity check box**, 105
Related Fields, 97
Related Views, 29, 30
relational database, 5, 69, 93, 94, 98, 99, 100, 265, 276
**Relational database**, 5
relational database technology, 5
Relationship window, 104, 182
**Relationships dialog box**, 104, 105, 106, 107
Relationships Tools, 109
**Relationships window**, 104, 105, 106, 108, 109, 110
Relationships window., 105, 106, 108, 109
**Remove Table option**, 207
RemoveAllTempVars, 371
RemoveTempVar, 371
Removing a table, 207
**rename field**, 39
repeating information, 355
Replace dialog box., 125, 130
**Replace tab**, 131
Replacing Values, 130
replication ID, 97
report design, 337, 341, 343, 344, 407, 412
Report design, 15
Report Footer section, 345
report header, 344, 352, 383
report header information, 344
Report Header section, 344
report layout, 15, 337, 356
report page size, 346
Report Wizard, 336, 337, 338, 339, 340, 341, 345, 363
Reports, 10, 29, 152, 336, 345, 356, 362, 388, 400, 406, 445
report's layout, 341
Resizing a section, 347
Ribbon, 31, 39, 74, 77, 104, 109, 112, 115, 117, 118, 119, 124, 130, 133, 135, 136, 138, 140, 141, 142, 143, 144, 146, 154, 170, 175, 178, 179, 183, 188, 191, 195, 201, 208, 219, 231, 235, 237, 241, 246, 274, 291, 292, 294, 298, 299, 300, 301, 302, 303, 304, 305, 307, 308, 316, 317, 318, 320, 327, 328, 335, 342, 343, 345, 346, 349, 350, 351, 352, 354, 365, 366, 367, 370, 375, 378, 379, 410, 433, 434,

436, 437, 438, 439, 440, 441, 442, 443, 444, 445, 446, 449
Round function, 256
row-and-column format, 9, 179
rows and columns, 5, 7, 92, 112, 156, 295, 296, 336, 427
rptFlexFormat, 359
RunMacro action, 370
Running Sum property, 345

## S

Sales Tax Rate, 16, 19
Salesforce, 151
sample data, 25
sandbox mode, 368
**save button option**, 77
Saving the record, 119, 335
schema files, 161, 162
Second normal form, 88
second table, 86, 93, 209, 266, 267
SELECT statement, 227, 265, 266, 268, 269, 271, 272, 277, 279
selection criteria, 199
Separator character, 63
sequence mode, 58, 182
SetTempVar, 371, 372
Setting relationships, 182
SharePoint, 25, 32, 151, 156, 380, 461, 462, 463, 464, 465
Short Text, 40, 41, 46, 48, 54, 55, 56, 57, 62, 68, 89, 121, 128, 255, 287
shortcut menu, 52, 71, 79, 81, 82, 84, 104, 111, 122, 132, 135, 142, 183, 191, 197, 199, 207, 210, 313, 327, 330, 346, 362, 417, 438, 439
simple string criteria, 199
single control, 300
single field, 70, 73, 83, 103, 104, 134, 193, 198, 218, 423
Single-field, 103
Single-Value Field Criteria, 218
snaking columns, 362, 363
Snaking columns, 362
software, 1, 13, 150, 177, 178, 384, 420
Solid, 137
Sort & Filter, 115, 143, 309
sort order, 44, 74, 198, 238, 268, 340

sorting, 32, 48, 49, 67, 74, 193, 198, 241, 268, 290, 340
Sorting Data, 354
Sound files, 122
**source database**, 152, 165
Special controls, 21
specific table, 29, 163, 230
specific value, 124, 127
Split form, 296
Split forms, 296
Splitter add-in, 187
spreadsheet, 5, 6, 7, 86, 92, 111, 113, 147, 148, 154, 162, 172, 178, 235, 293, 308
SQL (Structured Query Language)-, 1
SQL aggregate, 227, 268, 282
SQL aggregate function, 227, 268
SQL code, 269
SQL database, 182
SQL query, 219
SQL Server, 1, 151, 174, 177, 429
SQL statement, 222, 266, 267, 268, 269, 270, 274, 278, 280, 232, 315, 357, 361
SQL statements, 1, 192, 270, 271, 278, 426
SQL Statements, 267
**SQL view**, 192, 271, 272, 273, 276, 278
SQL-specific query, 272
Standard Deviation, 143
standard Microsoft, 78
standard PDF format, 342
**Standard Width check box**, 135
status bar, 44, 49, 112, 113, 305, 447, 448, 453
StDev, 227, 228
store files, 83
String, 211, 213, 215, 458
**Structure and Data**, 80
Structured Query Language (SQL), 265
structured Query Language (SQL)., 4
structured Query Language(SQL), 5
Subforms, 295, 324
Submacros, 370
Subqueries, 276, 277, 278, 279, 280
Subquery ground rules, 277
Subs and functions, 397
**Subtraction**, 212
surrogate primary keys, 103
switch function, 262, 263, 264, 288
Switchboard Form, 293

# T

Tab, 113, 119, 310, 317, 318, 324, 325, 330, 446
**tab button**, 51
**Table button**, 39, 104, 208, 231
table design, 38, 42, 49, 51, 52, 54, 58, 65, 68, 71, 77, 82, 86, 112, 121, 134, 223
Table design, 17, 89
Table Design, 34, 40, 42, 44, 45, 51, 77
**table design window**, 51, 52, 54, 68
table dialog box, 104
Table Events, 376
table modifications, 88
**Table Name field**, 231
Table pane, 206
Table Relationships, 92
TABLE RELATIONSHIPS, 85
**table structure**, 27, 51, 151, 245
Table tab, 376, 378
**Table Tools**, 89, 104, 118
Table Types, 36
table. Forms, 10
table. indexed Fields, 67
table-level rule, 66
tables, 1, 4, 5, 6, 7, 8, 9, 11, 12, 13, 17, 19, 20, 23, 25, 28, 30, 32, 34, 35, 36, 37, 38, 39, 43, 45, 47, 53, 55, 56, 65, 68, 69, 72, 73, 75, 76, 78, 79, 80, 81, 82, 83, 85, 86, 87, 88, 89, 91, 93, 94, 95, 96, 97, 98, 99, 102, 103, 104, 105, 106, 107, 108, 109, 110, 111, 116, 117, 123, 130, 149, 151, 152, 162, 163, 164, 165, 172, 173, 174, 175, 176, 177, 181, 182, 183, 184, 185, 186, 187, 188, 189, 190, 191, 192, 193, 201, 202, 204, 205, 206, 207, 208, 209, 210, 216, 222, 229, 234, 237, 240, 241, 251, 252, 255, 265, 266, 269, 270, 272, 273, 274, 276, 279, 290, 324, 345, 350, 382, 422, 425, 426, 427, 431, 433, 439, 448, 450, 454, 463, 464, 465
Tables, 6, 7, 9, 29, 30, 39, 72, 79, 176, 177, 181, 209, 448, 464
**table's design**, 38, 43, 44, 53
table's internal index, 75
**table's primary key**, 38, 70
Tabular reports, 336
Tag field, 48

Tallying check boxes, 325
TaxRate, 41
tbl customers, 50, 51
tbl Customers Field Properties, 68
tblAuthorBook., 37
tblCustomers, 36, 37, 45, 62, 68, 69, 70
TblCustomers, 45
**Teacher and student**, 95
Temporary Variables, 371
Text Align property, 56
text box, 64, 298, 303, 304, 305, 312, 314, 321, 323, 325, 331, 341, 345, 349, 351, 354, 355, 356, 357, 359, 360, 361, 363, 417, 433, 437
Text Box control, 321, 348, 349, 356
Text Box controls, 348, 349, 350
Text BOX controls, 348
Text boxes, 21, 330
text field, 54, 55, 62, 67, 117, 122, 247, 321
text file, 157, 158, 159, 160, 162, 163, 168, 169, 181
Text File, 151, 157, 159
**Text Files**, 174
Text Values, 48
Text-type field, 199
**the cursor**, 43, 45, 51, 118, 125, 126, 134, 137, 138, 198, 297
Third normal form, 90
Time Delimiter box., 160
Time Delimiter option, 160
time formats, 60
Time formats, 60
**title bar**, 64, 112, 206, 313, 314, 343, 346, 354, 362, 446
toggle button controls, 322
Toggle Button controls, 322
toggle buttons, 21, 66, 312, 436
TOP PERCENT Statement, 270
TOP statement, 270
total amount, 13
Total row, 112, 143, 144, 226, 229
**Totals button**, 143, 144
transaction table, 36, 37
Transformation Tasks, 247
Transparent Border, 137
Trust Center, 367, 368, 369
**Trust Center Settings**, 368, 369
**Trust Center tab**, 368, 369

two-pass report processing, 363

## U

**Unbound control**, 298
Understanding joins, 208
Undo Feature, 129
Unequal join, 209
unequal joins, 208
**Unhide Fields**, 138
Unicode, 57
**Unicode Compression**, 57
UNION operator, 271
unique index, 75, 97, 174, 205
university code key, 91
uppercase equivalents, 62
user interface, 1, 10, 22, 97, 291, 330, 337, 367, 379, 380, 414, 440, 451, 458
user's workspace, 330

## V

**Validation on a form**, 50
**validation rule**, 49, 50, 65, 66, 110, 119, 121, 229
**Validation Rule**, 50, 57, 65
validation rule property, 65, 66, 110, 119
Validation Rule property, 50
validation rules, 10, 40, 44, 49, 111, 119, 120, 211
**Validation Text**, 57, 65
Validation Text property, 65
Validation Text value, 65
VBA Branching Constructs, 386
VBA code, 10, 12, 53, 97, 291, 361, 365, 367, 372, 375, 376, 383, 389, 398, 400, 401, 411, 413, 414, 422, 447, 454, 457
VBA Code Basics, 382
VBA codes, 371
VBA modules, 1, 13
VBA operator, 215
VBA procedures, 10, 191, 372, 380, 382, 398
VBA statements, 374, 382, 387
VBA syntax, 385
**VBA window**, 398
**Video rentals and customers**, 96

viewing formats, 10
Views, 84, 115, 291, 307, 313
violate referential integrity, 97
Visual Basic button, 375
Visual Basic Editor, 389
Visual Basic for Application (VBA) code, 58
Visual Basic for Applications (VBA) programming., 2
Visual Basic process, 321

## W

wastes disk space, 87
Web Browser control, 323
Website, 41
Weekday functions, 256
welcome screen, 22, 34
Welcome Screen, 22
well-designed database, 9, 37
White space, 384
wildcards, 261
Window, 116, 309, 414, 417, 447
Windows applications, 147
Windows dialog boxes., 330
Windows events., 400
Windows settings, 58, 59, 60, 122
wizard screen, 64, 188, 341
Word document, 168, 169
**Words Mail Merge**, 169
worksheet, 27, 56, 92, 93, 155, 174, 178, 179

## X

XML, 147, 148, 150, 151, 160, 161, 162, 165, 379, 436, 440, 441, 442, 443, 445
XML document, 150, 165, 441
XML export, 161, 162
XML file, 147, 160, 162, 442
XML File, 151, 160, 162
XML format., 160, 161

## Z

Zero Length, 57, 67
Zipcode, 16, 18
Zoom window, 122

Made in United States
Troutdale, OR
08/24/2023

12338079R00283